An Introduction to

MUSIC TRAVEL CULTURE

Second Edition

Kendall Hunt
publishing company

Anthony J. Marra

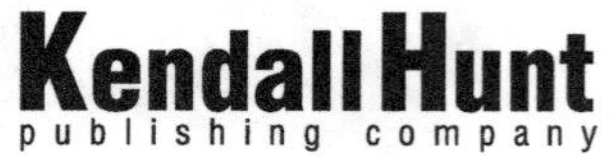

www.kendallhunt.com
Send all inquiries to:
4050 Westmark Drive
Dubuque, IA 52004-1840

Text Only ISBN: 978-1-5249-2136-1

Text with Napster ISBN: 978-1-5249-2137-8

Printed in the United States of America

Author

Anthony J. Marra is currently an Adjunct Professor of Music at Horry-Georgetown Technical College in South Carolina and has been for the past 20 years. In 2013, he was awarded Adjunct Faculty Member of the Year. He earned degrees from Adelphi University and C.W. Post College (Long Island University), both in New York. He has studied jazz and orchestral arranging with such noted people as Willie Strickland, Rich Iacona, and Philip J. Lang. Besides teaching and writing arrangements, his playing experiences are vast in that he has played in many nightclubs and hotels in New York City since age 15, as well as leading his own band Rosewood Music for over 20 years. Mr. Marra feels that the combining of his academic and professional playing careers has enabled him to be a more diverse instructor. Two of his star pupils from high-school music theory in New York are Ruth Ann Swenson and Craig Schulman, both noted vocalists with very prominent careers. Mr. Marra has always felt that music, travel, and culture are entities that coexist. In his travels to such places as Italy, Austria, Mexico, The Bahamas, Hawaii, and over 40 of the continental United States, he has gained a tremendous amount of knowledge and respect for people from other lands. He admits that there are music and cultural differences, but believes we as people have more in common. Mr. Marra hopes this textbook provides a reflection of good education and shared common values that should aid and help in the learning and teaching of music.

This book is dedicated to my wife Jean
who has been very patient and
an absolute pillar of strength
throughout this writing process.

Brief Contents

Contents

Acknowledgments

Writing a textbook of any kind is a humbling experience. It requires the input and expertise of many talented people. I would like to thank the following individuals and departments for their time, suggestions, guidance, and patience. This entire experience started when Brittanie Tucker found me at Horry Georgetown Technical College and convinced me to take on this project. Brittanie, thanks for all your hard work, advice, and suggestions. To you, I will be eternally grateful.

To Brenda Rolwes, a most incredibly helpful and talented project coordinator whose input and advice made my second addition effort go very smoothly. Thanks a million!

To Jenifer Fensterman, the talented artist who designed my book cover, I can only say, I absolutely love the design and you made me the happiest guy in the world. Thank you!

To the compositor's department I send my heartfelt thanks and gratitude for your hard work and expertise in putting all my loose ends together. Thank you!

To the permission's department, thanks for getting so many of the things I needed approved. Your department has been amazing and I can only say, WOW!

Finally, I would like to thank KendallHunt Publishing for believing in me and giving me an opportunity to fulfill a lifelong dream.

Book Purpose

This book is designed for the thousands of twenty-first century music students who want factual information in a compact format. This book is not the definitive book on music history, but rather a combination of music, travel, and culture. That being said, it is my ultimate hope each student will grasp a sufficient number of concepts so as to feel competent about picking out in sound special nuances in all types of music. Also, it is my hope that each student will become more aware of the connection between music, travel, and culture and their importance in our society.

Note: To all students and instructors, the listening choices in this text come from the Napster Program. Included in the price of the text is a one time, four months subscription to Napster.

Eight Surprising Ways Music Affects and Benefits Our Brains

Belle Beth Cooper

I'm a big fan of music, and use it a lot when working, but I had no idea about how it really affects our brains and bodies. Since music is such a big part of our lives, I thought it would be interesting and useful to have a look at some of the ways we react to it without even realizing.

Without music, life would be a mistake—Friedrich Nietzsche

1. Happy/sad music affects how we see neutral faces

We can usually pick if a piece of music is particularly happy or sad, but this isn't just a subjective idea that comes from how it makes us feel. In fact, our brains actually respond differently to happy and sad music.

Even short pieces of happy or sad music can affect us. One study showed that **after hearing a short piece of music, participants were more likely to interpret a neutral expression as happy or sad, to match the tone of the music they heard**. This also happened with other facial expressions but was most notable for those that were close to neutral.

Something else that's really interesting about how our emotions are affected by music is that **there are two kinds of emotions related to music: *perceived* emotions and *felt* emotions.**

This means that sometimes we can understand the emotions of a piece of music without actually feeling them, which explains why some of us find listening to sad music enjoyable, rather than depressing.

Unlike in real life situations, we don't feel any real threat or danger when listening to music, so we can *perceive* the related emotions without truly feeling them—almost like vicarious emotions.

2. Ambient noise can improve creativity

We all like to pump up the tunes when we're powering through our to-do lists, right? But when it comes to creative work, loud music may not be the best option.

It turns out that a moderate noise level **is the sweet spot for creativity**. Even more than low noise levels, ambient noise apparently gets our creative juices flowing, and doesn't put us off the way high levels of noise do.

The way this works is that **moderate noise levels increase processing difficulty which promotes abstract processing, leading to higher creativity**. In other words, when we struggle (just enough) to process things as we normally would, we resort to more creative approaches.

In high noise levels, however, our creative thinking is impaired because we're overwhelmed and struggle to process information efficiently.

This is very similar to how temperature and lighting can affect our productivity, where paradoxically a slightly more crowded place can be beneficial.

3. Our music choices can predict our personality

Take this one with a grain of salt, because it's only been tested on young adults (that I know of), but it's still really interesting.

In a study of couples who spent time getting to know each other, **looking at each other's top 10 favorite songs actually provided fairly reliable predictions as to the listener's personality traits.**

The study used five personality traits for the test: openness to experience, extraversion, agreeableness, conscientiousness, and emotional stability.

Interestingly, some traits were more accurately predicted based on the person's listening habits than others. For instance, openness to experience, extraversion, and emotional stability **were the easiest to guess correctly**. Conscientiousness, on the other hand, wasn't obvious based on musical taste.

Here is also a break-down of how the different genres correspond to our personality, according to a study conducted at Heriot-Watt University:

To break it down, here is the connection they have found:

- **Blues fans** have high self-esteem, are creative, outgoing, gentle, and at ease
- **Jazz fans** have high self-esteem, are creative, outgoing, and at ease
- **Classical music fans** have high self-esteem, are creative, introvert, and at ease
- **Rap fans** have high self-esteem and are outgoing
- **Opera fans** have high self-esteem, are creative and gentle
- **Country and western fans** are hardworking and outgoing
- **Reggae fans** have high self-esteem, are creative, not hardworking, outgoing, gentle, and at ease
- **Dance fans** are creative and outgoing but not gentle
- **Indie fans** have low self-esteem, are creative, not hard working, and not gentle

- **Bollywood fans** are creative and outgoing
- **Rock/heavy metal fans** have low self-esteem, are creative, not hard-working, not outgoing, gentle, and at ease
- **Chart pop fans** have high self-esteem, are hardworking, outgoing and gentle, but are not creative and not at ease
- **Soul fans** have high self-esteem, are creative, outgoing, gentle, and at ease

Of course, generalizing based on this study is very hard. However, looking at the science of introverts and extroverts, there is some clear overlap.

4. Music can significantly distract us while driving (contrary to common belief)

Another study done on teenagers and young adults focused on how their driving is affected by music.

Drivers were tested while listening to their own choice of music, silence or "safe" music choices provided by the researchers. Of course, their own music was preferred, but it also proved to be more distracting: **drivers made more mistakes and drove more aggressively when listening to their own choice of music.**

Even more surprising: music provided by the researchers proved to be more beneficial than no music at all. It seems that unfamiliar, or uninteresting, music is best for safe driving.

5. Music training can significantly improve our motor and reasoning skills

We generally assume that learning a musical instrument can be beneficial for kids, but it's actually useful in more ways than we might expect. One study showed that **children who had three years or more musical instrument training performed better than those who didn't learn an instrument in auditory discrimination abilities and fine motor skills.**

They also tested better on vocabulary and nonverbal reasoning skills, which involve understanding and analyzing visual information, such as identifying relationships, similarities and differences between shapes and patterns.

These two areas in particular are quite removed from musical training as we imagine it, so it's fascinating to see how learning to play an instrument can help kids develop such a wide variety of important skills.

Similar research shows this correlation for exercise and motor skills in the same way, which is also fascinating.

6. Classical music can improve visual attention

It's not just kids that can benefit from musical training or exposure. **Stroke patients in one small study showed improved visual attention while listening to classical music.**

The study also tried white noise and silence to compare the results, and found that, like the driving study mentioned earlier, **silence resulted in the worst scores.**

Because this study was so small, the conclusions need to be explored further for validation, but I find it really interesting how music and noise can affect our other senses and abilities—in this case, vision.

7. One-sided phone calls are more distracting than normal conversations

Another study focused on noise, rather than music, showed that **when it comes to being distracted by the conversations of others, phone calls where we can only hear one side of the conversation are the worst offenders.**

After a survey showed that **up to 82% of people find overhearing cellphone conversations annoying,** Veronica Galván, a cognitive psychologist at the University of San Diego, decided to study why these are such a pain.

In the study, participants completed word puzzles while one half of them overheard one side of a mundane phone conversation in the background. The other half of the volunteers heard the entire conversation as it took place between two people in the room.

Those who heard the one-sided phone conversation found it more distracting than those who heard both people speaking. They also remembered more of the conversation, showing that it had grabbed their attention more than those who heard both sides and didn't remember as much of the discussion.

The unpredictability of a one-sided conversation seems to be the cause of it grabbing our attention more. Hearing both sides of a conversation, on the other hand, gives us more contexts which makes it easier to tune out the distraction.

Then again, as we've explored before getting distracted is often not such a bad thing for various reasons.

8. Music helps us exercise

Back to music again, and we can see that just like silence doesn't help us to be more creative or better drivers, it's not much use when we're exercising, either.

Research on the effects of music during exercise has been done for years. In 1911, an American researcher, Leonard Ayres, found that cyclists pedaled faster while listening to music than they did in silence.

This happens because listening to music can drown out our brain's cries of fatigue. As our body realizes we're tired and wants to stop exercising, it sends signals to the brain to stop for a break. **Listening to music competes for our brain's attention, and can help us to override those signals of fatigue**, though this is mostly beneficial for low- and moderate-intensity exercise. During high-intensity exercise, music isn't as powerful at pulling our brain's attention away from the pain of the workout.

Not only can we push through the pain to exercise longer and harder when we listen to music, but it can actually help us to use our energy more efficiently. A 2012 study showed that **cyclists who listened to music required 7% less oxygen to do the same work as those who cycled in silence.**

Some recent research has shown that there's a ceiling effect on music at around 145 bpm, where anything higher doesn't seem to add much motivation, so keep that in mind when choosing your workout playlist. Here is how this breaks down for different genres:

Now if we team up these different "tempos" with the actual work-out we're doing, we can be in much better sync and find the right beat for our exercise. If you match up the above with the graphic below it should be super easy to get into a good groove:

So in the same way that exercising makes us happier, it's not surprising that music adds significantly to our work-out success.

What have you noticed about how music affects you? Let us know in the comments.

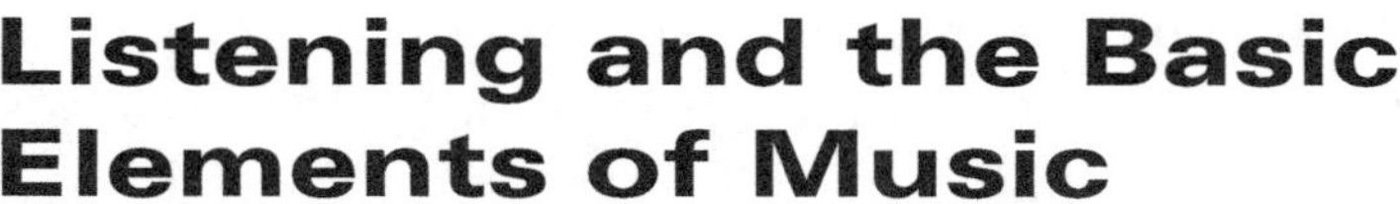

Listening and the Basic Elements of Music

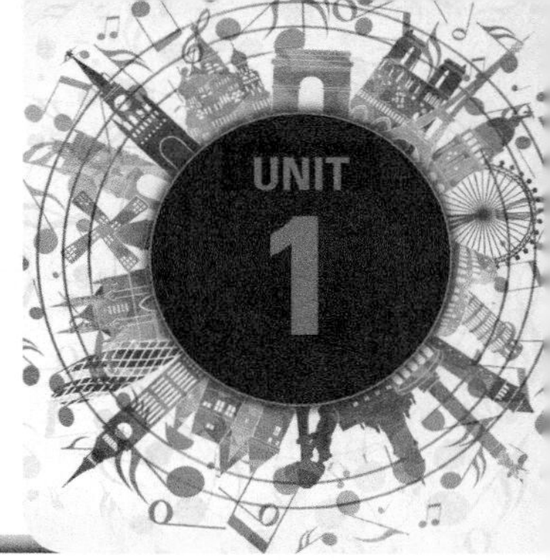

Unit Purpose

LISTENING

The purpose of this unit is to familiarize and give the students tools and information to become better listeners.

How Is a Musical Composition Put Together And How Does It Become Popular?

The Composer: This is the person who has the ability to create the music and in most cases write down the ideas. There are some cases where the composer cannot write music.

The Performer(s): The performer or performers interpret the music that is written.

Arranger(s): This is the person who sorts out the musical material and gives you the final sounds you hear.

The Audience: These are the people who decide what becomes popular. It is interesting that most listeners are not musicians.

What Is Music?

Music is **sound** caused by **vibration**. Sound can be music or noise.

The difference between music and noise is perception. How many of you have heard from your parents, how can you listen to that junk? When we were kids, we had good music. When parents react in this manner, we call this a generation gap. This at first glance might seem true, but it is not and let me explain.

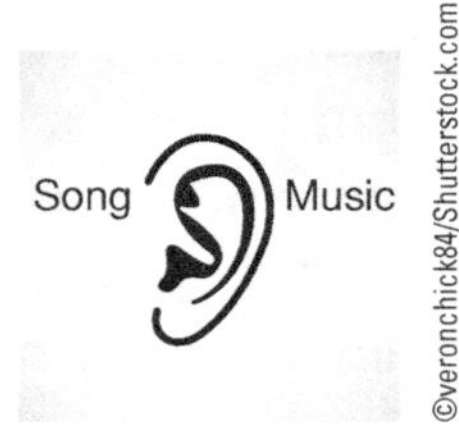

Your Ear

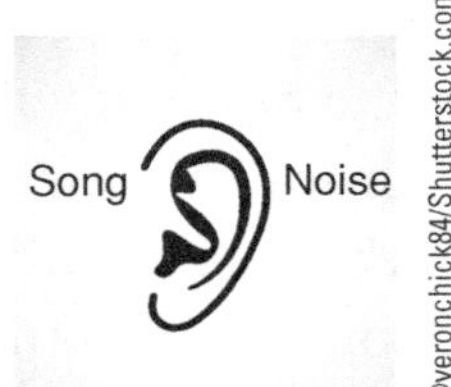

Mom's Ear

What happened here is that your mom was evaluating your music based on the standards of her music. This is not a generation gap, but rather a communication gap. In order to permanently fix this the following rule applies: You cannot listen to all different kinds of music with the same ears. This means if you like Rap or Taylor Swift and you listen to Mozart, you have to change your thinking. In summary, when your mom heard your song, she got a negative communication while you were getting a positive one.

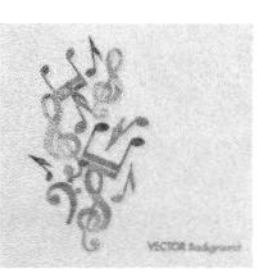

Listening Box 1

Type in Star Wars Theme and under Tracks choose Star Wars Theme, End Title (Your 2nd choice). Select Track 1, Star Wars Main Title.

How Do We Listen?

How we listen to anything or anyone depends on how we focus our attention. Listening to music necessitates that you listen many times to hear the structure of the arrangement. The most critical categories of listening are:

Emotionally: For everyone, music congers up emotions. Have you ever heard a song and thought to yourself, if I were a song writer, that is exactly what I would say about that subject? Often times it is difficult to verbalize the emotions you are feeling because they maybe deep rooted and personal.

Passively: This is not the best listening level. This listening level occurs when you are not giving the music much thought. For example, you may be washing your car on a nice day with the boom box going, you sing a few words, you stop singing to get a towel to dry off the car and when you get back to the car, you start singing again. The music is washing over you like the water washed over the car.

Adding a story line: You are at the beach and hear a song that has personal meaning for you. You start adding these personal thoughts to what you are hearing and in essence perhaps creating a new story. This listening level can happen with either a vocal or instrumental piece of music.

Music in context: I'm sure you have heard the phrase music for all occasions. This means if your sister is getting married, or you are going to a football game, or a Fourth of July celebration, there is specific music to go with these events. For example, you are probably not going to hear a symphony orchestra playing Mozart Symphonies during the half time show of a football game, as this would be out of context with the event. At this listening level the event is more important than the music, but the music must be in context and fit in with the event.

Subtleties of the musical arrangement: At this listening level, in my opinion, the listening fun begins. You begin to hear things that you were previously unaware of and the music starts to take on a new meaning. In order to understand a piece of music, you have to know what is going on in the arrangement. The nice part is that you do not have to be a musician to accomplish this.

My final point on these listening categories is that you can have more than one listening level going on at the same time. If your son is playing trumpet with the high school marching band you are probably listening on the music in context level as well as the emotional level because you are proud of his musical accomplishments and the music he is playing is in context with the event.

Class assignment: Each student must list and submit how they have listened in each of the above categories.

What Do We Listen For? The overall answer is, THE ARRANGEMENT!

There have been volumes written about how to listen to music, but the bottom line reveals the following:

1. First and foremost is the arrangement. All music is arranged so you have to know what is going on in sound.
2. Second, how you focus your attention is extremely important. Are you doing something besides listening carefully, or does the music have your undivided attention?
3. Third, what do you have in your listeners' toolbox?

The listeners' toolbox immediately takes us to the **Four Elements of Music**, and subdivision terms.

Melody

Melody is an organized succession of tones that make musical sense when perceived as a group and is a horizontal structure. Melody is one of the four main elements to listen for. Most melodies in Western Civilization Music are constructed from Major and Minor scales, but it is possible to use other scales or no scale at all. The most common scales used are Major and Minor.

Phrase: A phrase is really a melodic statement much like a phrase in an English sentence. We were taught that two phrases equal a sentence. In music, two phrases equal a complete melodic thought.

Cadence: A cadence is generally a resting spot at the end of a melodic phrase. Cadences make the melody sound like it is finished, or must keep going.

Motive: A motive is the shortest kind of melody.

Theme: Is a melody generally much longer than a motive.

Scales: Melody notes are usually taken from scales, and the most common scales in Western Civilization Music are Major and Minor.

Ornamentation: Melodies can be changed in various ways: See the following.

Repetition: A composer often times repeats a melody for two reasons. The first being to show the listener that the melody is the most important idea of his piece and also to extend his music without coming up with a new idea.

Sequence: Sequences are basically the same music on different pitch levels. Sequences generally come in groups of three.

Imitation: Imitation is very much like repetition but generally involves one voice or instrument imitating the melody previously stated.

Trills: Trills occur when a performer takes two different notes and goes back and forth in rapid succession.

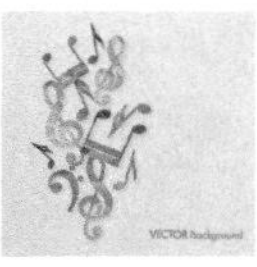

Listening Box 2

Type in Yoda's Theme and choose top box Yoda's Theme. Select Track 1, Yoda's Theme.

Harmony

Is basically a supporting structure to melody. You have to have a combination of notes sounding together to get harmony. Harmony is also a main element of music and is considered to be a vertical structure.

Interval: An interval occurs when you have two notes sounding together.

Chord: A chord occurs when you have three notes sounding together.

Add interval and chord examples here.

Harmony is frequently described as consonant or dissonant.

Consonant: Consonant harmony generally initiates a feeling of stability in the listener. The feeling is sometimes described as relaxing or without tension. What causes the stabile feeling is the vibrations of the notes numerically get along. A love scene in a movie would be a good example where consonant harmony would be used.

Dissonance: Dissonance is just the opposite of consonance in that it is harsh or unpleasant sounding and creates a tense feeling. What causes this tense feeling is that the vibrations of the notes do not numerically get along. A killer with a knife standing behind the door waiting for his prey would be a good example of where dissonant harmony would be used.

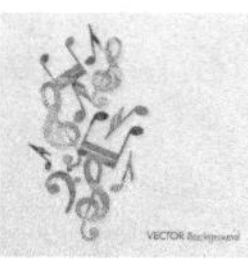

Listening Box 3

Type in Taylor Swift and choose top box Our Song, Taylor Swift. Select Track 3, Teardrops On My Guitar. (Consonant).

Type in Main Title Jaws and choose top box main Title (Jaws/Soundtrack Version). Select Track 1, Main Title (Jaws/Soundtrack Version). (Dissonant).

Rhythm

Rhythm is basically the measured flow or movement of the music. It is a very strong element of music because it has the ability to push or pull the music. By that I mean it can slow things down or speed things up. When people dance, even if the song has words, it is the rhythm that causes the dancing movements.

Beat: The beat is the pulse of music. The beat has two properties, strong and weak. The weak part of the beat is called the upbeat. The strong part of the beat is the actual hit you hear and respond to.

Tempo: Tempo refers to the speed of the beat. Are you listening or dancing to a slow song or a fast song?

Meter: Meter organizes beats into groups. The most common meters are Duple (two beats), Triple (three beats), and Quadruple (four beats). Most Western Civilization music is written in Quadruple Meter.

Syncopation: Syncopation is a shift of the normal accent. The actual strong part of the beat becomes the weak part and vice versa. Syncopation is an exciting rhythmic device which helps move the music forward and make it sound cool.

Rhythmic Ostinato: A rhythmic ostinato is a constantly recurring rhythmic pattern.

Rubato: A deliberate unsteady tempo.

Texture

Texture is basically how the musical elements are put together. There are three basic textures: monophonic, polyphonic, and homophonic. The illustrations and explanations in the following show what happens in the music.

Monophonic: Monophonic texture is just one melody without harmony and goes back to early Gregorian Chant.

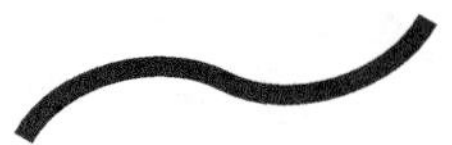

Polyphonic: Polyphonic texture is at least two or more melodies going on at the same time and goes back to the ninth century which is the first time two melodies were combined.

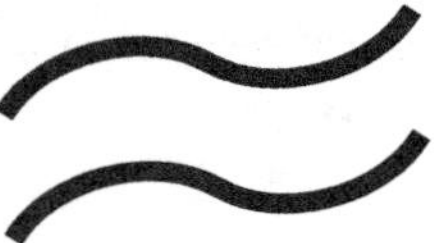

Homophonic: Homophonic texture consists of a melody and harmonic accompaniment. It is **also the texture of most of our modern-day music.**

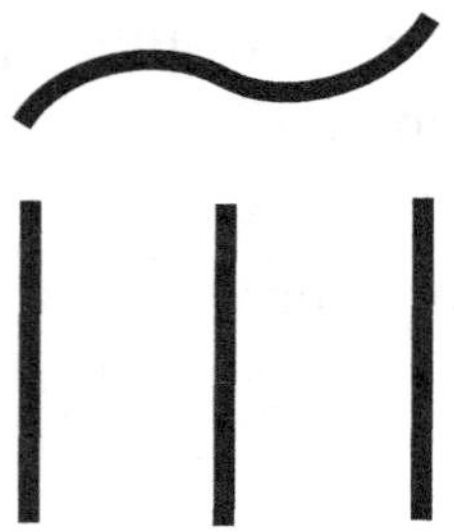

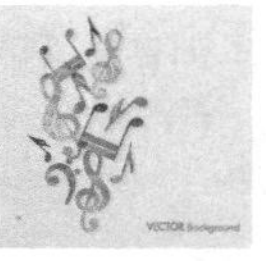

Listening Box 4

Type in Meditation With Gregorian Chants and choose top box Meditation With Gregorian Chants. Select Track 7, Kyrie. (**Monophonic**). Type in Best of Bach and choose top box Best of Bach: Inventions and Sinfonias. Select Track 4, Bach: Invention 4. (**Polyphonic**). Type in Alan Jackson and under Albums choose 34 Number Ones. Select Track 24, Little Bitty. (**Homophonic**).

Diagram of the Orchestra Seating Plan

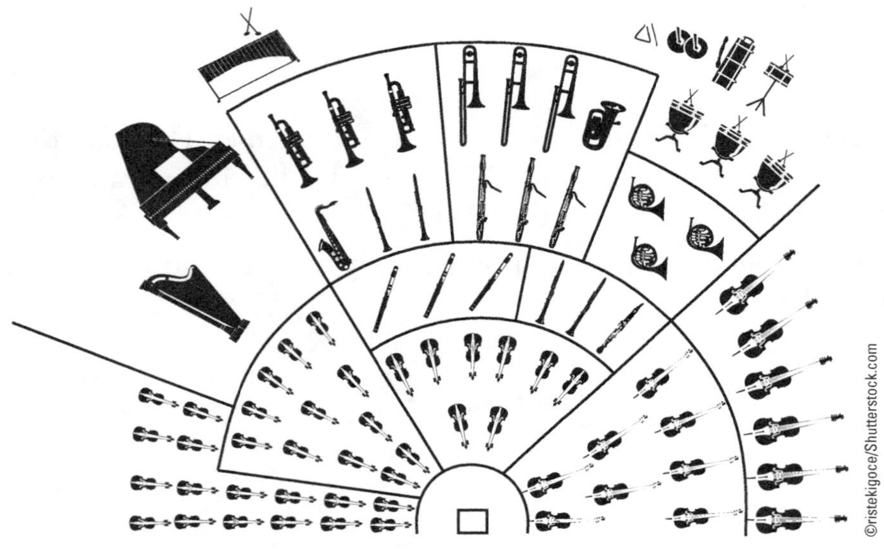

©ristekigoce/Shutterstock.com

String Notes

The violins are separated into first and second parts. All strings are placed at the front of the orchestra for sound reasons.

The rest of the instrument placement should be visibly self-explanatory. One of the best compositions for gaining instrument knowledge is, "**The Young Person's Guide to the Orchestra,**" by Benjamin Britten. This piece can be found in Napster, by the Royal Philharmonic Orchestra.

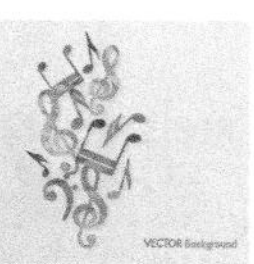

Listening Box 5

Type in The Young Persons Guide to The Orchestra and choose top box Variations on a Theme of Purcell, Op.34. Select disc 2, Track 1, Variations on a Theme of Purcell, Op. 34 (From "The Young Persons Guide to The Orchestra").

The Young Person's Guide to the Orchestra (1946) Op.34

By Benjamin Britten

Form: Theme, Variations, and Fugue. Below is a basic analysis of this piece. This composition has full orchestra and a narrator. It is designed to introduce the listener to the instruments of the orchestra and their different sounds.

Analysis: Main Theme

1. Main Theme—The Entire Orchestra
2. Main Theme—The Woodwind Section
3. Main Theme—The Brass Section
4. Main Theme—The String Section
5. Main Theme—The Percussion Section then the entire Orchestra again.

Variations

Variation 1 Flutes and Piccolo

Variation 2 Oboes

Variation 3 Clarinets

Variation 4 Bassoons

Variation 5 Violins

Variation 6 Violas

Variation 7 Cellos

Variation 8 String Basses

Variation 9 Harp

Variation 10 French Horns

Variation 11 Trumpets

Variation 12 Trombones and Tuba

Variation 13 Percussion (timpani, bass drum, cymbals, tambourine, triangle, snare drum, Chinese wood blocks, xylophone, castanets, gong, and whip).

Fugue: In a Fugue, the melody is called the subject.

Subject 1 Piccolo

Subject 2 Flutes

Subject 3 Oboes

Subject 4 Clarinets

Subject 5 Bassoons

Subject 6 First Violins

Subject 7 Second Violins

Subject 8 Violas

Subject 9 Cellos

Subject 10 String Basses

Subject 11 Harp

Subject 12 French Horns

Subject 13 Trumpets

Subject 14 Trombones and Tuba

Subject 15 Upper Strings and Woodwinds With Main Theme Added

Main Theme—Brass played in a slow speed

Coda: The coda is the ending and the percussion comes in followed by the orchestra answering. The final chord is played by the orchestra.

Note: This entire piece is based on a theme by Purcell.

The Conductor

The Conductor has a very important role in the production and interpretation of the music. Most of his work is done in rehearsal where he clears up any musical problems as well as any concerns on the part of the players. The conductor has basically four things he does on a consistent basis. First and foremost, he coordinates and interprets the music. He is also a scholar in that he will study previous interpretations of a piece. Finally, he generally uses a stick, which is called a baton, to help him keep time for the group.

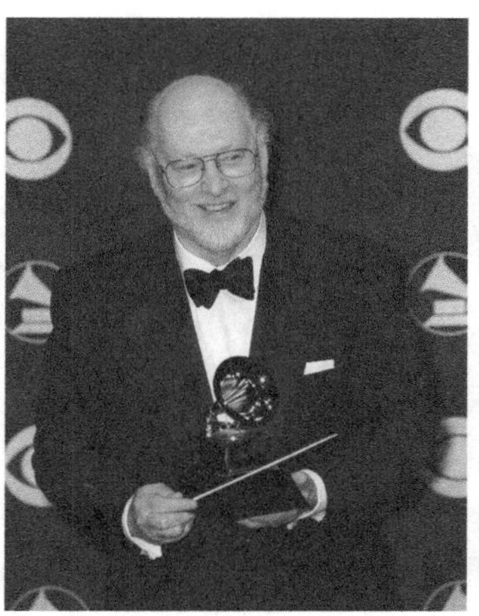

©Featureflash Photo Agency/Shutterstock.com

John Williams who has written musical scores for such movies as E.T, Jaws, Schindler's List, Towering Inferno, Close Encounters of the Third Kind, Raiders of the Lost Ark, Saving Private Ryan and Jurassic Park, to name a few. It is amazing that many people know this man's music, but do not know him. He is also a world renowned conductor.

The Concertmaster

The concertmaster is the last person to enter the stage before the conductor. He is responsible for making sure the orchestra is tuned before playing. A female concertmaster is called a concert mistress.

Tuning the Orchestra

The concertmaster comes on stage before the conductor and points to the oboe player to play the tuning note "A." All instruments tune to this note. The only time this is not true is when there is a piano soloist. When this happens, the concertmaster comes to the piano and plays the tuning note "A" on the piano. All instruments tune to this note.

Instruments and Voices (Timbre or Tone Color)

Timbre is the fourth element of music and refers to instruments and voices. How do we get sound from instruments and voices?

There are three things necessary for instruments and voices to get sound. They are: energy source, vibrating element(s), and resonating chamber. This is true for **all** instruments and voices.

The Four Sections of the Orchestra

Strings: Violin, Viola Cello, Bass, and Harp.

The violin, viola, cello, and bass all have four strings and all are played with a bow or the index finger plucking the strings. In all cases for these instruments, the bow or index finger is the energy source, the strings are the vibrating elements, and the hollow body of the instruments is the resonating chamber. Strings can be muted with a wooden device that covers all strings.

On a historical note, there were three famous string making families from the town of Cremona, Italy. The three famous men are Nicolò Amati (1596–1684), Antonio Stradivari

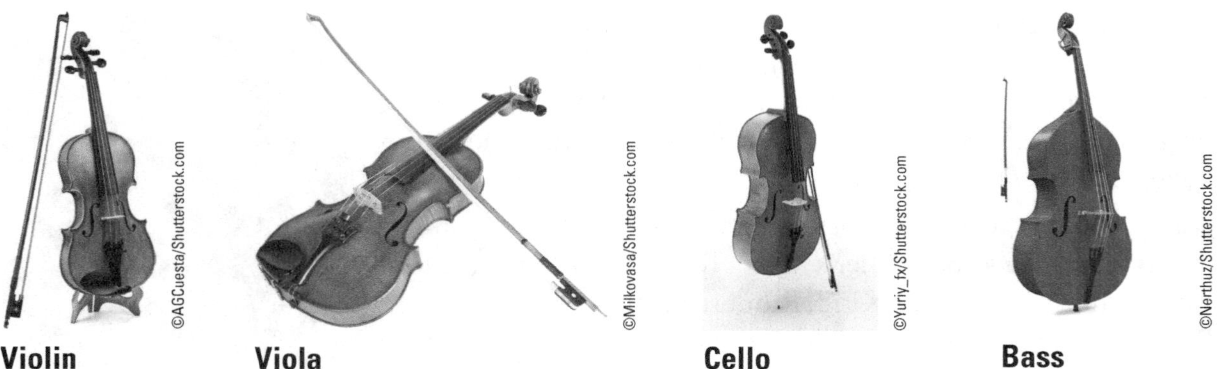

Violin ©AGCuesta/Shutterstock.com **Viola** ©Milkovasa/Shutterstock.com **Cello** ©Yuriy_fx/Shutterstock.com **Bass** ©Nerthuz/Shutterstock.com

(1644–1737), and Giuseppe Bartolomeo Guarneri (1698–1744). These men achieved perfection making string instruments, but were very secretive about the processes they used. They were all given credit for bringing string instrument making to its highest level.

The Harp

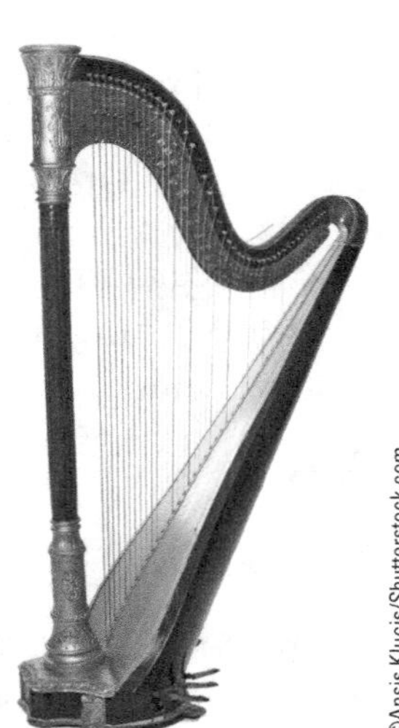

©Ansis Klucis/Shutterstock.com

There are forty-seven strings and seven pedals on the concert harp. The pedals are interesting in that they change the pitches of the strings. Pedals were first used in 1697 and they are separated. The three on the left are DCB and the four on the right are EFGA. Some of the strings are color coded to identify specific notes. The hands are used as the energy source, the strings are the vibrating elements, and the box on the bottom is the resonating chamber.

Woodwinds

There are three categories of woodwinds: no reed, single reed, and double reed. With no reed woodwinds, air is the energy source, air over mouth hole is the vibrator, and the resonating chambers are either the metal or wood tubes.

No Reed: Piccolo, Flute, and Alto Flute

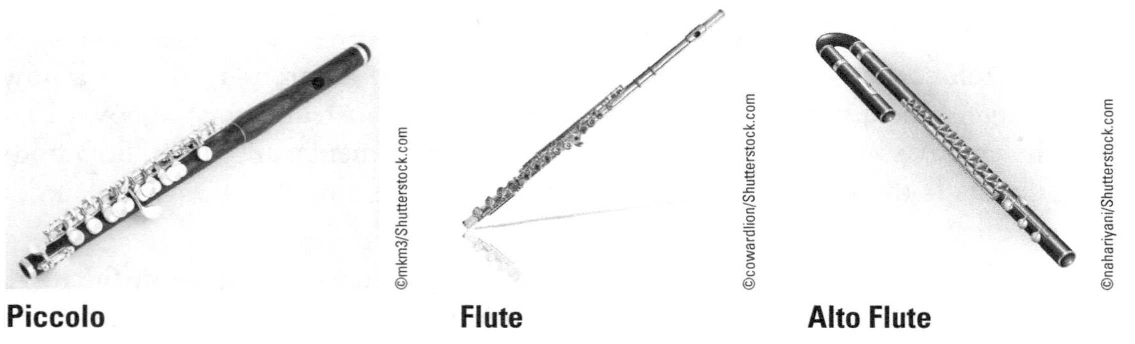

Piccolo ©mkm3/Shutterstock.com **Flute** ©cowardlion/Shutterstock.com **Alto Flute** ©nahariyani/Shutterstock.com

Single Reed: Clarinet and Bass Clarinet. With single-reed instruments, the reed is part of the mouthpiece and is held on with a clamp called a ligature. Air is the energy source, the reed is the vibrating element, and the wood tube is the resonating chamber.

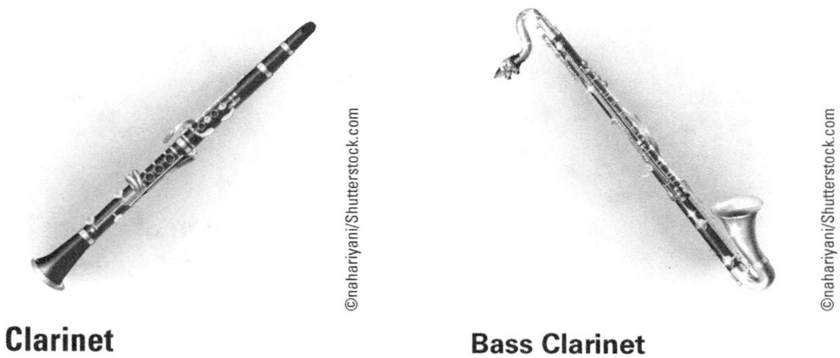
©nahariyani/Shutterstock.com
©nahariyani/Shutterstock.com

Clarinet **Bass Clarinet**

Bass Clarinet: Has a curved neck and curved bell.

Double Reeds: The double-reed instruments are the Oboe, English Horn, Bassoon, and Contra-Bassoon. With double-reed instruments, the reed is the mouthpiece and vibrating element. Air is the energy source and the wood tube is the resonating chamber.

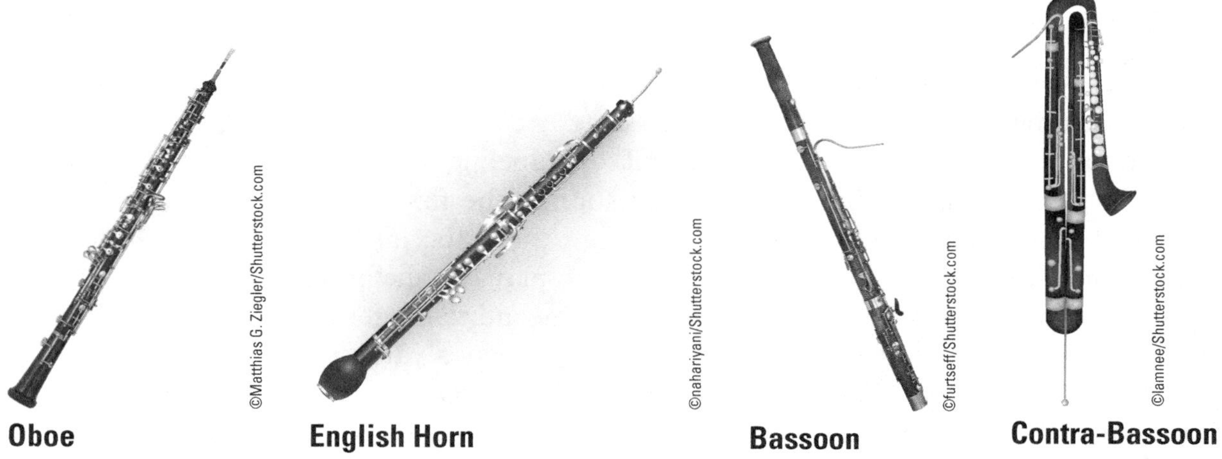
©Matthias G. Ziegler/Shutterstock.com
©nahariyani/Shutterstock.com
©furtseff/Shutterstock.com
©lamnee/Shutterstock.com

Oboe **English Horn** **Bassoon** **Contra-Bassoon**

Brass: Trumpet, Trombone, French Horn, Baritone Horn (Euphonium), and the Tuba

Brass instruments go back to Ancient Greek and Roman times, but evidence of modern brass instruments can be traced back to the fourteenth century. Modern-day brass instruments use either valves or a slide to change notes. I will indicate which instrument uses what mechanism. With brass, air is the energy source, lips on the mouthpiece are the vibrating elements, and the brass tubing of the horn is the resonating chamber. Trumpets and Trombones have the ability to change overall sound by using devices called mutes.

Some common mutes are straight (cone shaped) cup, wa-wa, and harmon. The French horn player can mute the horn by placing his right hand into the bell of the horn.

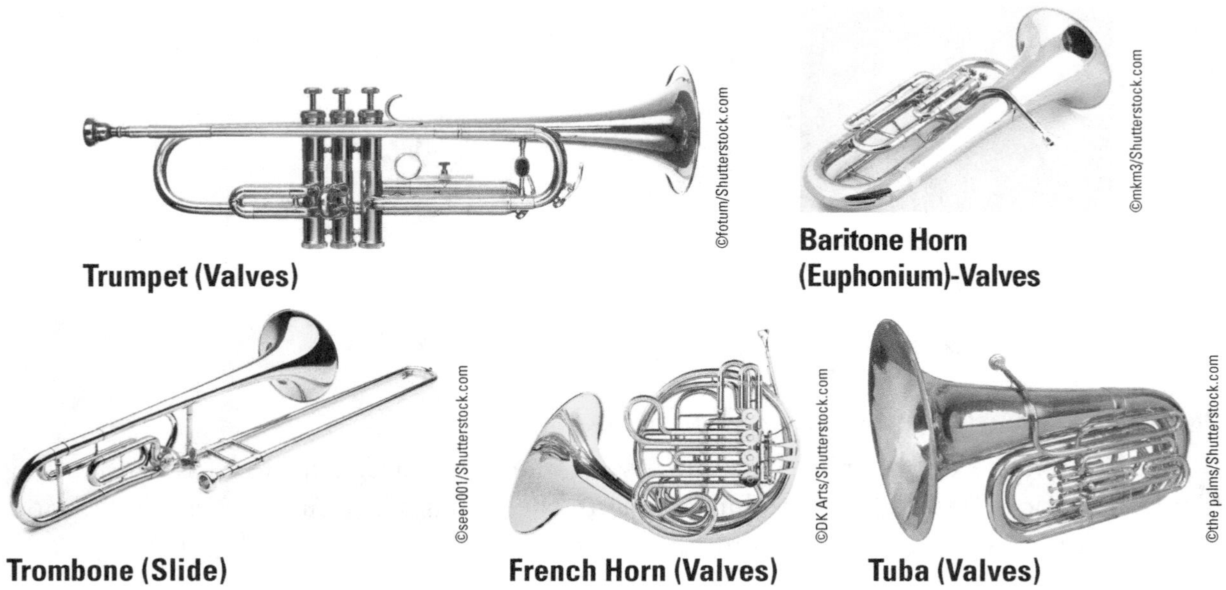

Trumpet (Valves)

Baritone Horn (Euphonium)-Valves

Trombone (Slide)

French Horn (Valves)

Tuba (Valves)

Percussion

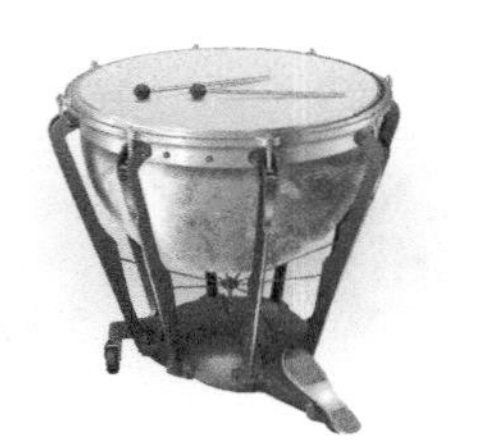

Timpani

The Percussion section of an orchestra has the most number of different instruments. Percussion players use different methods to get their sound. For example, a player can strike, scrape, jiggle, rub, or crash the instrument to obtain the desired sound. The first instrument to be presented is the Timpani. The Timpani is special for a few reasons; first it is the only drum to be able to play specific notes. Most Timpani can play an octave's worth of notes and the notes are changed on the drum with a pedal. Also, the player has a variety of mallets he can use to strike the drum. Mallets are basically sticks with different heads. Some heads are padded and others can be rubber. The second reason the Timpani is special is because it was the first drum to be added to the orchestra. The time frame of original appearance is the 1600s. With timpani, the mallets and hands are the energy source, the head is the vibrating element and the resonating chamber is the hollow body of the drum.

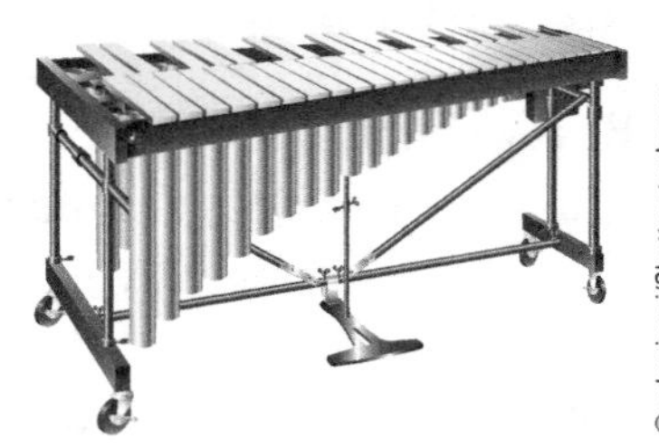

Vibraphone (Metal Bars)

Mallet Percussion: The mallet percussion instruments are set up like the piano keyboard. The bottom set of bars are like the white notes of the piano. The top set of bars are like the black keys on the piano. The mallets and hands are the energy source, the bars are the vibrating elements, and the resonating chambers are the metal tubes.

More Mallet Percussion

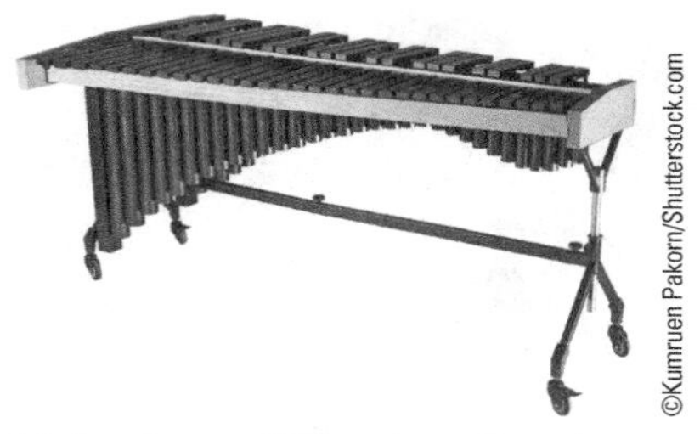

©Kumnuen Pakorn/Shutterstock.com

Xylophone (Wooden Bars)

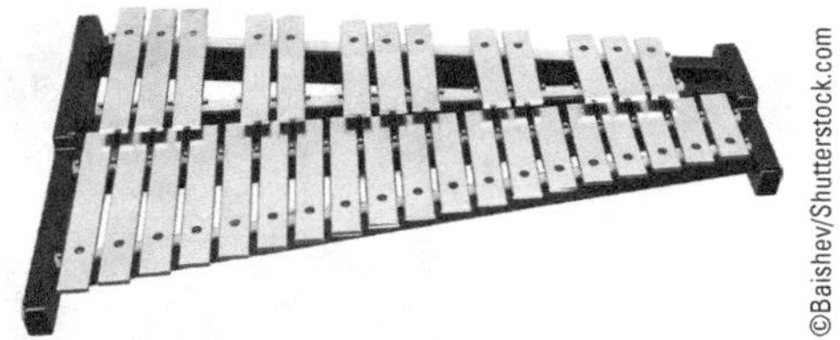

©Baishev/Shutterstock.com

Glockenspiele (Metal Bars)

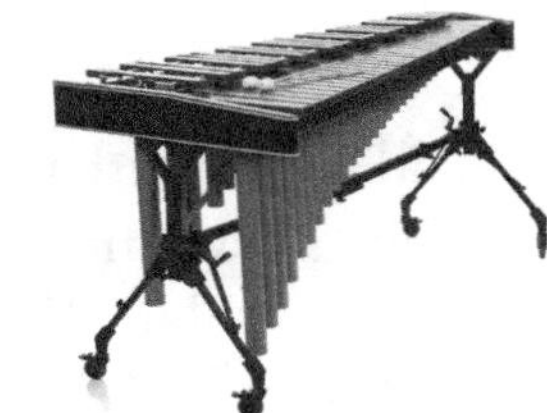

©Mike Flippo/Shutterstock.com

Marimba (Wooden Bars)

The following percussion instruments are commonly found in what is called a drum kit. A drum kit includes instruments that you see the Rock or Jazz drummer use. Note: The kit bass drum is different from the one used in orchestras. See photos below. With the exception of cymbals all sound production is the same as the timpani.

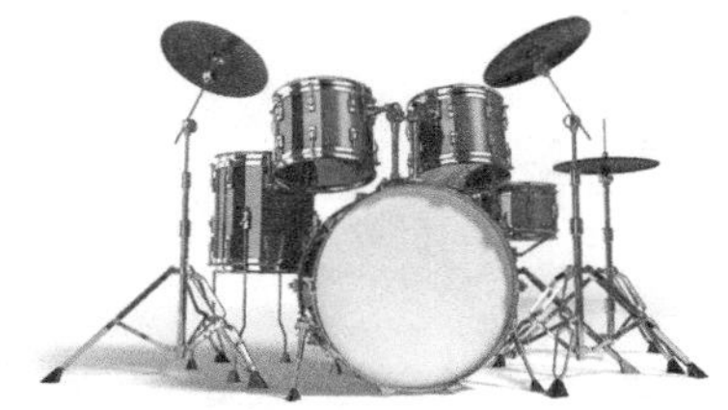

©Mikhail Bakunovich/Shutterstock.com

Drum Kit

The following is a basic list of instruments in the drum kit, including pictures: Snare Drum, Bass Drum, Cymbals, Hi-Hats, and Floor Tom-Tom.

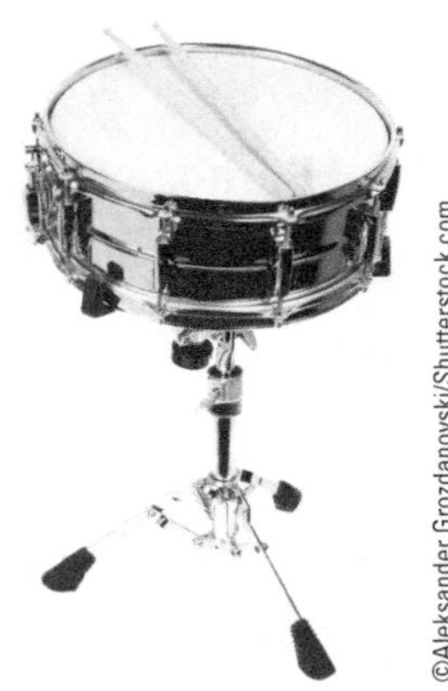

©Aleksander Grozdanovski/Shutterstock.com

Snare Drum

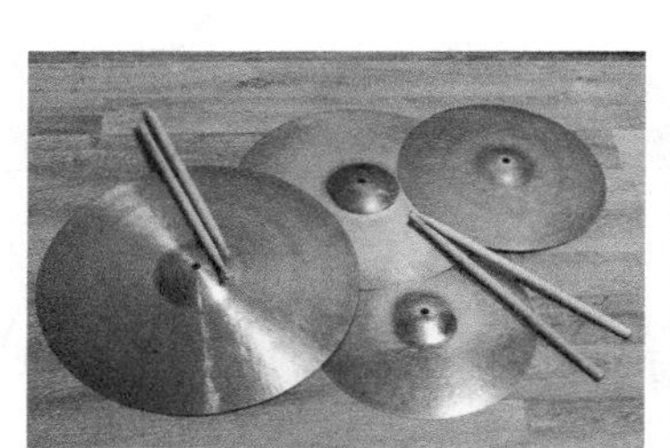

©Patramansky Oleg/Shutterstock.com

Cymbals

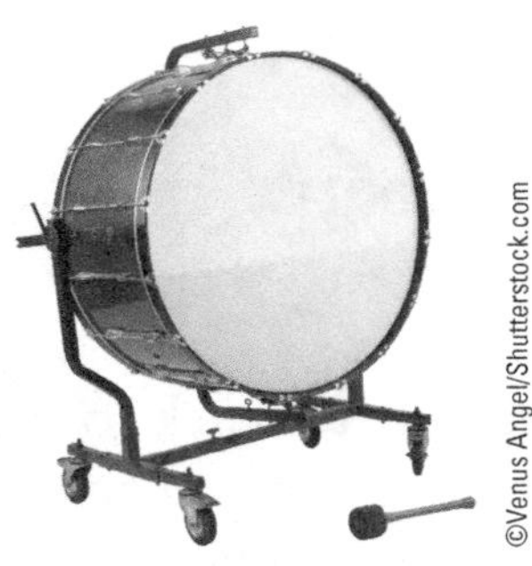

©Venus Angel/Shutterstock.com

Bass Drum (Orch.)

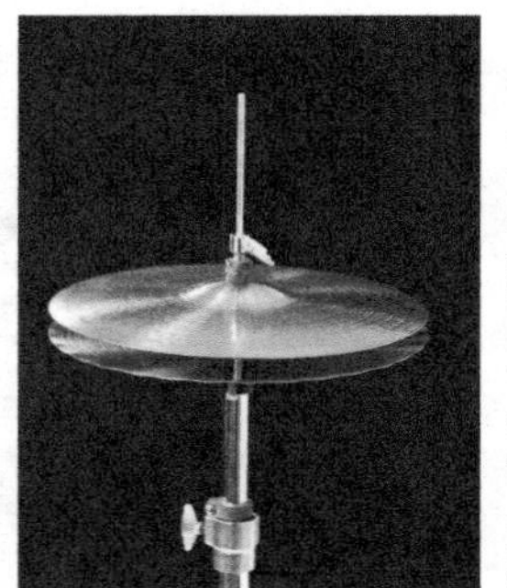
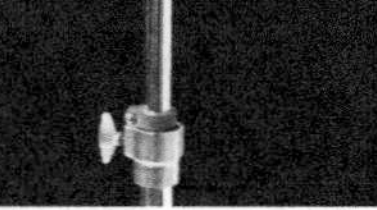

©Aleksander Grozdanovski/Shutterstock.com

Hi-Hats

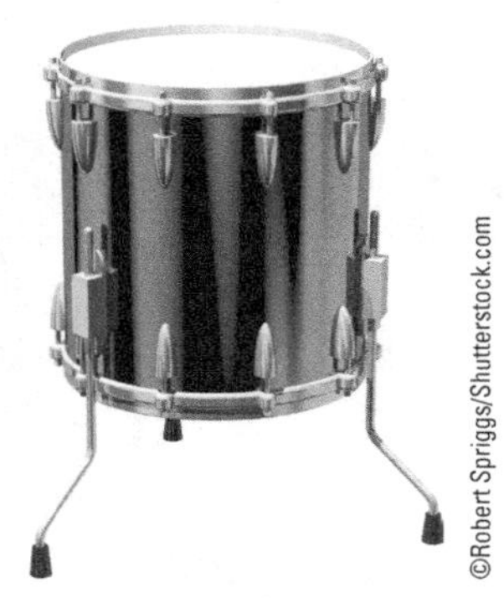

©Robert Spriggs/Shutterstock.com

Floor Tom-Toms

The Saxophones

While the saxophones are mainly considered band instruments, they have been used many times with the orchestra. To name a few instances, Rhapsody in Blue and An American in Paris by George Gershwin. Also, Bolero by Maurice Ravel. The saxophones were invented by a Belgian instrument designer, Adolph Sax, in the 1840s. The most commonly used saxophones are the Soprano, Alto, Tenor, and Baritone. With saxes, air is the energy source, the reed is the vibrating element, and the metal tube is the resonating chamber.

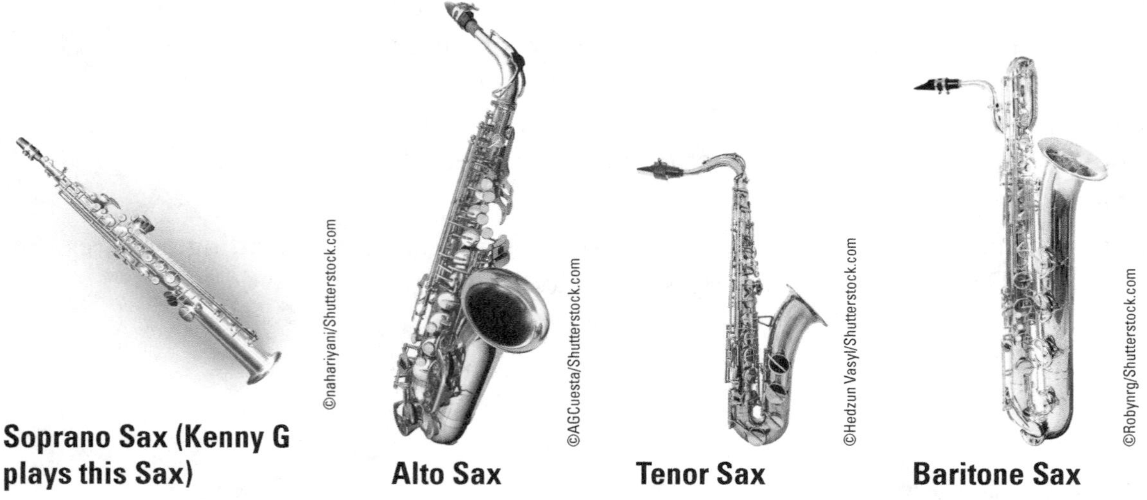

©nahariyani/Shutterstock.com

Soprano Sax (Kenny G plays this Sax)

©AGCuesta/Shutterstock.com

Alto Sax

©Hedzun Vasyl/Shutterstock.com

Tenor Sax

©Robynrg/Shutterstock.com

Baritone Sax

The Keyboards

Organ

The Organ dates back to the early hundreds and before in civilization. Some early concepts dealt with wheel and wind. Other concepts dealt with water. Below is a diagram of the wheel-wind concept.

Invented in the First Century by Heron of Alexandria, a Greek engineer.

© Science & Society Picture Library/SSPL/Getty Images

Heron's Wind Wheel

Hydraulis: The Hydraulis is a water organ that dates back to the third century BC. It was a pipe organ which used air powered by water from a water fall or manual pump. The water organ does not have a compressor, no bellows and no blower. See picture of Hydraulis.

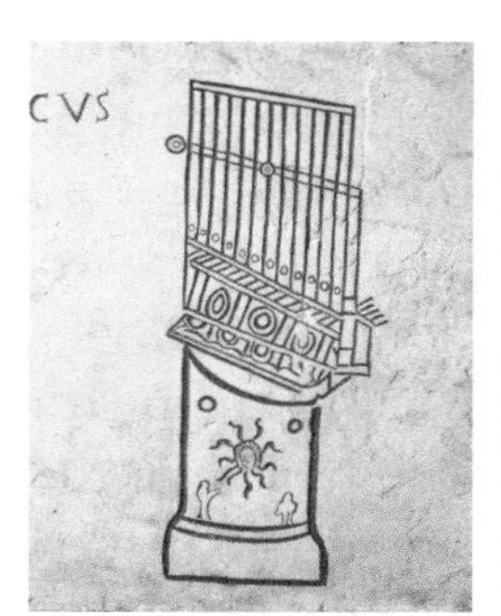

© DEA/A. DAGLIORTI/De Agostini/Getty Images

Pipe or Church Organ: The pipe or church organ concept goes back to the 700s and 800s. By the twelfth century, the organ began developing into a complex instrument. Below are pictures of the modern-day pipe organ. There are many pipes because each pipe yields one sound. The energy sources are the hands and air, the vibrating elements are the air columns and the resonating chambers are the metal or wood pipes.

The Pipes

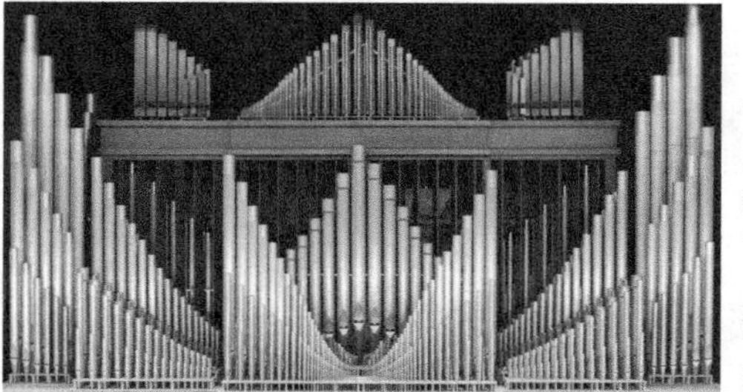

©Nagel Photography/Shutterstock.com

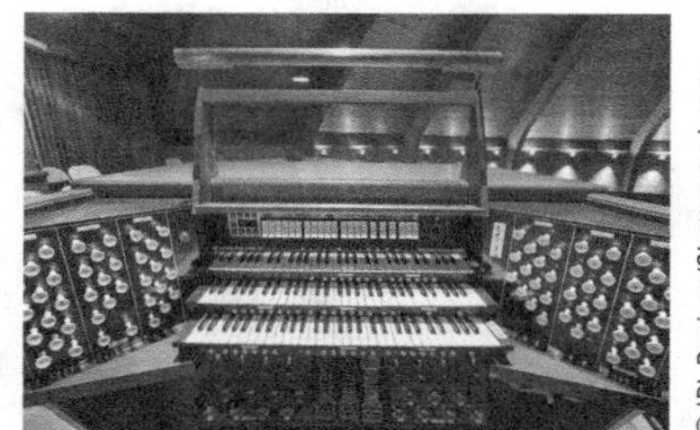

©JPL Designs/Shutterstock.com

The Keyboard and Pedals

For the next in line of keyboard development we turn to the clavichord and the harpsichord.

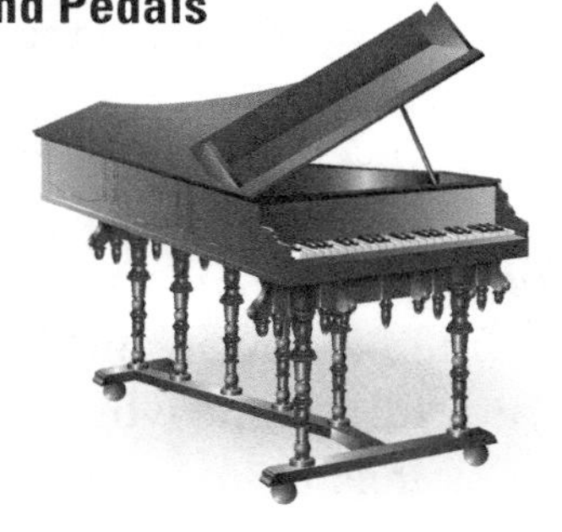

©nahariyani/Shutterstock.com

Clavichord

The Clavichord was invented in the early fourteenth century and was very popular from the sixteenth to the eighteenth century when the piano took over in popularity. The energy sources are the hands, the vibrating elements are the strings and the resonating chamber is the sound board. Overall sound production is caused by striking the strings with small metal blades called tangents.

Harpsichord

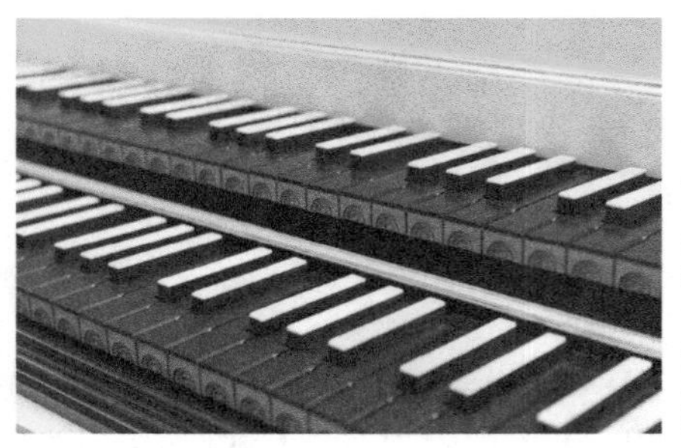
©Artem Furman/Shutterstock.com

The Harpsichord was originally constructed in 1646, by Andreas Ruckers. Its basic playing mechanism is a plectrum which is a wedge-shaped quill which plucks the strings. The energy sources are the hands and the plectrum, the vibrating elements are the strings, and the resonating chamber is the wood box.

The Piano

There is no doubt the piano was the most popular instrument in the eighteenth century. The invention of the piano is given to Bartolomeo Cristofori (1655–1731) of Padua, Italy. The first pianos were built in the 1700s and in Mozart's day they were only five octaves. They were later expanded to seven and one half octaves. The piano has eighty-eight keys, fifty-two are white and thirty-six are black. The current form of the piano dates back to the nineteenth century. There are two types of piano; the grand and the upright. The strings in the grand piano are mounted horizontally, while the strings in the upright are mounted vertically. The energy sources are the hands and hammers, the vibrating elements are the strings and the resonating chamber is the sound board and wood box.

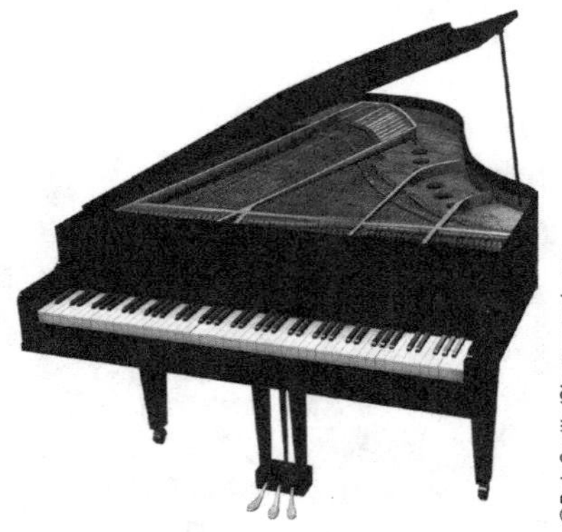
©Bob Orsillo/Shutterstock.com

Grand Piano

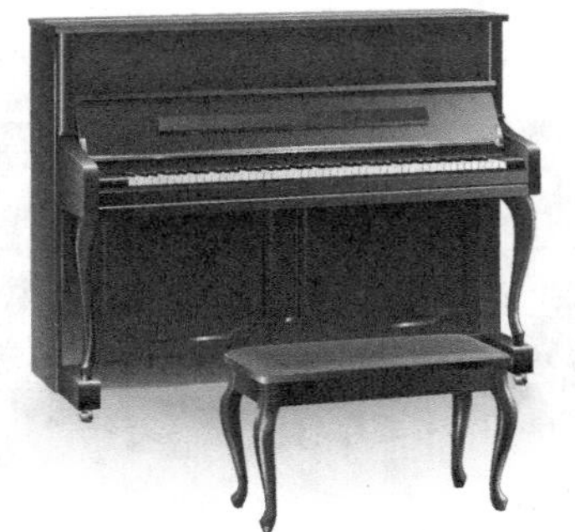
©nahariyani/Shutterstock.com

Upright Piano

The Celesta

The first Celesta was built by a Parisian, Victor Mustel in 1860, but his son Auguste, patented a newer and better instrument in 1886. The instrument is considered to be a struck idiophone which is any instrument that produces sound by its own vibration, without strings or membranes. The instrument can be anywhere from three to five octaves and some have two keyboards. The energy sources are hands and hammers, the vibrating elements are the strings and the resonating chamber is the box.

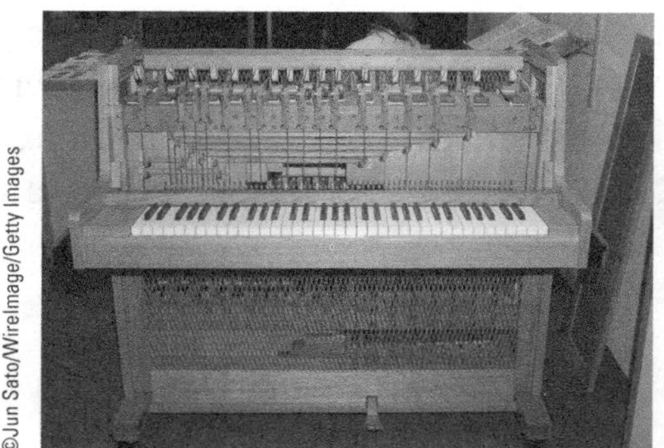

©Jun Sato/WireImage/Getty Images

Celesta (Five Octave)

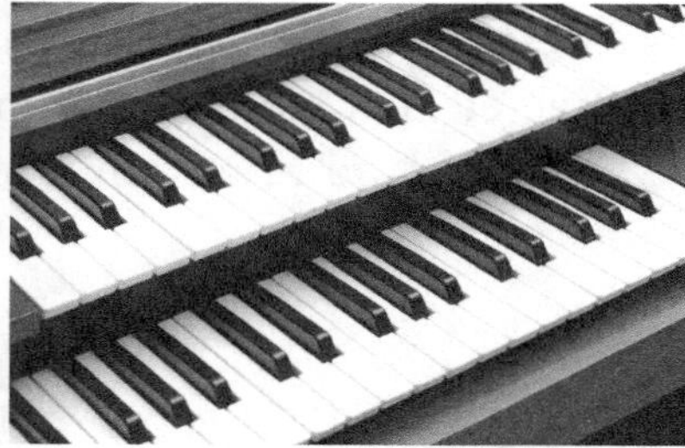

©cristi180884/Shutterstock.com

Celesta (Double Keyboard)

The Synthesizer

The modern-day synthesizer is a truly extraordinary instrument. The concept of it goes back to the 1950s and 1960s. Besides having its own sounds, it is designed to produce sounds of acoustical instruments. There are two types of synthesizers, the analog and the digital. Robert Moog, back in the 1950s was a leading pioneer in the development of the analog synthesizer. The Yamaha Company is noted for its digital synthesizer the DX7, which goes back to 1983. The energy sources are the hands and electricity, the vibrating elements are the transistors, and the resonating chamber is the loudspeaker or amplifier.

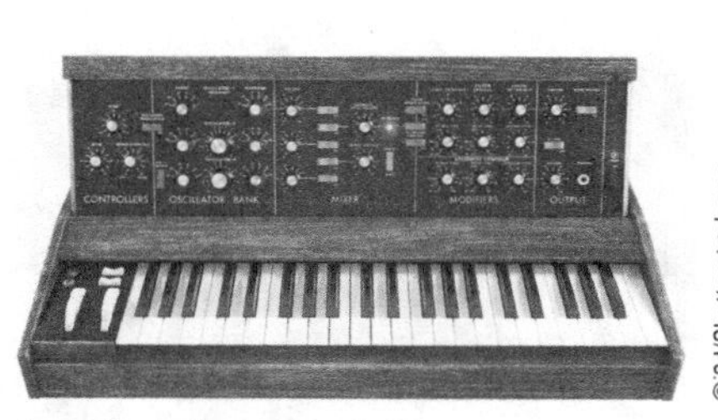

©i3d/Shutterstock.com

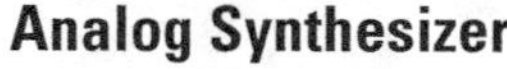

Analog Synthesizer

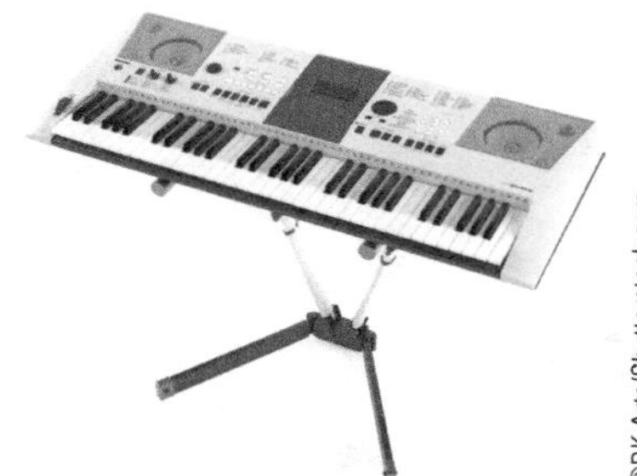

©DK Arts/Shutterstock.com

Digital Synthesizer

The Guitar

Since the guitar is very popular, I wanted to give the reader a bit more history on the instrument. First, the word guitar comes from the Latin, cithara. Guitars can vary from four to eighteen strings and are strummed or plucked. The main ancestor to the guitar is the Lute. The two Lutes that are cited as predecessors to the guitar are the European Lute and the four string Oud. Overall, much of modern guitar history is lost in Medieval Spain history. With the guitar, the energy source is the hand, the vibrating elements are the strings and the resonating chamber is the hollow body of the instrument.

Modern-day guitar designs go back to the late 1800s and early 1900s with designs from Orville Gibson. People like Les Paul and Adolph Rickenbacker were known for the solid-body guitar design. Les Paul was also known for innovative recording techniques as well as innovative electric guitar pickups. Other notable guitar makers are Clarence Fender, John D'Angelico, and Friedrich Gretsch.

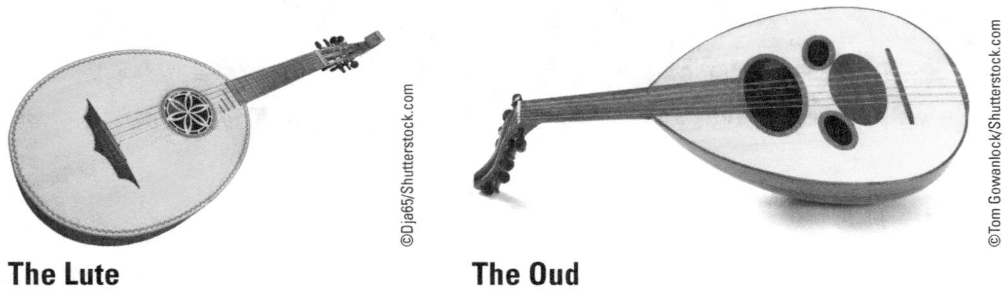

The Lute **The Oud**

Acoustical Guitars: The Classical Guitar (nylon strings), the Steel-String Guitar, and the Archtop Guitar.

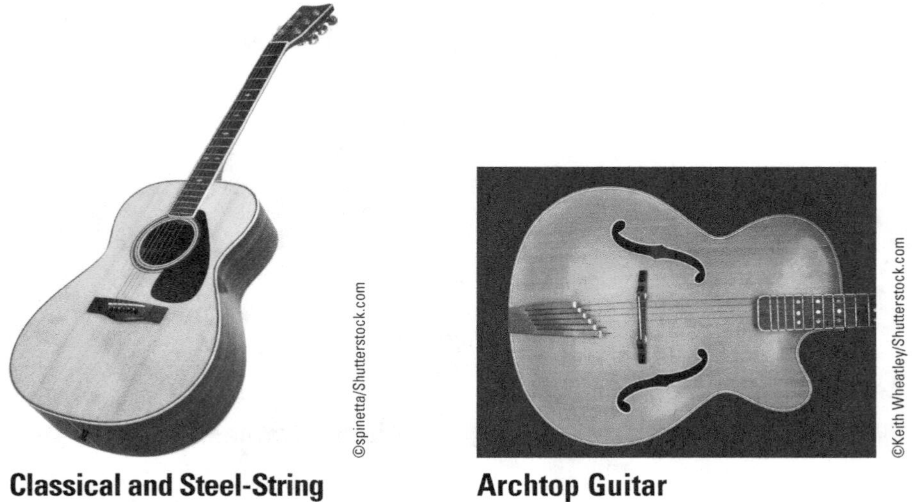

Classical and Steel-String **Archtop Guitar**

Electric Guitars: Electric guitars were first introduced in the 1930s. They can be either hollow body or solid body. As time went on, the solid body became the preferred choice because it was less prone to feedback than the hollow body. With the electric solid-body guitar, the energy source is the hand, the vibrating elements are the strings, and the sound is picked up by magnets and sent through the amplifier.

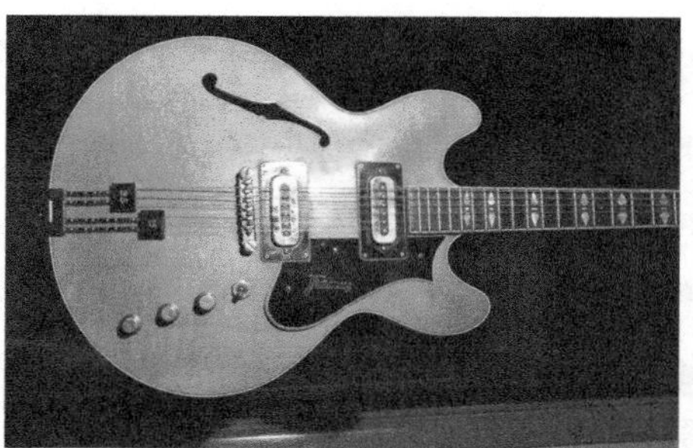
©Alan Heartfield/Shutterstock.com

Electric Guitar-Hollow Body

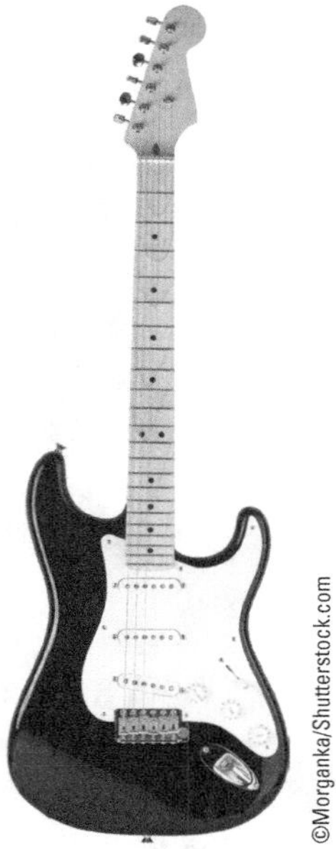
©Morganka/Shutterstock.com

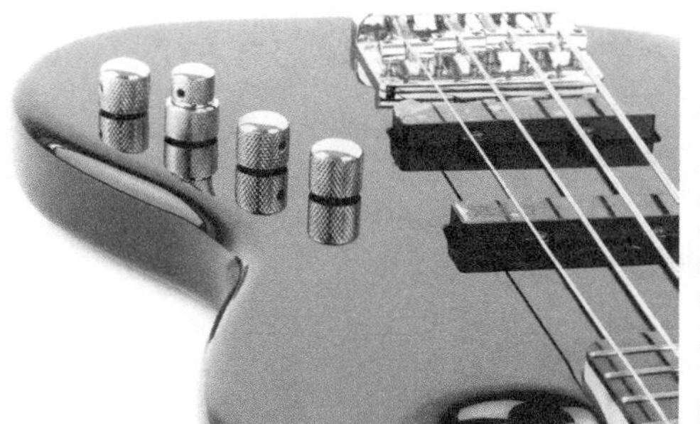
©I love photo/Shutterstock.com

Electric Bass (four strings)

Electric Guitar-Solid Body

The Four Sections of a Chorus: Soprano, Alto, Tenor, and Bass

These are listed from high to low range. The energy source for voices is air, the vocal chords are the vibrating elements and sound resonates in two places in the body, the chest and the head. **A cappella** is singing without instrumental accompaniment. An **Aria** is a vocal solo.

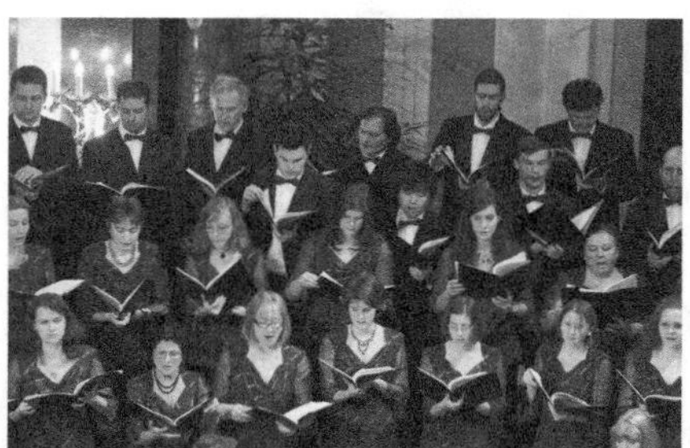
©posztos/Shutterstock.com

Bartok, Bela Choir

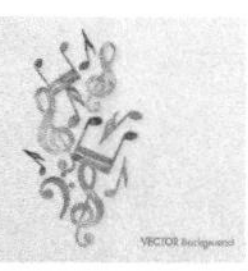

Listening Box 6

Type in the Mormon Tabernacle Choir and under Artists choose the Mormon Tabernacle Choir, Choral. Select track 47, 42. Chorus: "Hallelujah" (Four from the bottom).

A Cappella: Type in A Cappella Players and choose top box A Cappella Players, Vocal – Pop. Select Track 5, Eleanor Rigby, Track 6, All Will Be Well.

Aria: Type in Ruth Ann Swenson and choose top box Ruth Ann Swenson, Classical. Select Track 1, Linda di Chamonix "Ah! tardai troppo… O luce di quest anima."

Author's note. Ruth Ann is a personal friend of mine.

Small Ensembles

The Brass Quintet consists of two Trumpets, one Trombone, one French Horn, and a Tuba.

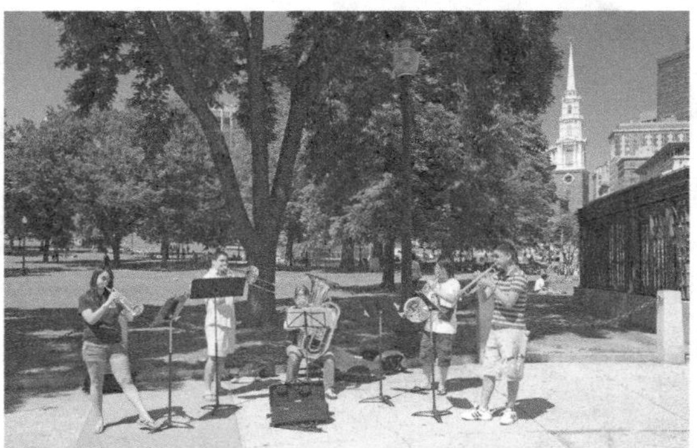

A Brass Quintet Performing in Boston

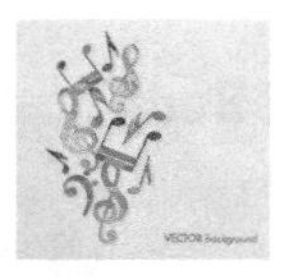

Listening Box 7

Type in Empire Brass in Japan and under Albums choose Empire Brass in Japan. Select Track 20, Boogie Woogie and Track 21, The Stars and Stripes Forever.

The Woodwind Quintet consists of one Flute, one Clarinet, one Oboe, one French Horn, and one Bassoon.

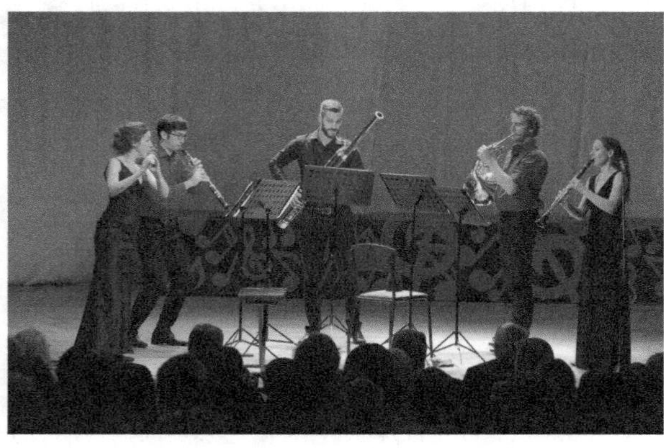

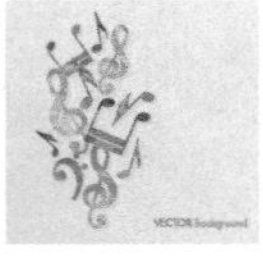

Listening Box 8

Type in The New York Woodwind Quintet and under Albums choose Woodwind Encores. Select Track 3, March and Track 5, Scherzo for Woodwind Quintet.

The String Quartet consists of two Violins—one Viola and a Cello.

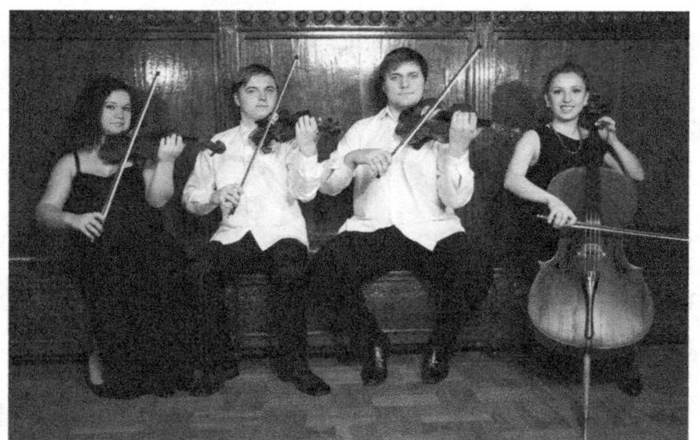

©kellyreekolibry/Shutterstock.com

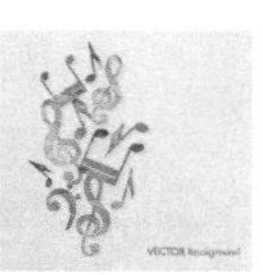

Listening Box 9

Type in The Dallas String Quartet-Red and under Listener Playlists choose the same name. Select Track 3, Paparazzi and Track 7, Don't Stop Believen.

Note: In the town of Cremona, Italy, string instrument making attained not only perfection, but this quality probably has never been equaled. Three men, Nicolò Amati (1596–1684), Antonio Stradivari (1644–1737), and Giuseppe Bartolomeo Guarneri (1698–1744) were master craftsmen and very secretive about the processes they used. The surviving instruments from these men go for very big dollars.

The String Trio consists of one Violin, one Viola, and one Cello.

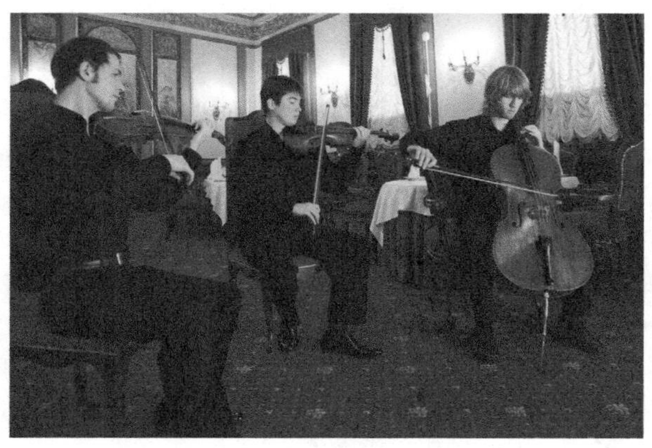

©Pavel L. Photo and Video/Shutterstock.com

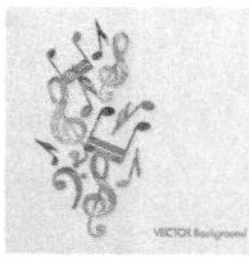

Listening Box 10

Type in Adaskin String Trio and under Top Result choose Trio in Eb, Op.3: Adagio. Select Track 4, Trio in Eb, Op.3: Adagio.

Summary of Unit 1 Terms

Composer, Performer, Arranger, and Audience. Also, Conductor and Concertmaster

Melody:	Harmony:	Rhythm:	Timbre: (Tone Color)
Phrase	Interval	Beat	Instruments
Cadence	Chord	Tempo	Voices:
Motive	Consonant	Meter	Soprano
Theme	Dissonant	Syncopation	Alto
Scales		Rhythmic Ostinato	Tenor
Ornamentation		Rubato	Bass
Repetition			
Sequence			
Imitation			
Trills			

Summary of the Listeners Toolbox (What do I Listen for?)

Introduction, Melody, Harmony, Rhythm, Instruments, Voices, Background Material, Style, Form, Genre, Story, Solos, Hooks and Fill-Ins, Tonic, Crescendo, Decrescendo, Forte, Piano, and Texture (Monophonic, Polyphonic, Homophonic).

Fill-Ins occur between melodic phrases and enhance the arrangement.

The Hook is designed to get you to buy the song and is made up of the song title and the main melody.

Tonic: The first note of a scale which is also called the keynote.

Crescendo: Gradually get louder. **Decrescendo:** Gradually get softer.

Forte: Loud. **Piano:** Soft.

Pertinent Questions

1. Can you hear what is going on in the introduction? Most people forget the intro and start listening when the singer starts.
2. Can you hear the instruments and voices?
3. Can you hear the background material?
4. Does the arrangement sound busy?
5. If a vocal, can you understand the words?

Listening Chart

Song Title	Intro	Melody	Harmony	Rhythm	Instr. Voices

Listening Assessment Sheet

The listening assessment sheet can be copied and used with any listening in the textbook.

1. What did you like about this piece?

2. What did you NOT like about this piece?

3. Do you feel this piece represents the era in which it was composed?

4. Overall, whether you liked the piece or not, did you appreciate how it was put together? (the arrangement)

Study Sheet for Unit 1 Test

The five listening levels:

1. Emotionally
2. Passively
3. Association and Context
4. Adding a story line
5. Subtleties of the musical arrangement.

Terms:

Melody: cadence, motive, sequence, theme, and trills.

Harmony: interval, chord, consonant, and dissonant.

Rhythm: beat, meter, tempo and syncopation, rhythmic ostinato.

Timbre: Know the four sections of the orchestra. Know all the instruments described in the instruments section. For example, know an oboe is a double-reed woodwind. Know the energy source, vibrating elements, and resonating chamber for each instrument.
Chorus: soprano, alto tenor, and bass. Know the energy source, vibrating elements, and resonating chambers of the human voice.
The Conductor's Role:

1. He coordinates and interprets.
2. He is a music scholar.
3. He keeps time with the baton.

Study Textures: Monophonic, Polyphonic, and Homophonic.

To The Student: The instructor may add or delete more study items at his or her discretion.

1. **Duet**: Two players.
2. **Trio**: Three players.
3. **Quartet**: Four players.
4. **Quintet**: Five players.
5. **Sextet**: Six players.
6. **Septet**: Seven players.
7. **Octet**: Eight players.
8. **Nonet**: Nine player.

Unit 1 Listening Box Playlist

LB1: Type in Star Wars Theme and under Tracks choose Star Wars Theme, End Title. (Your 2nd choice). Select Track 1, Star Wars Main Title.

LB2: Type in Yoda's Theme and choose top box Yoda's Theme. Select Track 1, Yoda's theme.

LB3: Type in Taylor Swift and choose top box Our Song, Taylor Swift. Select Track 3, Teardrops On My Guitar. (Consonant).

Type in Main Title Jaws and choose top box Main Title (Jaws/Soundtrack Version). Select Track 1, Main Title (Jaws/Soundtrack Version. (Dissonant).

LB4: Type in Meditation With Gregorian Chants and choose top box Meditation With Gregorian Chants. Select Track 7, Kyrie. (**Monophonic**). Type in Best of Bach and choose top box Best of Bach: Inventions and Sinfonias. Select Track 4, Bach: Invention 4. (**Polyphonic**). Type in Alan Jackson and under Albums choose 34 Number Ones. Select Track 24, Little Bitty. (**Homophonic**).

LB5: Type in the Young Person's Guide to the Orchestra and choose top box Variations on A Theme of Purcell, Op. 34. Select disc 2, Track 1, Variations on A Theme of Purcell, Op. 34 (From "The Young Person's Guide to the Orchestra").

LB6: Type in Mormon Tabernacle Choir and under Artists choose The Mormon Tabernacle Choir, Choral. Select Track 47, 42. Chorus: "Hallelujah" (Four from the bottom).

Type in A Cappella Players and choose top box A Cappella Players, Vocal—Pop. Select Track 5, Eleanor Rigby; Track 6, All Will Be Well.

Type in Ruth Ann Swenson and choose top box Ruth Ann Swenson, Classical. Select Track1, Linda di Chamonix "Ah! tardai troppo.. O luce di quest anima."

LB7: Type in Empire Brass in Japan and under Albums choose Empire Brass in Japan. Select Track 20, Boogie Woogie and Track 21, The Stars and Stripes Forever.

LB8: Type in The New York Woodwind Quintet and under Albums choose Woodwind Encores. Select Track 3, March and Track 5, Scherzo for Woodwind Quintet.

LB9: Type in The Dallas String Quartet-Red and under Listener Playlists choose the same name DSQ-Red. Select Track 3, Paparazzi and Track 7, Don't Stop Believen.

LB10: Type in Adaskin String Trio and under Top Result choose Trio in Eb, Op. 3: Adagio. Select Track 4, Trio in Eb, Op. 3: Adagio.

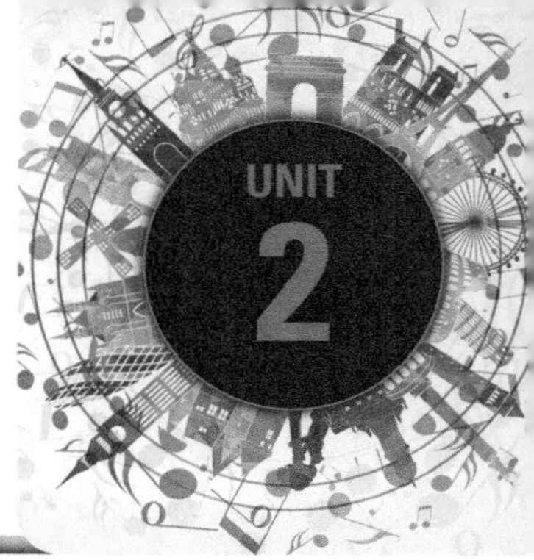

Basic Music Writing

Unit Purpose

The purpose of this unit is to immerse the student into some basic music writing. It has always been my contention if students can see how things are put together, they will derive a greater understanding about what they are studying.

To the Student: These worksheets are designed to be used in several ways. The instructor may use them as class assignments or for project submission.

Note: These worksheets are used with permission from the Finale Print Music Program © 2014. The material on all of these pages is original and nothing has been changed or modified.

The order of sheet usage in this unit is as follows:

1. The Staff
2. The Staff – Treble Clef
3. Musical Words – Treble Clef 1
4. The Staff – Bass Clef
5. Musical Words – Bass Clef 1
6. Treble Clef – Ledger Lines
7. Bass Clef – Ledger Lines
8. The Grand Staff
9. Time Signatures – 4/4
10. Time Signature – 3/4
11. Time Signatures – 2/4
12. Time Signatures – 2/2, ¢
13. Rests
14. Notes and Rests
15. Eighth Notes and Eighth Rests
16. Slurs and Ties
17. Stems
18. Intervals
19. Sharps and Flats 1
20. Sharps, Flats, and Naturals

21. Enharmonic Notes 1
22. Enharmonic Notes II
23. Half Steps and Whole Steps 1
24. The Circle of Fifths 1
25. The Circle of Fifths III – 𝄞
26. Major Scale Ia – 𝄞
27. Major Scales and Key Signatures IIa – 𝄞
28. Major Scale Ia – 𝄢
29. Major Scales and Key Signatures IIa – 𝄢

Name________________________ Date____________________

The Staff

The musical **staff** is made up of five **lines** and four **spaces**. Lines and spaces are both numbered from low to high.

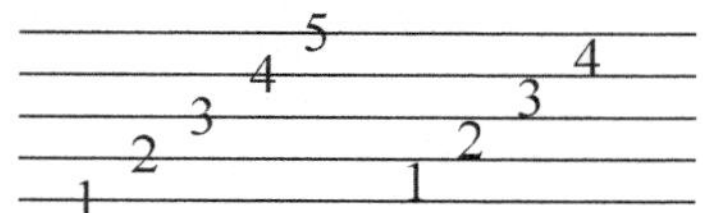

---

1. Practice drawing two staffs by connecting the dots. Use a ruler to help draw straight lines.

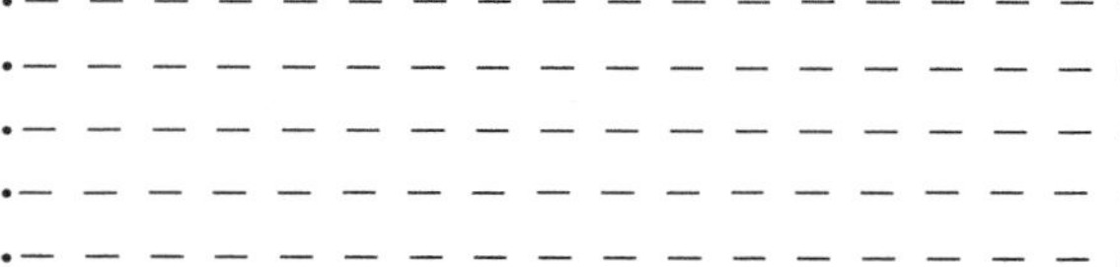

2. On the first staff, number the lines from low to high.

3. On the second staff, number the spaces from low to high.

4. Draw a note on each line of the staff below.

5. Draw a note on each space of the staff below.

Name________________________ Date____________________

The Staff - Treble Clef

A **clef** appears at the beginning of each staff. The clef shown here is a **treble clef**.

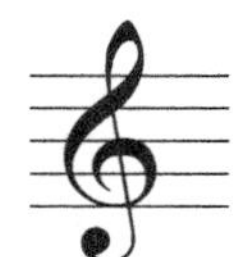

Each note on the treble clef staff has a letter name.

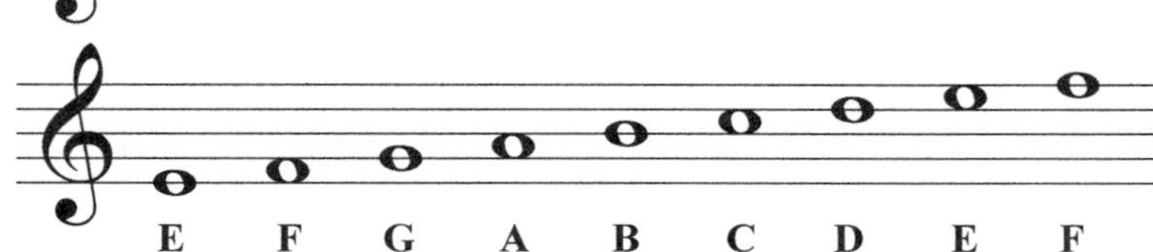

1. Practice drawing the treble clef sign by tracing over the guidelines. Draw five more in the remaining space.

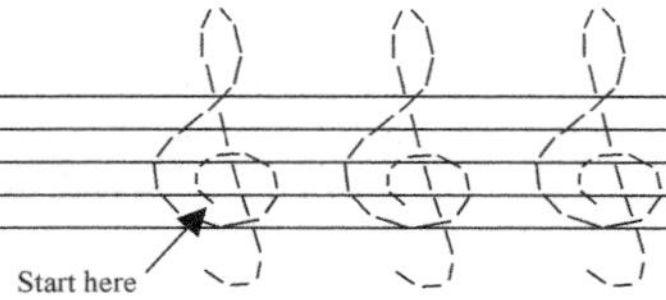

2. Draw a treble clef at the beginning of the staff and write the letter name of each note.

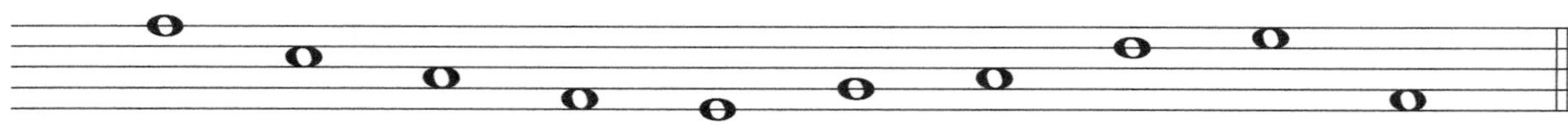

___ ___ ___ ___ ___ ___ ___ ___ ___ ___

3. Draw the treble clef at the beginning of the staff and then draw the notes indicated.
If a note can be drawn in more than one place on the staff, choose which one you want to draw.

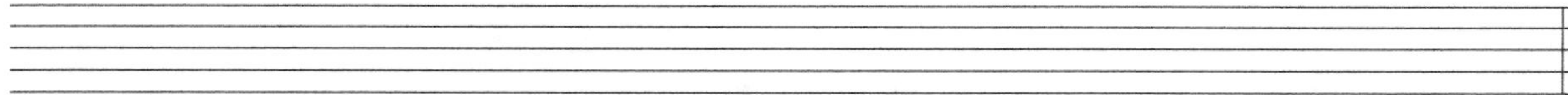

A C E F D B A F D G

4. Draw the treble clef at the beginning of the staff.
Write the letter name for each note, then circle the higher note in each pair.

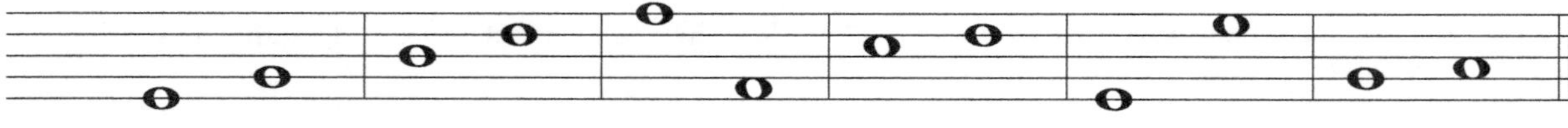

___ ___ ___ ___ ___ ___ ___ ___ ___ ___ ___ ___

5. Draw the treble clef at the beginning of the staff.
Write the letter name for each note, then circle the lower note in each pair.

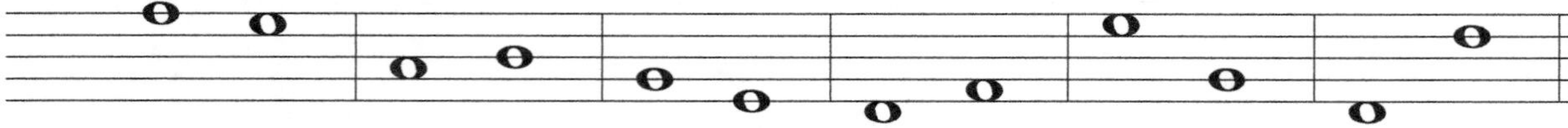

___ ___ ___ ___ ___ ___ ___ ___ ___ ___ ___ ___

Name______________________ Date____________________

Musical Words - Treble Clef I

Each group of notes spells a word.
Write the word that each group spells.

Example

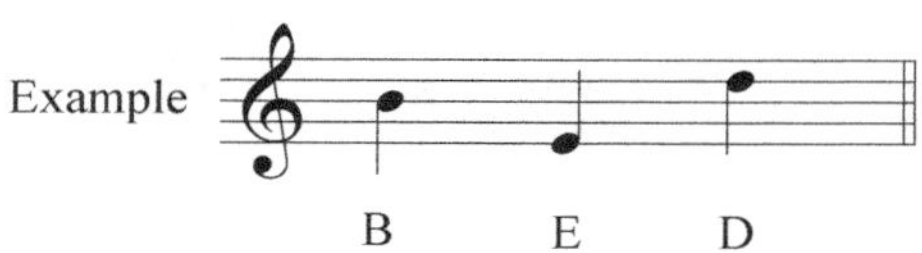

1

2

3

4

5

6

7

8

9

10

11

12

13

14

15

16

17

18

Name________________________ Date____________________

The Staff - Bass Clef

A **clef** appears at the beginning of each staff. The clef shown here is a **bass clef**.

Each note on the bass clef staff has a letter name.

G A B C D E F G A

---

1. Practice drawing the bass clef sign by tracing over the guidelines. Draw five more in the remaining space.

2. Draw a bass clef at the beginning of the staff and write the letter name of each note.

___ ___ ___ ___ ___ ___ ___ ___ ___ ___

3. Draw the bass clef at the beginning of the staff and then draw the notes indicated.
If a note can be drawn in more than one place on the staff, choose which one you want to draw.

C A E D F G B C D G

4. Draw the bass clef at the beginning of the staff.
Write the letter name for each note, then circle the higher note in each pair.

___ ___ ___ ___ ___ ___ ___ ___ ___ ___ ___ ___

5. Draw the bass clef at the beginning of the staff.
Write the letter name for each note, then circle the lower note in each pair.

___ ___ ___ ___ ___ ___ ___ ___ ___ ___ ___ ___

Name________________________ Date____________________

Musical Words - Bass Clef I

Each group of notes spells a word.
Write the word that each group spells.

Example 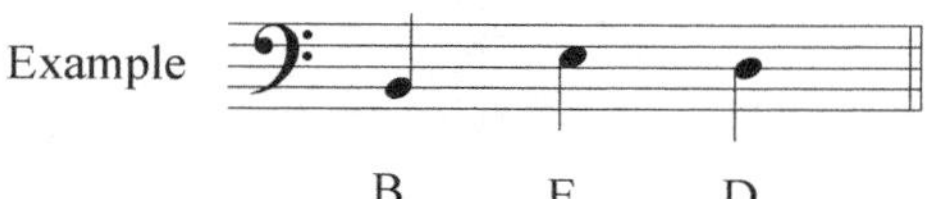

B E D

1 ___ ___ ___

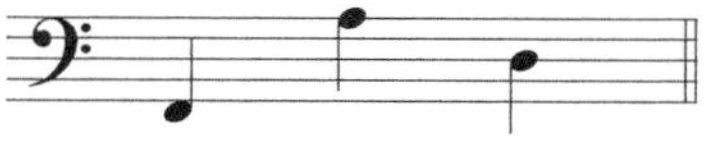

2 ___ ___ ___

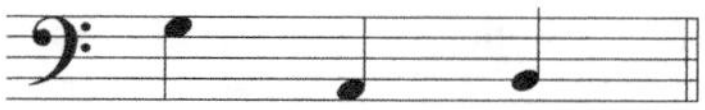

3 ___ ___ ___

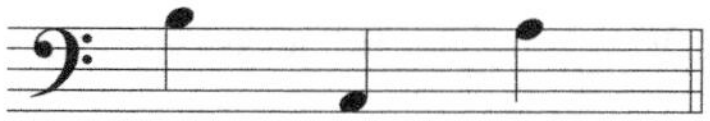

4 ___ ___ ___

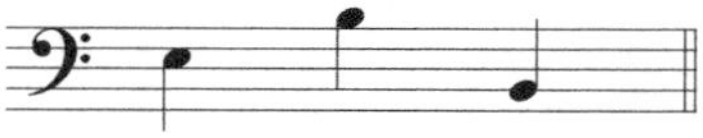

5 ___ ___ ___

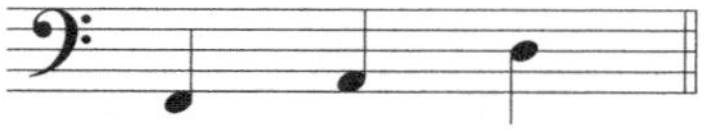

6 ___ ___ ___

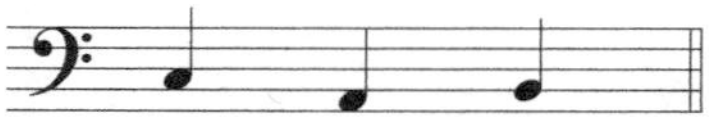

7 ___ ___ ___ ___

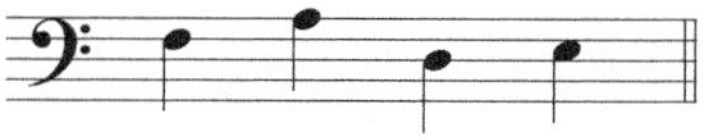

8 ___ ___ ___ ___

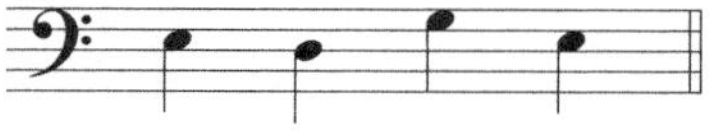

9 ___ ___ ___

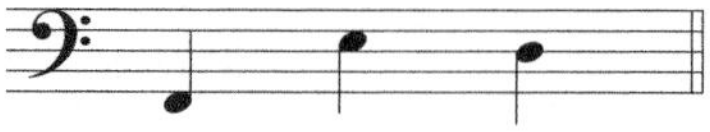

10 ___ ___ ___

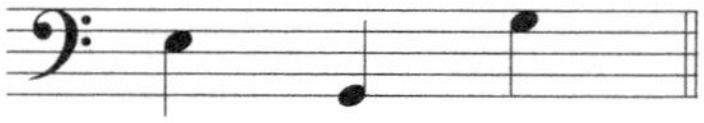

11 ___ ___ ___ ___

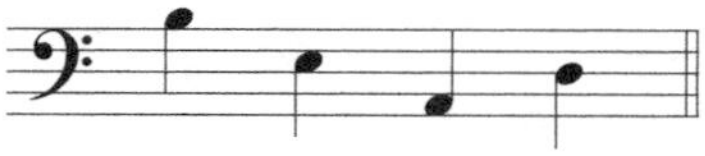

12 ___ ___ ___ ___

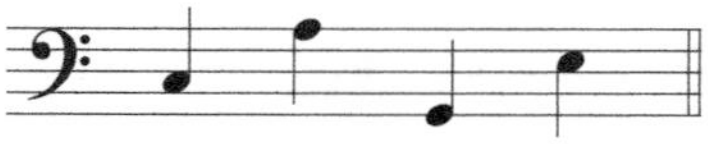

13 ___ ___ ___

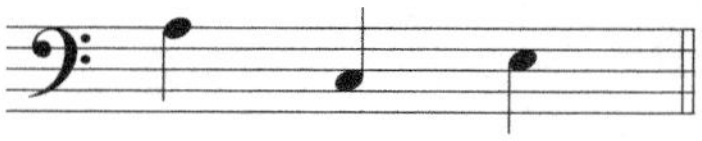

14 ___ ___ ___

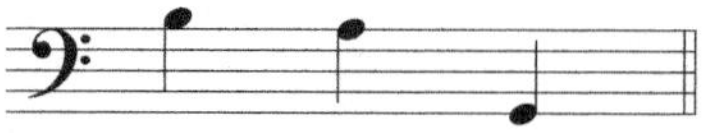

15 ___ ___ ___

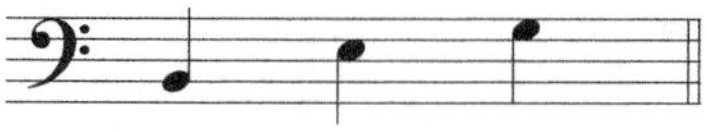

16 ___ ___ ___ ___

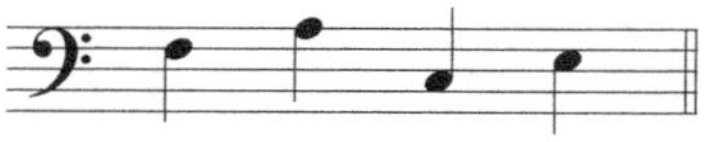

17 ___ ___ ___ ___

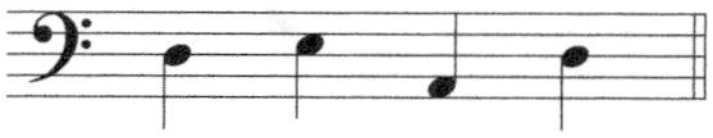

18 ___ ___ ___

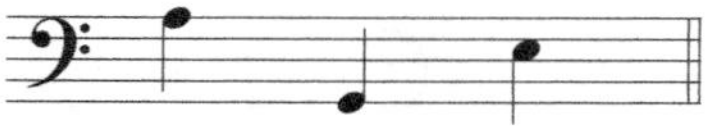

Name________________________ Date____________________

Treble Clef - Ledger Lines

Ledger lines can be used to extend the upper and lower ranges of a staff.

This example includes notes which can be written above and below the treble clef using **ledger lines**.

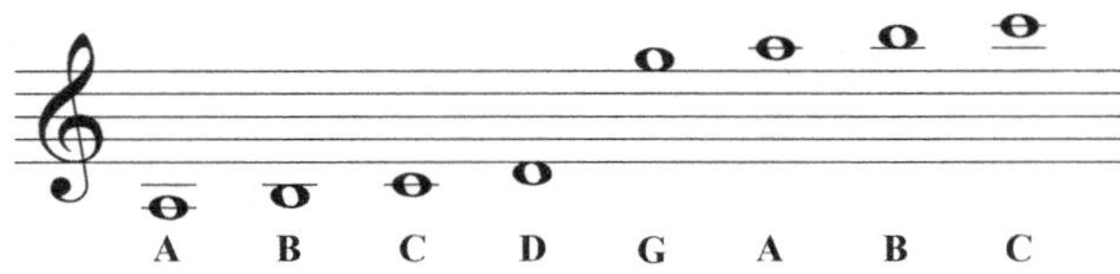

1. Draw a treble clef at the beginning of the staff and write the letter name of each note.

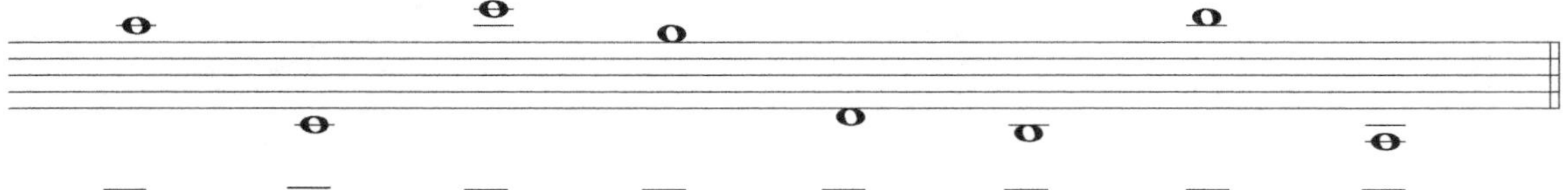

2. Draw a treble clef at the beginning of the staff and write the letter name of each note.

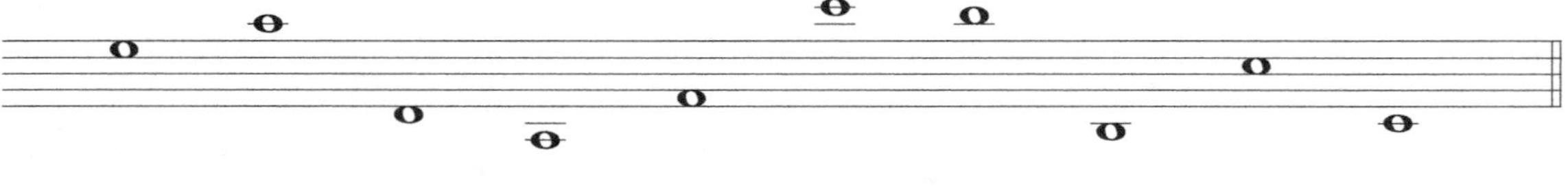

3. Draw the indicated notes. Use ledger lines to draw the specified number of pitches without duplication.

Example

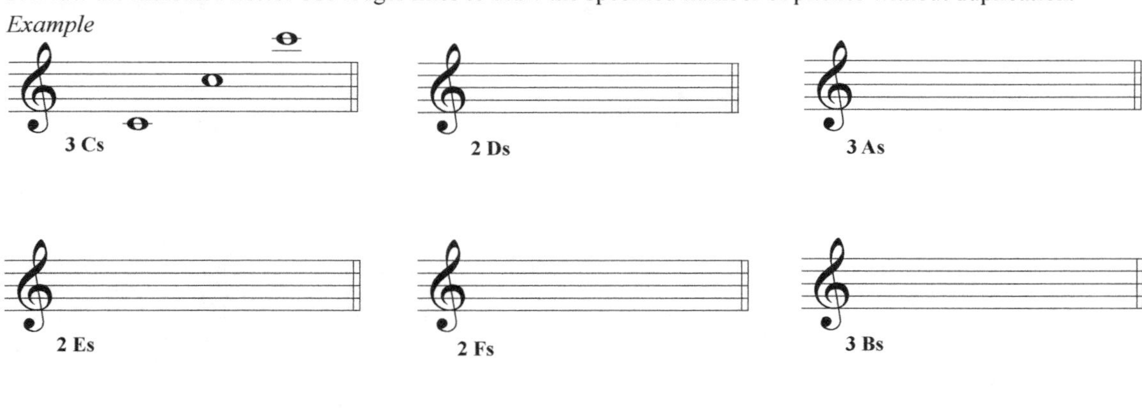

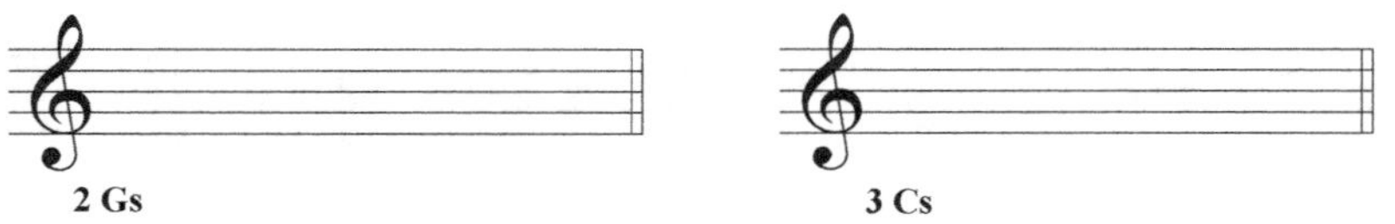

Name________________________ Date____________________

Bass Clef - Ledger Lines

Ledger lines can be used to extend the upper and lower ranges of a staff.

This example includes notes which can be written above and below the bass clef using **ledger lines**.

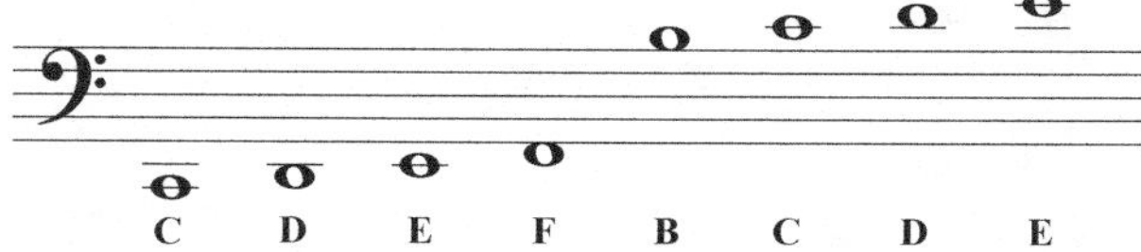

1. Draw a bass clef at the beginning of the staff and write the letter name of each note.

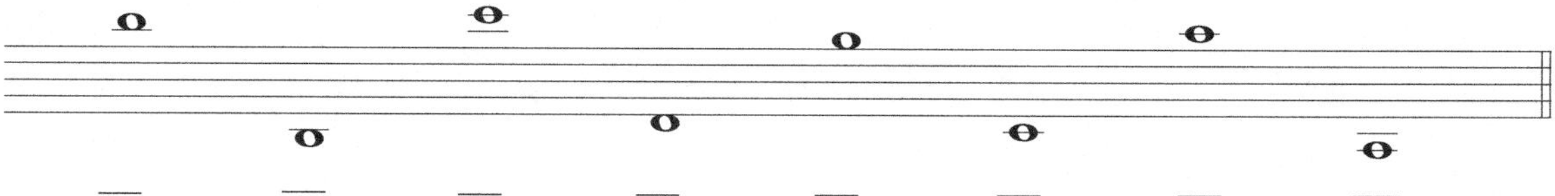

2. Draw a bass clef at the beginning of the staff and write the letter name of each note.

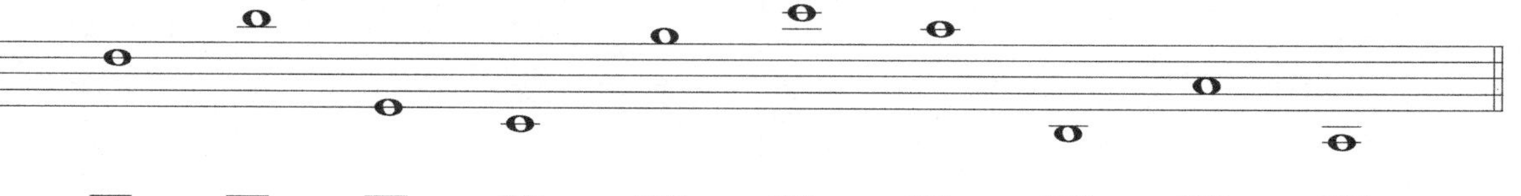

3. Draw the indicated notes. Use ledger lines to draw the specified number of pitches without duplication.

Example

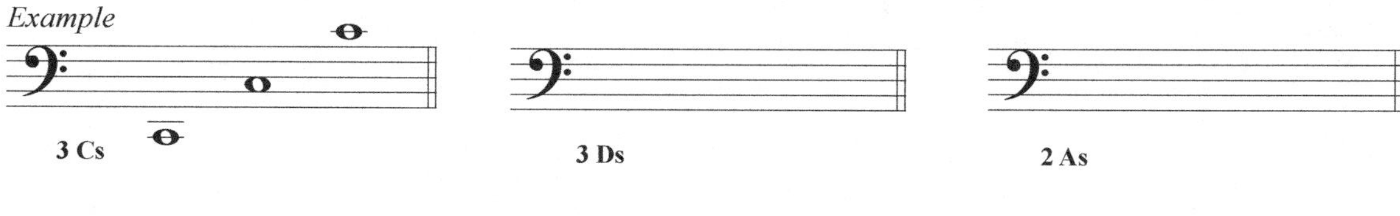

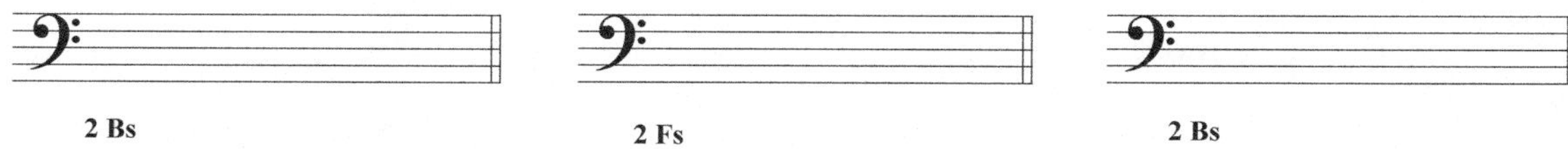

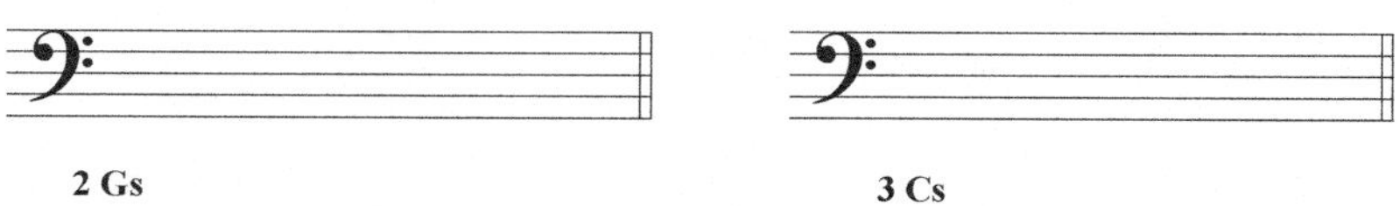

Name________________________ Date____________________

The Grand Staff

The **grand staff** is created by joining the treble staff and the bass staff with a **brace** and **bar line.**

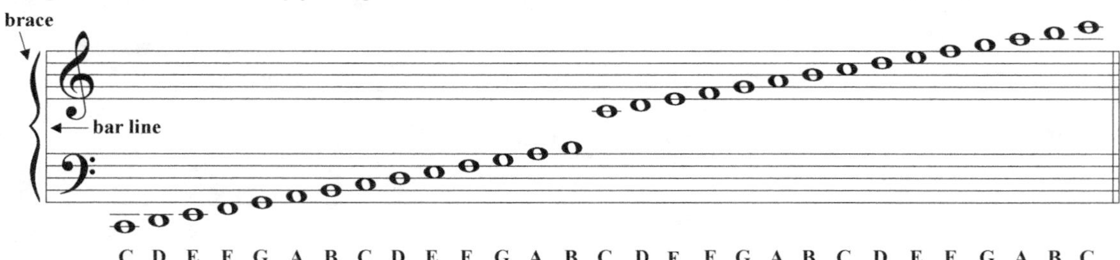

1. Practice creating the grand staff by tracing the braces, bar lines, and clefs.

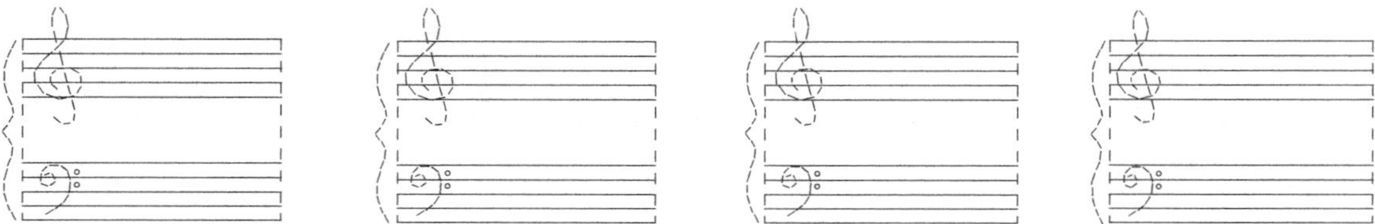

2. Using the staffs below, create four grand staffs by adding braces, bar lines, and clefs.

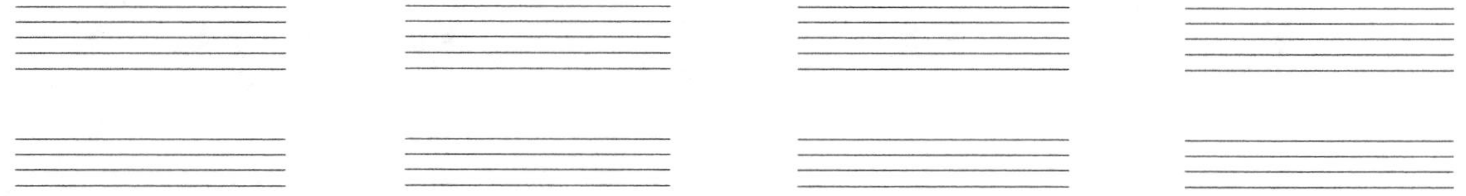

3. Write the letter name for each note.

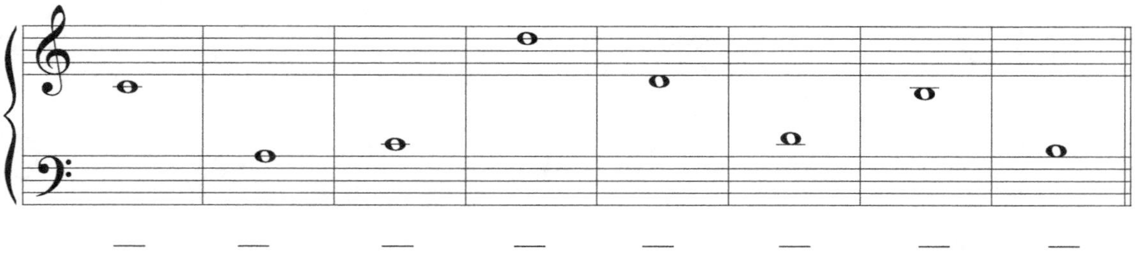

___ ___ ___ ___ ___ ___ ___ ___

Name________________________ Date____________________

Time Signatures - $\frac{4}{4}$

Time signatures appear at the beginning of a piece of music music. They are made up of two numbers.

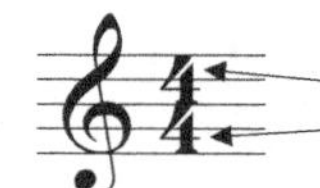

The top number indicates the number of beats per measure.
The bottom number indicates which note will get one beat.

In $\frac{4}{4}$ time there are four beats in each measure.

A **quarter note** (♩) = 1 beat
A **half note** (𝅗𝅥) = 2 beats
A **whole note** (𝅝) = 4 beats

---

1. Clap the rhythm while counting the beats out loud.

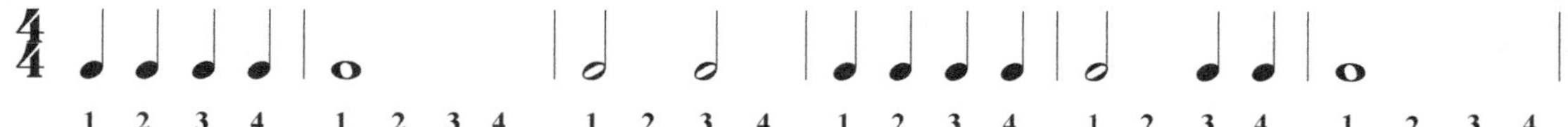

2. Write the count below the notes and then clap the rhythm while counting the beats out loud.

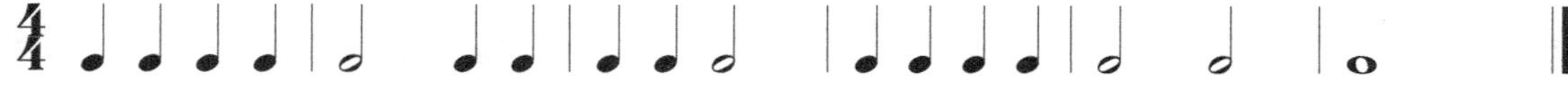

3. Write a $\frac{4}{4}$ time signature after the clef sign.
Write the count below the notes and then clap the rhythm while counting the beats out loud.

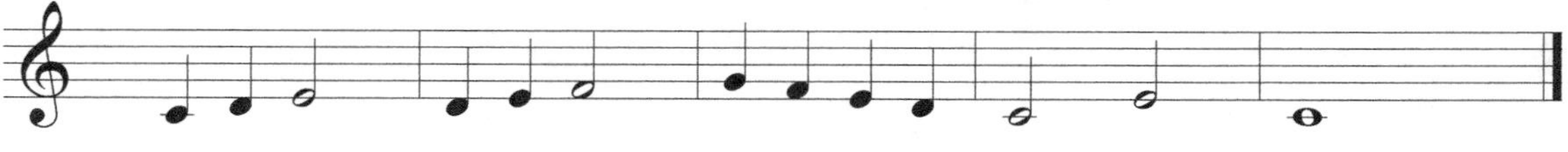

4. Write a $\frac{4}{4}$ time signature after the clef sign.
Write in the count below the notes.
Draw the missing bar lines.

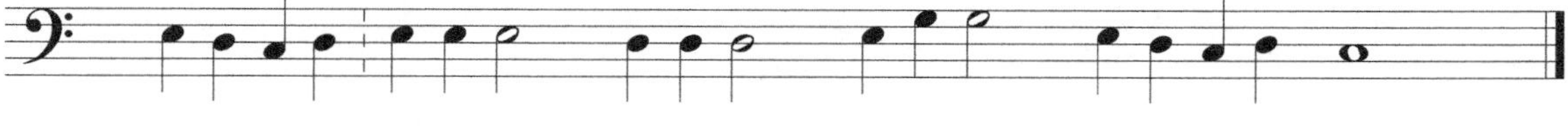

5. Write in the count below the notes and add the missing barlines.

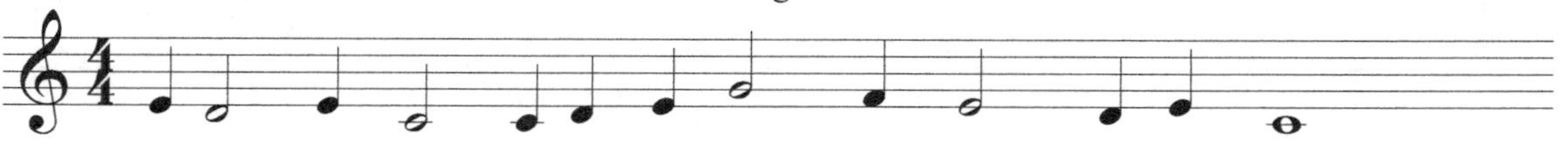

Name________________________ Date___________________

Time Signatures - $\frac{3}{4}$

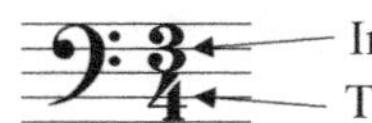

In $\frac{3}{4}$ time there are three beats in each measure.
The quarter note gets one beat.

Rhythmic values
- A quarter note (♩) = 1 beat
- A half note (𝅗𝅥) = 2 beats
- A dotted half note (𝅗𝅥.) = 3 beats

The dotted half note gets three beats. 𝅗𝅥. = 3 beats

---

1. Clap the rhythm while counting the beats out loud.

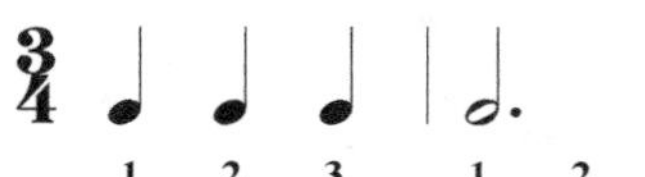
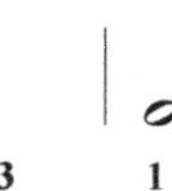
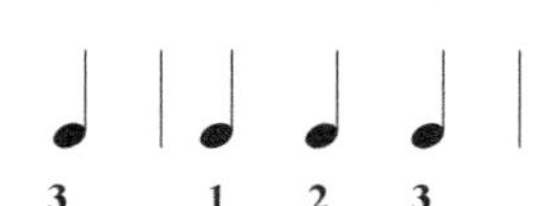
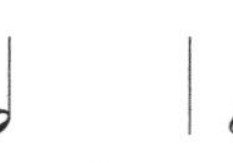
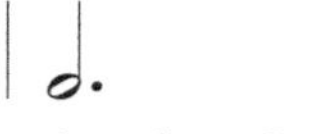

2. Write the count below the notes and then clap the rhythm while counting the beats out loud.

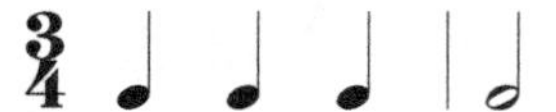
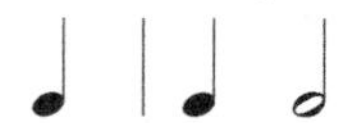
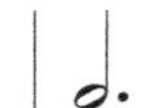
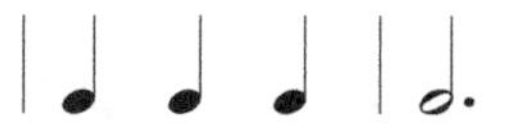

3. Write a $\frac{3}{4}$ time signature after the clef sign.
Write the count below the notes and then clap the rhythm while counting the beats out loud.

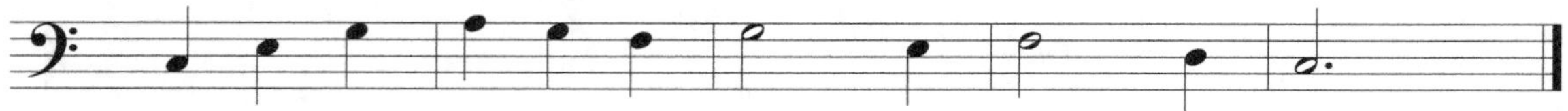

4. Write a $\frac{3}{4}$ time signature after the clef sign. Write in the count below the notes. Draw the missing bar lines.

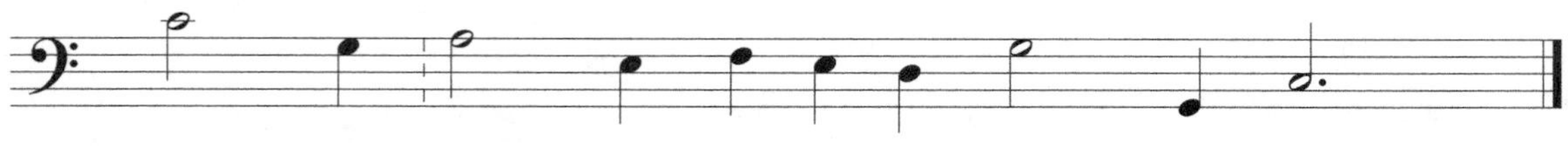

5. Write in the count below the notes and add the missing barlines.

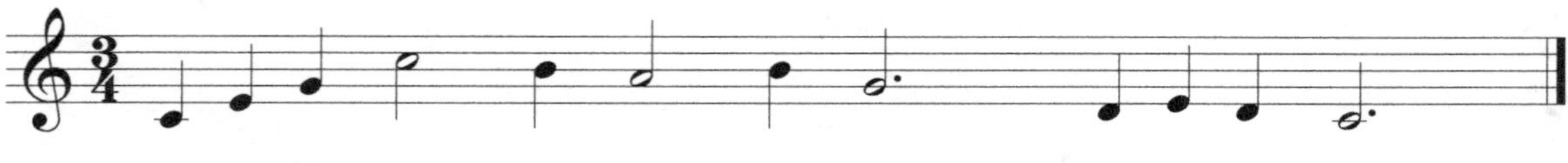

Name________________________ Date__________________

Time Signatures - 2/4

In 2/4 time there are two beats in each measure.
The quarter note gets one beat.

Rhythmic values
- An eighth note (♪) = 1/2 beat
- A quarter note (♩) = 1 beat
- A half note (𝅗𝅥) = 2 beats

---

1. Clap the rhythm while counting the beats out loud.

1 2 | 1 + 2 + | 1 2 | 1 2 | 1 2 + | 1 2

2. Write the count below the notes and then clap the rhythm while counting the beats out loud.

3. Write a 2/4 time signature after the clef sign.
Write the count below the notes and then clap the rhythm while counting the beats out loud.

4. Write a 2/4 time signature after the clef sign. Write in the count below the notes. Draw the missing bar lines.

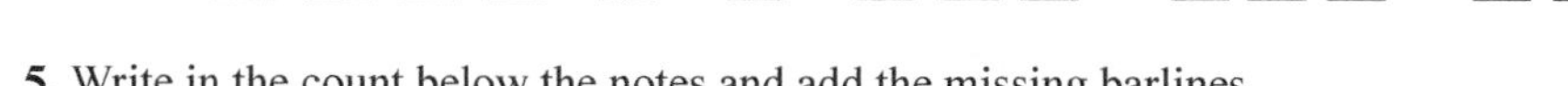

5. Write in the count below the notes and add the missing barlines.

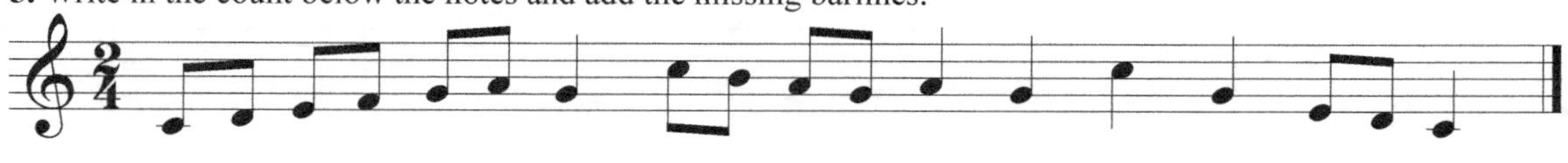

Name________________________ Date____________________

Time Signatures - $\frac{2}{2}$, ¢

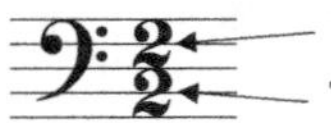

In $\frac{2}{2}$ time there are two beats in each measure.
The half note gets one beat.

$\frac{2}{2}$ is often referred to as "cut" time.

$\frac{2}{2}$ may also be displayed as ¢.

Rhythmic values
- A quarter note (♩) = 1/2 beat
- A half note (𝅗𝅥) = 1 beat
- A whole note (𝅝) = 2 beats

---

1. Clap the rhythm while counting out loud.

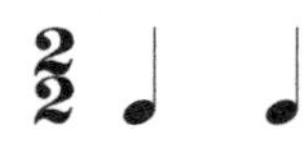
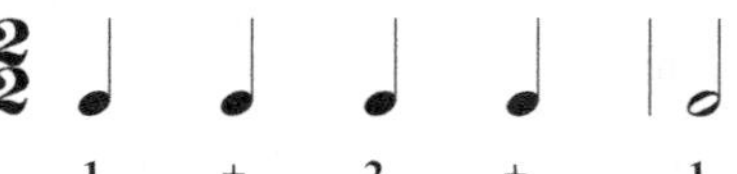

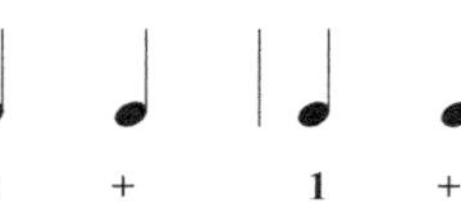
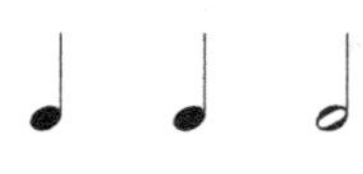
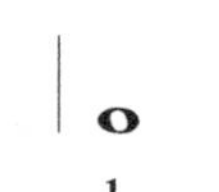

2. Write the count below the notes and then clap the rhythm while counting out loud.

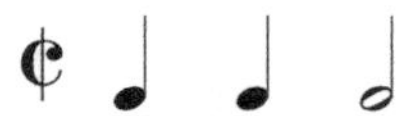
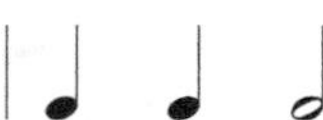
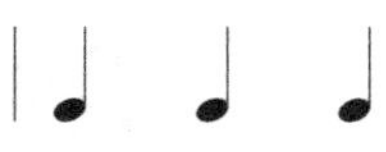
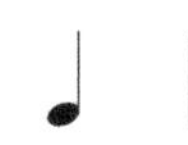
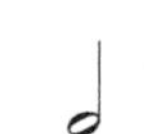

3. Write a $\frac{2}{2}$ time signature after the clef sign.
Write the count below the notes and then clap the rhythm while counting out loud.

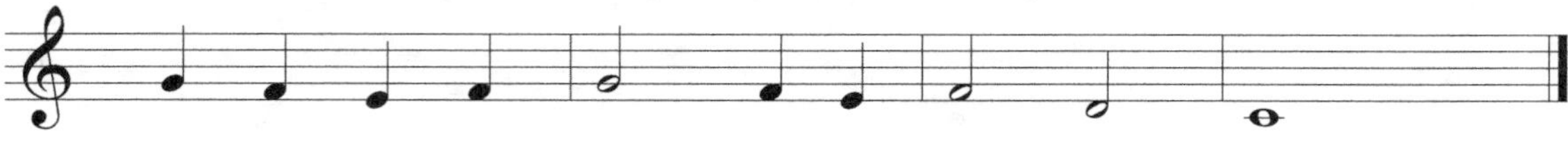

4. Write a $\frac{2}{2}$ time signature after the clef sign. Write in the count below the notes. Draw the missing bar lines.

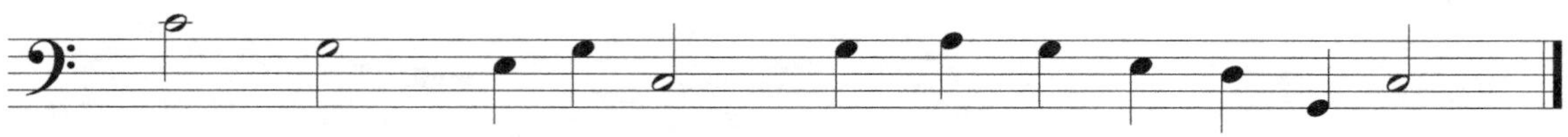

5. Write in the count below the notes and add the missing barlines.

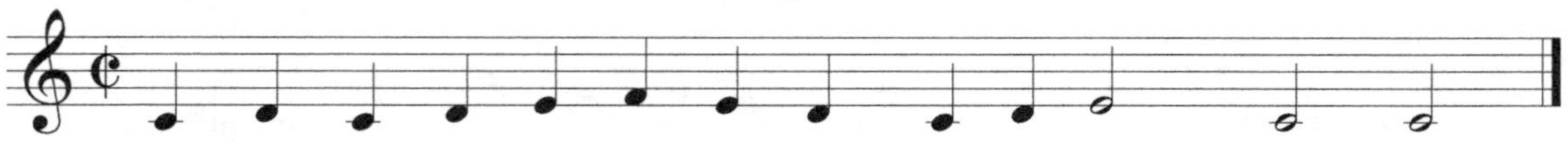

Name________________________ Date____________________

Rests

Rests are used in music to indicate silence.

A **quarter rest** (𝄽) = 1 beat
A **half rest** (▬) = 2 beats
A **whole rest** (▬) = 4 beats

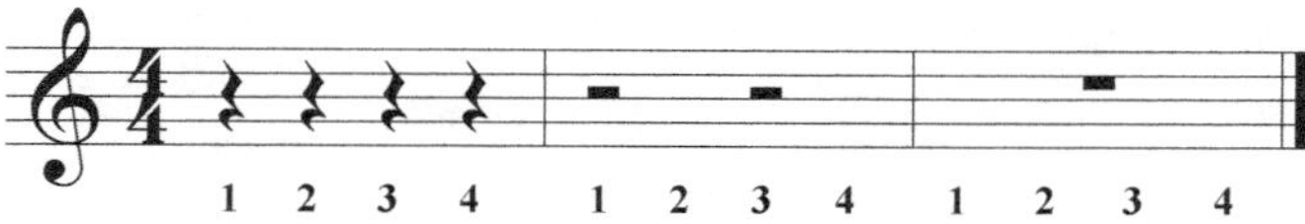

1. Practice drawing quarter rests by tracing over the outlines.
Draw four quarter rests in each blank measure.

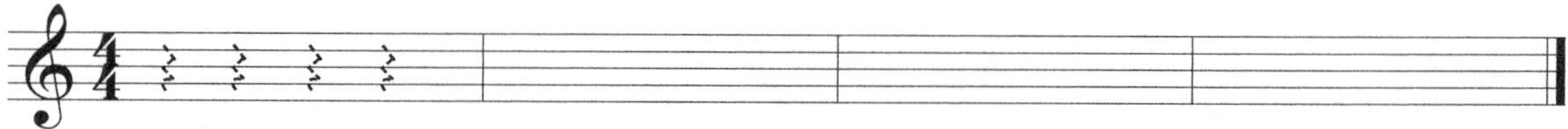

2. Draw two half rests in each blank measure.

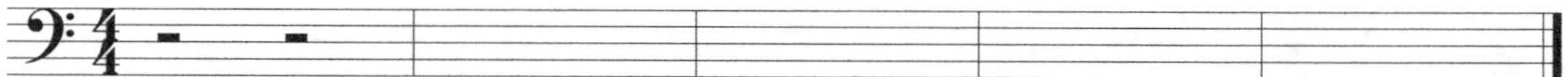

3. Draw one whole rest in each blank measure.

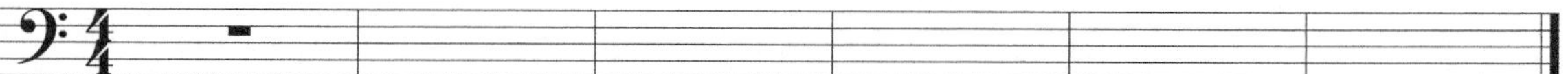

4. Write the count below the rests.

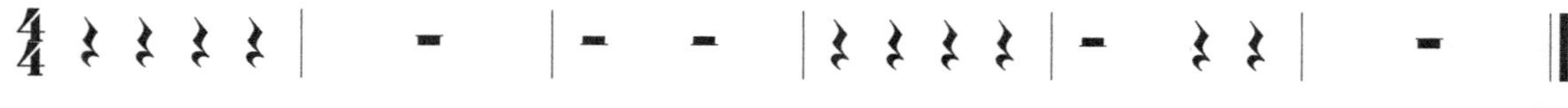

5. Write the count below the notes and rests, then clap and count the rhythm out loud.

6. Write the count below the notes and rests, then add the missing bar lines.

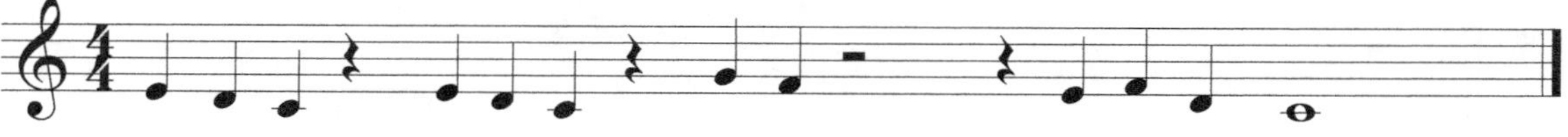

Name______________________ Date__________________

Notes and Rests

Complete these exercises.

Make sure each measure contains four beats.

A **quarter note** (♩) = 1 beat
A **half note** (𝅗𝅥) = 2 beats
A **whole note** (𝅝) = 4 beats

A **quarter rest** (𝄽) = 1 beat
A **half rest** (𝄼) = 2 beats
A **whole rest** (𝄻) = 4 beats

1. Each measure in the next two exercises is missing one rest.
Complete each measure by adding the appropriate rest.

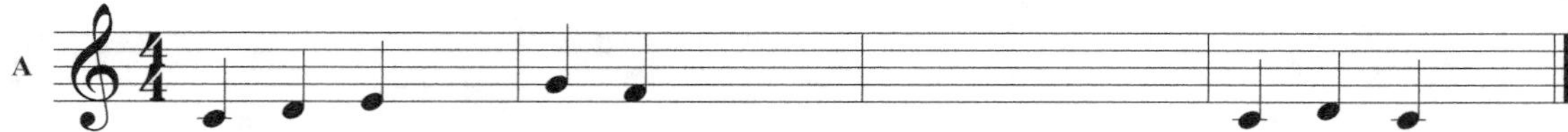

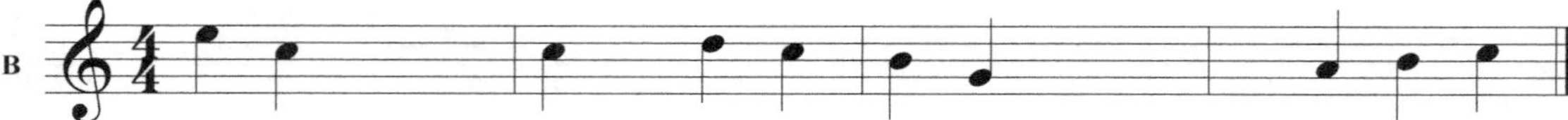

2. This song is missing bar lines. Fill in the missing barlines

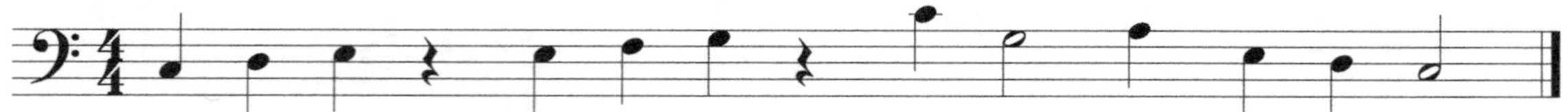

3. Some of the measures in this song are missing a rest. Complete each measure by adding the appropriate rest.
Remember, some measures are complete.

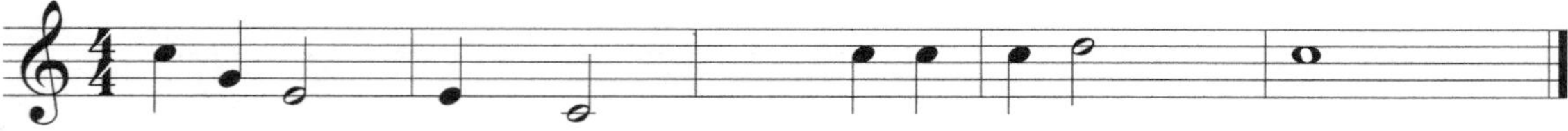

4. Fill in the missing rests. Some measures are missing more than one rest.

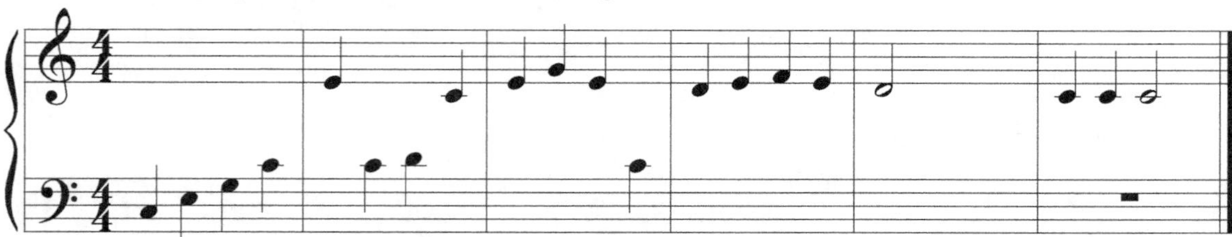

Name________________________ Date____________________

Eighth Notes and Eighth Rests

The rhythmic value of an **eighth rest** is one half of a beat.

An **eighth rest** (𝄾) = 1/2 beat

An **eighth note** (♪) = 1/2 beat

Use a plus sign (+) when writing the count for eighth notes and eighth rests.

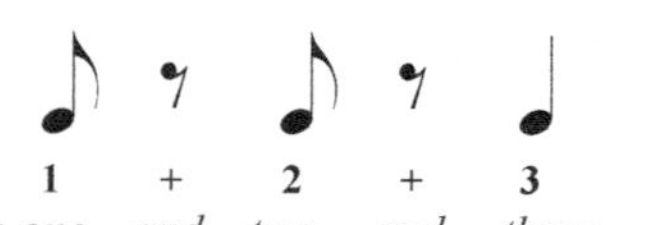

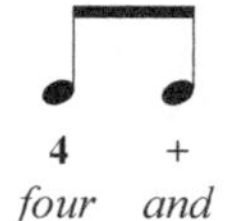

1. Clap the rhythm while counting out loud.

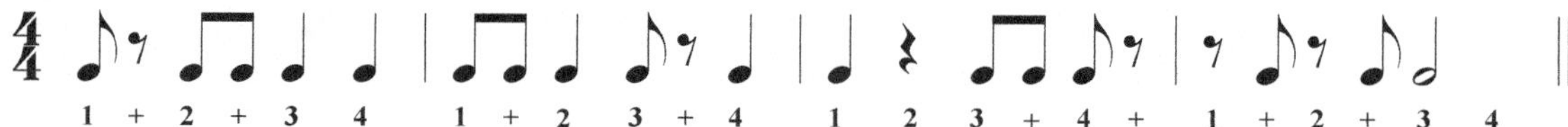

2. Write the count below the notes and then clap the rhythm while counting out loud.

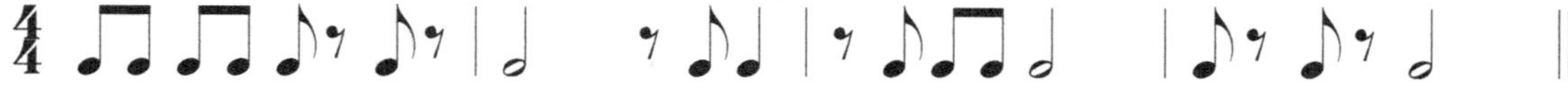

3. Write the count below the notes and then clap the rhythm while counting out loud.

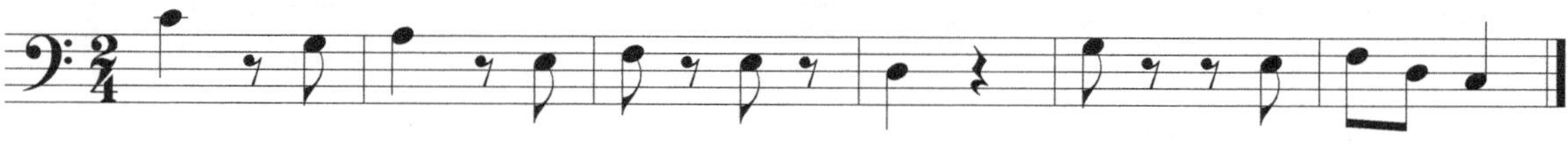

4. Some eighth notes are missing their flags or beams. Draw the missing flags and beams.

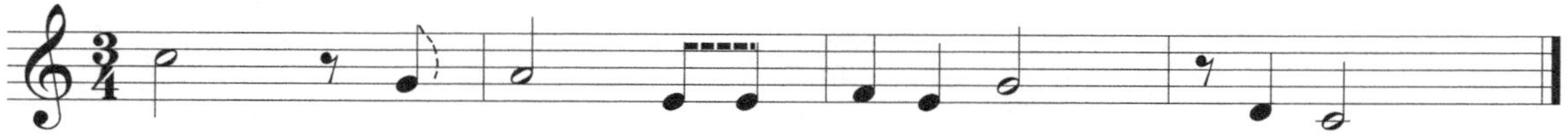

5. Write in the count below the notes and then add the missing barlines.

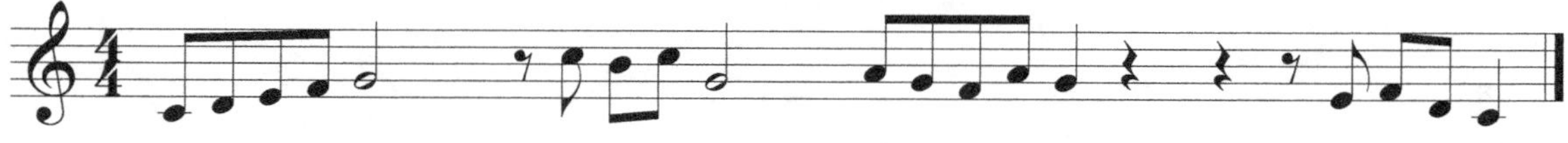

6. Some eighth notes are missing their flags or beams. Draw the missing flags and beams.

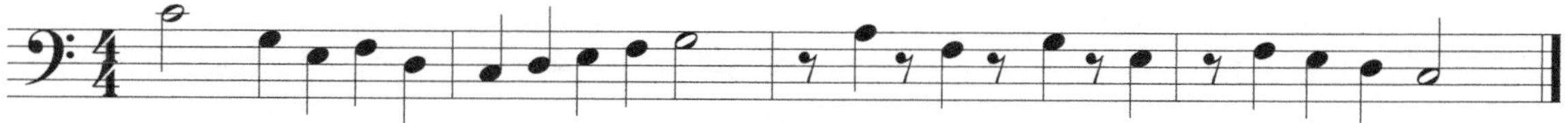

Name________________________ Date____________________

Slurs and Ties

A **slur** is a curved line connection *two or more* notes of *different* pitches.
Slurred passages should be played as smoothly as possible.

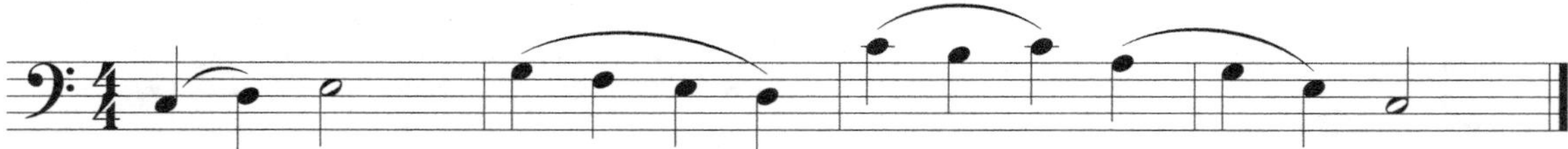

A **tie** is a curved line which connects *two* notes of the *same* pitch.

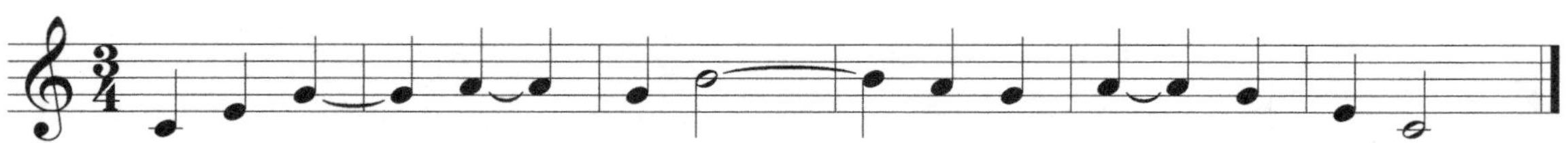

Tied notes are played as one note. The rhythmic value is the sum of the two notes.

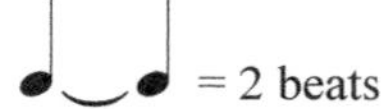

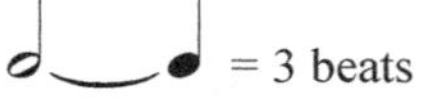

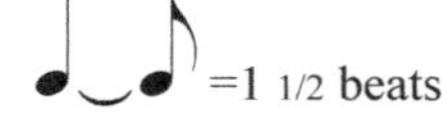

---

1. Circle the ties in this example.

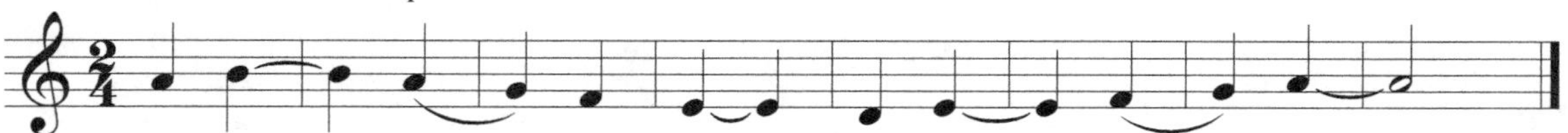

2. Circle the slurs in this example.

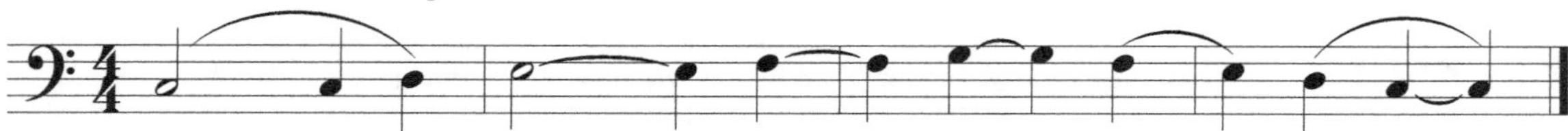

3. Write the number of beats each pair of tied notes should receive.

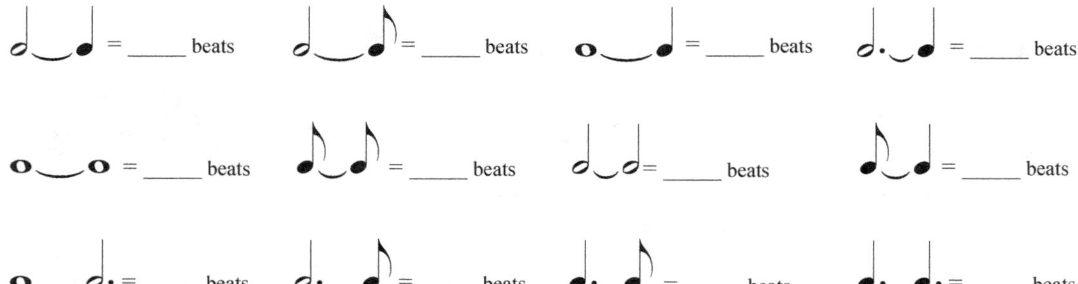

Name________________________ Date____________________

Stems

Stems are used to help determine what rhythmic value a note will have. By adding a stem to an open notehead you change the value of the note from a whole note to a half note

𝅝 = 4 𝅗𝅥 = 2

It is important to draw stems on the proper side of the notehead and draw them in the proper direction. Notes that appear on or above the middle staff line have downward stems drawn on the left side of the notehead. Notes that appear below the middle staff line have upward stems drawn on the right side of the notehead.

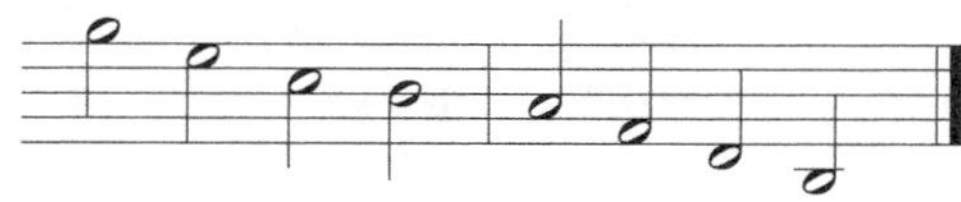

---

1. Practice drawing stems by adding the proper stem to each notehead.

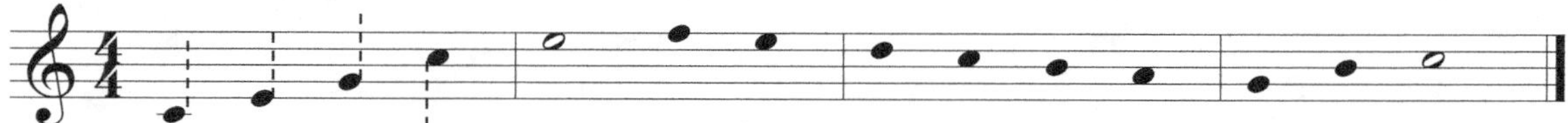

2. Practice drawing stems by adding the proper stem to each notehead.

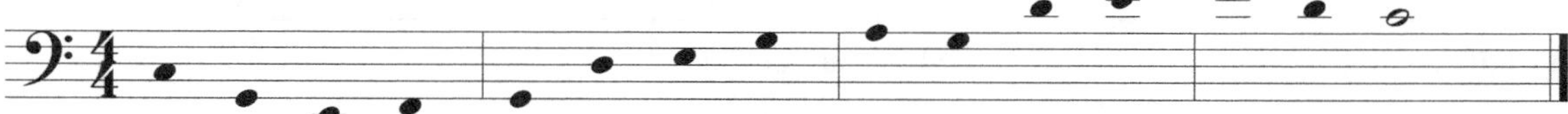

3. Some of these stems are drawn incorrectly. Circle the incorrect stems.

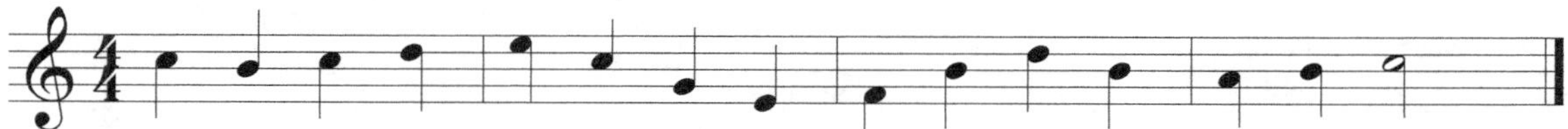

4. Some of these stems are drawn incorrectly. Circle the incorrect stems.

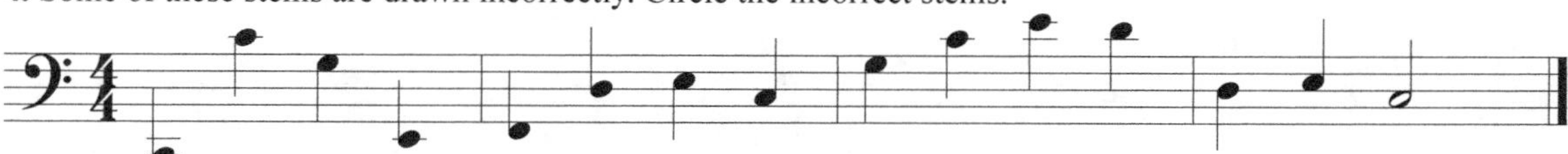

5. Some of these notes are missing stems. Add stems where needed.
Make sure that each measure has four beats.

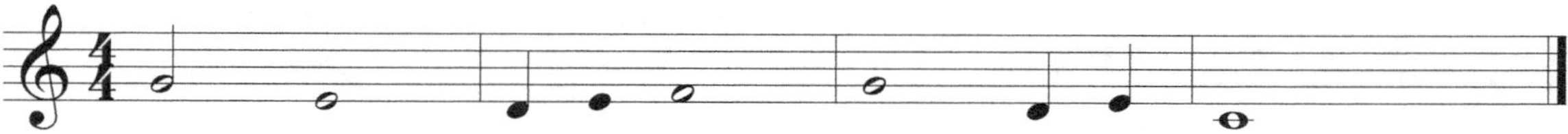

6. Some of these notes are missing stems. Add stems where needed.
Make sure that each measure has four beats.

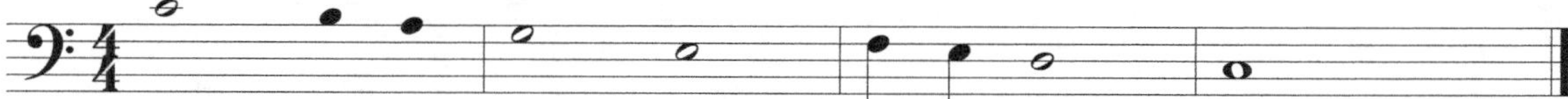

Name________________________ Date____________________

Intervals I

In music, an **interval** is the distance between two notes.
A **melodic interval** is the distance between two notes shich are played one at a time.
A **harmonic interval** is the distance between two notes which are played at the same time.

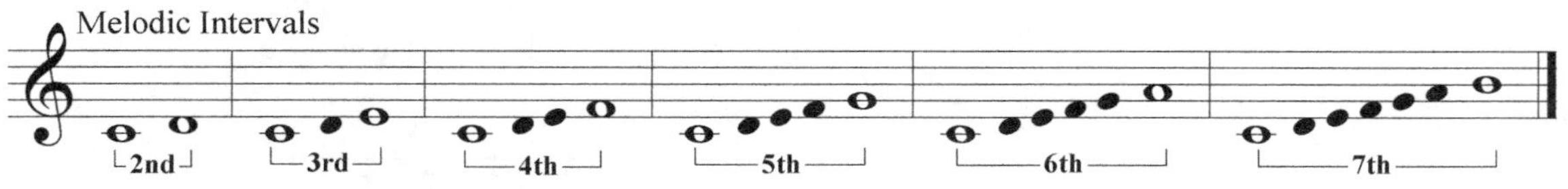

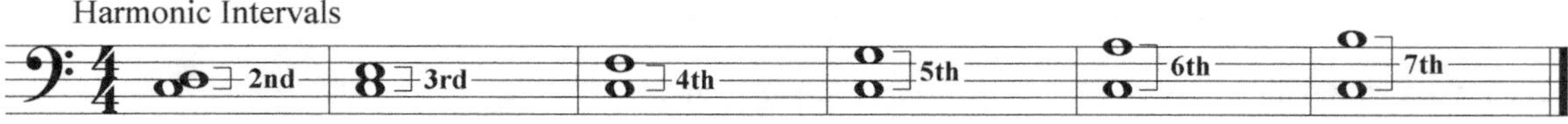

The interval between two identical notes is called a **unison**.

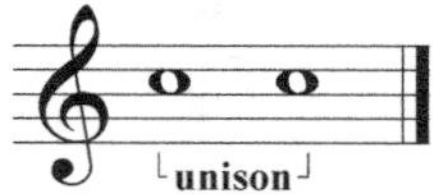

The interval of an eighth is called an **octave**.

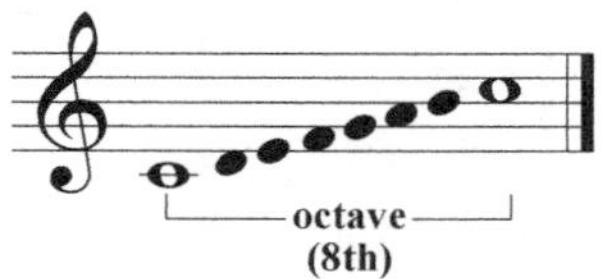

1. Identify the following intervals as melodic (M) or harmonic (H).

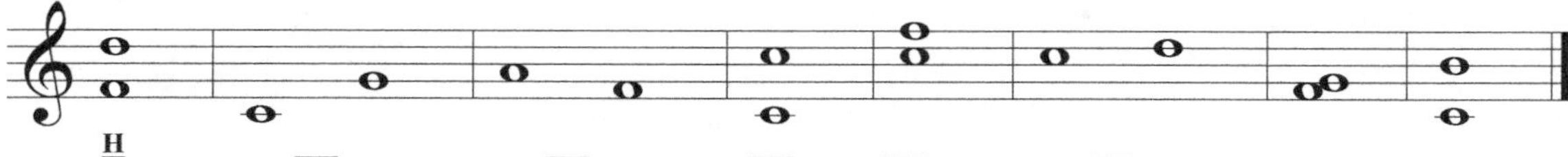

2. Name these melodic intervals.

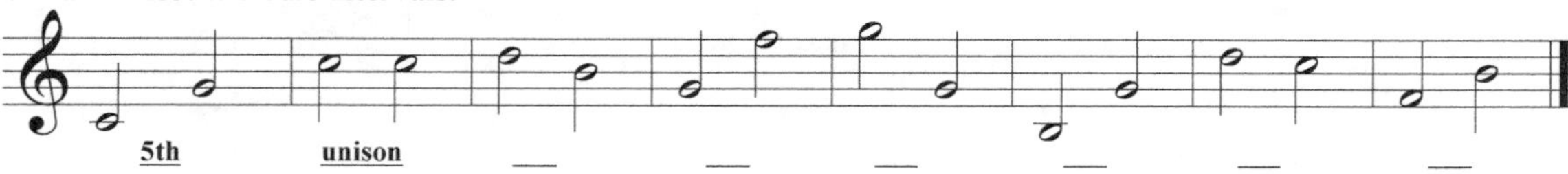

3. Name these harmonic intervals.

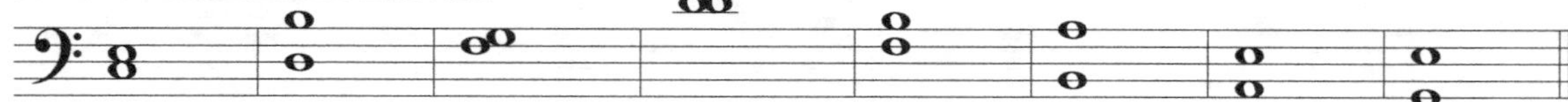

4. Write the indicated harmonic interval above the given note.

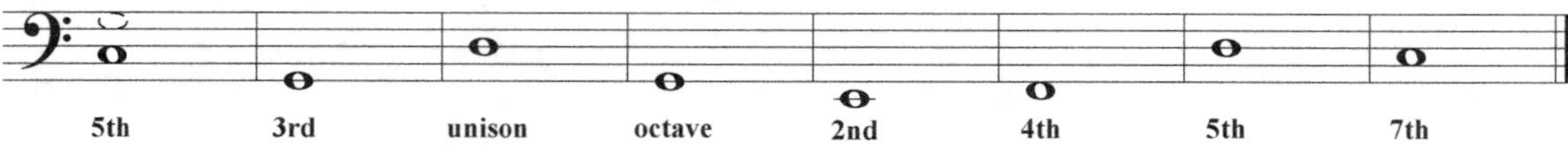

5. Write the indicated harmonic interval above the given note.

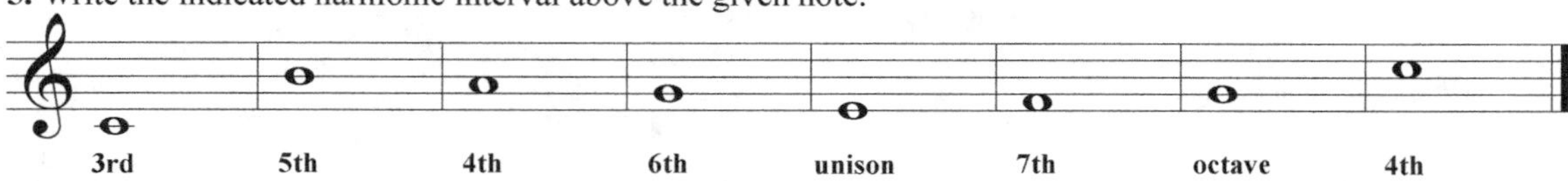

Name________________________ Date____________________

Sharps and Flats I

A **sharp** sign (♯) placed in front of a note (♯♩) *raises* its pitch a half step.

A **flat** sign (♭) placed in front of a note (♭♩) *lowers* its pitch a half step.

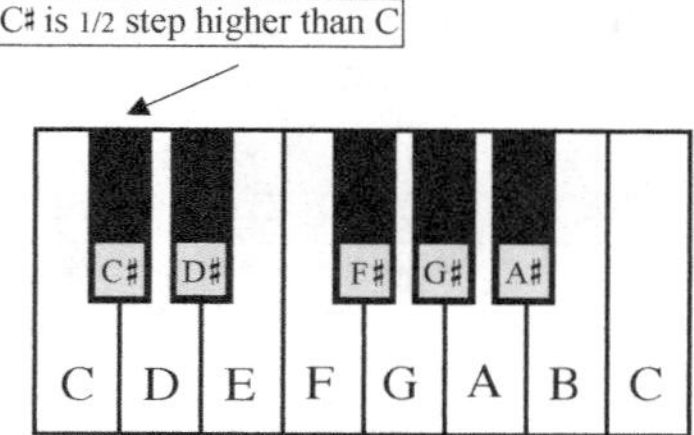

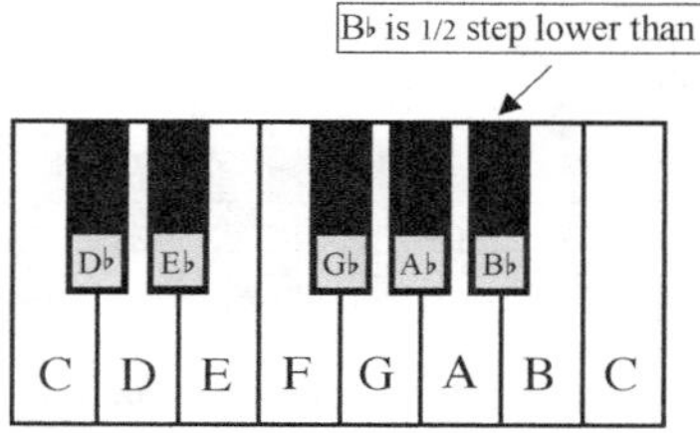

It is easy to see, on the piano keyboard, how the black keys to the right (1/2 step higher) of a note are sharps and the black keys to the left (1/2 step lower) of a note are flats.

---

1. Practice drawing sharps by tracing over the guidelines. Draw six more in the remaining space.

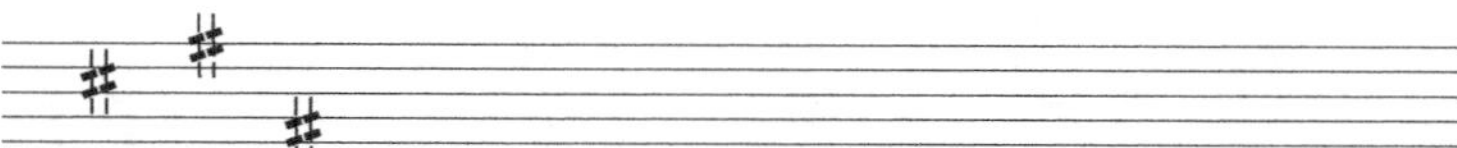

2. Practice drawing flats by tracing over the guidelines. Draw six more in the remaining space.

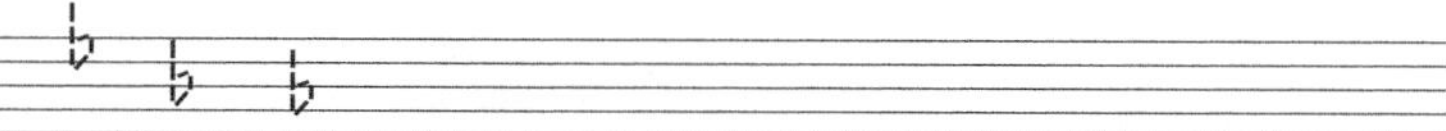

3. Write a flat sign in front of each note and then name the note.

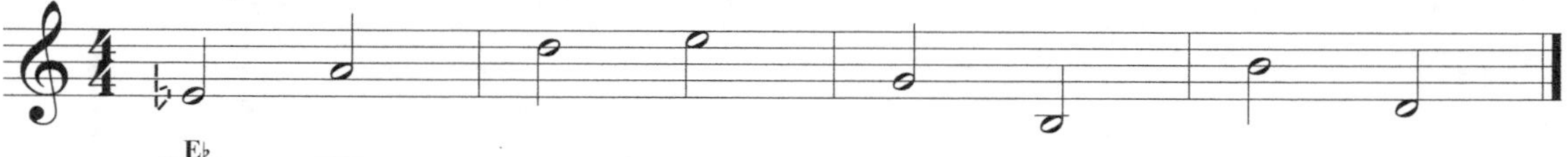

4. Write a flat sign in front of each note and then name the note.

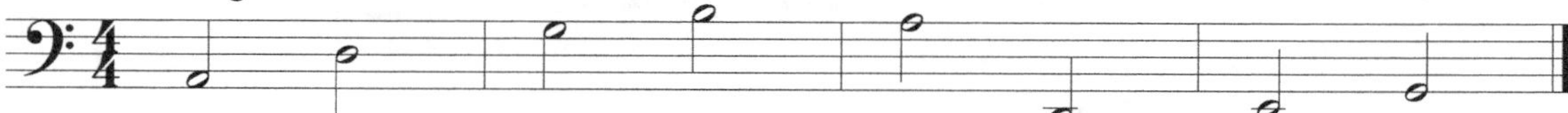

5. Write a sharp sign in front of each note and then name the note.

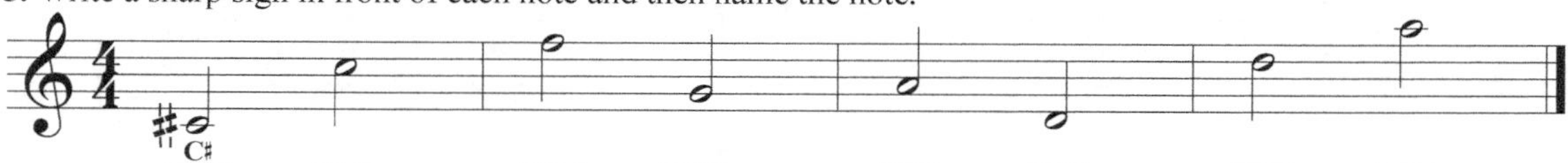

6. Write a sharp sign in front of each note and then name the note.

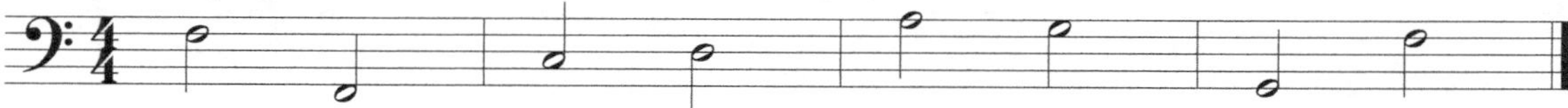

Name________________________ Date_____________________

Sharps, Flats and Naturals

A **natural** sign (♮) placed before a note cancels a sharp or flat.

Sharps, flats and naturals are all called **accidentals.**

Accidentals affect every note on the same line or space for the remainder of the measure.
Bar lines cancel all accidentals from the previous measure unless a note is tied across the bar line.

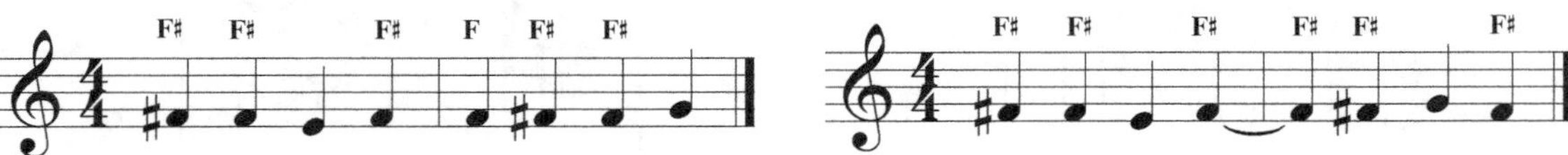

A natural is used to cancel sharps and flats.

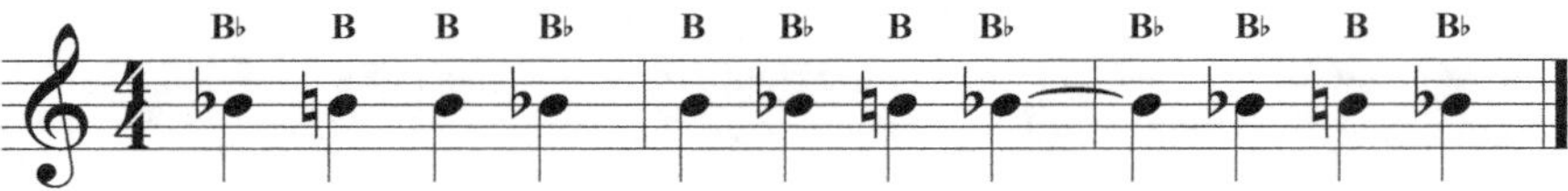

Write the name of each note.

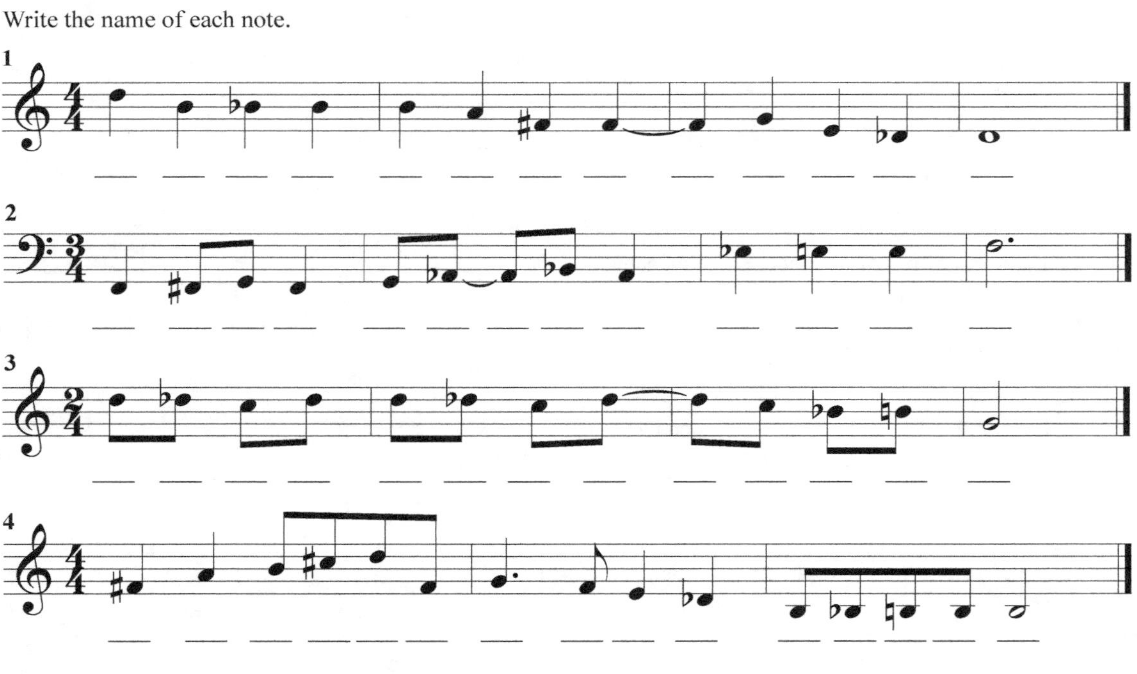

Name________________________ Date____________________

Enharmonic Notes I

In music there are many notes that have more than one name.
Enharmonic notes sound the same but are spelled differently.

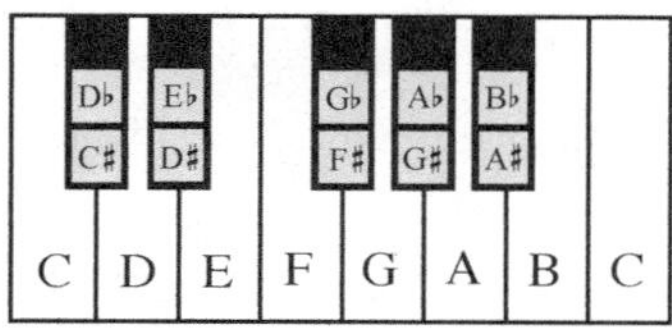

If you look at a piano keyboard you will see that D♯ and E♭ are played with the same key.

---

1. Use a quarter note to write in the enharmonic equivalent of the given note.

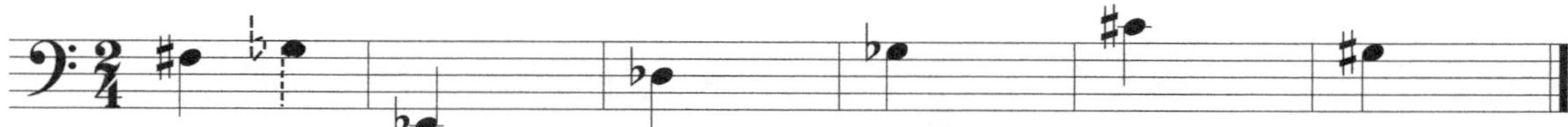

2. Use a quarter note to write in the enharmonic equivalent of the given note.

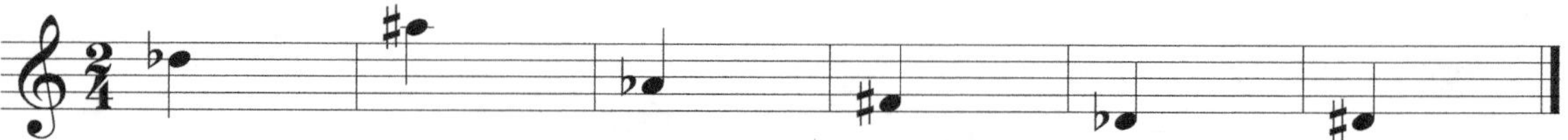

3. Use a quarter note to write in the enharmonic equivalent of the given note.

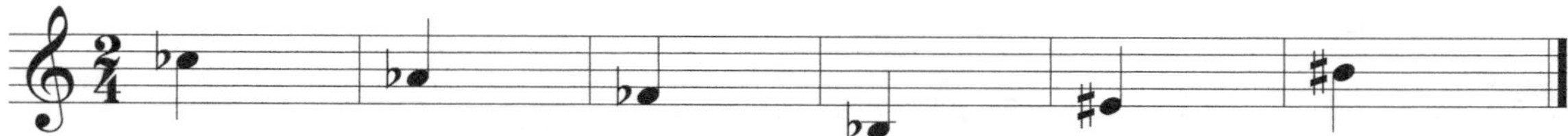

4. Use a quarter note to write in the enharmonic equivalent of the given note.

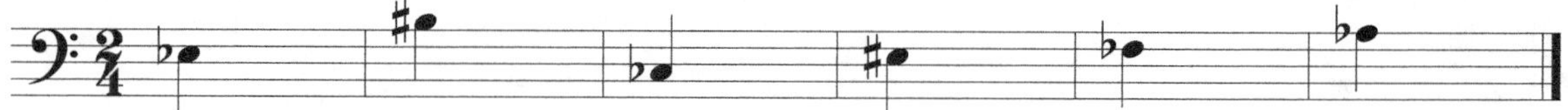

5. This is the first part of a familiar song written with many enharmonic notes.
Identify the song and write the name here: ________________

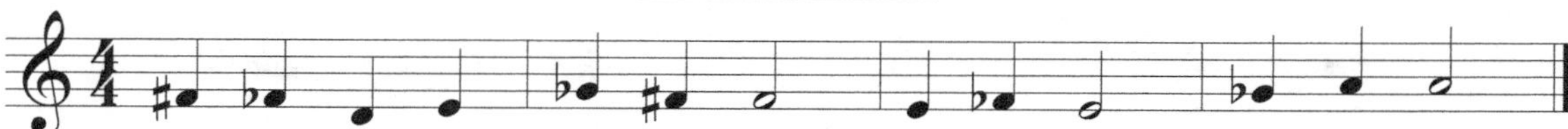

Name______________________ Date__________________

Enharmonic Notes II

Complete these exercises.

1. Circle the measures in which the notes are *not* enharmonically equivalent.

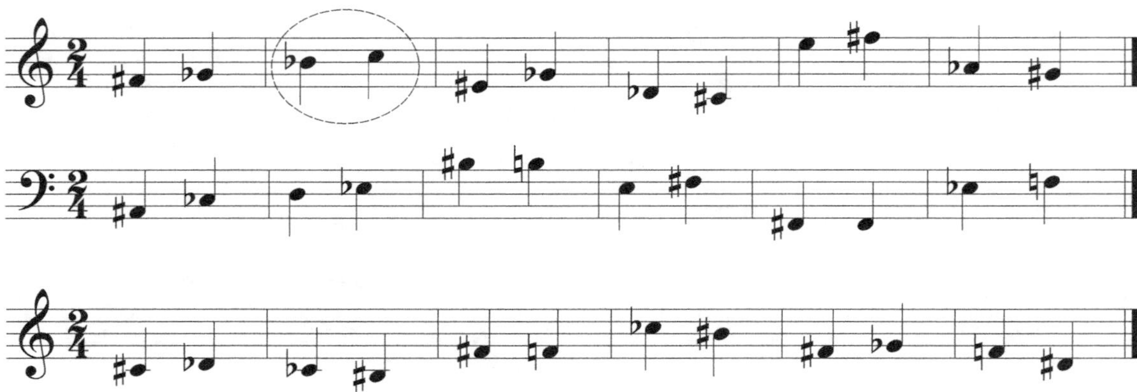

2. Identify these familiar songs.

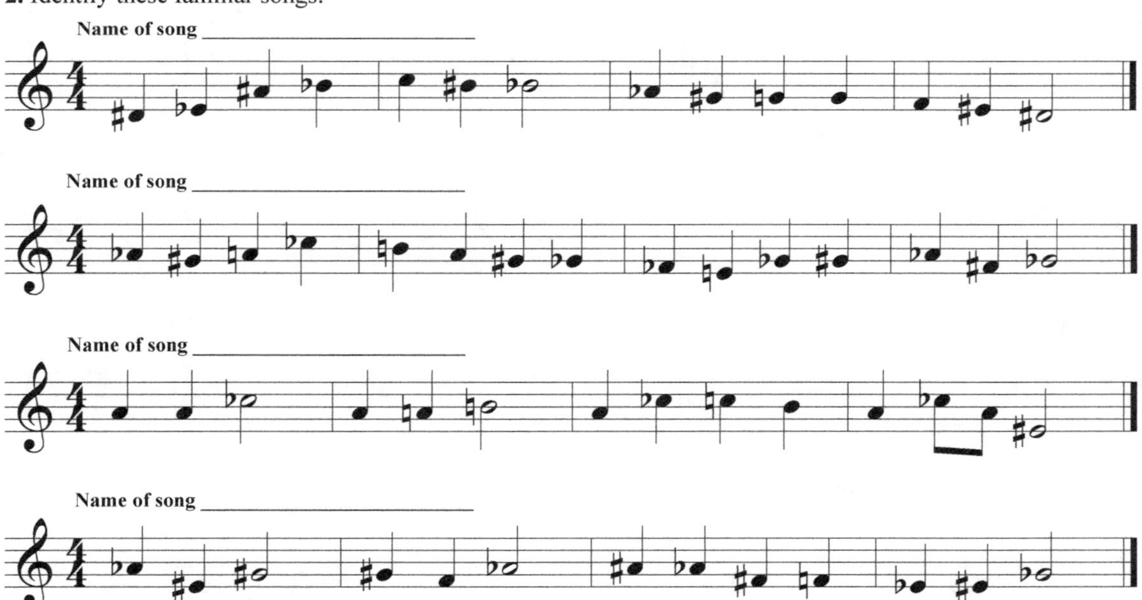

Elements of Music: 0030

Half Steps and Whole Steps I

The **half step** (H) is the smallest interval used in traditional Western music. The piano keyboard is arranged in half steps; the distance between two adjacent keys on the piano is a half step.

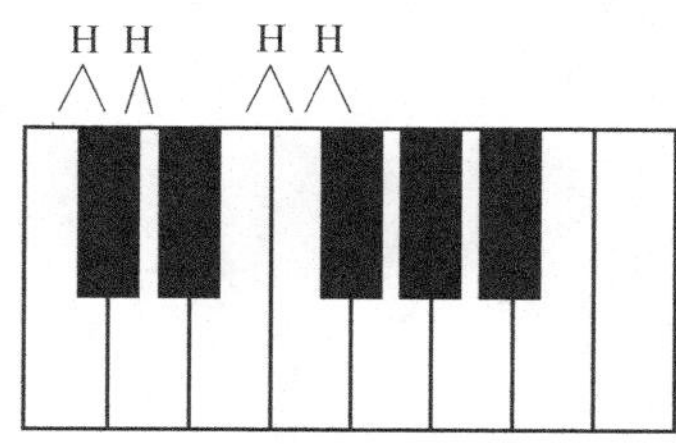

The **whole step** (W) is an interval made by combining two half steps.

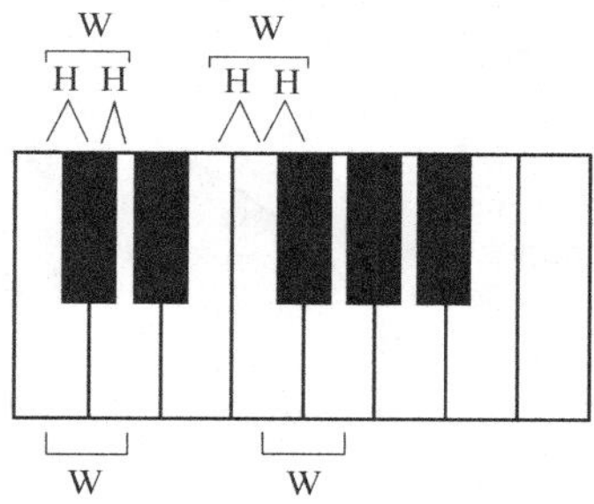

Using the keyboards below, write the interval (whole step or half step) that is created by the Os.

1. ___________________

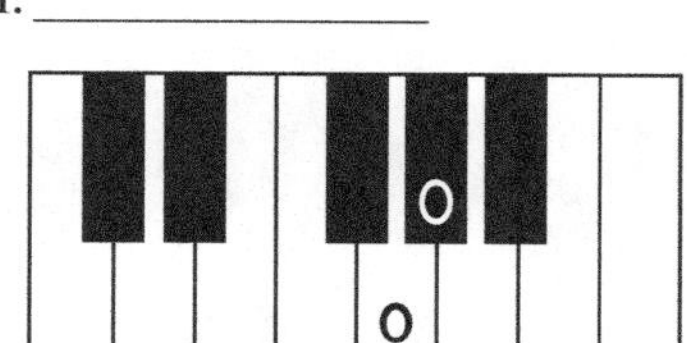

2. ___________________

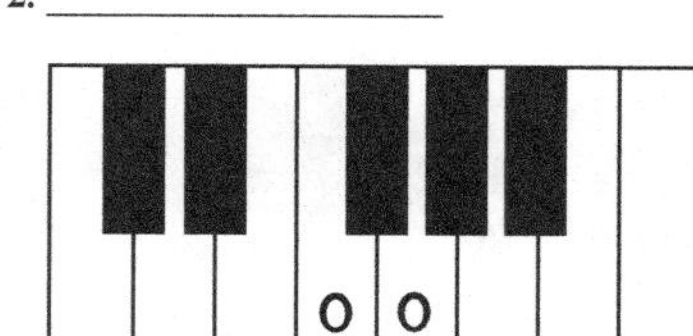

3. ___________________

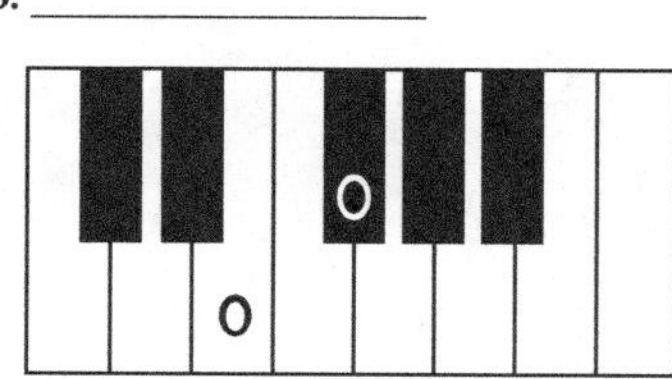

4. ___________________

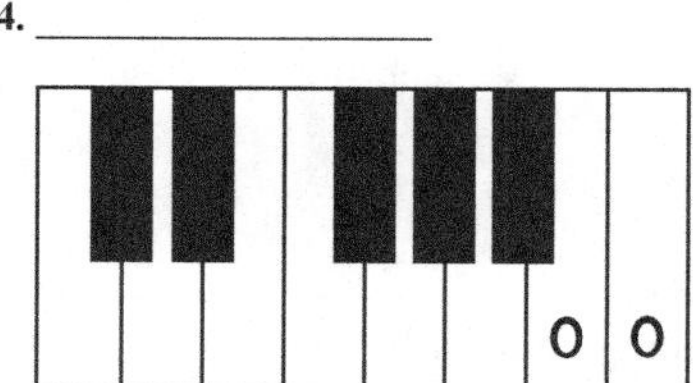

5. ___________________

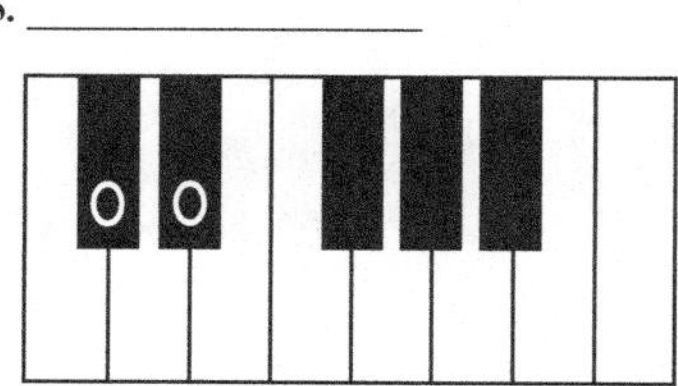

6. ___________________

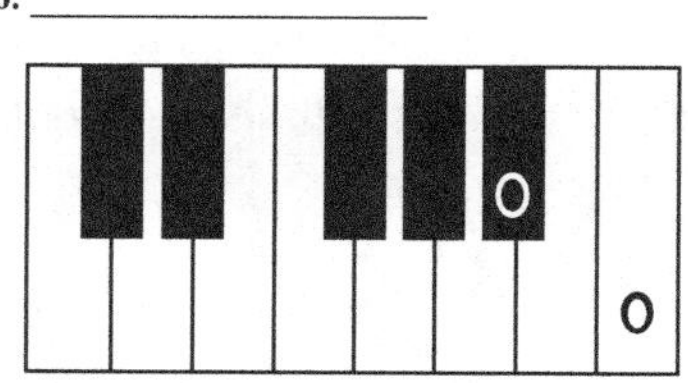

Name_______________________ Date___________________

The Circle of Fifths I - 𝄞

The **Circle of Fifths** diagram shows the clockwise arrangement of major keys in an order of ascending fifths for sharp key signatures. With each added sharp the key advances five letter names and the tonic moves up a perfect fifth.

Flat keys are presented in an order of descending fifths. With each added flat the key moves back five letter names and the tonic moves down a perfect fifth.

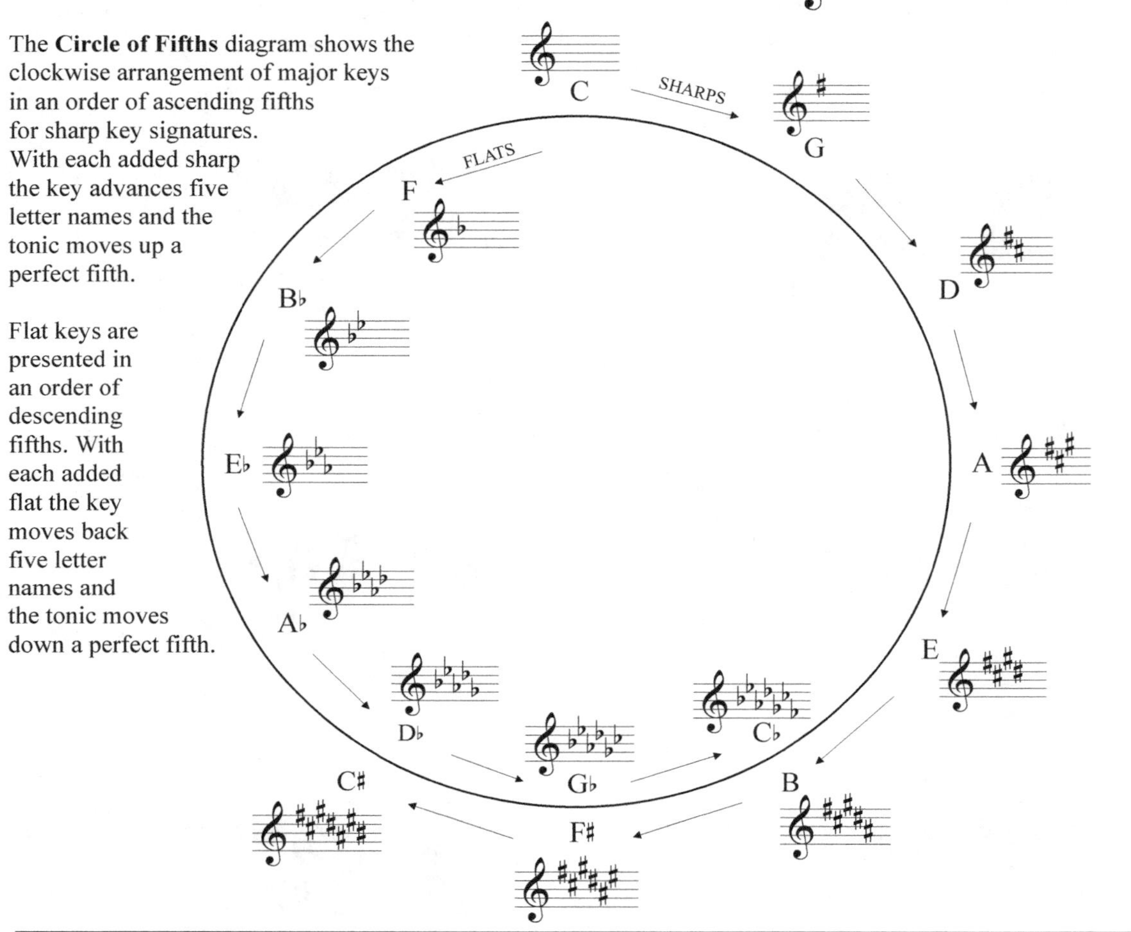

1. Write the flats in the order in which they are added as you go around the circle of fifths.

   B♭ ______ ______ ______ ______ ______ ______

2. Write the sharps in the order in which they are added as you go around the circle of fifths.

   F♯ ______ ______ ______ ______ ______ ______

3. Write the names of the keys with sharps in order as they appear on the circle of fifths.

   G ______ ______ ______ ______ ______ ______

4. Write the names of the keys with flats in order as they appear on the circle of fifths.

   F ______ ______ ______ ______ ______ ______

Name________________________ Date____________________

The Circle of Fifths III - 𝄞

Complete the circle of fifths by adding the missing key signatures.

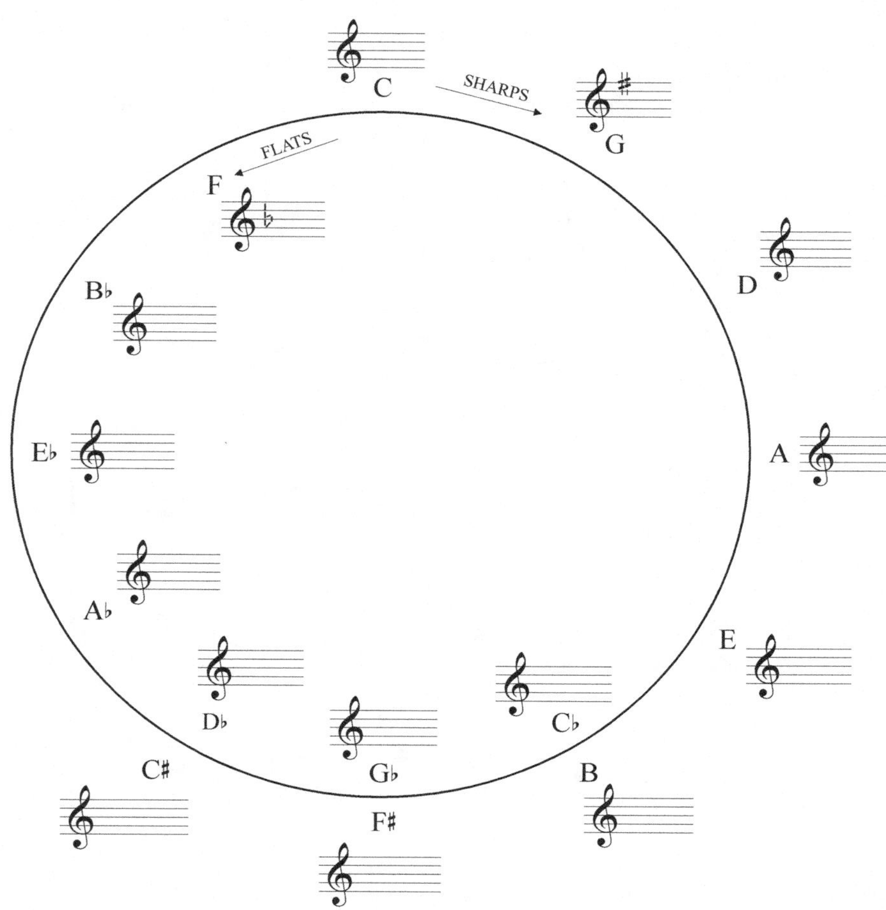

Name______________________ Date____________________

Major Scale Ia - 𝄞

All major scales are made up of the following pattern of whole steps and half steps:

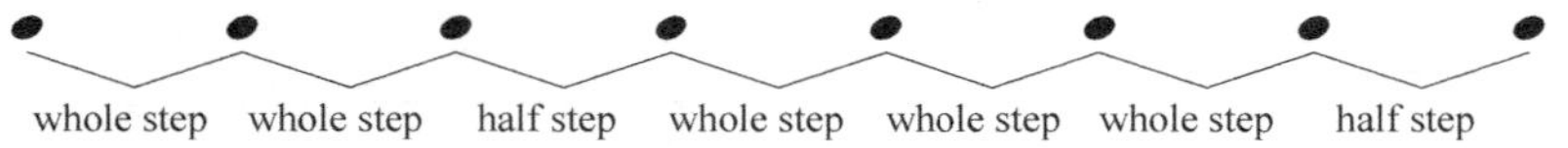

Add sharps or flats to the exercises below to create major scales.
Use the pattern of whole and half steps to determine which accidentals you will need to add.

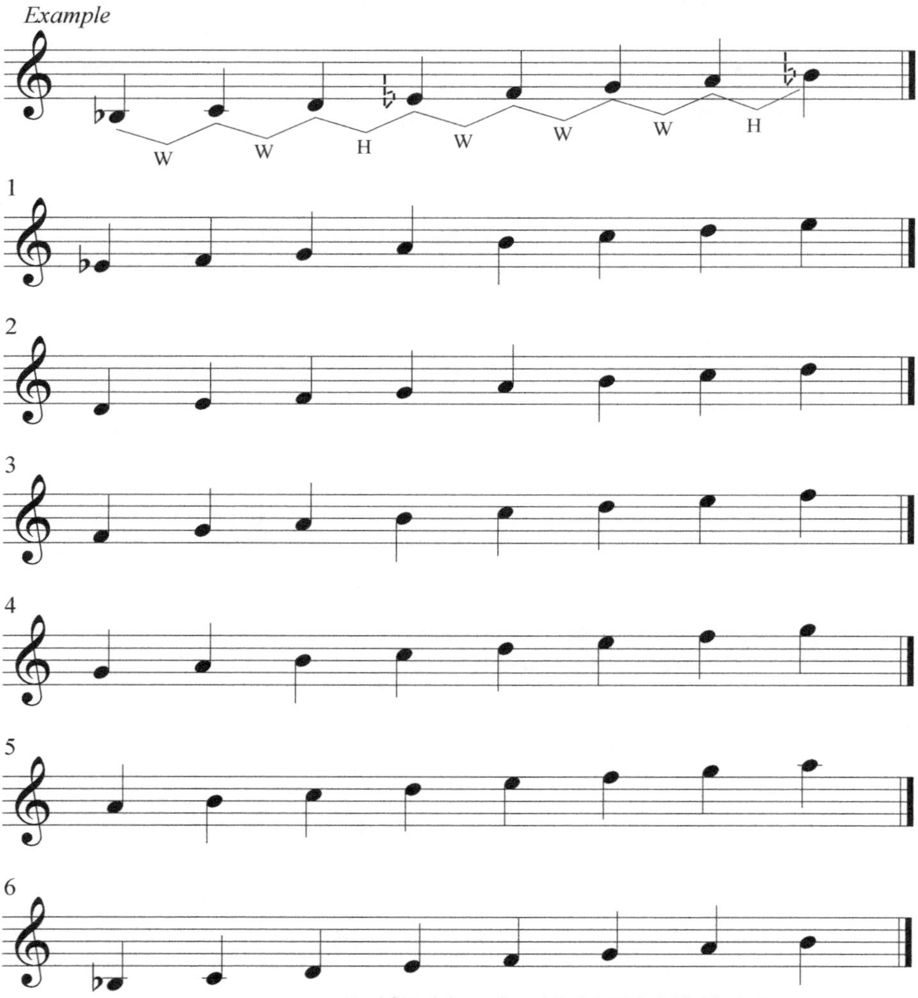

Name______________________ Date____________________

Major Scales and Key Signatures IIa - 𝄞

Use this major scale pattern to help complete the exercises:

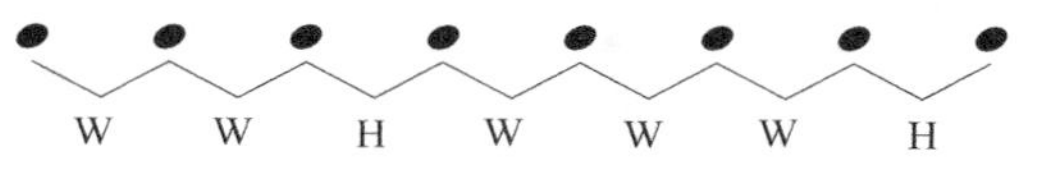

When writing key signatures the order of flats and sharps must always remain the same.

The order of sharps:

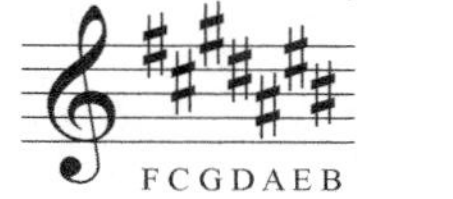

The order of flats:

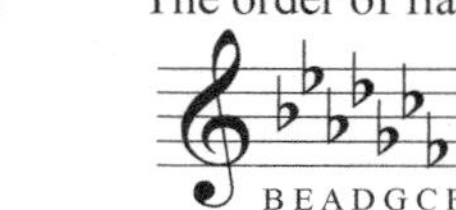

Starting with the given note, complete each major scale.
Then write the name of the scale and fill in its key signature.

Example

Name of Scale: D Major

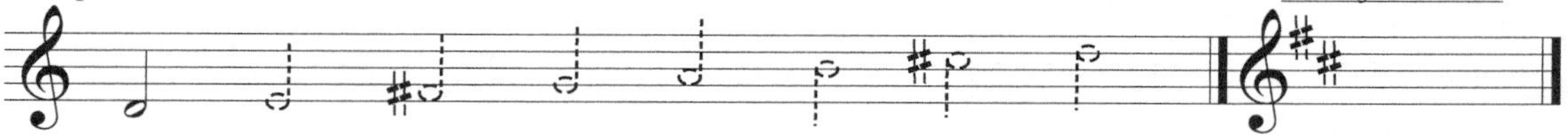

1

Name of Scale: ____________

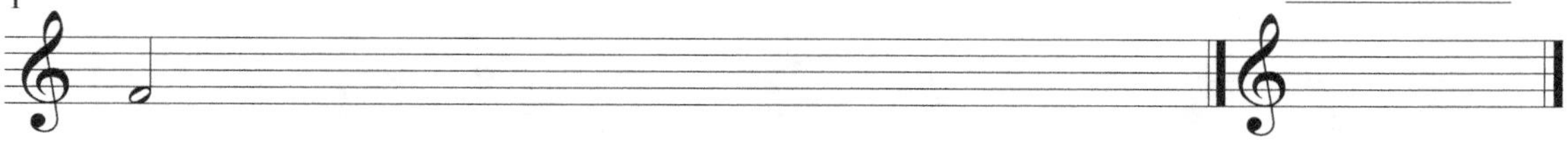

2

Name of Scale: ____________

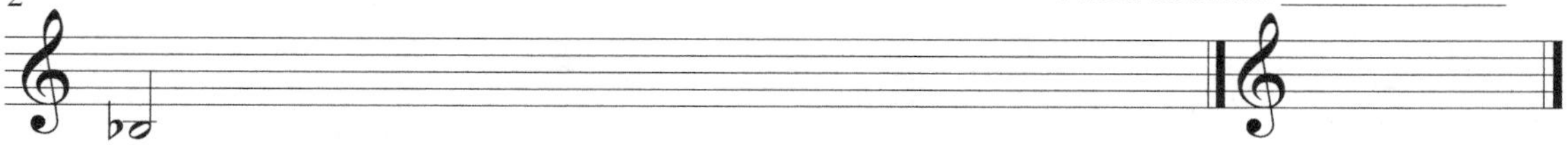

3

Name of Scale: ____________

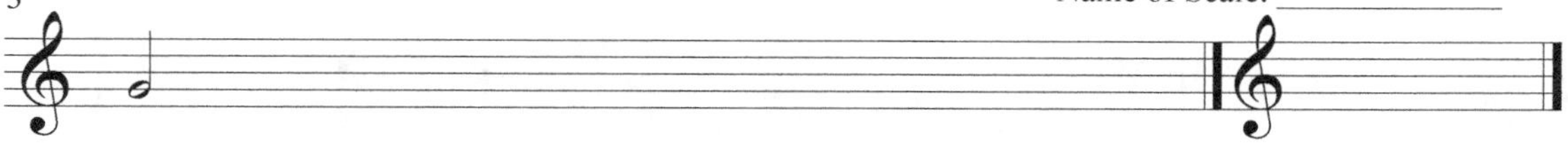

4

Name of Scale: ____________

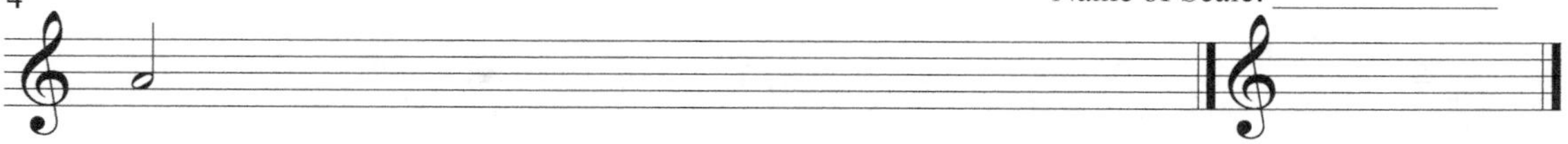

5

Name of Scale: ____________

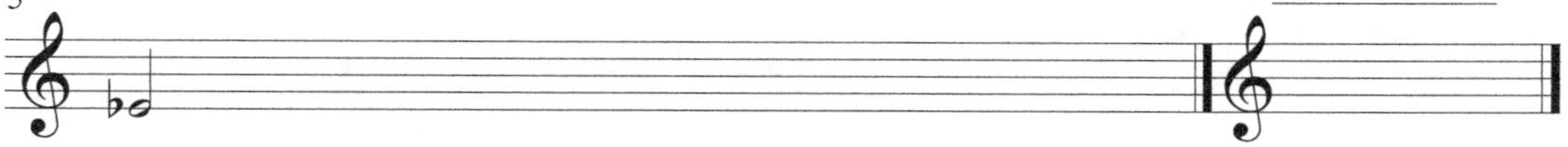

6

Name of Scale: ____________

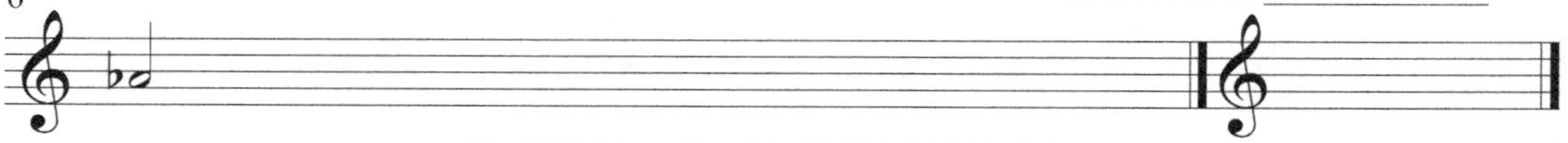

Name________________________ Date_____________________

Major Scale Ia - 𝄢

All major scales are made up of the following pattern of whole steps and half steps:

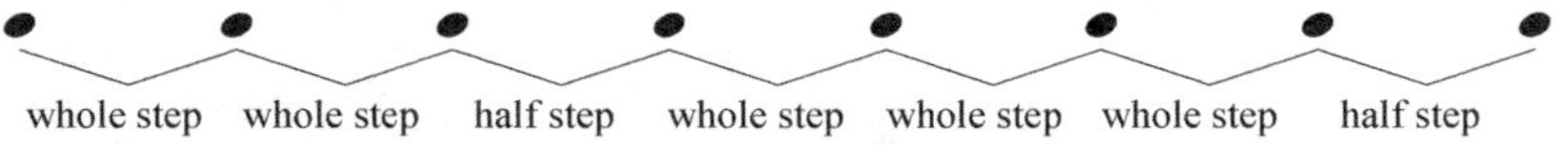

Add sharps or flats to the exercises below to create major scales.
Use the pattern of whole and half steps to determine which accidentals you will need to add.

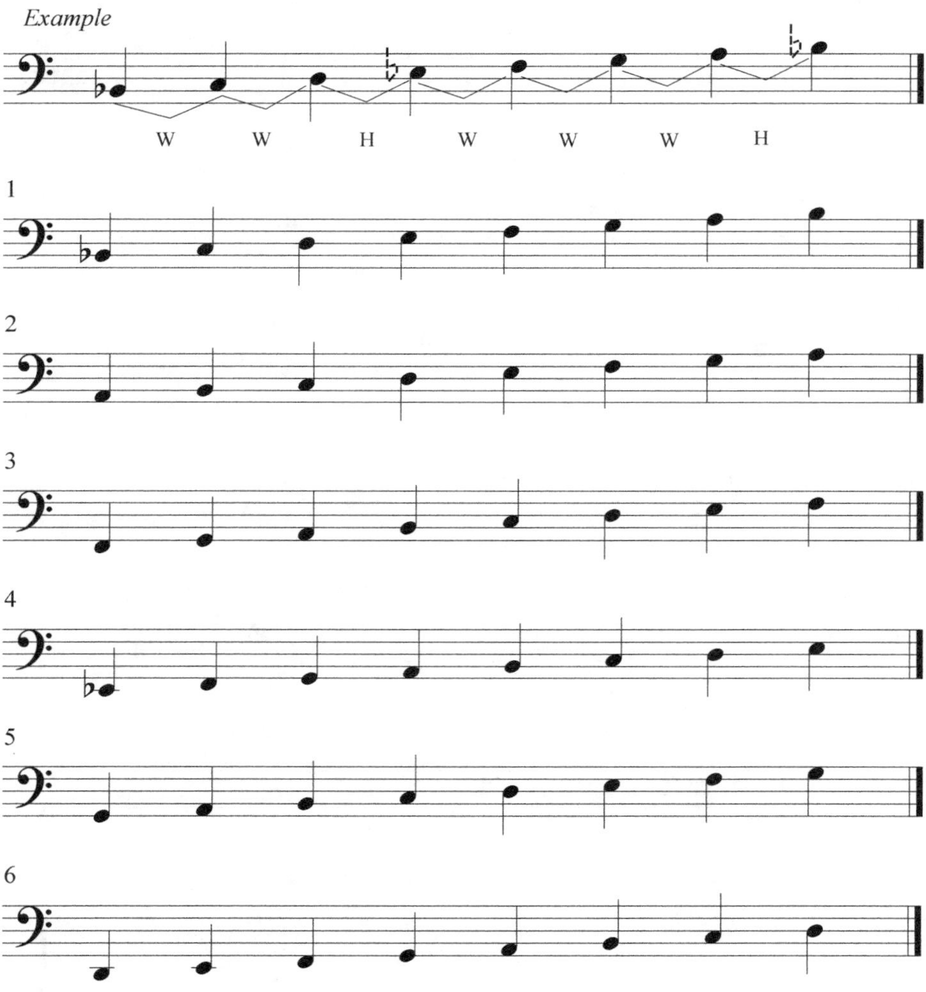

Name______________________ Date__________________

Major Scales and Key Signatures IIa - 𝄢

Use this major scale pattern to help complete the exercises:

W W H W W W H

When writing key signatures the order of flats and sharps must always remain the same.

The order of sharps: F C G D A E B

The order of flats: B E A D G C F

Starting with the given note, complete each major scale.
Then write the name of the scale and fill in its key signature.

Example

Name of Scale: D Major

1 Name of Scale: _____________

2 Name of Scale: _____________

3 Name of Scale: _____________

4 Name of Scale: _____________

5 Name of Scale: _____________

6 Name of Scale: _____________

Summary of Unit 2 Terms

1. **Staff**: The five lines and four spaces on which music is written.
2. **Treble Clef**: The Treble or G clef tells us that the note g is on the second line of the staff from the bottom. It also indicates a middle to high range of music.
3. **Bass Clef**: The Bass or F clef tells us that the F is on the fourth line of the staff from the bottom. It also indicates a middle to low range of music.
4. **Ledger Lines**: Ledger lines are shortened staff lines that are used to write notes above or below the staff.
5. **Grand Staff**: The Grand Staff is eleven lines and ten spaces and combines the Treble and Bass clefs.
6. **Time Signatures**: Time signatures are most often two numbers at the beginning of the staff. Each number has a specific function. The top number tells us how many beats in on measure and the bottom number tells us what kind of note gets one beat.
7. **Rests**: Musical rests indicate silence and each note has a specific symbol that represents silence or rest.
8. **Slur**: A slur is a curved line connecting two or more notes of different pitch.
9. **Tie**: A tie is a curved line connecting notes of the same pitch.
10. **Note Stems**: Note stems are primarily used to help determine what rhythmic value a note will have.
11. **Interval**: Intervals are the distances in pitch from one note to another.
12. **Sharp Sign ♯**: Sharp signs are symbols that are used to raise musical notes.
13. **Flat Sign b**: Flat signs are symbols that are used to lower musical notes.
14. **Natural Sign ♮**: The natural sign placed before a note cancels out a sharp or flat.
15. **Sharp, Flat, and Natural signs** are called accidentals.
16. **Enharmonic**: An enharmonic is a note that sounds the same but has two different spellings. For example on the piano, the note C sharp is the same in sound as D flat. When written, the scale of C sharp has seven sharps and the scale of D flat has five flats, but when played they both sound the same.
17. **Half Step-Whole Step**: Half steps and whole steps are used to describe the distances between notes in a scale. For example, the pattern for a major scale is 1-1-1/2-1-1-1-1/2.
18. **Circle of Fifths**: The Circle of Fifths diagrams (worksheets 24, 25) show the clockwise arrangement of major keys. Sharp keys go to the right and flat keys go to the left. (To be explained by the instructor.)
19. **Major Scale**: The whole step-half step major scale pattern is cited above in number 17.
20. **Key Signatures**: Key signatures are the sharps and flats that are placed at the beginning of a piece to inform the player or singer what notes are altered. These sharps and flats come after the G Clef or F clef and before the time signature.

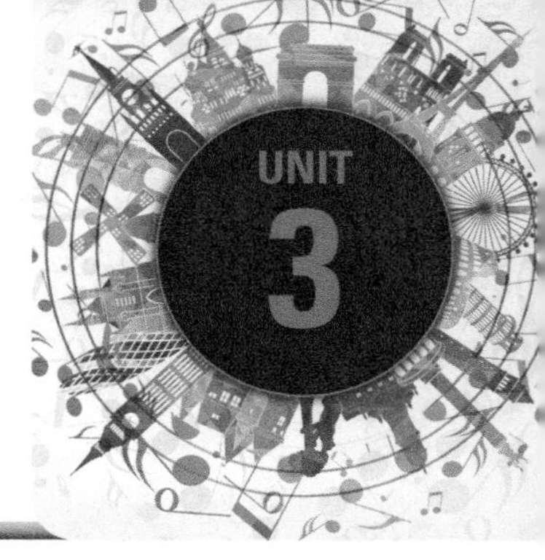

Understanding Music History and Style Changes

Unit Purpose

The purpose of this unit is to enlighten students on past music history and hopefully enhance their understanding. This task will be accomplished by examining different style periods. It is important for the student to understand at the very outset that musical style periods do not start on January 1 and do not end on December 31 of the dates listed. Style periods are primarily based on when there was sufficient evidence of the music changing and the lives of the important composers of that time.

History experts have divided the style periods into six major areas:

1. Middle Ages, Medieval, "Dark Ages" 450–1450
2. Renaissance 1450–1600
3. Baroque 1600–1750
4. Classical 1750–1820
5. Romantic 1820–1900 and Nationalism (Russia)
6. Impressionism 1880–1920 (see the following)

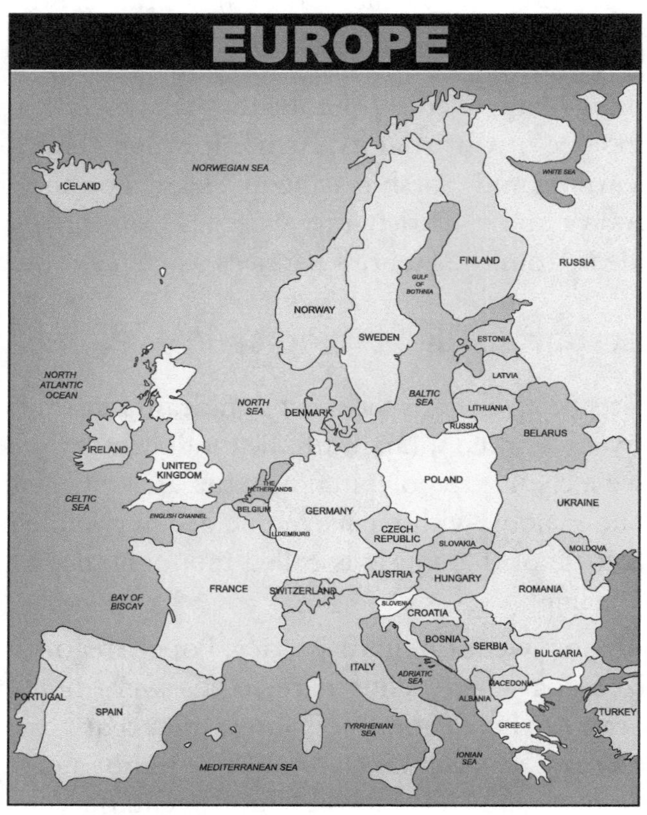

Modern 1900 till today

For some reason, historians do not always include Impressionism, 1880–1920, in the list. Later, I will include it as it has very distinct sounds and flavors you have heard. I am also putting in Nationalism with the Romantic Era as they occur at the same time.

Note: I am including a map to show where the music was born.

CHAPTER 1 MIDDLE AGES, MEDIEVAL, "DARK AGES" (450–1450)

What Do We Find in This Period?

1. **Music**: Primarily sacred (religious) vocal music.
2. **Texture**: Monophonic, Polyphonic enters in the ninth century.
3. **Forms**: Chant, mass, organum (polyphony), motet, and madrigal.
4. **Composers**: This list will not be complete, but will include what I deem to be the trend setters: Leonin, Perotin, Guillaume de Machaut, and Hildegarde of Bingen. I have to include Pope Gregory; although not a musician, he initiated the codification of chant.
5. **Travel To:** Rome, Italy, Paris, France, and Germany.

Historically and culturally for 1,000 years of Western European history, many interesting things happened. Probably, the most significant was the fall of the Roman Empire and the rise of Christianity. As life for many was not good, the church became the center of learning and worship as people leaned on the church with hopes of improving their lives. As we know, Christianity emerges from Judaic roots as the early liturgy took most of its ideas from the Hebrew services as well as using Hebrew melodies.

Gregorian Chant (Plainsong or Plainchant) and Pope Gregory 1 (590–604)

Gregorian chant is the most significant music of the sixth century but more importantly, this style was predominant till the ninth century when we see a change to polyphonic texture. Chant is basically one melody without harmonic accompaniment. The texture of this music is called monophonic, meaning one line.

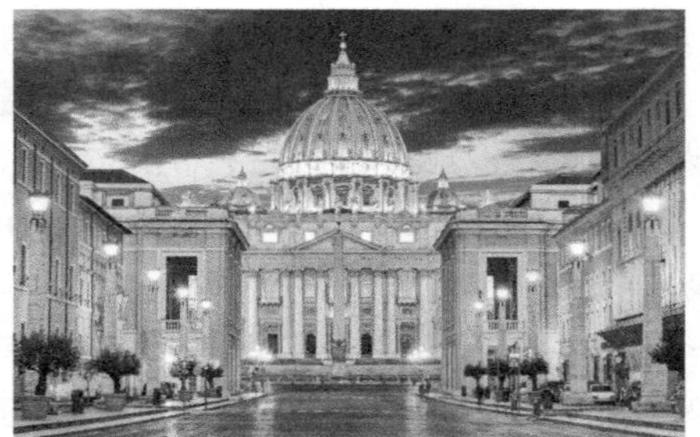

The Vatican

As time went on in his papacy, Pope Gregory 1 realized that many church melodies were not in any organized collection. It is interesting that he focused on these musical treasures as he was not a composer or musician. As a preservation technique, he eventually charged his minions with the responsibility of putting this church music together.

At the time, this collection had no categorical name and, thus, the Pope was honored by calling this music Gregorian Chant.

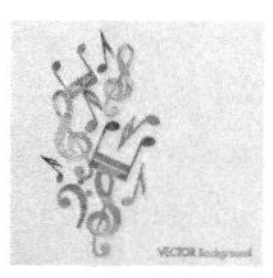

Listening Box 1

Type in Meditation with Gregorian Chants and choose top box with the same name, Select Track 2, Inno: Conditor; Track 7, Kyrie.

The Mass

The Mass is basically a celebration and a reenactment of the Last Supper of Jesus Christ. There are two types of Mass, the Proper and the Ordinary.

Proper Mass

The Proper Mass is used for specific holidays or occasions in the church calendar and the text changes as the events change. The components of the Proper Mass are: Introit, Gradual, Alleluia or Tract, Sequence, Offertory, and Communion.

Ordinary Mass

The Ordinary Mass is the everyday mass and has a fixed text. The components of the Ordinary Mass are: Kyrie, Gloria, Credo, Sanctus, and Agnus Dei.

Note I: Pope Gregory was very influential in organizing the mass.

Note II: Sacred means religious and secular means nonreligious.

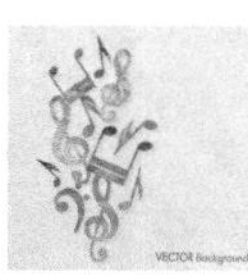

Listening Box 2

Type in More Sublime Chant and under Albums choose More Sublime Chant: The Art of . . . Select Track 2, Kyrie Eleison; Track 4, Sanctus; Track 5, Agnus Dei.

Ninth Century: Polyphony (Organum)—The Beginning of Harmony

As unbelievable as it might seem, we had almost a thousand years of music before composers had the idea to combine two lines. The overall story here is that we go from one line of music (monophonic) to two lines (polyphonic). There are several theories as to how this happened and the one I favor the most is that composers took an existing chant melody called the cantus firmus (fixed voice) and added a second line. It is important to note, church musicians referred to this early harmony as organum.

Twelfth Century—The School of Notre-Dame

The School of Notre-Dame gives us two important musicians—clerics. Leonin (Leo), 1150s–1201 and Perotin (Pierre), 1180–1225. Historically, these dates cannot be proven and are approximate. Both these men worked at the Cathedral and were very good at writing polyphonic texture.

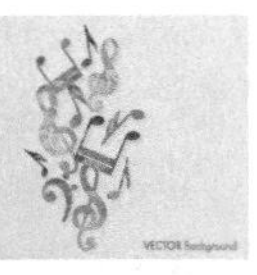

Listening Box 3

Type in Leonin/Perotin and under Albums choose Leonin/Perotin: Sacred Music from . . . Select Track 5, notem fecit; Track 9, Viderunt omnes (both are 2 part organum).

To the Listener

Notice that one part sustains or holds notes while the other puts many notes to one syllable.

Melisma or Melismatic

The process of putting many notes to one syllable in a melody.

The Motet

The earliest motets go back to the thirteenth century. Many were two to three part vocal compositions with several different texts. On occasion, vernacular languages were sung over a Latin cantus firmus (fixed voice—melody). Motets could be sacred or secular. If they were secular, they often praised a reigning Monarch.

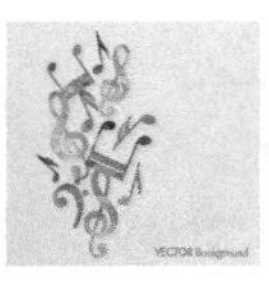

Listening Box 4

Type in Giacomo Carissimi and choose top box Giacomo Carissimi, Baroque. Select Track 5, In te, Domine, sperava.

The Madrigal

Madrigals are vocal pieces for small groups of singers that were invented by the Italians in the early 1500s and were used for court entertainment. The madrigal is generally a mix of polyphonic and homophonic textures. The words were often poems that dealt with love, but there were times the subjects were humorous or political with double entendres. It is also important to note madrigals were very popular and spread throughout Europe, especially in England around Shakespeare's time.

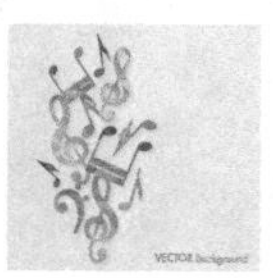

Listening Box 5

Type in Claudio Monteverdi and under Albums choose Madrigals book 1, Claudio Monteverdi. Select Track 9, Fumia la Pastorella—Prima Parte.

There are some contributors in this era that sometimes fly under the radar. I have chosen three to mention.

Guido D'Arezzo (991/992 – after1033) was a monk and a musician from the Provence of Arezzo, Italy. He made a very significant contribution to music as he is given credit for inventing the scale, albeit, the first six notes.

Hildegard of Bingen, Germany(1098–1179), was a nun who is given credit for writing over 69 compositions which represent one of the largest surviving collections of Medieval music.

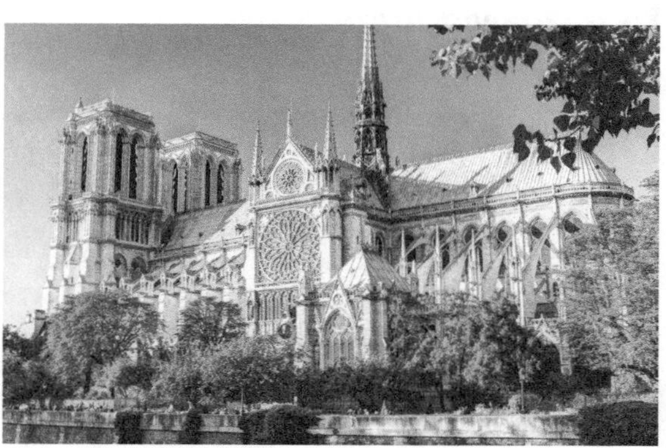

The Cathedral of Notre-Dame (Our Lady), Paris, France

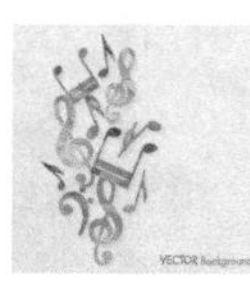

Listening Box 6

Type in Ave generosa and choose top box Ave generosa, Hildegard of Bingen. Select Track 3, Ave generosa.

Guillaume de Machaut (c. 1300–1377) was a poet and a composer who helped develop the motet and other song forms. It is said that his poetry was so good and admired by Chaucer.

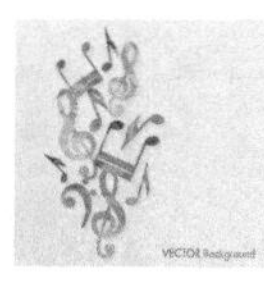

Listening Box 7

Type in Guillaume de Machaut and under Tracks choose Agnus Dei. Select Track 5, Agnus Dei.

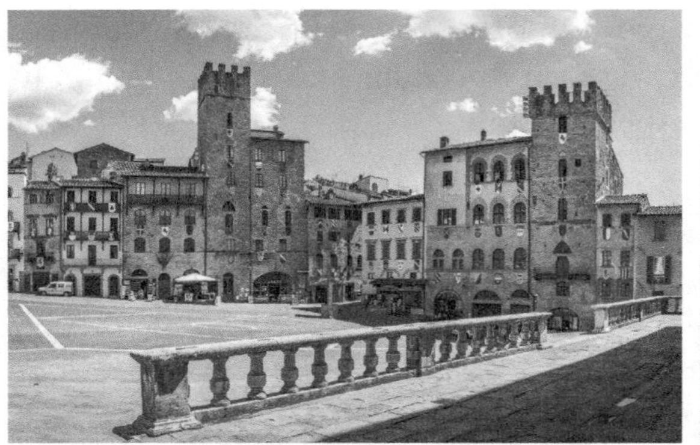

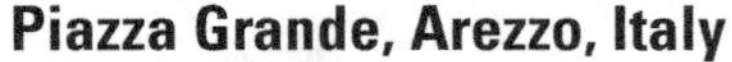
Piazza Grande, Arezzo, Italy

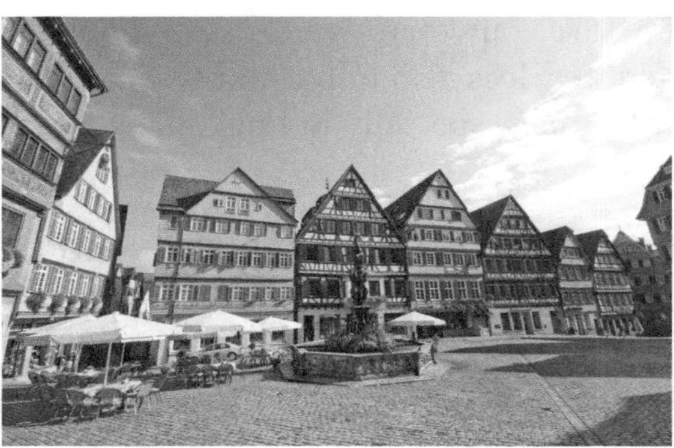

Market Square, Bingen, Germany

Middle Ages and Secular Music (Nonreligious)

It is assumed in some circles that the only music in the Middle Ages was sacred. What causes this mentality is that no written examples are there as the performers did not have knowledge in music notation. What we have as evidence comes basically from paintings and illuminated manuscripts. We go to two countries to find evidence that secular music existed. In France, we find the Minstrels, the Troubadours, and the Trouvères. In Germany, we find the Minnesingers and the Meistersingers.

The Minstrels (Tenth Century, France)

The Minstrels, starting around the tenth century, were musicians, story tellers, and poets, who made their living moving from town to town entertaining people. For the most part, they were very talented and engaged in such activities as doing magic tricks, exhibiting trained animals, acrobatics, and juggling. For some reason, they were considered social outcasts by many and often had to scurry away from oncoming officials. There is no written song documentation from these people as they were too busy traveling and probably did not have music writing knowledge.

The Troubadours (Twelfth Century, France)

The Troubadours were knights in the courts in southern France. They sang about love, the beauty of women, honor, and the Crusades. Some of their songs were actually notated which gives us information that they were more skilled than the Minstrels.

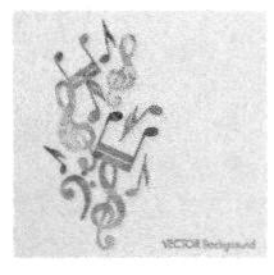

Listening Box 8

Type in Troubadour Music and under Albums choose Faidit: Troubadour Music from the . . . Select Track 8, Mon cor e mi e mas bonas chansos.

The Trouvères (Twelfth to Thirteenth Centuries, France)

The Trouvères were knights in the courts of northern France. They too sang about love, the beauty of women, honor, and chivalry. Their songs were notated and were written in their dialect.

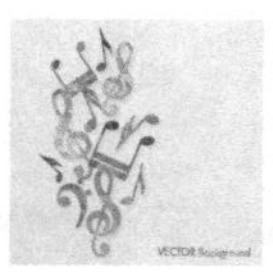

Listening Box 9

Type in Music of the Trouvères and choose top box with the same name. Select Track 6, On parole—A Paris—Frese nouvele.

The Minnesingers (Twelfth to Fourteenth Centuries, Germany)

The Minnesingers were knights in the courts of Germany and were the counterparts to the Troubadours and Trouvères. The word "minne" in old German means love and their main subject as poets was love so they got the title Minnesingers. They also sang about nature, the beauty of women, and were considered aristocrats.

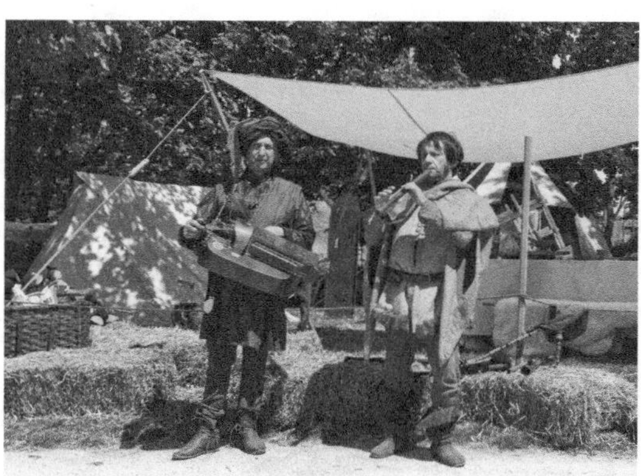

Modern Day Troubadours

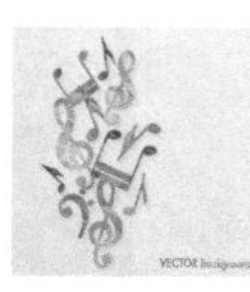

Listening Box 10

Type in Marc Lewon and choose top box Marc Lewon, Vocal. Select Track 1, Mir ist ummaten leyde.

The Meistersingers (Fourteenth to Sixteenth Centuries, Germany)

The Meistersingers (German for "master singer") were probably the best of all the secular groups mentioned here. A group of people who were taken from the middle class built on the structures and techniques of the Minnesingers for three centuries. In order to insure knowledge and consistency in music writing, they formed guilds where aspiring songwriters had to demonstrate their knowledge of the rules before they could become members. Many of their songs were sung without accompaniment and the first Meistersinger school goes back to the fourteenth century in the city of Mainz, Germany.

Hans Sachs, Leader of the Meistersinger School, Sixteenth Century

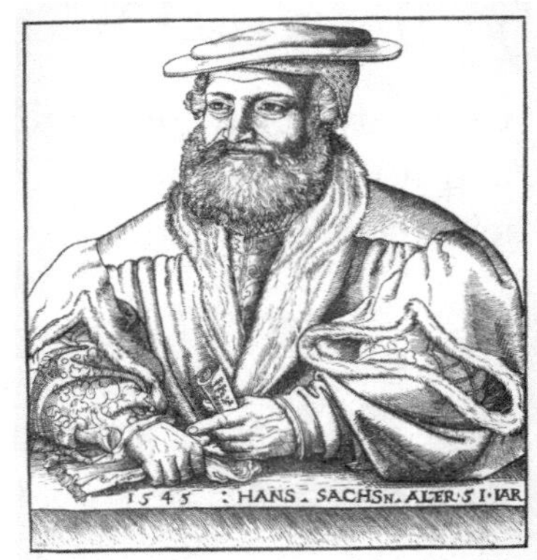

Note to the student: The song selections in this chapter are old. They were chosen for two reasons; first to give you sound examples of what music was like and second to point out how much more advanced we are now. As you can well imagine, technology has caused a meteoric rise in the sound of music.

Some Instruments from the Middle Ages

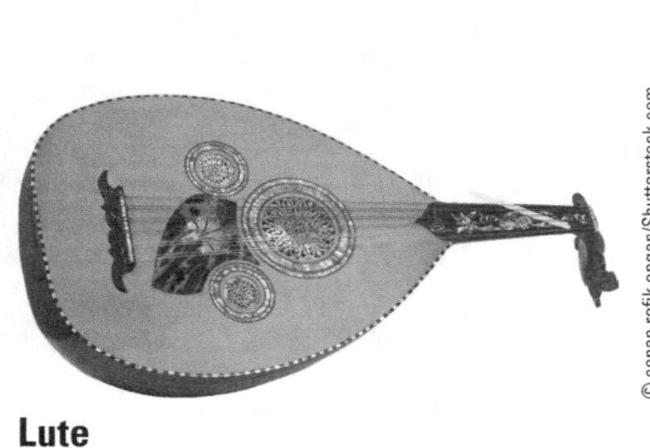

Lute

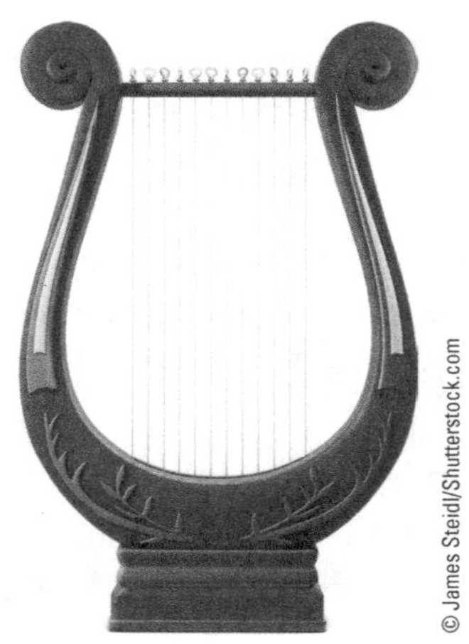

Lyre

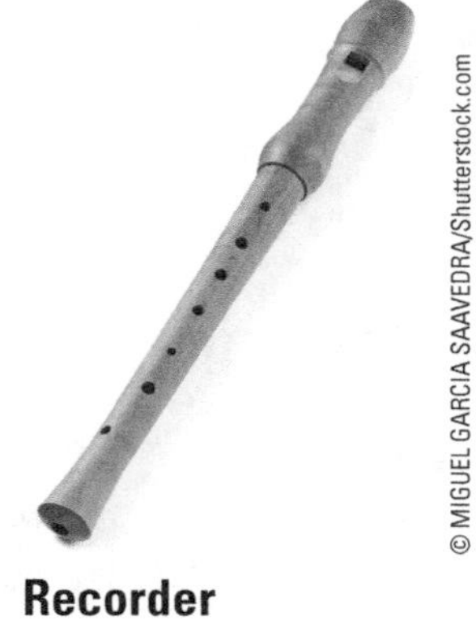

Recorder

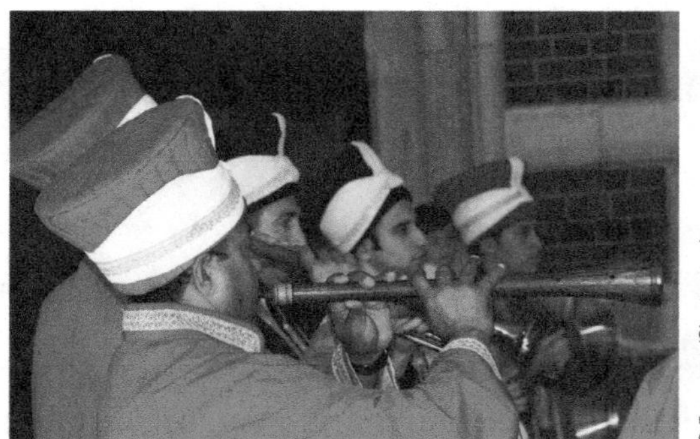

Shawm

Summary of Unit 3, Chapter 1 Terms and Study Sheet

1. Middle Ages time period, 450–1450
2. Sacred Vocal Music (Religious)
3. Sixth Century Gregorian Chant—monophonic texture
4. The Mass (Proper and Ordinary)

   Proper Sections: Introit, Gradual, Alleluia or Tract, Sequence, Offertory, and Communion.

   Ordinary Sections: Kyrie, Gloria, Credo, Sanctus, and Agnus Dei.
5. Nineth Century, Polyphony (Organum), the beginning of harmony
6. Tenth Century, Guido D'Arezzo invents the scale
7. Twelfth Century, "School of Notre Dame," Leonin and Perotin
8. Motet and Madrigal
9. Secular Music (Nonreligious), France and Germany

   France: Tenth century, Minstrels; Twelfth century, Troubadours and Trouveres.

   Germany: Twelfth century, Minnesingers; fourteenth—to sixteenth centuries, Meistersingers.

Instruments: Lute, Fiddle, Lyre, Recorder, Shawm (Oboe like instrument), Early Flutes.

Summary of Listeners Toolbox

The music for about 1,000 years was one melodic line called monophonic texture and was mostly religious. In the ninth century, we switch to polyphonic texture as a melodic line was added to an existing chant.

In the tenth through the sixteenth centuries we see the appearance of secular music, which gives people another choice besides sacred music. This does not mean sacred music disappeared, but rather we have an addition of a new style.

Note: As music develops, we start to see more evidence of counterpoint being used. Counterpoint is described as note against note and tends to provide the listener with a busy sound as you have melodies going against each other.

To The Student: The instructor may add or delete study items at his or her discretion.

Unit 3, Chapter 1 Listening Box Playlist

LB1: Type in Meditation With Gregorian Chant and choose top box with the same name. Select Track 2, Inno: Conditor; Track 7, Kyrie.

LB2: Type in More Sublime Chant and under Albums choose More Sublime Chant: The Art of . . . Select Track 2, Kyrie Eleison; Track 4, Sanctus; Track 5, Agnus Dei.

LB3: Type in Leonin/Perotin and under Albums choose Leonin/Perotin: Sacred Music From . . . Select Track 5, Notem fecit; Track 9 Viderunt omnes (both listening are examples of 2 part organum).

LB4: Type in Giacomo Carissimi and choose top box Giacomo Carissimi, Baroque. Select Track 5, In te, domine, speravi.

LB5: Type in Claudio Monteverdi and under Albums choose Madrigals Book 1, Claudio Monteverdi. Select Track 9, Fumia la Pastorella—Prima Parte.

LB6: Type in Ave generosa and choose top box Ave generosa, Hildegard von Bingen. Select Track 3, Ave generosa.

LB7: Type in Guillaume de Machaut and under Tracks choose Agnus Dei. Select Track 5, Agnus Dei.

LB8: Type in Troubadour Music and under Albums choose Faidit: Troubadour Music From The . . . Select Track 8, Mon cor e mie mas bonas chansos.

LB9: Type in Music of the Trouvères and choose top box with the same name. Select Track 6, On parole—A Paris—Frese nouvele.

LB10: Type in Marc Lewon and choose top box Marc Lewon, Vocal. Select Track 1, Mir ist ummaten leyde.

CHAPTER 2 THE RENAISSANCE (1450–1600)

What Do We Find in This Period?

Music: Sacred and secular music with polyphonic texture.

Texture: Mainly polyphonic texture.

Forms: A continuation of Masses, Motets, Madrigals, Chansons, evidence of Concertos (to be discussed in a later chapter).

Composers: I will submit a list of composers later in this chapter. They are Franco-Flemish, Italian, and English.

Travel To: Italy, France, and England.

The word Renaissance means "rebirth" in French and represents a revival of the human spirit. What caused such a dismal outlook on life in this period was the plague, famine, pestilence and the Hundred Years' War between France and England from 1337 to 1453. These issues caused people to turn away from the church and favor the secular world.

There is a general consensus among history experts that the Renaissance started in the fourteenth century in Florence, Italy, as a cultural movement. Its influence affected subjects such as art, politics, science, religion, literature, philosophy, and music. The unifying musical language of the day was a polyphonic style. In this era the distribution of music greatly improved as music printing was invented by Ottaviano Petrucci, from Venice, Italy, in 1501. Such forms as motets, masses, madrigals and chansons (songs) spread throughout Europe as composers were becoming increasingly popular with the general public.

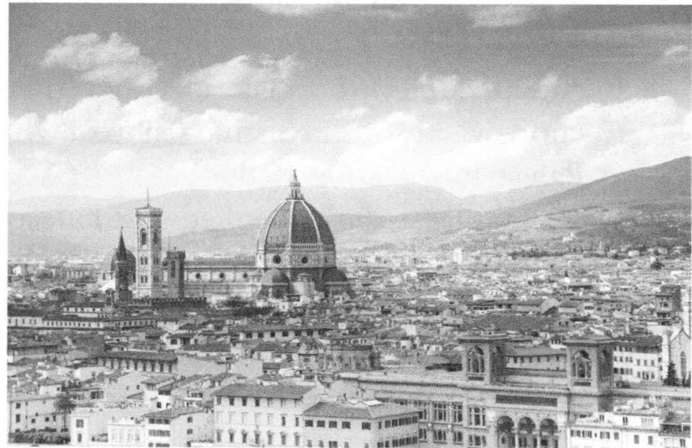

Florence, Italy

Musical Forms in the Renaissance

There were not any new forms in the Renaissance, but there was rather an increasing improvement of older ones with advancements of polyphonic texture.

The Renaissance Madrigal

The madrigal was the most important secular vocal form of its time and was invented by the Italians in the early 1500s. Several years later, the English became very adept at writing in this form. These pieces were written for small groups of singers and were used for court entertainment. The number of voices used ranged from three to eight, but most were three to six. Most madrigal subjects dealt with nature, love, and religious devotions. As opera emerged as a new vocal form, the madrigal became less popular. This information is a restatement from Chapter 1 and applies to the advancement of the madrigal in the Renaissance.

The Music: Italy

Since madrigals were invented in Italy, I will start with the composers and music from this country. Also, in the best interest of avoiding lengthy paragraphs about the composers' lives, I will use outline form.

Giovanni da Palestrina (c.1525–1594)

1. Born in Palestrina, a small town near Rome.
2. Got his musical education in Rome and returned to Palestrina in 1544.
3. The local Bishop appointed him choirmaster and organist at the church of Sant Agapito.
4. Eventually, the Bishop was elevated to Pope in 1553 and he appointed Palestrina to choirmaster of the Sistine Chapel, which was not met well with Vatican officials as Palestrina was married.
5. Five years later the Pope died and Palestrina left the Vatican, but stayed in Rome.
6. Musically, Palestrina wrote some secular madrigals, but he is most noted for his sacred vocal music which also included the Mass. He was well respected by everyone and was a master at writing counterpoint and polyphonic texture.

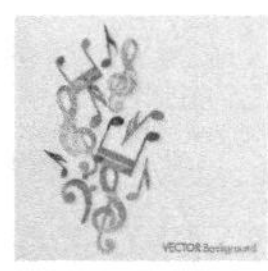

Listening Box 11

Type in S'il disse mai and under Tracks choose Madrigals Book 1 (IL primo libro . . .). Select Track 2, S'il disse mai, ch'io veng' in odio a quella.

Palestrina wrote a huge amount of sacred music and the Mass discussed in Chapter I. That being said, I feel obligated to include one listening from Palestrina's Mass music.

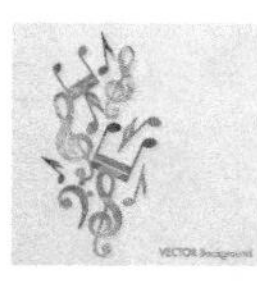

Listening Box 12

Type in Palestrina Masses and Motets and under Albums choose Palestrina: Masses and Motets (Your 1st choice). Select Track 5, Missa Ecce ego Johannes: Sanctus.

The Renaissance Motet

The motet in the Renaissance was a very popular form. It was quite advanced as it included polyphonic settings, imitative counterpoint, and sacred texts in Latin. It is interesting to note that secular motets in this era often praised Monarchs.

The Music: The Franco-Flemish School

Josquin des Prez (c.1450/1455–1521)

1. Born in France but spent most of his life in Italy, in particular, Rome and Milan.
2. He was very popular and was considered one of the best composers of his era.
3. Although being so popular, there is not much known about his personal life or personality.
4. A strange event occurred in 1466 when his father died and his uncle and aunt left him an inheritance. For some reason they changed his name to Gille Lebloitte dit Desprez and Jacque Banestonne. It is conjectured that his uncle and aunt did not want this inheritance known or stolen.
5. Some of his music was printed in 1502 by Petrucci of Venice, Italy. This project turned out to be so successful that Petrucci published more in 1504 and 1514.

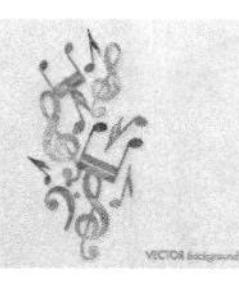

Listening Box 13

Type in Qui velatus and under Tracks choose Qui velatus facie fuisti. Select Track 10, Qui velatus facie fuisti.

The Music: England

Thomas Morely (c.1557–1602)

1. Known for writing English madrigals and keyboard music.
2. Lived during Shakespeare's time and was an organist at St. Paul's Cathedral.
3. He was the most famous composer of secular music in Elizabethan England and received a bachelor's degree from Oxford in 1588.

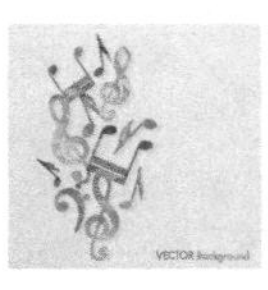

Listening Box 14

Type in arise, get up my dear and under Tracks choose Madrigals: No. 20 Arise, Get Up My . . . Select Track 1, Now is the Month of Maying; Track 6, Madrigals: No. 20, Arise, Get Up My Dear.

The mention of the Renaissance would not be complete without mentioning some of the great artisans, philosophers, and writers of the period. You probably have heard of the term "Renaissance Man." This is a person who has knowledge and skills in different subjects. Some of the most prominent are Michelangelo Buonarroti, Leonardo da Vinci, Galileo Galilei, Niccolo Machiavelli, and William Shakespeare. I will cite a few here.

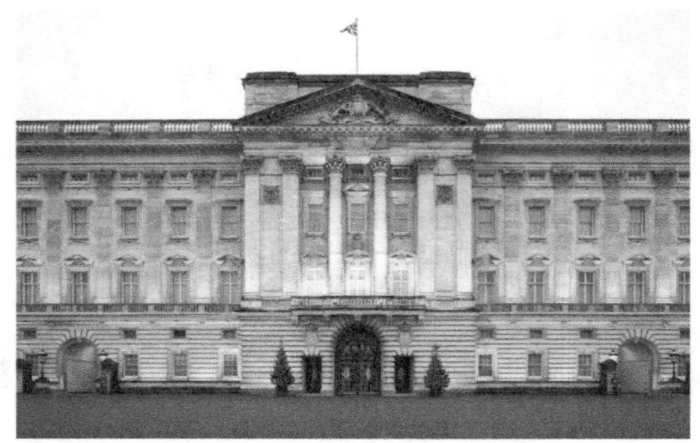

Buckingham Palace

Michelangelo di Lodovico Buonnarti Simoni (1475–1564)

1. Born in Caprese near Arezzo.
2. He was a painter, sculptor, architect, poet, and engineer.
3. His most notable works are: Pieta, David, The Last Judgement, Painting of Sistine Chapel, and the Cupola of the Vatican.
4. He was often called "il divino," the divine one and was considered the best in his era.

He once said, "If there is some good in me, it is because I was born in the subtle atmosphere of your country Arezzo. Along with the milk of my nurse I received the knack of handling chisel and hammer, with which I make my figures."

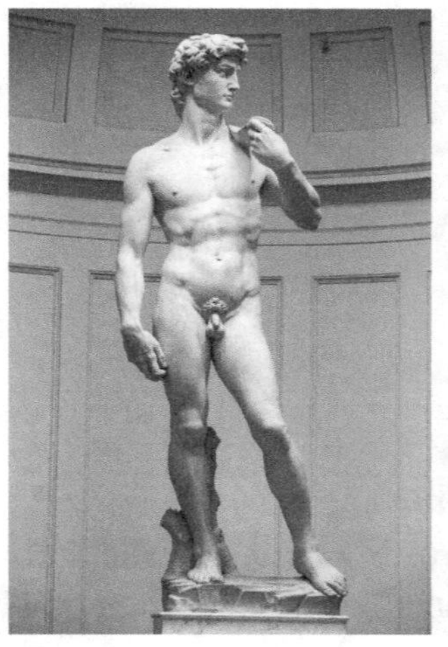

David

Pieta

Leonardo di ser Piero da Vinci (1452–1519)

1. Born in Vinci, Republic of Florence (Present-day Italy).
2. Considered a Renaissance Man, his subjects of interest were music, math, painting, inventions, science, engineering, literature, geology, astronomy, cartography, history, sculpting, and architecture. WOW! Believe it or not, he was at times considered to be a procrastinator in that he did not always finish his works.
3. He was given credit for the basic inventions of the helicopter, parachute, and the armored tank.
4. Interesting to note, he was born out of wedlock to a notary and gentleman Piero da Vinci and his mother was a peasant woman called Caterina. Leonardo had no official last name and da Vinci means "of Vinci."
5. Some of his greatest works are MonaLisa, St. John The Baptist, The Last Supper, The Vitruvian Man, and Lady With an Ermine.

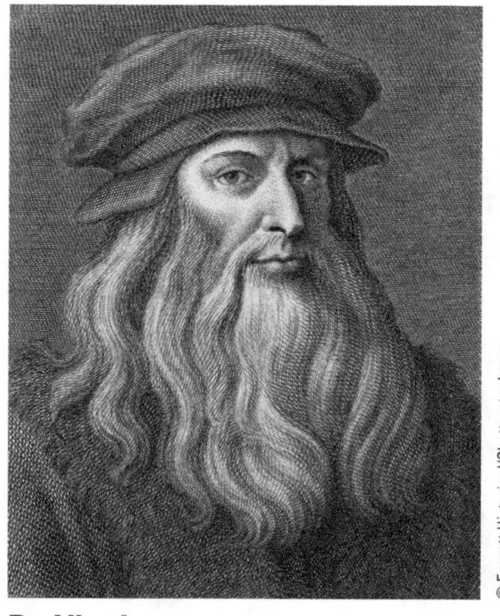

Da Vinci

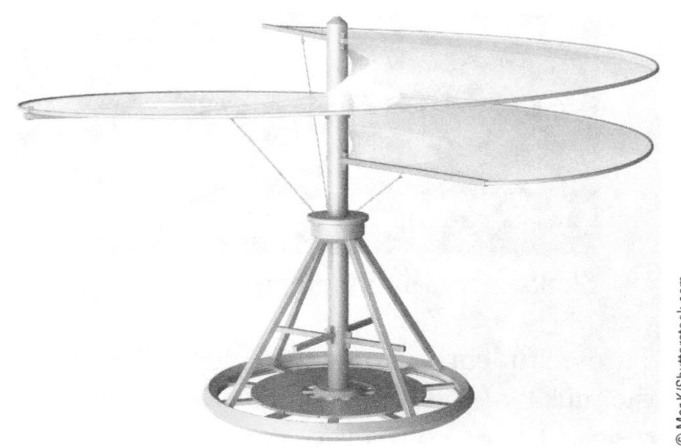

Helicopter

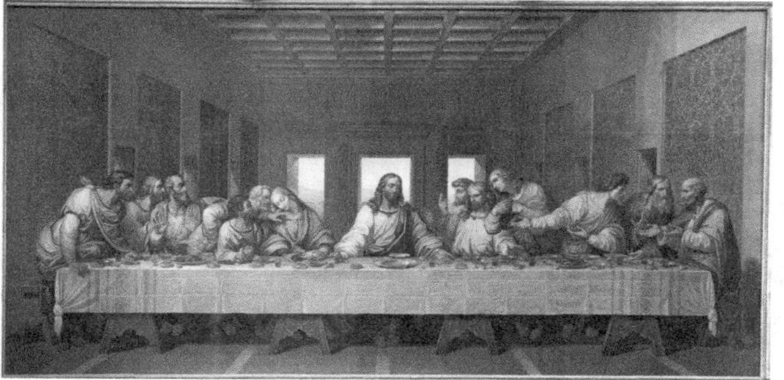
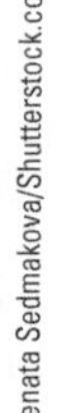

The Last Supper

William Shakespeare (Baptized April, 1564–1616)

1. Born in Stratford-upon-Avon, Warwickshire.
2. He was a playwright, actor, and poet.
3. At the age of 18, he married Anne Hathaway, who was 26, and they had three children. First born was Susanna, Hamnet, a son, and Judith were the next and were twins.
4. Some of his best known works are Hamlet, Othello, Macbeth, and King Lear.

A quote from Shakespeare's, Hamlet:

> What a piece of work is a man, how noble in reason, how infinite in faculties, in form and moving how expressive and admirable, in action how like an angel, in apprehension how like a God.

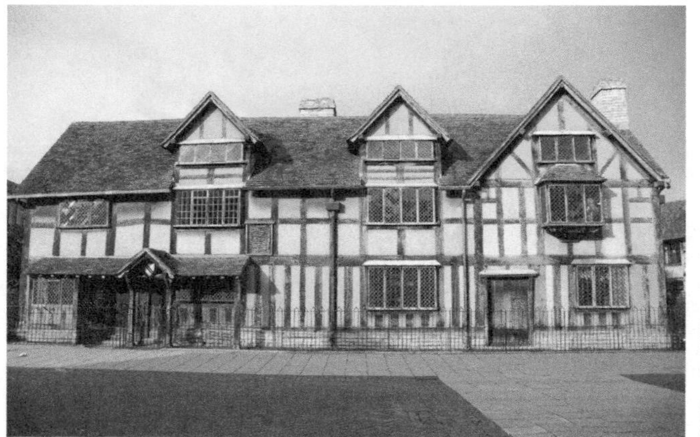

Shakespeare's Birthplace

William Shakespeare

Shakespeare

For those students who want to go further in the music of the Renaissance, I am submitting a list of composers that I believe really culminate and exemplify their style period.

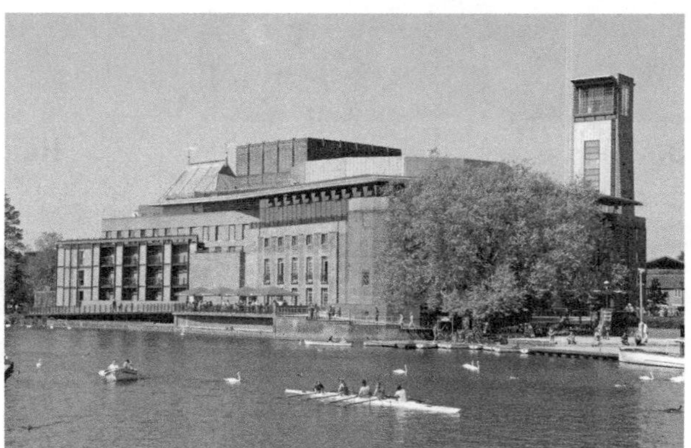

Shakespeare's Theater, Stratford, Avon

Italy:

Giovanni da Palestrina (1525–1594), known for his sacred vocal music.

Andrea Gabrieli (c.1533–1585), known for his church music and madrigals.

Giovanni Gabrieli (c.1555–1612), known for his church music, instrumental music, concertos, and madrigals. Also, the nephew of Andrea Gabrieli.

Luca Marenzio (c.1553–1599), known for sacred motets and madrigals.

Claudio Monteverdi (1567–1643), known for madrigals and opera, he also invented the overture.

Franco-Flemish:

Guillaume Dufay (c.1400–1474), known for masses and motets for the church and chansons (songs) for the courts.

Johannes Ockeghem (c.1430–1497), known for canons and sacred as well as secular music.

Josquin des Prez (c.1440–1521), known for his masses and secular chansons.

Jacob Arcadelt (c.1505–1567), known for his chansons and madrigals.

Orlando di Lasso [(Lassus) 1532–1594)], known for his sacred and secular vocal music. He was considered one of the greatest of his time.

England:

John Taverner (c.1490–1545), known for being one of England's finest church composers.

William Byrd (1543–1623), known for his church music, songs, and keyboard music. He was considered one of England's best before the Baroque Era.

Thomas Morley (c.1557–1602), known for his English madrigals.

Summary of Unit 3, Chapter 2 Terms and Study Sheet

Basically, the summary terms and styles of music were pretty similar to Chapter 1. Again, the music was both sacred and secular and contained polyphonic texture and counterpoint. Rather than having a summary list, I am proposing a few questions that may be used for class assignment and discussion, or, submitted as a short paper.

Questions

1. How did the music of the Middle Ages and Renaissance affect you personally? Did you like it and would you listen to more of it?
2. Do you think we still have Troubadours in our present society? If so, where might we find them?
3. Do you think the people of the Middle Ages and Renaissance had a difficult time choosing between sacred and secular music as their favorite?
4. The Renaissance fostered for the people a new hope of dignity and belief in the individual. In our present society have we lost these values or have we still maintained them?

Unit 3, Chapter 2 Listening Box Playlist

LB11: Type in S' il disse mai and under Tracks choose Madrigals Book 1 (Il primo libro di . . .). Select Track 2, S' il disse mai, ch'io veng in odio a quella.

LB12: Type in Palestrina Masses and Motets and under Albums choose Palestrina: Masses and Motets (your 1st choice). Select Track 5, Missa Ecce ego Johannes: Sanctus.

LB13: Type in Qui velatus and under Tracks choose Qui velatusfacie fuisti. Select Track 10, Qui velatus facie fuisti.

LB14: Type in Arise, Get up My Dear and under Tracks choose Madrigals: No. 20, Arise, Get Up My . . . Select Track 1, Now is the Month of Maying; Track 6, Arise, Get Up My Dear.

CHAPTER 3 THE BAROQUE (1600–1750)

What Do We Find in This Period?

Music: New forms, counterpoint, polyphonic texture sacred and secular music. We also see an infusion of the Germanic influence.

Texture: Mainly polyphonic.

Forms: Oratorio, Opera, Cantata (sacred and secular), Overture, Concerto (Solo Concerto and Concerto Grosso), and Fugue.

Composers: Andrea Gabrieli, Giovanni Gabrieli, Claudio Monteverdi, Antonio Vivaldi, George Frideric Handel, and Johann Sebastian Bach. I will cite most, but not all of these.

Travel To: Italy and Germany.

The Baroque Era represents many firsts in music. First, the term Baroque is a Portuguese word which means irregular shape or irregular pearls. This period was actually named after its existence as future composers thought the music was too ornate (fancy) and not structured very well. Second, it is a very important era as it has come to represent the first period of our current concert music.

At this point, I would like to digress for a moment and explain the term "Classical Music." In most cases much of the older music is termed "Classical," but it is not correct. As you will see the next era represents "Classical" in music. For example, composers such as Vivaldi and Bach are Baroque composers, not Classical.

Giovanni Gabrieli (c.1554/1557–1612)

1. Born in Venice, Italy, and was one of five children.
2. He was a composer and organist and represents the culmination of the Venetian School of Music.
3. He was principal organist at Saint Mark's Basilica starting in 1585 and not only composed music, but spent much of his time editing the music of his uncle Andrea.
4. Eventually, he took an additional organist post at Scuola Grand di San Rocco which enabled his reputation and career to grow further.

5. He preferred sacred vocal music and instrumental music.
6. He worked with antiphonal sound (sound coming from different directions) to create spatial effects.
7. He used specific word notations in his music because he wanted his music to sound the same all the time, regardless of who was performing. For example, forte (loud), piano (soft), as well as many others.
8. He died in 1612, due to complications of a kidney stone.

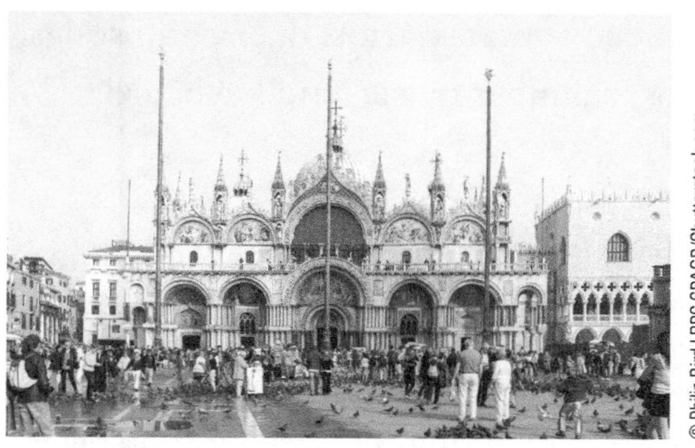

Saint Mark's Basilica, Venice, Italy, where Gabrieli worked

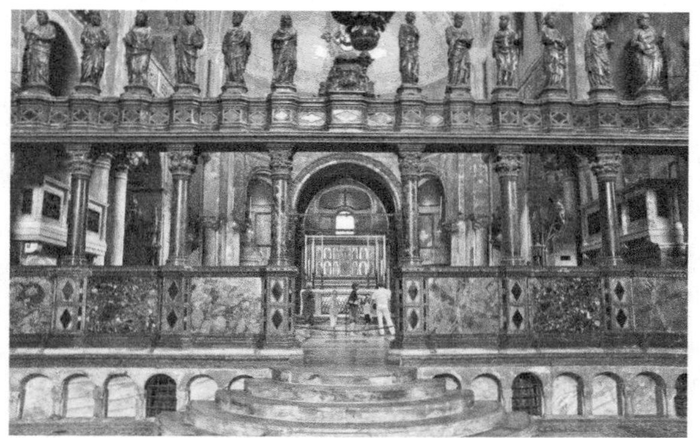

Interior of St Mark's Basilica

Some music from Giovanni Gabrieli. Please pay close attention to the polyphonic texture and how the melodic lines go against each other, but come together as a whole.

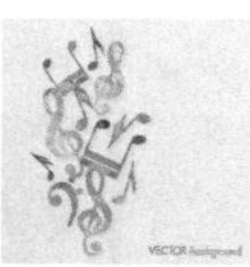

Listening Box 15

Type in Music for Brass and under Albums choose Music for Brass Vol. 1, Giovanni Gabrieli. Select Track 1, Canzon XVII; Track 3, Canzon IX.

George Frideric Handel (1685–1759) the Oratorio and Opera

1. Born in Halle, Germany, which is near Berlin.
2. At 18, he entered the University of Halle and eventually accepted a one year contract as church organist at Domkirche. This position provided Handel with lodging, money, and prestige. He also had income from his father's estate.
3. After one year his contract expired at Domkirche and he moved to Hamburg and got a position playing violin in the orchestra.
4. After a while he traveled to Hamburg and Venice, Italy, which was the opera capitol at the time.

5. His final two moves were back to Hannover, Germany and London, England.
6. In his later years he is partially blind and he dies in England.
7. Some of his main compositions are:

   Over forty operas in Italian. Two of the most famous are Giulio Cesare and Rinaldo.

   Over thirty oratorios, the most famous of which is Messiah, in 1741.

   He wrote instrumental music and two of his famous pieces are Water Music (1717) and Music for Royal Fireworks (1749).

   He also wrote secular vocal music which included cantatas, trios, duets, and songs.

   Last but not least, he also composed concertos, chamber music, and keyboard music. WOW!

The Oratorio (Meaning a Small Prayer Chapel Where These Works Were Performed)

The Church of England banned all stage productions during Lent. Oratorios provided a loophole in which they had sacred subjects; there was no acting, no staging, no special scenery, or costumes. Messiah, written by Handel in 1741, in just twenty-four days is probably one of the worlds' most famous. It was first heard in 1742, in the Dublin Music Hall, Ireland. In a later charity performance at the Dublin Cathedral enough money was raised to free 142 people from debtor's prison.

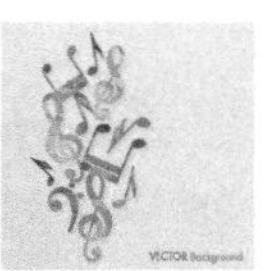

Listening Box 16

Type in For unto us and under Tracks choose Chorus: For unto us a Child is born, The Mormon Tabernacle Choir. Select Track 10, Chorus: For unto us a Child is born.

The Words: For unto us a Child is born, unto us a son is given

And the government shall be upon his shoulder, and his name shall be called

Wonderful, Counselor, the Mighty God, the Everlasting Father, the Prince of Peace.

Note: Go to YouTube and type in lyrics to, For unto us a Child is born in addition to Napster.

Also, listen to how the strings kick in on the words Wonderful and Counselor.

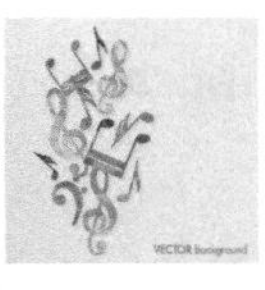

Listening Box 17

Type in Chorus: Hallelujah! and under Tracks choose Chorus: Hallelujah!, The Mormon Tabernacle Choir. Select Track 11, Chorus: Hallelujah!

The Words: Hallelujah, repeats 10× (sequence)

For the Lord god omnipotent reigneth, (answer hallelujah 4×). All of this keeps repeating.

The kingdom of this world, is becoming, the kingdom of our Lord

And of his Christ and of his Christ

And he shall reign forever and ever (4×)

King of Kings and Lord of Lords (repeats) (sequence)

And he shall reign forever and ever (repeats) (stretto)

Hallelujah, Hallelujah.

Sequence

A sequence is the same musical material on different pitch levels.

Stretto: Stretto means "tight" and refers to the voice parts entering in close succession.

Features of an Oratorio: Basically, a concert with a sacred subject and not a full blown show.

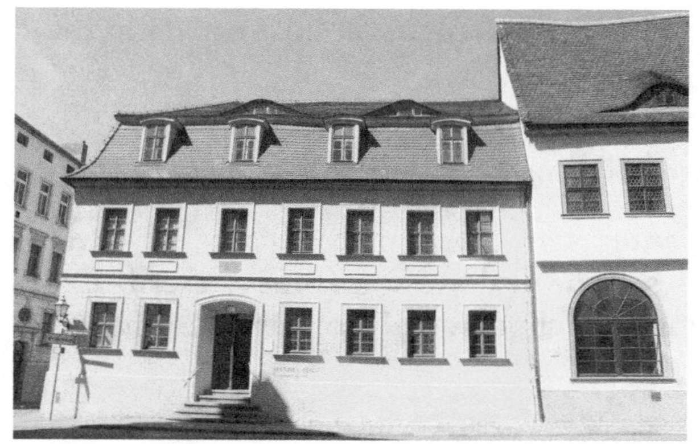

G. F. Handel Birth House in Halle, Germany

Opera

Opera started in Northern Italy around 1573. There was an elitist group of people who met at the home of Count Bardi to discuss the arts, music, and the important issues of the day. These people became to be known as the Florentine Camerata. They eventually felt there was a need to change vocal music and they went back to investigate Ancient Greek Dramas. These investigations turned up stories, but no music. The obvious connection here is music was added to these stories and opera was born. The first opera composer was Jacopo Peri (1561–1633), who was a Camerata member. His first opera, Dafne in 1597, met with a terrible fate in which the music was eventually lost. His second opera, Euridice, in 1600, became the first opera for which we have music. As time goes on, Venice, Italy, becomes the city with the most opera houses as it was a major commercial trading center. The first one was called Teatro San Cassiano which was built in 1565 and destroyed by fire in 1629. It reopened in 1637 and its last performances were in 1807. It was finally demolished for good in 1812.

Features of Opera

Operas in this era had secular subjects, overtures, arias, recitatives, librettos, solos, and chorus. These terms will be defined at the end of the chapter in the study sheet.

Claudio Monteverdi (1567–1643)

1. Born in Cremona, Italy, the famous string making town.
2. He was a composer and string player who replaced Giovanni Gabrieli at St. Mark's Basilica in 1612, after Gabrieli's death.
3. Invented and pioneered the use of the overture, which is instrumental music that provides an introduction to the opera or oratorio before the action starts.
4. He wrote opera and two of his most famous are Orfeo (1607) and the Coronation of the Pope (1642).
5. He eventually took holy orders in the church and concentrated on writing sacred music.

Cantata

Cantatas are vocal pieces that were developed in the Baroque Era. They can be sacred or secular and are sometimes described as small oratorios. They generally include solo voices, a chorus, and various instruments.

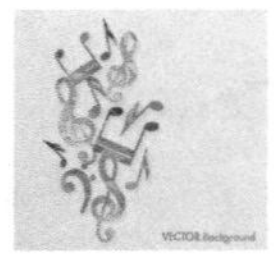

Listening Box 18

Type in Bach Sacred Cantatas and choose top box Bach: Sacred Cantatas Vol. 2: BWV 20–36. Select Track 1, "O Ewigkeit, du Donnerwart;" Track 3, "Gott ist gerecht."

Note: O ewigkeit, du Donnerwart means, O eternity, you Thunder Word.

Gott ist gerecht means, God is just.

Castrato

A castrato is a surgically altered male who sang high parts in operas. Opera producers in the seventeenth and eighteenth centuries arranged for young boys to be castrated before their voices changed. Primarily, this was the result of women not being allowed on stage in many places. A castrato was treated like a hero and the last of the castrati was Alessandro Moreschi who died in 1922.

Antonio Vivaldi (1678–1741) "maestro de' concerti," master of the concerto

1. Born in Venice, Italy, he was one of the six children.
2. His father was a barber and played violin in the orchestra of St. Mark's.
3. Vivaldi was a composer, violin virtuoso, teacher, and cleric.

4. He became a priest at the age of 25 and was also known as, "il prete rosso," the red head.
5. In 1703, he begins to work in Pio Ospedale della Pieta (Devout Hospital of Mercy), an orphanage. He had some very talented students and for the next 20+ years he writes most of his major works here.
6. Vivaldi's health was never good and at the age of 49 he moved to Vienna, Austria, to accept the post of court composer.
7. In his lifetime he wrote almost 800 compositions, unfortunately, most were lost.

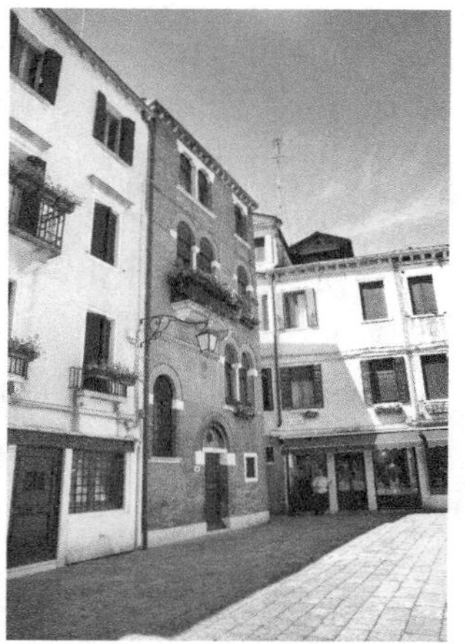

The House of Antonio Vivaldi, Venice, Italy

The Concerto

There are two kinds of concerto, the solo concerto and the concerto grosso. Both types are instrumental pieces that have three sections, fast, slow, fast and were written for small orchestra. The difference is the solo concert has one solo instrument and the concerto grosso has more than one solo instrument. Grosso in Italian means big or large and the composers of the day did not want to change the overall structure of the concerto, as this form was very popular with the people. They added several soloists to provide variety for the listener.

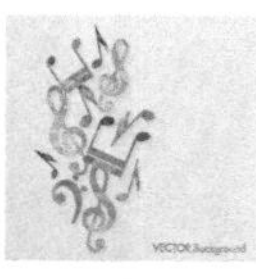

Listening Box 19

Type in Baroque for Babies and choose top box Baroque for Babies. Select Track 2, The Four Seasons—Spring—Vivaldi. Here I decided to have some fun with this listening and introduce you to a great disc for young kids. This disc has a variety of classical pieces and very appropriate for young children.

Note: One of my favorite videos of Spring, by Vivaldi, is on YouTube. Go to YouTube, go to videos, type in Spring, Julia Fischer. You will have several choices, take your pick. Also, this is an example of a solo concerto.

Johann Sebastian Bach (1685–1750)

1. Born in Eisenach, Germany, he was one of the eight children.
2. He worked and lived within a one hundred mile radius of his birthplace.
3. He came from a family of musicians which included his father, older brother, and uncles.
4. His mother died in 1694 and his father died eight months later. Bach was orphaned at the age of 10 and he later moved in with his oldest brother Johann Christoph Bach.

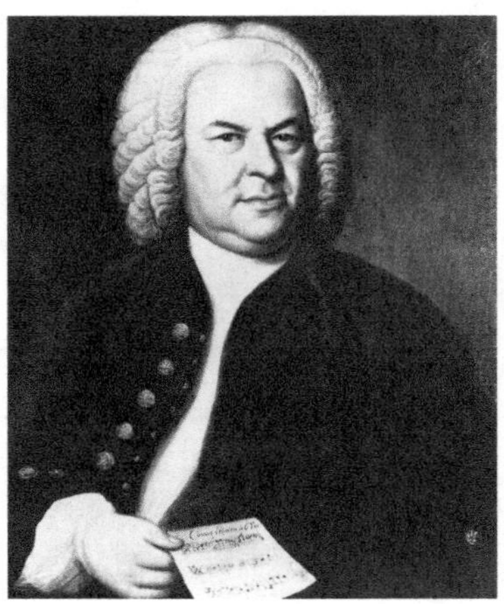

5. He received extensive music training from his brother who taught him organ, clavichord, and composition.
6. Bach was not only a master keyboardist, but also a master at writing polyphonic texture and counterpoint.
7. In 1706, Bach married a cousin on his father's side, Maria Barbara. They had seven children, four lived into adulthood.
8. In 1717, Bach did not get his desired position of Kapellmeister for the court. He made a fuss and asked for his release. The Duke was so angered, he put Bach in prison for four weeks. After his time in jail, Bach was dismissed.
9. In 1720, Maria Barbara dies and Bach meets a wonderful singer, Anna Magdalena Wilke. Anna was 16 years younger than Bach.
10. In 1721, Bach marries Anna and they had 13 children, 6 live into adulthood.
11. In his later years Bach went blind and he eventually passed in 1750, at the age of 65.
12. Some of his most famous compositions are:

    6 Brandenburg Concertos

    The Well-Tempered Clavier (48 Preludes and Fugues)

    Mass in B minor

    Goldberg Variations

    St. Matthew Passion

    St. John Passion

    Over 300 cantatas, of which around 200 survived. And The Art of the Fugue.

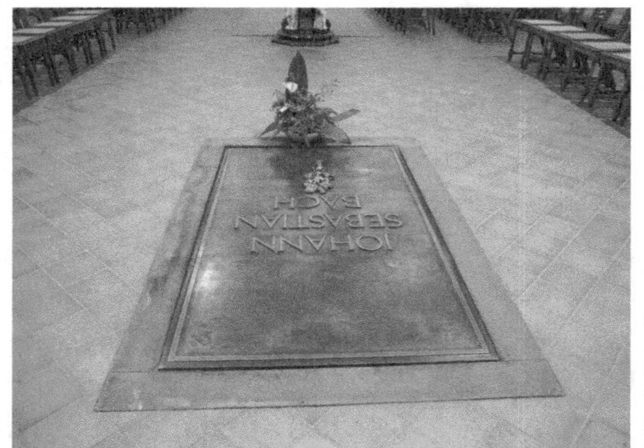

Bach's Grave in St. Thomas Church, Leipzig, Germany

Concerto Grosso

As previously stated, the main difference between solo concerto and concerto grosso is that concerto grosso has more than one soloist.

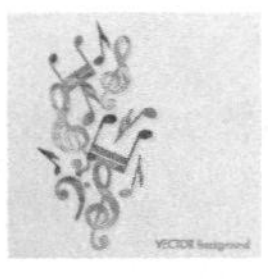

Listening Box 20

Type in Bach's Greatest Hits and choose top box Bach's Greatest Hits: The Brandenburg Concertos. Select Track 8, No. 2 in F Major: 3rd mvt: Allegro assai; Track 18, No. 5 in D Major: 1st mvt: Allegro.

Note: This listening from Brandenburg 2 was written for chamber (small) orchestra and solo trumpet, flute, oboe, and violin. It was written in 1721, and is the third movement. Listen for the interaction of the instruments and melodies. In Brandenburg 5, listen for the great Harpsichord solo. Good Baroque Rock n Roll!

The Fugue

The fugue is an instrumental composition that contains a subject (melody), imitation, counterpoint, and polyphonic texture. As the instruments present their parts and interact, the music has a very busy type sound. This style of composition can also be written for voices. As a matter of fact, the individual parts are referred to as voice parts as they reflect a certain voice range.

Construction of the Fugue Form (A-B-A)

1. **No Introduction**
2. **Exposition (A):** In this section, the main melody (subject) is introduced. When all the parts have completed their entry with the melody, the exposition is finished.
3. **Development (B):** In this section the composer takes parts of the main melody, adds some new material and creates somewhat of a different sound. Development sections are put in for sound variety.
4. **Recapitulation (A):** This section restates the main melody. This generally happens before the fugue ends.
5. **Coda:** The coda is the ending of the piece and can be as long or as short as the composer wishes.

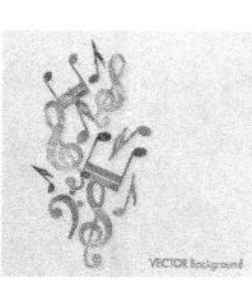

Listening Box 21

Type in Bach: Great Organ Favorites and under Albums choose Bach: Great Organ favorites, E. Power Biggs. Select Track 8, Fugue in G minor (The Little).

I would like to introduce you to a fantastic a cappella singing group called The Swingle Singers. They consist of eight voices: 2 sopranos, 2 altos, 2 tenors, and 2 basses. I have chosen two selections which demonstrate what a fugue sounds like a cappella.

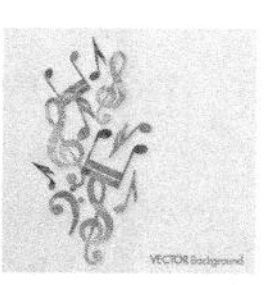

Listening Box 22

Type in Spotlight on Bach and under Albums choose Spotlight on Bach, The Swingle Singers. Select Track 1, Organ Fugue BWV 542; Track 13, Fugue a La Gigue.

Summary of Unit 3, Chapter 3 Terms and Study Sheet

New Forms

Vocal: Oratorio, Opera, and Cantata. **Instrumental**: Overture, Concerto, and Fugue.

Terms

Antiphonal: Sound coming from different directions creating spatial effects.

Aria: A vocal solo.

Baroque: A Portuguese word meaning irregular shape or irregular pearls.

Cantata: A vocal piece which can be sacred or secular with solo voices, instruments, and chorus.

Canzon: A canzon is a song.

Castrato: A surgically altered male who sang high parts in operas.

Chorus: There are four sections in a chorus, soprano, alto, tenor, and bass.

Coda: A tail or tag ending.

Concerto: A concerto is an instrumental piece in three sections, fast, slow, and fast. It was originally written for solo instrument and small orchestra.

Concerto Grosso: Similar to concerto, but has more than one soloist.

Counterpoint: Note against note.

Fugue: A composition where the subject is presented in several parts and also contains imitation, counterpoint, and polyphonic texture; the sections are exposition, development, recapitulation, and coda.

Libretto: It is the story of an opera or oratorio.

Opera: An opera is basically a full blown show with acting, staging, scenery, costumes, chorus, orchestra, vocal soloists, and generally a secular subject.

Oratorio: A vocal piece with a sacred subject, chorus, orchestra and vocal soloists. Also, no special scenery, acting or costumes.

Overture: An overture is instrumental music that comes before the opera or oratorio begins. It is designed to set a mood and introduce songs you will hear later.

Recitative: Recitative is a speech-like style of singing found in operas, oratorios, and cantatas.

Solo: One person playing an instrument or just singing.

Stretto: Stretto is generally found in a fugue and is the process where the main melody is imitated in close succession.

Composers: Andrea Gabrieli, Giovanni Gabrieli, Claudio Monteverdi, Antonio Vivaldi, Johann Sebastian Bach, and George Frideric Handel.

Summary of Listeners Toolbox

In two words, polyphonic texture. The key here is to listen for the entrances of the melody and how the parts interact.

To The Student: The instructor may add or delete study items at his or her discretion.

Unit 3, Chapter 3 Listening Box Playlist

LB15: Type in Music for Brass and under Albums choose Music for Brass Vol. 1, Giovanni Gabrieli. Select Track 1, Canzon XVII; Track 3, Canzon IX.

LB16: Type in For unto us and under Tracks choose Chorus: For unto us a Child is born, The Mormon Tabernacle Choir. Select disc 1, Track 10, Chorus: For unto us a Child is born.

LB17: Type in Chorus: Hallelujah! and under Tracks choose Chorus: Hallelujah! The Mormon Tabernacle Choir. Select disc 2, Track 11, Chorus: Hallelujah!

LB18: Type in Bach Sacred Cantatas and choose top box Bach: Sacred Cantatas Vol. 2: BWV 20–36. Select Track 1, Cantata No. 20, "O Ewigkeit, du Donnerwort;" Track 3, "Gott ist gerecht."

LB19: Type in Baroque for Babies and choose top box Baroque for Babies. Select Track 2, The Four Seasons—Spring—Vivaldi.

LB20: Type in Bach's Greatest Hits and choose top box Bach's Greatest Hits: The Brandenburg Concertos. Select Track 8, No. 2 in F Major: 3rd mvt. Allegro assai; Track 18, No. 5 in D Major: 1st mvt. Allegro.

LB21: Type in Bach: Great Organ Favorites and under Albums choose Bach: Great Organ Favorites, E. Power Biggs. Select Track 8, Fugue in G Minor (The Little).

LB22: Type in Spotlight on Bach and under Albums choose Spotlight on Bach, The Swingle Singers. Select Track 1, Organ Fugue BWV 542; Track 13, Fugue a La Gigue.

CHAPTER 4 THE CLASSICAL (1750–1820)

What Do We Find in This Period?

Music: The era of the symphony and sonata form. The music was elegant, formal, and restrained.

Texture: Mainly homophonic which is a melody over a chordal accompaniment.

Forms: Some new forms—Theme and Variations, Rondo, Minuet, Sonata, and Symphony.

Old forms—Concerto, Mass, Opera, Overture, and Oratorio.

Composers: Franz Joseph Haydn, Wolfgang Amadeus Mozart, and Ludwig van Beethoven.

Travel to: Austria, Germany, and London.

Amazingly, the concepts of Classical Music go back to 79 A.D. when the cities of Pompeii and Herculaneum were buried under volcanic ash from Mt. Vesuvius. When archeologists excavated these ruins in 1748, they uncovered Roman and Greek art, artifacts, and architecture. Many of these discoveries displayed in appearance balance, clarity, simplicity, and symmetry. As applied to music of this period, the ideas of symmetry of form and clarity of sound come from this earlier mentality. In addition, these discoveries in 1748, sparked a renewed interest in ancient Greek and Roman Art.

Note: The term Classical Music has always been used to describe older music history. As you can see, this is an incorrect name in which Classical only refers to music from 1750 to 1820.

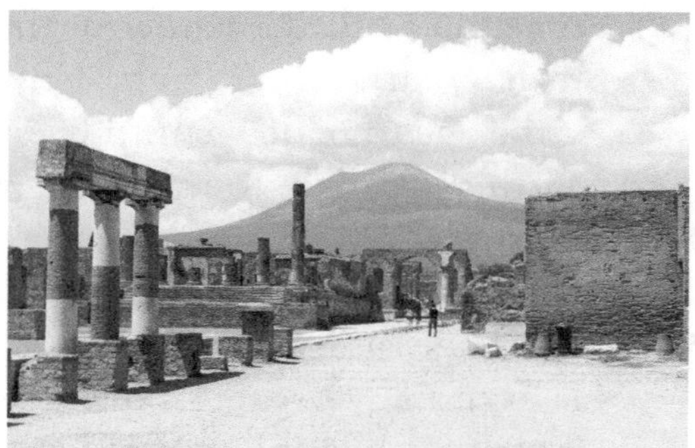

Mount Vesuvius and Pompeii

Music and Events at Court

1. After an event was scheduled, it was the job of the servants to deliver invitations and collect responses.
2. On the day of the event, guests would arrive and mingle, chat and have something to eat (snacks). After a while they would perhaps take a nap before changing their clothes for dinner.

3. After dinner, guests would go to the music room for a concert. Many times they would be disrespectful in that they would talk, not pay attention, and even sleep while the musicians were playing.
4. After the concert, the guests would again retire to their rooms to rest, change their clothes, and get ready for the evening dance (the Ball). These dances would go till the wee hours of the morning. In general, people did not go to bed at 7 p.m. every evening because they did not have 50 in. flat screen TVs. There was not much happening and this was a good way to keep the fun going.

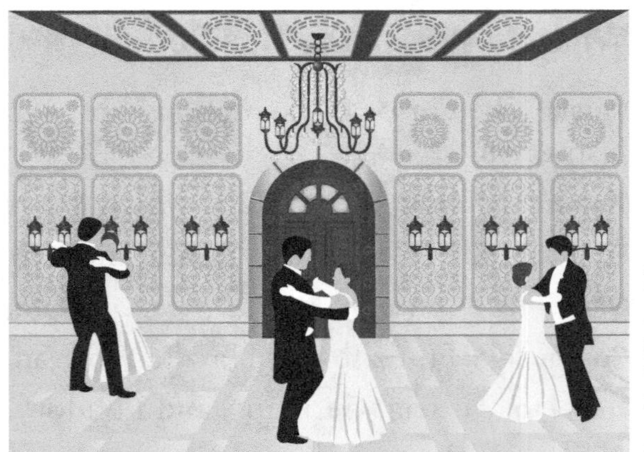

Waltzing in the Ballroom

Note: It is important to note that musicians of the day were considered servants of the people. Many times their assignments included serving food and cleaning up before playing music. As the eighteenth century progresses, the nobility becomes the primary patrons of art and music.

Franz Joseph Haydn (1732–1809)

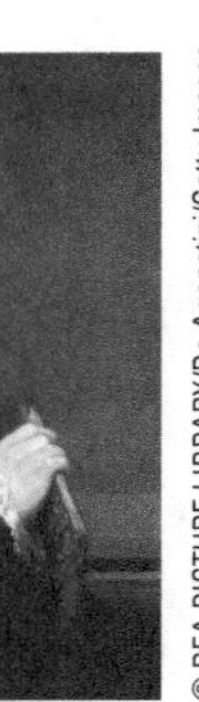

Portrait by Thomas Hardy, 1792

1. Born in Rohrau, Austria.
2. Sometimes called, "Father of the Symphony," "Father of the String Quartet," or "Pappa Haydn."
3. At the age of 6, he went to live with a relative Johann Matthias Frankh, to train as a musician. Although Frankh's house was only 7.5 miles away from where Haydn lived, he never again lived with his parents.
4. At the age of 8, he received a scholarship to study in Vienna. He eventually became a member of the famous Vienna Boys' Choir, which is still in existence.
5. He did not have a good career as a freelance musician, but as he got older, he held different positions in court such as violinist, music director, and composer.
6. In 1760, he married Maria Anna Keller. This marriage was neither pleasant nor peaceful and produced no children. Apparently, Maria could not care about Haydn's career or music and it is said she showed such disdain that she used his manuscript paper for pastry pan linings or curl papers.

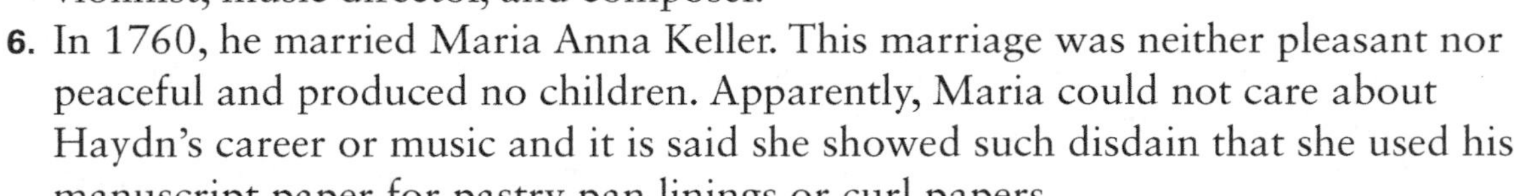

7. In 1761, he secured a position with the wealthy Esterhazy family for whom he worked for about 30 years. The Esterhazy's had two palaces, one in Hungary and another in Austria. Haydn traveled back and forth to both places.
8. After the death of his Esterhazy patron, Haydn moved to London where he wrote his famous London (Salomon) Symphonies, numbers 93–104.

9. In his later years, he moved back to Austria to serve Prince Miklos II, the new head of the Esterhazy family. There he wrote his two famous oratorios, The Creation and The Seasons.
10. Some of his most famous compositions are:
    104 symphonies (London 93–104)
    Two oratorios, The Creation and The Seasons
    The Seven Last Words of Christ
    Fifteen operas in Italian, many of which were lost
    Fifty-four piano sonatas
    Over seventy string quartets
    Concertos
    Fourteen Masses.

I would like to cite Haydn's symphony number 45, the famous "Farewell Symphony." Apparently, Haydn was in the midst of a labor dispute because his musicians were not allowed to bring their wives and families to the Esterhazy Palace in Eisenstadt, which was about thirty miles south of Vienna. Living in servant's quarters and being away from families for a long time was not good for morale.

In his Farewell Symphony, Haydn comes up with a very clever scheme. The first three movements were pretty much conventional. However, in the fourth movement, about midway, Haydn instructed his second horn player and first oboist to pack up their instruments, blow out their reading candles, and leave the hall. Soon after, other musicians followed, the bassoonist, the second oboist, cello and bass players, then violin, and viola players. The symphony ended with just two violin players. Prince Esterhazy got the message and decided to give extended leave to the musicians to visit their families.

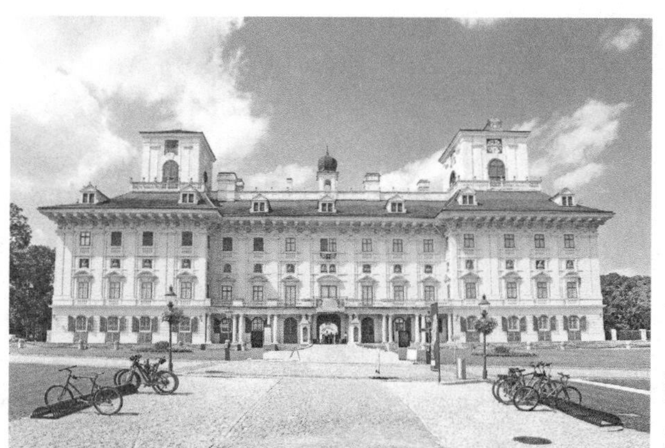

The Esterhazy Palace in Eisenstadt, Austria

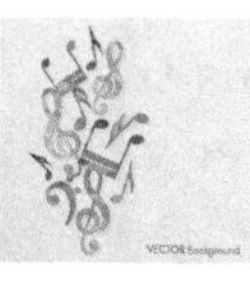

Listening Box 23

Type in Haydn Symphony 45 and choose top box Haydn Symphony No. 45 & 94. Select Track 1, Symphony No. 45 in F—Sharp Minor "Farewell": I Allegro assai; Track 8, Symphony No. 94 in G Major "Surprise": III. Allegro Di Molto.

Wolfgang Amadeus Mozart (1756–1791)

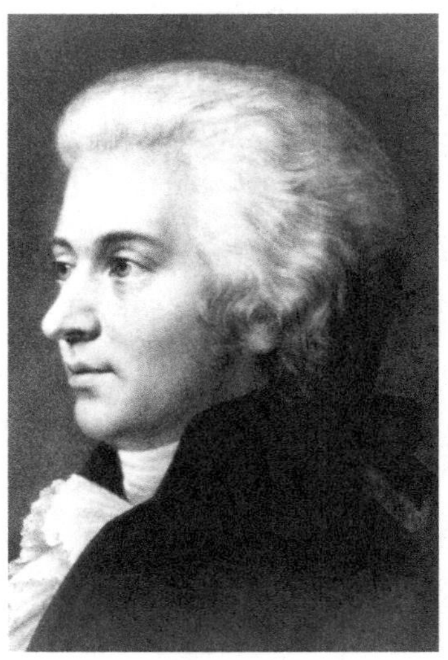

© Everett Historical/Shutterstock.com

1. Born in Salzburg, Austria.
2. Mozart was definitely a child prodigy as he was composing and concertizing at the age of 4 and 5. He wrote over 600 compositions in only 35 years. He is still considered "the greatest natural genius" of all the composers.
3. Some of his early age accomplishments were his first symphony at the age of 8, his first oratorio at the age of 11, and his first opera at the age of 12.
4. Mozart never went to school and was taught all aspects of music by his father Leopold, who was a violinist in the court orchestra in Salzburg. Mozart's main instruments were the piano and the violin, but he also played viola and organ. He studied a bit with Haydn.
5. Mozart had an elder sister Maria Anna, also known as Nannerl, who was a very good musician in her own right.
6. Leopold would take his two talented children all over Europe to concertize. Being among the aristocracy so often had an effect on Mozart's attitude later in life. He actually thought he was a member of the upper class rather than a servant of the people.
7. Mozart spent the first twenty-five years of his life in Salzburg and the last ten years in Vienna.
8. In 1782, he married Constanza Weber, six years his junior and they had six children. Only two lived into adulthood, Karl Thomas and Franz Xavier. Mozart's father did not approve of this marriage as Mozart did not have a steady job.
9. Several stories had circulated about Mozart, some were true and some were not. First, he was a pauper. This is not true as Mozart made a great deal of money from opera commissions and other sources. Truth is, Mozart had a very lavish lifestyle and out spent what he made. He died owing money. Second, he was murdered by a rival, Antonio Salieri. This is not true, but it had spread like wild fire because Salieri was one of the last people to see Mozart alive and Salieri was somewhat of a musical rival in Vienna. Third, he was buried in a communal grave which was true. In 1784, Emperor Joseph II decreed that all people were to be buried as follows: covered in a linen sack without a coffin, put in a communal grave with other people and buried far from the city, sprinkled with lime and the grave left unmarked. The Emperor put these rules into effect so people could conserve their resources and prevent water contamination.
10. It is important to note that Mozart's father had set a very high bar for his son and the father was very demanding. By today's standards, Mozart's father would probably be considered a control freak. It is also important to note Mozart had a great deal of difficulty with his superiors as he did not consider himself a servant.

11. Mozart died on December 5th, 1791 from a kidney ailment, rheumatic fever, and a streptococcal infection.
12. Some of his most important compositions are:

    Forty-one Symphonies

    Concertos

    Eine Kleine Nachtmusik

    Chamber Music

    Piano Music

    Twenty Operas, several written in German as opposed to the traditional Italian language

    Choral music: The Requiem (a death Mass) was Mozart's last composition and was completed by a friend Sussmeyer.

Note: Recommended reading: Mozart's Letters, Mozart's Life by Robert Spaethling.

Popular Forms

Sonata Form

Sonata form is most frequently used in the first movement of symphonies. In a fast movement it is called Sonata-Allegro. It can be used in other movements of the same work. In the Classical Era, the form was so popular that it was used in concertos, string quartets, and just about any two, three, or four movement compositions.

Mozart's Birth House in Salzburg, Austria

The Plan

1. **Optional introduction.**
2. **Exposition (A):** The main melody is exposed or introduced in this section.
3. **Development (B):** In this section the composer takes melody A, adds new material to come up with a bit of a different sound. Development sections provide sound variety.
4. **Recapitulation (A):** In the recapitulation section, the main melody A is restated.
5. **Coda:** The coda is the tag or tail ending. In this section musical events are summarized.

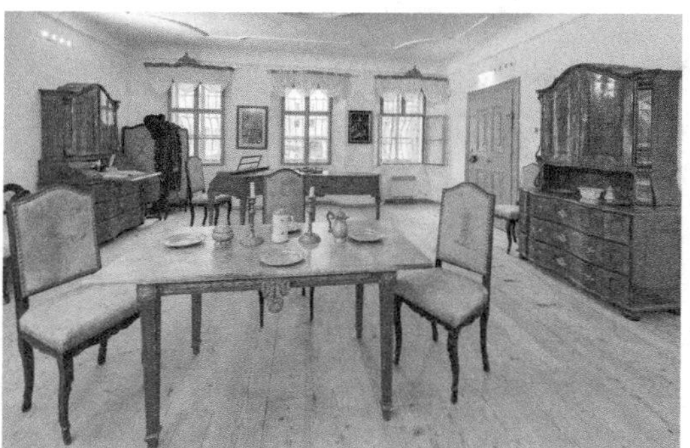

Interior of Birth House

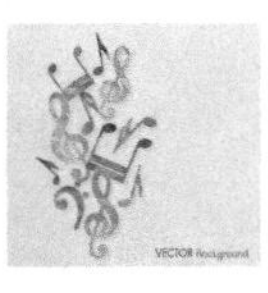

Listening Box 24

Type in Beethoven Classical Best and choose top box Beethoven—Classical Best of. Select Track 8, Symphony No. 5 in C Minor Op. 67 Part 1.

Theme and Variations

Theme and variations are basically melody and variety (changes made to the melody).

The Plan and Diagram

INTRODUCTION	MELODY A	VARIATION 1	VARIATION 2	ENDS WITH MELODY

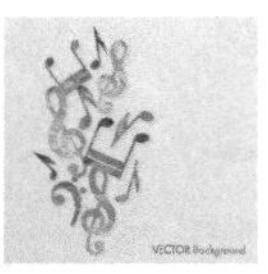

Listening Box 25

Type in Mozart for Baby and under Tracks choose Twinkle Twinkle Little Star (Baby Cla . . . Select Track 4, Twinkle Twinkle Little Star (Baby Classical Sleepin Song).

Note: Caution! Do not be fooled by this listening. I purposely chose this melody because you know it and will be able to hear the variations as they are very clear. While listening, follow the diagram I put for you preceding Listening Box 25.

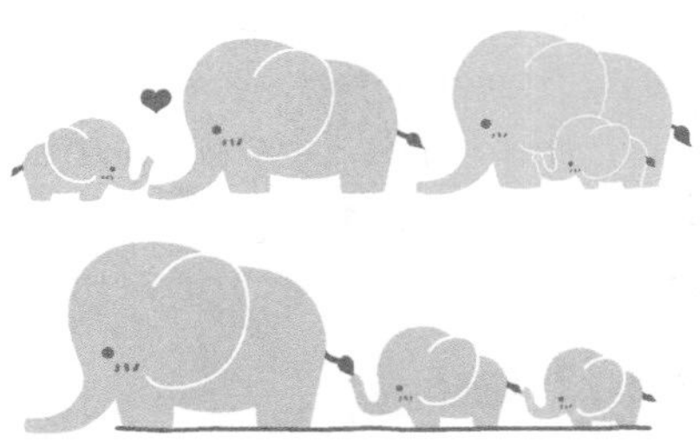

Overture Form

I previously discussed the overture in bio notes about Claudio Monteverdi and in the Chapter 3 Summary. With that being said, I would be remiss if I do not mention the Overture to the Marriage of Figaro (Le nozze di Figaro).

1. Written in 1786, by Mozart and with Lorenzo Da Ponte as librettist.
2. The four main characters are: Count Almaviva, Countess Rosina Almaviva, Susanna the countess's maid and fiancée to Figaro and Figaro, personal valet to the count, and fiancée to Susanna.

Synopsis of Story

The story takes place in a single day of court life. Figaro is to marry Susanna. Count Almaviva has turned into a lecherous, skirt chasing individual who wants to be with Susanna. The Count tries to stall the wedding and compel Figaro to marry a much older woman who happens to be Figaro's mother. Things heat up and Figaro, Susanna, and the Countess embarrass the Count by publicly exposing his scheme. In the end, the Count apologizes to the Countess and in so doing restores his love for her. As you might have guessed, Susanna and Figaro get married and live happily ever after.

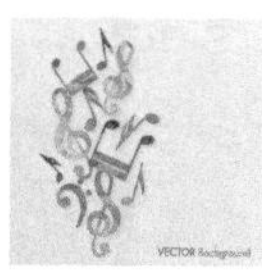

Listening Box 26

Type in Big Mozart Box and under Tracks choose Overture To Marriage of Figaro, Vienna Symphony Orch. Select Track 37, Overture to Marriage of Figaro K.492.

Note: Go to YouTube and type in Overture to the Marriage of Figaro. Select the one that says Mozart Overture the Marriage of Figaro Muti Vienna Philharmonic Orchestra. Riccardo Muti is the conductor. Good Classical Era Rock n Roll.

Rondo Form

Rondo form was one of the most popular forms in music composition. It was used most frequently in symphonies, sonatas, concertos, and string quartets. Rondo means return of the main theme, so the listener is always listening for the return of melody A.

One of the most popular piano pieces by Beethoven is Fur Elise (For Elise). This is a good example of rondo form.

Melody A	Melody B	Melody A	Melody C	Melody A

The Plan and Diagram

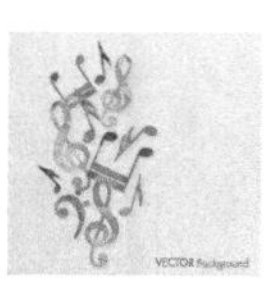

Listening Box 27

Type in Fur Elise and choose top box Fur Elise. Select Track 7, Fur Elise.

Minuet Form

The minuet was a very popular dance in the seventeenth and eighteenth centuries. It is written in triple meter, also called ¾ time. Composers often used the minuet in the third movement of the symphony as this dance was popular with the general public.

I have choosen three Mozart minuets. These pieces are short and your listening objective here, if possible, is to count the three beats in a measure. In this rhythm, the accent is on the first beat.

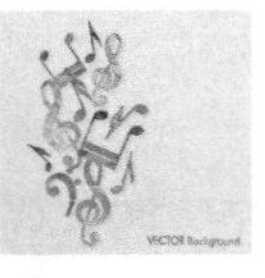

Listening Box 28

Type in menuetto first and choose top box III. Menuetto (First Version . . . Select Tracks 15, 19, and 23. They will all say III. Menuetto—Trio and are from different Mozart Symphonies.

Symphony Form

The symphony is an instrumental piece usually in four movements. Traditionally, the first movement is fast, the second movement is slow, the third movement is the dance movement (minuet), and the fourth movement is fast. An exception to this four movement form is Beethoven's Symphony No. 6, The Pastoral, which is in five movements.

For the symphony listening I chose Beethoven's Symphony No. 9, the fourth movement. The symphony is called the Choral Symphony which is the first time vocal soloists and a chorus is performed in a symphony. Beethoven based his musical ideas on a poem by Friedrich Schiller, "Ode to Joy." This was Beethoven's last symphony and he wrote it when he was totally deaf. There is much emotion in this section and I chose it because you know the melody, but probably never heard the original setting. Most people have heard this melody as a vocal, but Beethoven presents the melody in the bass section. The range of music is low and being played in the bass section provides the listener with very dark colors. This symphony was completed in 1824 and was first performed in the same year in Vienna, Austria. Also, listen how the melody takes on different flavors as Beethoven brings it to a higher range.

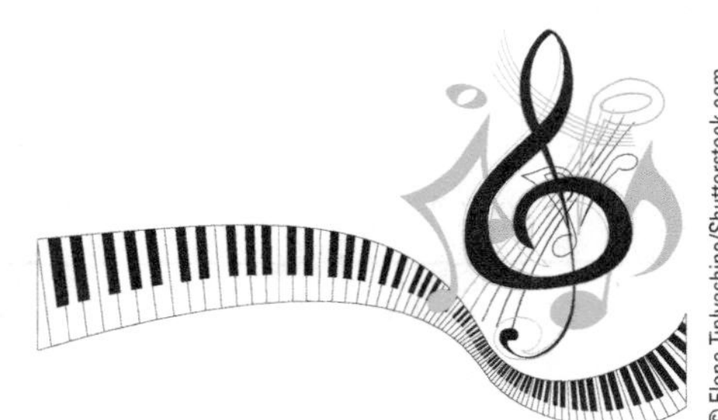

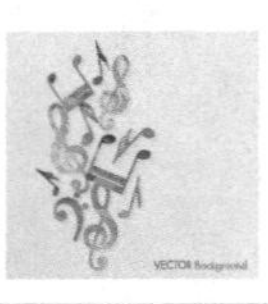

Listening Box 29

Type in Classical Blast and choose top box Symphony #9: Ode To Joy. Select Track 7, Symphony #9: IV. Ode To Joy.

In the summer of 1788, Mozart wrote three symphonies, 39 was finished on June 26th, 40 was finished on July 25th, and 41 was completed on August 10th. These three combined are called "The Trilogy" and are his last symphonies. I have chosen the fourth movement of the 41st as a final symphony listening for this period. The section starts off with no introduction and a four note melody. The section is written in sonata form and has a total of five melodies. Toward the end, Mozart has a five voice fugue which represents all five melodies. This will be a good test for you in the symphony listening category. Listen to it several times and do not panic if you cannot hear everything. It is a mind blower!

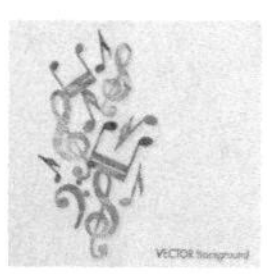

Listening Box 30

Type in Jupiter Symphony and under Tracks take first choice. This will take you right to Track 4. Select Track 4, as this is the last movement of Symphony 41, The Jupiter.

Suggested Video

Go to YouTube videos and type in, Mozart Symphony No. 41 Kazuo Yamada NHKso 4th movement. Yamada is the conductor and I think you are going to like this guy.

Ludwig van Beethoven (1770–1827)

1. Born in Bonn, Germany, baptized on December 17th, 1770, and died on March 26, 1827.
2. At an early age he was taught music by his father Johann who was a court musician.
3. Beethoven's parents Johann and Maria had seven children. Beethoven was second oldest and he had two younger brothers Casper (Carl) and Nikolas Johann.
4. Beethoven's father realized that his son had talent and he tried to promote his son as a prodigy. On concert programs he would say Beethoven was 6 when he really was 7. Beethoven's father had heard of the success Leopold Mozart had with his children and he tried to copy him.
5. At the age of 21 he moved to Vienna to study composition with Haydn. Beethoven remained in Vienna until death.
6. His main physical impediment was his hearing loss and in 1802 he went to the town of Heiligenstadt to take thermal baths in hopes of a cure. These treatments did not work and he became very depressed and on October 2, 1802, he wrote the famous Heiligenstadt Testament. Beethoven considered this document to be his last will and testament as he clearly stated considering suicide. He went completely deaf in 1819.
7. Beethoven had many "firsts" in music. Because of his hearing loss he demanded piano makers construct larger instruments for better sound. He also increased

the size of the orchestra for the same reason. As previously stated, he was the first composer to use vocals in a symphony and was unorthodoxed in his symphony writing as he sometimes went from one movement to the next without stopping.

8. He was considered "The Bridge to Romanticism" as he was a freelance musician and broke many traditions of how composers earned a living. He made a great deal of money from publishing and concerts. He was a good businessman and a much better negotiator than Mozart.
9. His personal life also reveals he had relationships with several women, but he never married and supposedly had no children.
10. Some of his most important compositions are:

    Nine Symphonies

    One Violin Concerto

    Five Piano concerts

    Thirty-two Piano Sonatas

    Sixteen String Quartets

    Missa Solemnis (Mass)

    One Opera, Fidelio.

To My Brothers Carl and Johann Beethoven

Heiligenstadt, Oct. 6, 1802.

Oh! ye who think or declare me to be hostile, morose, and misanthropical, how unjust you are, and how little you know the secret cause of what appears thus to you! My heart and mind were ever from childhood prone to the most tender feelings of affection, and I was always disposed to accomplish something great. But you must remember that six years ago I was attacked by an incurable malady, aggravated by unskilful physicians, deluded from year to year, too, by the hope of relief, and at length forced to the conviction of a *lasting affliction* (the cure of which may go on for years, and perhaps after all prove impracticable).

Born with a passionate and excitable temperament, keenly susceptible to the pleasures of society, I was yet obliged early in life to isolate myself, and to pass my existence in solitude. If I at any time resolved to surmount all this, oh! how cruelly was I again repelled by the experience, sadder than ever, of my defective hearing!--and yet I found it impossible to say to others: Speak louder; shout! for I am deaf! Alas! how could I proclaim the deficiency of a sense which ought to have been more perfect with me than with other men,--a sense which I once possessed in the highest perfection, to an extent, indeed, that few of my profession ever enjoyed! Alas, I cannot do this! Forgive me therefore when you see me withdraw from you with whom I would so gladly mingle. My misfortune is doubly severe from causing me to be misunderstood. No longer can I enjoy recreation in social intercourse, refined conversation, or mutual outpourings of thought. Completely isolated, I only enter society when compelled to do so. I must live like an exile. In company I am assailed by the most painful apprehensions, from the dread of being exposed to the risk of my condition being observed. It was the same during the last six months I spent in the country. My intelligent physician recommended me to spare my hearing as much as possible, which was quite in accordance with my present disposition, though sometimes, tempted by my natural inclination for society, I allowed myself to be beguiled into it. But what humiliation when any one beside me heard a flute in the far distance, while I heard *nothing,* or when others heard *a shepherd singing*, and I still heard *nothing*! Such things brought me to the verge of desperation, and wellnigh caused me to put an end to my life. *Art! art* alone, deterred me. Ah! how could I possibly quit the world before bringing forth all that I felt it was my vocation to produce? And thus I spared this miserable life--so utterly miserable that any sudden change may reduce me at any moment from my best condition into the worst. It is decreed that I must now choose *Patience* for my guide! This I have done. I hope the resolve will not fail me, steadfastly to persevere till it may please the inexorable Fates to cut the thread of my life. Perhaps I may get better, perhaps not. I am prepared for either. Constrained to become a philosopher in my twenty-eighth year! This is no slight trial, and more severe on an artist than on any one else. God looks into my heart, He searches it, and knows that love for man and feelings of benevolence have their abode there! Oh! ye who may one day read this, think that you have done me injustice, and let any one similarly afflicted be consoled, by finding one like himself, who, in defiance of all the obstacles of Nature, has done all in his power to be included in the ranks of estimable artists and men. My brothers Carl and Johann, as soon as I am no more, if Professor Schmidt [see Nos. 18 and 23] be still alive, beg him in my name to describe my malady, and to add these pages to the analysis of my disease, that at least, so far as possible, the world may be reconciled to me after my death. I also hereby declare you both heirs of my small fortune (if so it may be called). Share it fairly, agree together and assist each other. You know that anything you did to give me pain has been long forgiven. I thank you, my brother Carl in particular, for the attachment you have shown me of late. My wish is that you may enjoy a happier life, and one more free from care, than mine has been. Recommend *Virtue* to your children; that alone, and not wealth, can ensure happiness. I speak from experience. It was *Virtue* alone which sustained me in my misery; I have to thank her and Art for not having ended my life by suicide. Farewell! Love each other. I gratefully thank all my friends, especially Prince Lichnowsky and Professor Schmidt. I wish one of you to keep Prince L----'s instruments; but I trust this will give rise to no dissension between you. If you think it more beneficial, however, you have only to dispose of them. How much I shall rejoice if I can serve you even in the grave! So be it then! I joyfully hasten to meet Death. If he comes before I have had the opportunity of developing all my artistic powers, then, notwithstanding my cruel fate, he will come too early for me, and I should wish for him at a more distant period; but even then I shall be content, for his advent will release me from a state of endless suffering. Come when he may, I shall meet him with courage. Farewell! Do not quite forget me, even in death; I deserve this from you, because during my life I so often thought of you, and wished to make you happy. Amen!

LUDWIG VAN BEETHOVEN

Source: *Beethoven's Letters 1790–1826*, by Ludwig Beethoven, translated by Lady Wallace.

Summary of Unit 3, Chapter 4 Terms and Study Sheet

Terms

Theme and Variations: A melody and variety.

Rondo: A return of the main melody (A).

Minuet: *A dance in ¾ time.*

Sonata Form: Optional introduction, exposition, development, recapitulation, and coda.

Symphony: An orchestral piece, usually in four movements.

Overture: An instrumental section that comes before an opera or oratorio begins.

Composers: Haydn, Mozart, and Beethoven.

Cadenza: An instrumental solo.

Summary of Listeners Toolbox

This era is definitely the era of the symphony. Try to add some of these listenings to your daily routine and use them for enjoyment and relaxation.

Questions

How did the events at Pompeii and Herculaneum in 79 A.D. affect the mentality of music in the Classical Era? How were social events at the courts handled? Why did it bother musicians to be considered servants?

To The Student: The instructor may add or delete study items at his or her discretion.

Unit 3, Chapter 4 Listening Box Playlist

LB23: Type in Haydn Symphony 45 and choose top box Haydn Symphony No. 45 & 94. Select Track 1, Symphony No. 45 in F—Sharp Minor "Farewell": I Allegro assai; Track 8, Symphony No. 94 in G Major "Surprise": III. Allegro Di Molto.

LB24: Type in Beethoven Classical Best and choose top box Beethoven—Classical Best of. Select Track 8, Symphony No. 5 in C Minor Op. 67 Part I.

LB25: Type in Mozart for Baby and under Tracks choose Twinkle Twinkle Little Star (Baby Cla . . .Select Track 4, Twinkle Twinkle Little Star (Baby Classical Sleeping Song).

LB26: Type in Big Mozart Box and under Tracks choose Overture to Marriage of Figaro, Vienna Symphony Orchestra. Select Track 37, Overture to Marriage of Figaro. K492.

LB27: Type in Fur Elise and choose top box Fur Elise. Select Track 7, Fur Elise.

LB28: Type in Menuetto First and choose top box III. Menuetto (First version . . . Select Tracks 15, 19, and 23. They will all say III. Menuetto—Trio and they are from different Mozart Symphonies.

LB29: Type in Classical Blast and choose top box Symphony #9: Ode to Joy. Select Track 7, Symphony #9: IV. Ode To Joy.

LB31: Type in Jupiter Symphony and under Tracks take first choice. This will take you right to Track 4. Select Track 4, as this is the last movement of Symphony 41, The Jupiter.

CHAPTER 5 THE ROMANTIC (1820–1900)

What Do We Find in This Period?

Music: Music of emotional extremes, more freelance composers, larger orchestras, small intimate groups, long beautiful melodies, more chromaticism, new forms invented, and music written for the general public. The piano was the most popular instrument in this era. It is important to note that not all musical subjects were about love because the era is called Romantic. Favorite subjects included nature, superheroes, brotherhood of man, philosophy, death, love, nationalism, mystic and supernatural, poetry, and literature.

Texture: Mostly homophonic, but sometimes polyphonic texture was used.

Forms: (Vocal): Lied, Sacred and Secular, Requiems, Opera (Italian, French, and German).

Instrumental Large Forms: Symphonic Poem (new), Sonata, Symphony, Concerto, Ballet, Ballade, and Impromptu.

Instrumental Small Forms: Waltz, Nocturne, Etude, Fantasy, Mazurka, Variations, and Rhapsody. The instrumental small forms listed are basically piano forms.

Composers: I could easily cite between 30 and 40 composers. In the best interest of highlighting the points of the era I have chosen the following: Hector Berlioz, Franz Schubert, Frederic Chopin, Franz Liszt, Felix and Fanny Mendelsohn, Robert and Clara Schumann, Richard Strauss, and Johannes Brahms. When I discuss opera and nationalism, I will have to add other composers.

Travel to: France, Germany, Austria, Russia, and Italy.

A Few Interesting Facts about Issues in the Romantic Era

1. In previous eras, composers depended heavily on the church and aristocracy to make a living. Now many composers were freelance musicians who made a living from concerts, publishing, and private teaching.
2. Women composers were marginalized and wrote primarily in smaller forms like art songs. Not writing grand works like symphonies and operas, women were considered inferior.
3. Inventions in the Industrial Revolution led to advancements and improvements in the mechanical valves and keys used by brass and woodwind instruments.

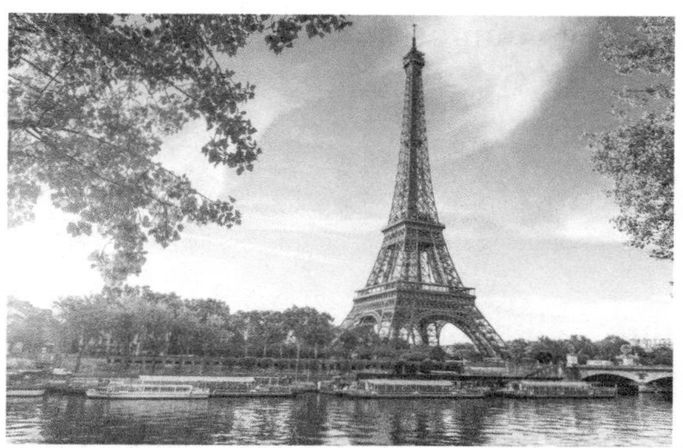

Eiffel Tower, Paris, France

Hector Berlioz (1803–1869)

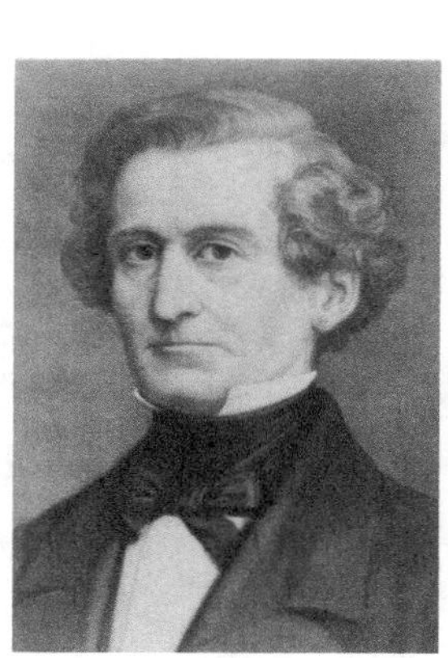

1. Born in La Cote Saint-Andre, a small town near Lyon, France.
2. Berlioz's father was a doctor and at the age of 18 Hector was sent to Paris to study medicine. In 1824, despite his parents' disapproval, he abandoned his medical studies to pursue a career in music.
3. In 1827, while still in Paris, he attended performances of Hamlet and Romeo and Juliet. He became infatuated with the lead actress Harriet Smithson and began sending letters to her hotel room, which not only confused but scared her.
4. 1830 was a big year for Berlioz. On his fourth try, he won the prestigious Prix de Rome, met and started a relationship with a young, talented pianist, Camille Moke, and they eventually got engaged. In this same year, he wrote his famous Symphony fantastique in Harriet's honor.
5. In 1831, his luck changed. He received a letter from Camille's mother stating that her daughter has called off their engagement and is going to marry someone else. Berlioz decided to leave Italy and go back to Paris to take revenge on all three, but eventually calmed down and did nothing.
6. In 1833, he rekindled his relationship with Harriet and they got married on October, 3rd. In 1834, a son Louis was born.
7. In 1841, while still married to Harriet, he started a relationship with singer Marie Recio.
8. In 1844, he separated from Harriet and moved in with Marie and from this time on, Berlioz maintained two households. The bottom line of this soap opera occurred in 1854 when in March, Harriet died and Berlioz married Marie in October.
9. His writings include The Orchestral Conductor and Treatise on Instrumentation.

10. Some of his most important compositions are:
    Symphony Fantastiqe
    Harold in Italy
    Romeo and Juliet
    The Roman Carnival
    Three operas [Benvenuto Cellini (1838); Les Troyens (1858); Beatrice et Benedict (1862)],
    Three choral works [Requiem (1837); Te Deum (1849); Childhood of Christ (1854)].
11. Berlioz had traveled extensively throughout his life, but his later years show he had become isolated and depressed. He once wrote, "I am in my 61st year; past hopes, past illusions, past high thoughts and lofty conceptions. My son is almost always far away from me. I am alone. My contempt for the folly and baseness of mankind, my hatred of its atrocious cruelty, have never been so intense. And I say hourly to Death, 'When you will.' Why does he delay?"

Symphony Fantastique (1830), Hector Berlioz

Fifth Movement: "Dream of a Witches' Sabbath"

This symphony is called program music which means it is based on a story. The overall message concerns itself with the various things that happen in an artists' life. Berlioz dedicated this composition to Harriet Smithson and wrote a melody about her which permeates all five movements. He called this central theme idee fixe (fixed idea). There were over 90 instruments used in the orchestra for this piece, the most ever to this point.

"Dream of a Witches' Sabbath" has three melodies. They are: Beloved Theme, Dies irae, and Witches' Round Dance. The phrase Dies irae, dies illa, basically means "Day of wrath, O judgment day." Berlioz's program notes for this movement state: He sees himself at a witches' Sabbath, in the midst of a hideous gathering of shades, sorcerers, and monsters of every kind who have come together for his funeral. Strange sounds, groans, outbursts of laughter, and distant shouts which seem to be answered by more shouts. The beloved melody appears once more, but has now lost its noble and shy character, it is now no more than a vulgar dance tune, trivial, and grotesque: it is she who is coming to the Sabbath . . . . Roar of delight at her arrival . . . she joins the diabolical orgy . . . the funeral bells toll, burlesque parody of the Dies irae, the dance of the witches. The dance of the witches combined with the Dies irae.

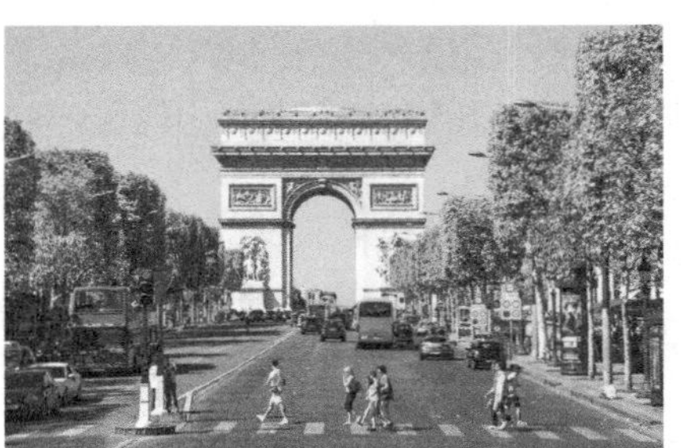

Arc de Triomphe, Paris, France

Note: There are many who honestly believe Berlioz was under the influence of opium when he wrote this. Since none of this has been proven, you will just have to decide for yourself.

Note to the listener: This fifth movement is an excellent example of music of emotional extremes. As you listen, try to get the highs and lows of emotion in this piece.

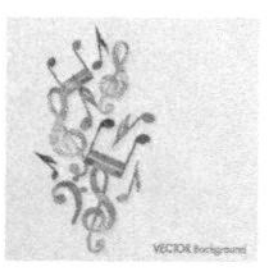

Listening Box 31

Type in Dream of a Witches' Sabbath and choose top box V: Dream of a Witches' Sabbath. Select track 5, V: Dream of a Witches' Sabbath.

Franz Schubert (1797–1828)

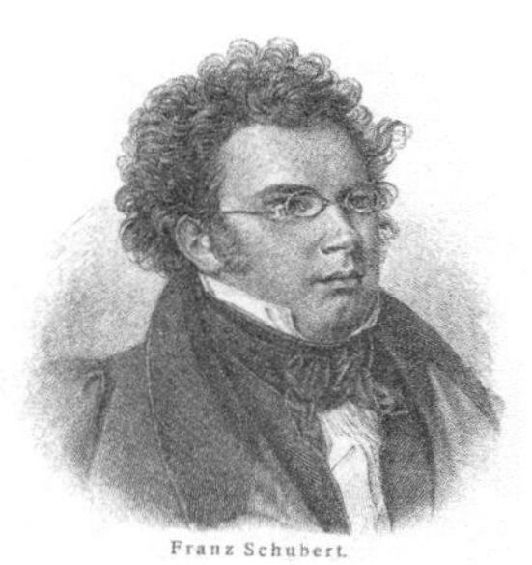

1. Born in Himmelpfortgrund, now Alsergrund. This is the ninth district of Vienna and is located just north of the first district.
2. Schubert learned to play violin from his father and piano from his brother. He also played viola and organ.
3. He was a good singer and eventually earned a scholarship which enabled him to become a member of the Vienna Boys Choir.
4. Schubert was short, not quite 5 feet tall and his nickname was "schwammerl" which means "tubby" or "mushroom."
5. He studied composition with Antonio Salieri who thought he was a genius.
6. He was very good in school and at the age of 18 he became a school master, like his dad. Unhappy with teaching young students, he left teaching at the age of 21.
7. In his lifetime, he wrote over 1,500 works, many of them not published, and he made very little money. He often had to be subsidized by friends.
8. Some of his most important compositions are:

   Rosamunde

   Nine Symphonies, No. 8 unfinished

   Fifteen String Quartets

   Piano Music: Twenty-one Sonatas, impromptus, fantasies, dances, variation, and marches

   Songs: Over 600 and some of the most famous are: The Erlking, To Music, Ave Maria, The Wanderer, The Trout, and The Beautiful Maid of the Mill

   Opera: Alfonso und Estrello (1822), Fierabras (1823)

   Choral Works: Seven Masses as well as thirty other choral works.

The Romantic Art Song

Romantic Art Songs were small intimate songs called Lied in German. Basically, they were poems set to music and were often used in the homes of the wealthy for an evening of entertainment. They became so popular that concerts were given in small concert halls for the general public. The performers were generally a piano player and a singer who had roles of equal importance as they both worked together to highlight the poem meaning and the accompanying music.

The Erlking

The Erlking is a messenger of death who kills everyone he touches. In this song he kills a young child and, believe it or not, this is considered a Romantic Art Song in which it describes death and the supernatural.

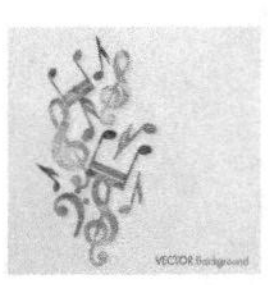

Listening Box 32

Type in The Erlking and under Tracks choose The Erlking, Steve Gillette. Select Track 1, The Erlking. Also, under the same Tracks choose The Erlking, Sequester. Select Track 3, The Erlking (both are modern versions).

Felix Mendelsohn (1809–1847)

1. Born in Hamburg, Germany.
2. Considered a musical prodigy, he gave his first concert at the age of 9, published his first work at the age of 13, a piano quartet, and wrote his first symphony at the age of 15.
3. His grandfather Moses was a noted philosopher and his father Abraham was a well-respected banker. The family had money and were among the elites of the day. It was not uncommon for the Mendelsohn's to have famous writers, thinkers, and artists to the house for concerts.

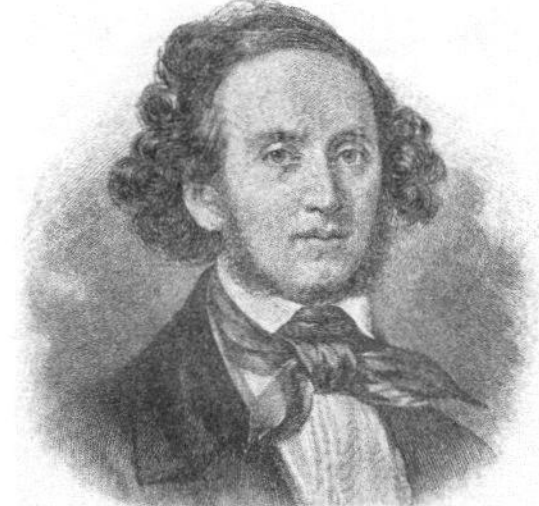

4. In order to circumvent anti-Semitism, Mendelsohn's father renounced the Jewish religion and changed his last name to Bartholdy. Both Felix and his sister Fanny were unhappy with this change.
5. In 1835, he was named conductor of the Leipzig Gewandhaus Orchestra. Mendelsohn wanted to improve the quality of the orchestra and promised to increase the member pay and start a pension fund. Eventually, the orchestra became the best in Europe and Mendelsohn kept his promises.
6. In 1837, he married Cecile Jeanrenaud, a clergyman's daughter. They had five children, Carl, Marie, Paul, Lilli, and Felix.

7. In 1843, he founded the Leipzig Conservatory of Music, a very prestigious school that is still in existence and is now called The University of Music and Theater "Felix Mendelsohn Bartholdy" Leipzig.
8. Throughout his life, Mendelsohn worked very hard and traveled to places such as London, Italy, Scotland, and Switzerland.
9. In May 1847, his sister Fanny died suddenly while rehearsing one of his cantatas. Felix was so depressed and in failing health himself, he passed in November of the same year from a ruptured blood vessel.
10. Some of his most important compositions are:

Thirteen String Symphonies

Five full Orchestra Symphonies

Four Concert Overtures: A Midsummer Night's Dream (1826), Calm Sea and Prosperous Voyage (1828), The Hebrides–Fingal's Cave (1830), Ruy Blas (1839)

Two Piano Concertos: No. 1 in g minor (1831), No. 2 in d minor (1837)

Two Piano Concertos for Two Pianos: one E Major (1823)and another in Ab Major (1824)

One Violin Concerto in e minor (1844)

Chamber Music: Over seventy pieces

Keyboard Music: Over 200 pieces mostly for piano and some for organ

Forty-eight Leider ohne worte (Songs without words)

Two Oratorios: St. Paul (1836), Elijah (1846).

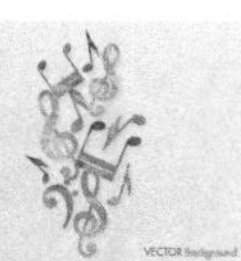

Listening Box 33

Type in Mendelssohn and choose top box Felix Mendelssohn, Romantic. Select Track 1, Italian Symphony: Saltarello. (The Saltarello is an Italian dance that uses a big jump as one of the moves. The word saltare means to jump in Italian.)

Fanny Mendelsohn Bartholdy Hensel (1805–1847)

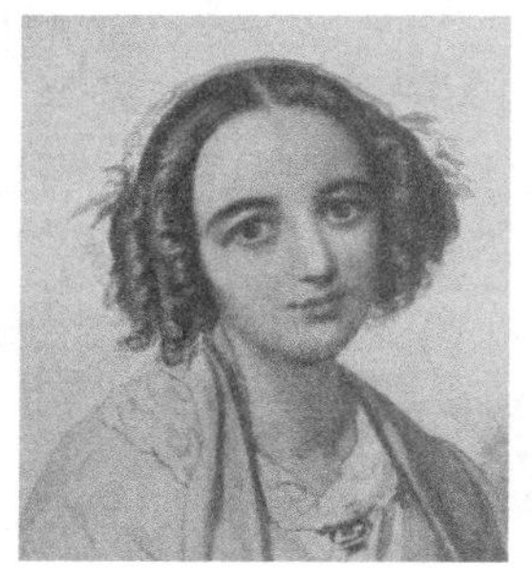

© Universal History Archive/Universal Images Group/Getty Images

1. Born in Hamburg, Germany, she was the eldest of the four children.
2. Fanny and her brother Felix shared a great love and passion for music. They were both talented and got along very well.
3. In her lifetime she wrote over 460 pieces of music and was considered to be a very skilled piano player.
4. She was hampered by the prevailing attitudes and prejudices toward women in her time which made it difficult for her to

publish her music. Some of her songs were published under Felix's name, three in his Op. 8 collection and three more in his Op. 9 collection.

5. In 1829, she married a painter, Wilhelm Hensel, after a very long courtship and the following year she had her only child, a son, Sebastian.
6. As stated in Felix's bio notes, in May, 1847, Fanny was rehearsing one of his cantatas and suddenly passed from an apparent stroke.
7. Some of her most important compositions are:

   Piano Music: Das Jahr (The Year), a suite of 12 pieces depicting the 12 months

   Sonatas

   Chamber Music: Trio in d minor for Violin, Cello and Piano (Op. 11).

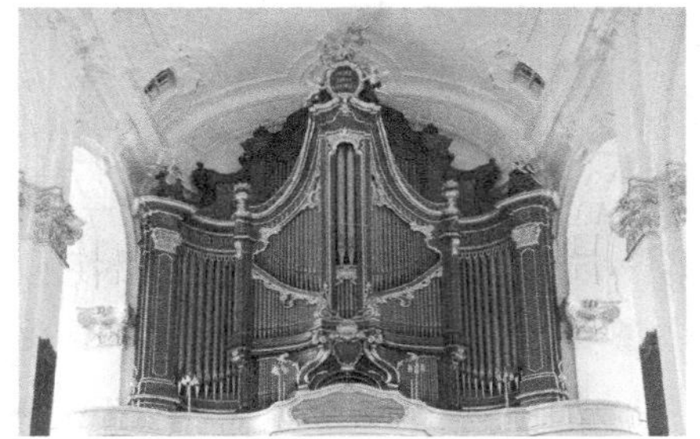

Organ, St. Michaelis Church, Hamburg, Germany

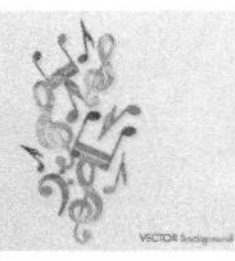

Listening Box 34

Type in Fanny Hensel and choose top box Fanny Hensel—Mendelsohn. Select Track 1, Vier Lieder ohne Worte, Op. 8: 1. Allegro moderato

Note: Lieder ohne worte means songs without words.

Robert Schumann (1810–1856)

1. Born in Zwickau, a town near Leipzig, Germany.
2. Robert showed early signs of musical talent and began to compose before the age of 7.
3. Schumann also had a great interest in literature and some of his favorite writers were Schiller, Goethe, Byron, Richter and he loved Greek tragedies. His father was a book seller, so it makes sense Robert might have an interest in literature.

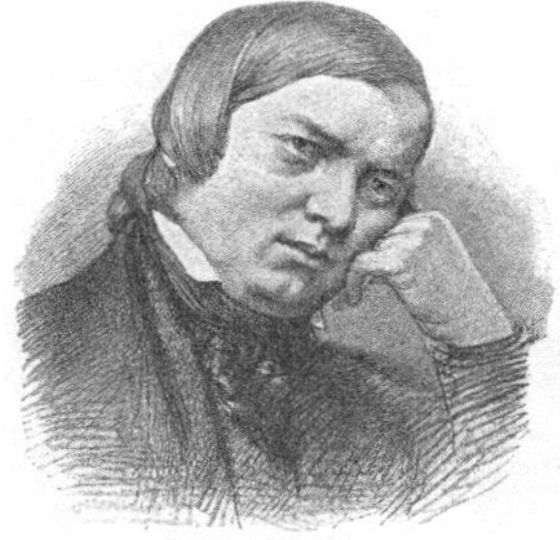

4. In 1826, his father died and as per his inheritance conditions, he was mandated to study law. Robert was not interested in law and after a few years left law school to pursue a career in music.
5. In 1830, he started studying piano with the noted teacher Friederich Wieck in Leipzig. At the Wieck household he met Clara Wieck who was about 10 years his junior. Robert remained at the Wieck residence as a boarder and shared many musical interests with Clara who was a good musician in her own right. As time passed, Robert and Clara fell in love and wanted to get married. Clara's father opposed and the couple had to go to

court for permission since Clara was not 21 years old. The court decided in their favor and on September 12, 1840, Robert and Clara got married.

6. The marriage produced eight children, seven lived in to adulthood. In 1846, first born Emil lived only one year. Then came Marie, Elise, Julie, Ludwig, Ferdinand, Eugenie, and Felix.
7. During his lifetime, Schumann had physical issues. First, he apparently injured his hand with a mechanical device used to strengthen the fingers. Second, he had syphilis, which is presumed he got as a student. Both conditions shut him down from playing piano and concertizing which made Robert very hostile and jealous of Clara who was enjoying playing piano for the general public.
8. Schumann's physical conditions forced him to turn to his second love, writing and publishing. In 1834, he started the "New Journal for Music," which became the first music magazine. This publication is still in existence.
9. In his later years his behavior became erratic and in 1854, he attempted suicide by throwing himself into the Rhine River. He was rescued and put in an asylum where he remained until his death in 1856.
10. Some of his most important compositions are:

    Piano Music: "Abegg" Variations Op. 1 (1830), Papillons (Butterflies), Op. 2 (1831), Carnival Op. 9 (1835), and Kinderszenen (Scenes from Childhood) (1838)

    Orchestral Music: four Symphonies, Symphony five was unfinished, The Bride of Messina, and Julius Caesar Overture.

    Chamber Music: twenty-three works for different chamber groups

    Songs: Over 275 songs.

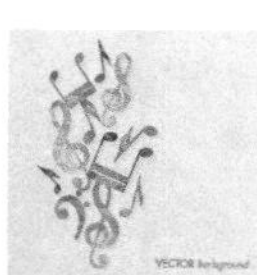

Listening Box 35

Type in Schumann: Symphonies & Concertos, Disc 1 #9. Sinfonie Nr. 3 Es-Dur Op. 97 "Rheinische": 5. Satz: Lebhaft.

Clara Wieck Schumann (1819–1896)

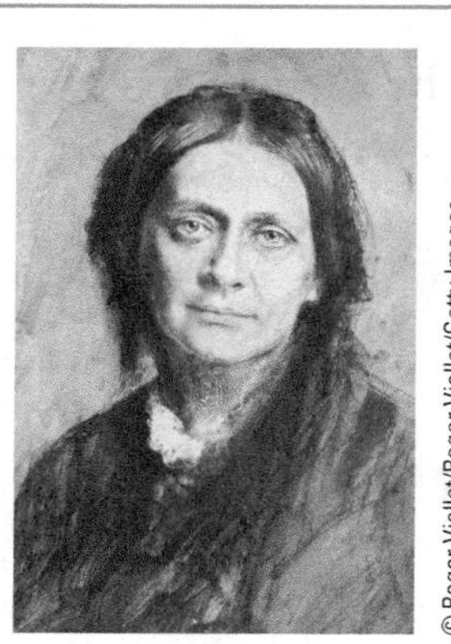

© Roger Viollet/Roger Viollet/Getty Images

Portrait by Franz von Lenbach, 1878

1. Born in Leipzig, Germany.
2. Her mother was a singer and her father was a piano teacher.
3. In 1824, her parents divorced and she remained with her father.
4. She was recognized as one of the best piano players of her day and she concertized in major cities such as Paris, Vienna, Leipzig, London, Glasgow, and Edinburgh. She

was also noted for playing music from memory and won many awards for playing excellence.

5. As stated in Robert's bio notes, she married in 1840 and had eight children. After Robert's death, she spent most of her life promoting his music.
6. In 1853, a young Johannes Brahms arrived at her house to study piano with Robert. As years passed by, it was rumored that she and Brahms had a relationship. Apparently, the two would correspond by letter, but both destroyed the letters. Eventually, Clara's eldest daughter Marie convinced her to stop burning the letters.
7. There was much tragedy in her life as four of her children and her husband died before her. She was forced to take care of the grandchildren and provide everyone money she made from concerts and teaching.
8. In 1878, she was appointed a piano teacher at the Hoch Conservatory, in Frankfurt, a position she held until 1892.
9. She passed at the age of 76 from an apparent stroke.
10. Some of her most important compositions are:

Orchestral: Concerto in a minor (1837), Trio in g minor for Violin, Cello and Piano (1846), Three Romances for Violin and Piano (1853)

Choral Music: Many songs for mixed a cappella choir (1848)

Piano Music: Soiree Musicales (1836), Romance—Variations on a Theme of Robert Schumann

Works in different forms such as polonaises, waltzes, scherzos, caprices, mazurkas, and nocturnes

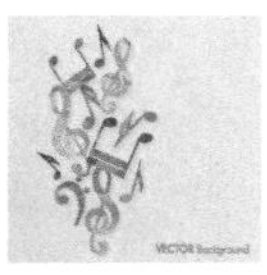

Listening Box 36

Type in Clara Schumann and select Judith Alstadter, Clara Schumann. The selection is Impromptu, Op. 9—Scherzo in c minor, Op. 14.

Note: Scherzo comes from the Italian word scherzare which means to joke or jest or frolic. As applied to music, it is an upbeat, lively piece. Impromptu denotes improvised and without preparation.

Frederic Chopin (1810–1849)

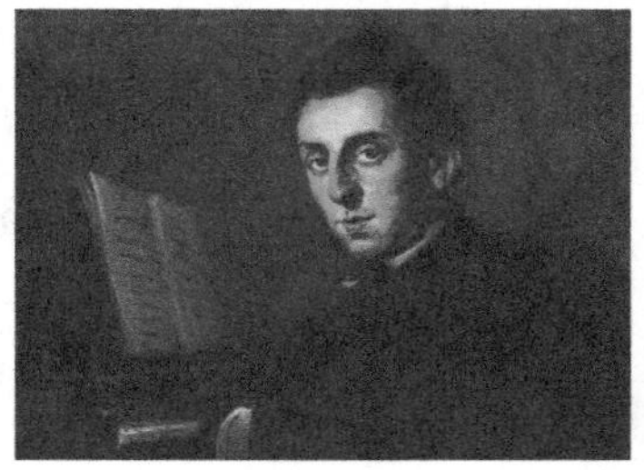

1. Born in Zelazowa Wola, Poland, about 30 miles west of Warsaw.
2. Frederic was the second child of Nicholas and Justyna Chopin. He had one older sister, Ludwika, and two younger sisters, Izabela and Emilia.
3. Chopin grew up in Warsaw as his parents moved there when he was only six months old.

4. His parents were musicians. His father played flute and violin and his mother played piano.
5. He was considered a child prodigy as he was composing and concertizing at the age of 7.
6. In 1828, Chopin had traveled back and forth from Warsaw to Berlin and as time went on, traveled to Vienna, England, and Scotland to concertize.
7. In 1831, he traveled to France, became a French citizen, and never left. Amazingly, he always considered himself Polish and not French.
8. Chopin did meet Franz Liszt, exactly when is not known, but they lived within a few blocks of each other in Paris and concertized together on several occasions.
9. Frederic was a great piano player, well liked, and was accepted into the artistic community in Paris which had members such as Berlioz, Liszt, Victor Hugo, Delacroix, George Sand.
10. George Sand was really a female writer, Aurore Dudevant, who changed her name in order to get her works published. Sand and Chopin lived together for years and she helped him with his tuberculosis issues. There is some question as to whether Chopin had tuberculosis or cystic fibrosis. His physical symptoms align more with cystic fibrosis, but the disease was not known in his time.
11. In 1849, Chopin passed and he had a very strange burial request which was granted. He wanted his body to be buried in France and his heart to be buried in Poland. As recently as 2007, DNA scientists wanted to test Chopin's heart to put to rest once and for all the cause of death. The Polish government denied their request.
12. Some of his most important compositions are:

    He mostly wrote for piano and used many different forms. Some of those forms are impromptus, fantasies, etudes, polonaises, waltzes, nocturnes, and others

    Orchestral Music: Two concertos for Piano and Orchestra, No. 1 in e minor (1830), and No. 2 in f minor (1830).

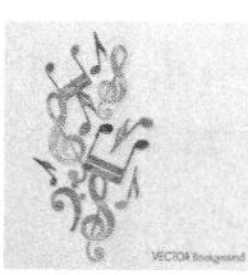

Listening Box 37

Type in Fantasie Impromptu. Under Track Results select the first option, Fantasie Impromptu Opus 66 in c sharp minor by Chopin. It is Track 12. This piece is a good example of A-B-A form.

Franz Liszt (1811–1886)

1. Born in Doborjan, which was in Sopron County and part of the Austro-Hungarian Empire.
2. Liszt began taking piano lessons from his father Adam at the age of 7 and began composing at the age of 8. Some say Liszt started concertizing at 7 years, but officially it was probably 9 years.

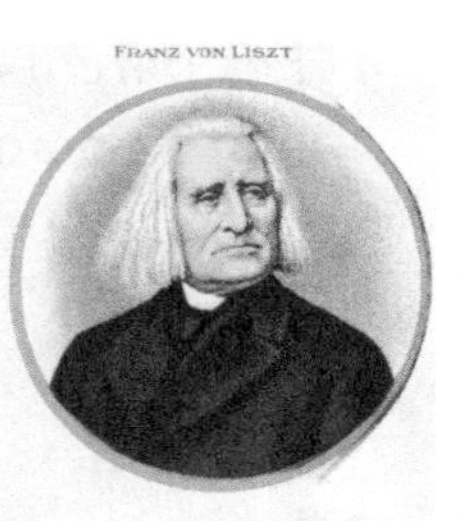

3. Franz was a very talented young musician and was eventually sent to Vienna to study piano with Carl Czerny and composition with Antonio Salieri.
4. He moved to Paris in 1837, after his father's death, and moved into a small apartment with his mother. He gave lessons in piano and composition to make a living.
5. In 1833, Liszt had a relationship with Countess Marie d' Agoult and she left her family in 1835 to join Franz in Geneva. They eventually had three children, Blandine, Daniel, and Cosima.
6. In 1842, Liszt received an Honorary Doctorate from the University of Konigsberg for his musical achievements.
7. In 1844, he and Marie separated as he was rarely home, touring all over Europe.
8. In 1847, he met Princess Carolyne zu Sayn-Wittgenstein, who persuaded him to concentrate on composing. This forced him to virtually give up touring as a concert pianist. Overall, Liszt made a great deal of money and by 1857, he gave all his performance fees to charity.
9. Tragedy struck in 1859, when he lost his son Daniel. More tragedy occurred in 1862, when his eldest daughter Blandine passed. At this point, he decided to pull back to a more solitary life.
10. In his late forties, he began taking minor orders in the Catholic Church, and in 1865 he received the orders of porter, lector, exorcist, and acolyte. At this time, he became known as Abbe Liszt and he eventually became an honorary canon of Albano.
11. He invented the symphonic poem which is basically a one movement orchestral work. He wrote a total of thirteen pieces in this form.
12. Liszt was very good friends with Richard Wagner and Wagner eventually married Liszt's daughter Cosima.
13. In his later years, Liszt became very ill and he passed at the age of 74, in Bayreuth, Germany. The official cause was pneumonia, but he also had heart issues.
14. Some of his most important compositions are:
    Piano Music: Traveler's Album (1836), Six Consolations (1850), Transcendental Studies (1851), Sonata in b minor (1853 and Hungarian Rhapsody (1847).
    Orchestral Music: Symphonic Poems: Tosso (1849), Les Preludes (1854), Totentanz for Piano and Orchestra (1849) Piano Concertos: No. 1 in E flat (1849) and No. 2 in A (1849), Faust Symphony (1854), Dante Symphony (1856).
15. It is important to note in 1866, Liszt wrote the Coronation Ceremony Music for Emperor Franz Joseph and Elizabeth of Bavaria. It was first performed in 1867.

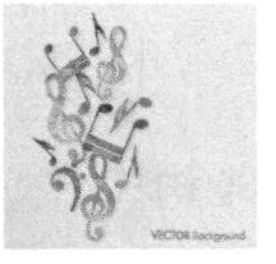

Listening Box 38

Type in Franz Liszt and under Track Results choose Liebestraum No. 3. This selection is Track 6. This piece has a very famous melody.

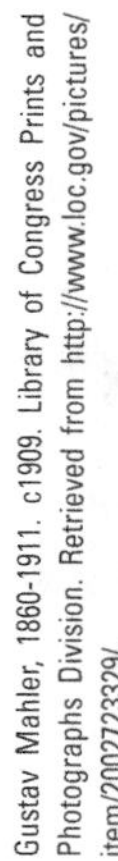

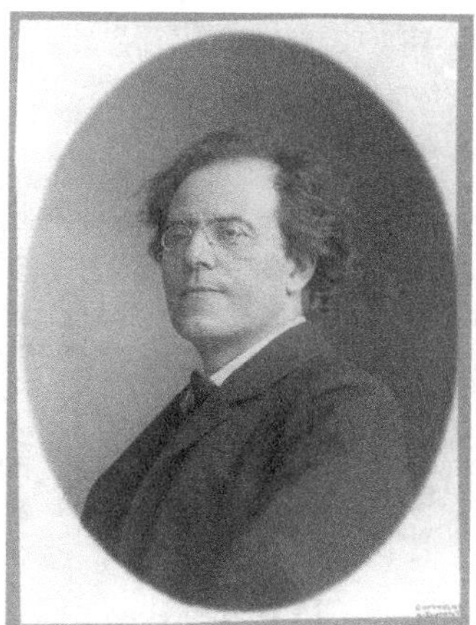

Gustav Mahler (1860–1911)

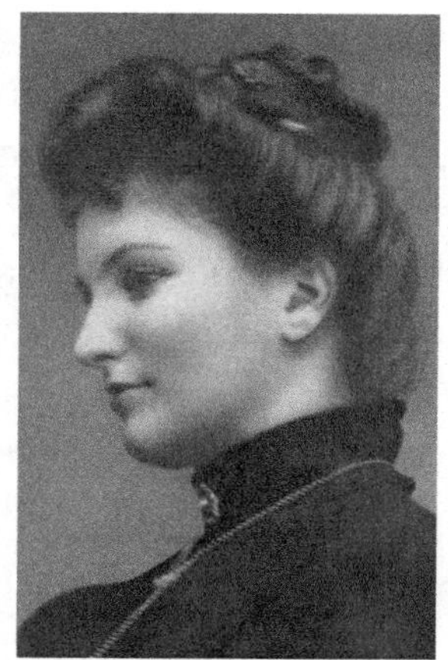

Alma Schindler Mahler (1879–1964)

1. Gustav was born in the Bohemian region of Austria. He was the second of the fourteen children born to Bernhard and Marie Mahler. Only six children lived to adulthood.
2. Gustav started playing his grandparents piano at the age of 4. Through the early years he became very skilled and gave his first concert at the age of 10.
3. Supported by his father, Mahler got accepted into the Vienna Conservatory in 1875. He eventually studied harmony and composition with Franz Krenn and Robert Fuchs.
4. Gustav was Jewish, but was very interested in German philosophy, in particular, the works of Nietzsche, Schopenhauer, and Lotze.
5. At the age of 37, Mahler converted to Christianity in order to secure a position as a conductor of the Vienna State Opera. Nevertheless, he was hounded by bigots and the anti-Semitic press.
6. In 1901, Mahler met Alma Schindler and in March,1902, they married. Apparently, Alma was pregnant as their first daughter Maria Anna was born in November, 1902. A second daughter Anna was born in 1904.
7. In 1907, tragedy struck the Mahler household as both daughters came down with diphtheria and scarlet fever. Anna survived, but Maria passed. Needless to say, the Mahler's were devastated.
8. Gustav always had a reputation for being moody and a tyrant. The loss of his daughter aggravated this situation and he eventually sought help from Sigmund Freud.
9. Although Mahler never wrote operas, he conducted many, and in 1908, made his American conducting debut in New York.
10. In his second year in New York, Mahler became ill and returned to Vienna where he passed in 1911.

11. Alma outlived Gustav by more than fifty years and she married twice more before passing in 1964. Their surviving daughter Anna became a well-known sculptor and was married five times. She eventually passed in Hampstead, London, England in 1988.
12. Some of his most important compositions are:

    Choral Music: The Song of Sorrow, **Songs with Orchestra**: Songs of a Wayfarer (1888), Songs on the Death of Children (1904), Youth's Magic Horn (1893–1898), The Song of the Earth (1909)

    10 Symphonies: No. 1 (The Titan, 1888), No. 2 (The Resurrection, 1894) with soprano, No. 3, the longest in history at 1 hour and 35 minutes, No. 4 (1900), with soprano, No. 8, "Symphony of a Thousand," the largest in history with 1000 performers.

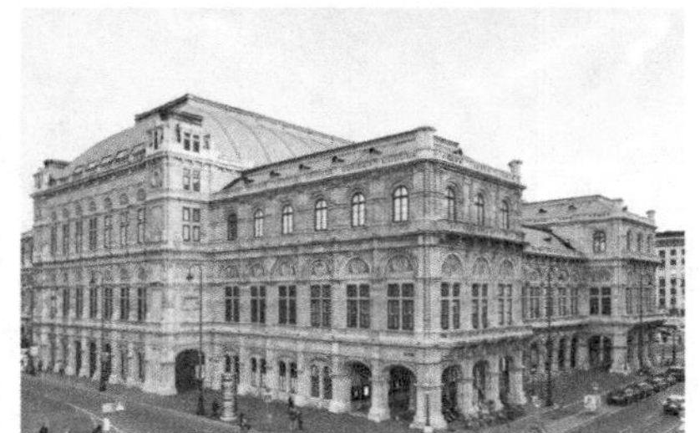

The Vienna State Opera (German: Wiener Staatsoper)

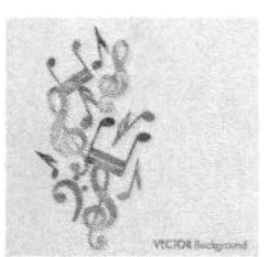

Listening Box 39

Type in Gustav Mahler and under Album Results choose Symphony No. 10, then select Track 2, Scherzo.

Note: Mahler's music is filled with one of the Romantic Era's concepts of emotional extremes. One of the things I do when listening to Mahler is try and put a story line to the music. I suggest you do the same.

Johannes Brahms (1833–1897)

1. Born in Hamburg, Germany.
2. His first music teacher was his father and at an early age, Brahms had to play in dance halls to supplement the family income.
3. Brahms had a very strange personality which vacillated between perfectionist and introvert. He often destroyed many of his works, he took small music jobs, and seemed to have difficulty in relationships with women.
4. At the age of 20, he got an introductory letter from Joseph Joachim to study with Robert Schumann. Schumann was immediately impressed and Brahms became not only a student but a boarder.
5. During the years Schumann was in an asylum, Brahms and Clara Schumann were very close friends and some say intimate. Nevertheless, Brahms helped Clara with her eight children until Schumann's death. He left their home and corresponded

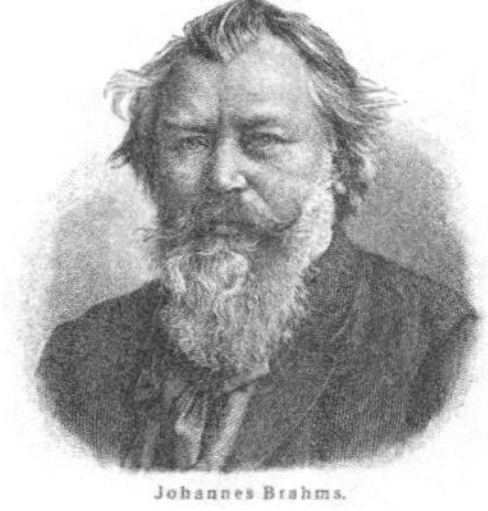

with Clara through extensive letter writing. Much of this correspondence was destroyed by both.

6. Brahms made Vienna his permanent home and spent the rest of his life composing conducting and traveling. One of his favorite places to visit was Venice in the springtime.
7. In 1879, he was awarded an honorary Doctor of Philosophy degree from the University of Breslau. In appreciation, he wrote "The Academic Festival Overture." By his own admission, he described the piece as a "very boisterous potpourri of student songs."
8. In his last years, he wound up with cancer and passed in 1897. The jury is out as to whether it was in the liver or pancreas.
9. Some of his most important compositions are:

Orchestral: Four Symphonies; No. 1 in c minor (1855–1876), No. 2 in D Major (1877), No. 3 in F Major (1883), No. 4 in e minor (1885). Two Piano Concertos: No. 1 in d minor (1858), No. 2 in B-Flat Major (1881) Violin Concerto (1878), Academical Festival Overture (1880), Tragic Overture (1881)

Choral Music: A German Requiem (1868), Alto Rhapsody (1869), and over 180 songs

Piano Music: Different forms such as capricios, ballades rhapsodies, and others. Hungarian Dances and Liebeslieder Walzer

Chamber Music: Included are string quartets, quintets, and sextets. Piano trios and quartets, violin sonatas, and Clarinet Quintet.

Note: This overture has eight different melodies. Your challenge is to see if you can hear the differences between all eight. Do not be surprised if you have to listen to this piece more than once.

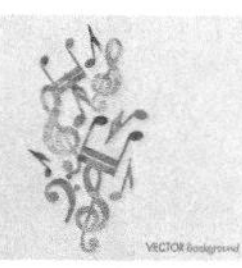

Listening Box 40

Type in Academic Festival Overture, choose top box Academic Festival Overture, Op. 80, Chicago Symphony Orchestra. Selection is on disc 3, Track 5.

Richard Strauss (1864–1949)

1. Born in Munich, Germany.
2. Richard's father was a horn player at the Court Opera in Munich. Subsequently, Richard received extensive musical training at home and wrote his first composition at the age of 6.

3. In his early years, he studied music theory, composition, and violin with members of the orchestra who were his father's friends.
4. In 1882, he entered Ludwig Maximilian University in Munich, where he studied philosophy and history. He left the university after a year to take an assistant conductor's position under Hans von Bulow.
5. In 1894, Strauss married soprano Pauline de Ahna. They had one son, Franz, born in 1897.
6. In 1919, he was made the Director of the Vienna State Opera, a position once held by Gustav Mahler.
7. In 1933, Richard desperately avoided dealings with the Nazi's and he tried to stay apolitical. Unfortunately, he did have dealings with Joseph Goebbels who appointed him the president of Reichmusikkamer, The State Music Bureau. Strauss was not asked if he wanted this position, but accepted in order to protect his Jewish daughter-in-law and his Jewish grandchildren.

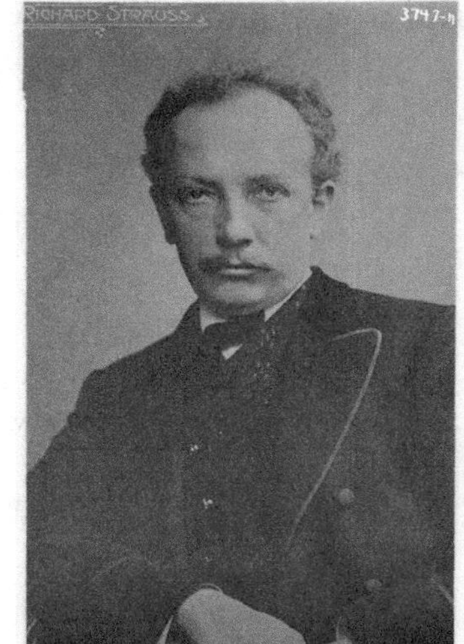

Strauss in Amsterdam (1924)

Richard Strauss. Between ca. 1915 and ca. 1920. Library of Congress, George Grantham Bain Collection, Prints & Photographs Division. Retrieved from http://www.loc.gov/pictures/item/ggb2005020996/.

8. During his lifetime, he received many awards from different organizations and is still recognized as a first rate composer and conductor. In 1949, at the age of 85, he died in Garmisch-Partenkirchen, Bavaria.
9. Some of his most important compositions are:

Operas: Salome (1905), Elektra (1909), Der Rosenkavalier (1911), Ariadne auf Naxos (1912), Die Frau ohne Schatten (The Woman without a Shadow,1919), Arabella (1933)

Orchestral, Symphonic Poems: Aus Italien (1886),Don Juan (1889), Death and Transfiguration (1889), Till Eulenspiegel's Merry Pranks (1895), Also sprach Zarathustra (1896), Don Quixote (1897), A Hero's Life (1898), Symphonie Domestica (1903)

Concertos: No. 1 in e-Flat (1883), No. 2 in E-Flat (1942), both horn concertos. Oboe Concerto (1945)

Songs: Four Last Songs (with orchestra, 1948) and approximately 200 songs with piano.

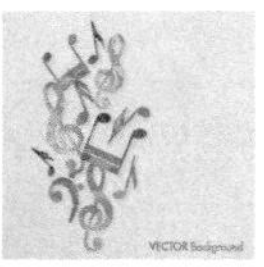

Listening Box 41

Type in Also Sprach and select the top box Also Sprach Zarathustra, Track 2. If this piece sounds familiar, it was used in the movie 2001, A Space Odyssey. This is a good example of older music used in a modern context.

Summary of Unit 3, Chapter 5 Terms and Study Sheet

Terms

Ballade: A ballade is a piano composition in freestyle. It was very popular in the Romantic Era.

Ballet: A storyline set to dancing and music. The dance movements are of most importance.

Etude: It is a study piece designed to display the technical ability of the player, usually piano.

Fantasie: A piano piece that in sound denotes whimsical or fantasy; generally, a short piece.

Impromptu: A piano piece that in sound denotes improvisation, but is really written out.

Idée fixe: A fixed musical idea, usually a melody representing something or someone.

Lied: The German term for art song. Plural is Lieder.

Mazurka: A Polish dance in triple meter (three beats per measure).

Nocturne: A short piano piece inspired by association with the night time.

Requiem: A requiem is music for a death mass.

Symphonic Poem: An orchestral piece in one movement sometimes called a tone poem.

Waltz: A dance in 3/4 meter, considered to be a ballroom dance.

Composers: Felix Mendelsohn, Fanny Mendelsohn Hensel, Franz Schubert, Robert Schumann, Clara Schumann, Frederic Chopin, Franz Liszt, Gustav Mahler, Alma Schindler Mahler, Johannes Brahms, and Richard Strauss.

Summary of Listeners Toolbox

The Romantic Era provides the listener with many new things. Among them are emotional extremes, orchestras were larger, music from a variety of composers and countries, program music, music with evocative titles, tons of piano music, and some new forms. Take advantage of the diversity.

To The Student: The instructor may add or delete study items at his or her discretion.

Unit 3, Chapter 5 Listening Box Playlist

LB31: Type in Dream of a Witches' Sabbath and choose top box V: Dream of a Witches' Sabbath. Select Track 5, V: Dream of a Witches' Sabbath.

LB32: Type in The Erlking and under Tracks choose The Erlking, Steve Gillette. Select Track 1, The Erlking. Also, under the same Tracks choose The Earlking, Sequester. Select Track 3, The Erlking. (Both are modern versions).

LB33: Type in Mendelssohn and choose top box Felix Mendelssohn, Romantic. Select Track 1, Italian Symphony: Saltarello.

LB34: Type in Fanny Hensel and choose top box Fanny Hensel-Mendelsohn. Select Track 1, Vier Lieder ohne Worte, Op. 8: 1. Allegro moderato.

LB35: Type in Schumann: Symphonies and Concertos, disc 1, # 9, Sinfonie Nr. 3 Es-Dur Op. 97 "Rheinische": 5. Satz: Lebhaft.

LB36: Type in Clara Schumann select Judith Alstadter, Clara Schumann, Impromptu Op. 9-Scherzo in cminor, Op. 14.

LB37: Type in Fantasie Impromptu. Under Track Results select the first option, Fantasie Impromptu Opus 66, in c sharp minor by Chopin. Track 2.

LB38: Type in Franz Liszt and under Track Results choose Liebestraum No. 3. Track 6.

LB39: Type in Gustav Mahler and under Album Results choose Symphony No. 10, then select Track 2, Scherzo.

LB40: Type in Academic Festival Overture. Choose top box academic festival Overture, Op. 80, Chicago Symphony Orchestra, Disc 3, Track 5.

LB41: Type in Also sprach and select the top box Also sprach Zarathustra, Track 2.

CHAPTER 6 NATIONALISM IN MUSIC (AS PART OF ROMANTICISM)

What Do We Find in This Period?

Music: Nationalism in music is an outgrowth of musicians wanting to honor and promote their own countries in terms of history, legends, instruments, and anything native. While nationalistic music existed in several countries, Russia was the dominant producer in the Romantic Era. Apparently, there is no official start to this time period, but most historians believe it started in the late eighteenth century.

Texture: Mostly homophonic

Forms: Composers primarily used existing forms such as symphony, opera, tone poems, songs, piano music, and various types of chamber music.

Composers: In Russia, five composers came together to form a group calledThe Mighty Five. They are Mily Balakirev, Alexander Borodin, Cesar Cui, Modest Mussorgsky, and Nikolai Rimsky-Korsakov. It is interesting to note that Peter Tchaikovsky, who did write Russian Nationalistic music, was not a member of the five. I will get into some of the reasons later.

Travel to: St Petersburg, Russia, and Spain.

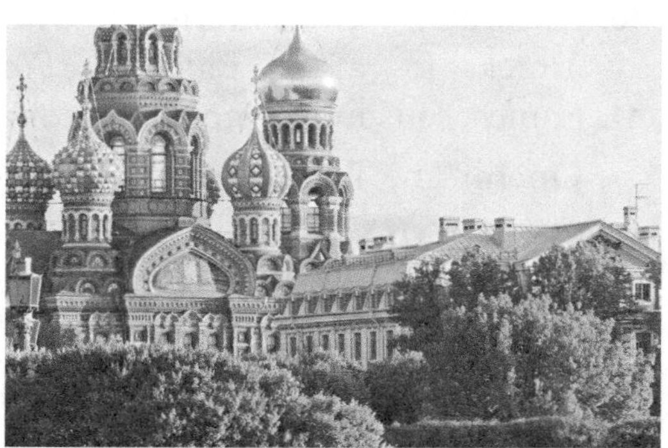

Orthodox Church, St Petersburg, Russia

Alexander Borodin (1833–1887)

1. Born in St. Petersburg, Russia.
2. Alexander was not only a composer, but a noted doctor and a chemist. In his lifetime he won several awards for scientific experiments.
3. To say the least, his beginnings were unconventional. He was the illegitimate son of a sixty-two-year-old nobleman and a twenty-five-year-old married woman. In his lifetime his mother was affectionate, but he referred to her "aunt."
4. In order to cover his tracks, the father named the son after a serf named Porfiry Borodin. Serfdom status was lifted at the age of 7 by his real father.

5. At the age of 17, he entered the Medical-Surgical Academy in St. Petersburg and after graduation spent a year in a military hospital, as a surgeon.
6. Although Borodin was a cellist, music was his avocation and in 1862, he met Mily Balakirev. He studied composition with Balakirev and completed his first symphony in 1869.
7. In 1862, he married a pianist, Ekaterina Protopopova. A year later a daughter was born.
8. Throughout his lifetime, Borodin was known as an advocate for women's rights. He promoted education for women and eventually was the founder of the School of Medicine for Women in St. Petersburg.
9. Borodin's melodies were adapted in the musical Kismet in 1953 by George Forrest and Robert Wright. Two popular songs are, "And This Is My Beloved" and "Stranger in Paradise."

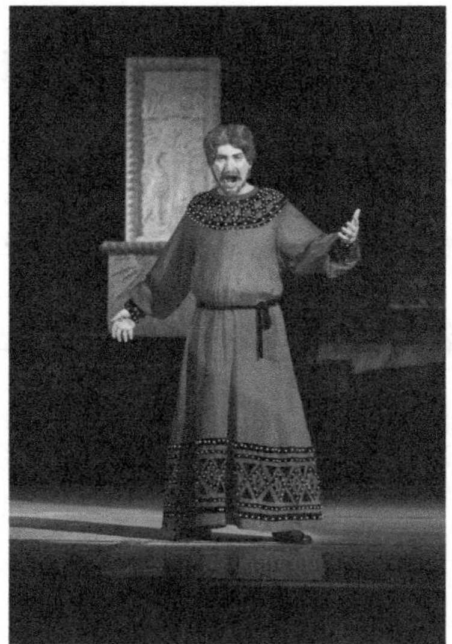

Prince Igor performance by members of the Dniprpetrovsk Opera and Ballet Theatre

10. Alexander had health issues with cholera and heart attacks. It was at a Ball at the Academy that he suddenly passed.
11. Some of his most important compositions are:

Opera: The Tsar's Bride (1868), Mlada (1872), Bogatyri (1878), Prince Igor (1887)

Orchestral: Symphony 1 in E-Flat (1867), Symphony 2 in b minor (1876), In the Steppes of Central Asia (1880), Symphony 3 in a minor (1887), was left unfinished, but was finished by Glazunov. He also wrote piano music, songs and chamber music. Unfortunately at least seven of his compositions were lost.

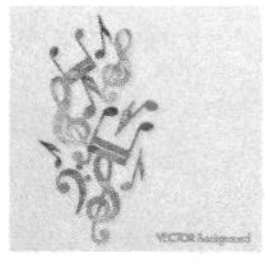

Listening Box 42

Type in Alexander Borodin and select top box Alexander Borodin. Go to Track 4, Polovtsain Dance No. 17 (Stranger in Paradise). For the second listening go to Track 12, Borodin: Polovtsain Dance. If you are a Sarah Brightman fan, just type in Stranger in Paradise and under Track Results select Sarah Brightman, then select Track 12. She has a wonderful arrangement of this piece.

Nikolai Rimsky-Korsakov (1844–1908)

1. Born in Tikhvin, Russia, into an aristocratic family.
2. Although he played the piano at the age of 6 and started to compose at the age of 10, his early interests were in literature and the ocean.His elder brother Voin encouraged him to join the Navy, so he decided to attend the School for

Mathematical and Navigational Sciences. In 1862, at the age of 18, he took his final exam.

3. It was Mily Balakirev who showed interest In Korsakov and suggested he should become a composer. This was a difficult transition as Nikolai was military trained and he eventually became a Naval Cadet. He was later made the Inspector of Naval Bands.
4. From 1871 to 1906, he taught music at the St. Petersburg Conservatory. He continued composing all the while maintaining his military status.
5. In 1872, Nikolai married Nadezhda Purgold, a pianist herself, and they eventually had seven children.
6. Rimsky-Korsakov is known for being one of the greatest orchestrators in music history. In his lifetime he was friends with Peter Tchaikovsky and on many occasions edited many musical works of "The Five." One of his famous pupils was Igor Stravinsky.
7. Some of his most important compositions are:

   Opera: May Night (1878–1879),The Snow Maiden (1880–1881), Christmas Eve (1894–1895), Mozart and Salieri (1897), Sadko (1898, a popular song from this opera is Song of India), The Tsar's Bride (1899), The Tale of Tsar Sultan (1900, a popular song from this opera is Flight of the Bumblebee)

   Orchestral: Capriccio Espagñol (1887), Russian Easter Overture (1887–1888), Scheherezade (1888). Three symphonies and works for smaller groups such as chamber music, songs, piano music, and choral works.

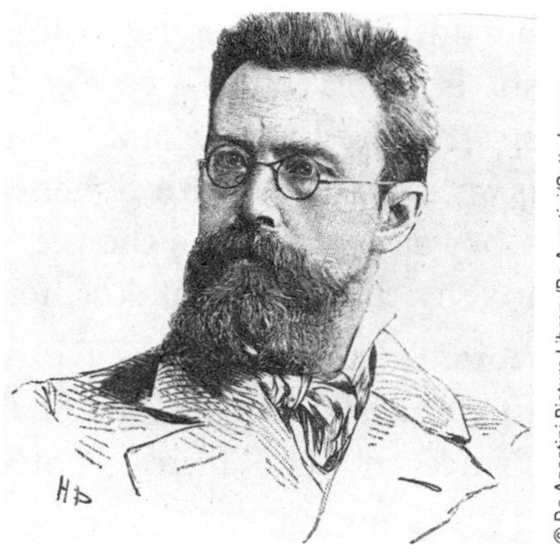

Portrait by Valentin Serov (1898)

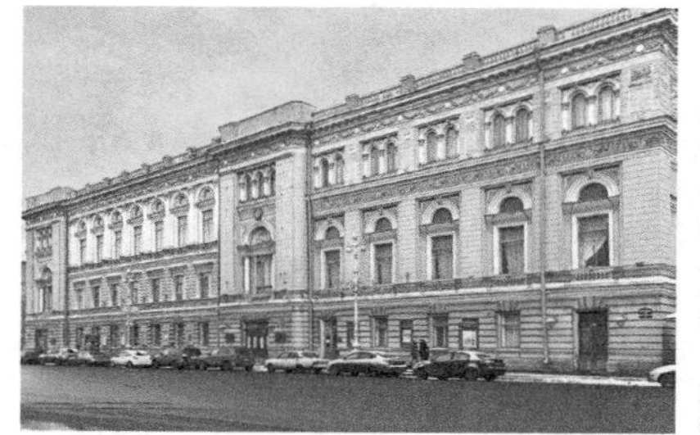

St. Petersburg Conservatory

Scheherezade, Rimsky-Korsakov (1888)

The story of Scheherezade is based on "One Thousand and One Nights" sometimes called "The Arabian Nights."

Story Synopsis

Apparently, the King of Persia finds out his wife has been unfaithful. He decides to marry a new virgin each day then behead her the next day to make sure she is not unfaithful. Amazingly, he killed 1000 wives before meeting Scheherezade, the daughter of a high ranking political advisor. Scheherezade is very intelligent and well read, but goes against her father's wishes by volunteering to spend one night with the King. She realizes that she is going to die the next day and asks the King if she could bid one last farewell to her sister by telling a story. She is granted permission and the King listens intently. The King is so impressed with Scheherezade's story telling, he keeps asking her to tell a different story each night. As the nights pass, 1001, Scheherezade's life is spared. The King falls in love with her and makes her his Queen.

Note: **Scheherezade,** by Rimsky-Korsakov, is an orchestral piece in four movements. The movements are: (1) The Sea and Sinbad's Ship, (2) The Kalendar Prince, (3) The Young Prince and The Young Princess, and (4) Festival at Baghdad—The Sea.

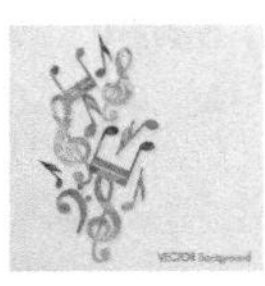

Listening Box 43

Type in Festival at Baghdad and select the top box, Festival at Baghdad—The Sea. Select Track 4. This movement contains the Scheherezade Theme, shipwreck music, musical statements from other movements and has a very calm and tranquil ending.

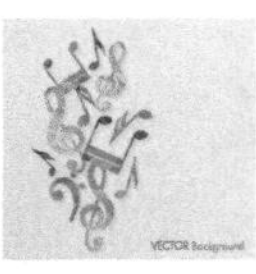

Listening Box 44

Type in Flight of the Bumblebee and under Trach Results select the London Philharmonic Orchestra. Select Track 11. This piece is from Korsakov's opera, The Tale of Tsar Sultan.

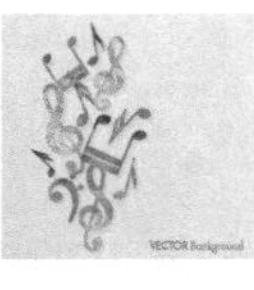

Listening Box 45

Type in Fandango asturiano and under Track Results select New York Philharmonic. Choose Track 9.

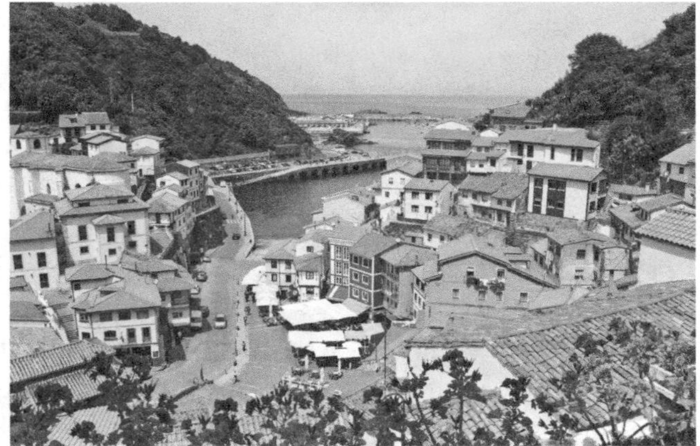

Town of Cudillero, Asturias, Spain

Note: In 1887, Rimsky-Korsakov writes a piece called Cappricio Espagñol. It basically represents his travels to Spain. It is an orchestral piece in five movements. The movements are: (1) Alborada, (2) Variazioni, (3) Alborada, (4) Scena e canto Gitano (Scene and gypsy song), and (5) Fandango asturiano. The Asturias region is in Northern Spain.

Pyotr (Peter) Ilyich Tchaikovsky (1840–1893)

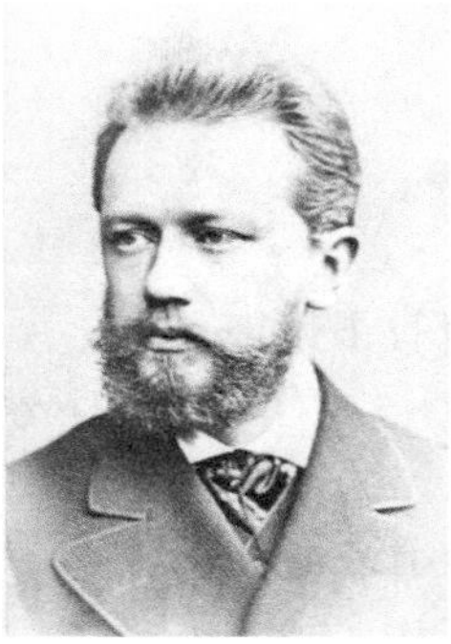

1. Born in Votkinsk, Russia.
2. His mother was the second of his father's three wives and eighteen years his junior.
3. Peter began piano lessons at the age of 5 and at the age of 10 was sent to St. Petersburg to enter the Imperial School of Jurisprudence. A student had to be 12 years old to enter, so Tchaikovsky had to spend two years at the Preparatory School.
4. In 1854, Peter's mother passed from cholera and the loss stayed with him the rest of his life.
5. Although he was not a member of "The Five," he maintained a decent relationship with several members. In 1865, he graduated from the St. Petersburg Conservatory. In 1866, he received a Professorship from the Moscow Conservatory.
6. Tchaikovsky had deep personal and emotional issues. In 1886, he met soprano Desiree Artot. She refused to give up her career and the relationship ended.
7. In 1887, he married a former student Antonina Miliukova. The marriage did not work out and Tchaikovsky left after two and a half months. In this same year, he started a 13 year relationship with Nadezhda von Meck who was a patroness and confidante.
8. For most of his life he lived alone and traveled extensively throughout Europe and the United States.
9. In 1891, he was invited by the New York Philharmonic to be the guest conductor for the opening of Carnegie Hall.
10. During his lifetime he was a prolific composer who experienced severe bouts of depression. He was homosexual and was constantly hounded by bigots. He also drank and smoked heavily.
11. As stated, he was not a member of "The Five" as they considered him to be too cosmopolitan and too influenced by music from other countries such as America.
12. In 1893, at the age of 53, he passed from the disease cholera. While nothing has been proven, many historians believe he committed suicide.
13. Some of his most important compositions are:

    Orchestral: Six symphonies, No. 1 (1866), No. 2 (1872), No. 3 (1875), No. 4 (1878), No. 5 (1888), and No. 6 (1893). Violin Concerto (1878), Piano Concerto No. 1 (1874–1875), Piano Concerto No. 2 (1879–1880), Piano Concerto No. 3 (reworked in 1893)

Ballets: Swan Lake(1877), Sleeping Beauty (1889), and The Nutcracker (1892)

Overtures: Romeo and Juliet (1869), Francesca da Rimini (1876), Capriccio Italien (1880), 1812 Overture (1882), Marche slave (1876)

Operas: Eugene Onegin (1865), Mazeppo (1884), The Queen of Spades (1880)

Chamber Music: Three String Quartets, One String Sextet, Piano and Choral Music.

The 1812 Overture, Tchaikovsky (1882)

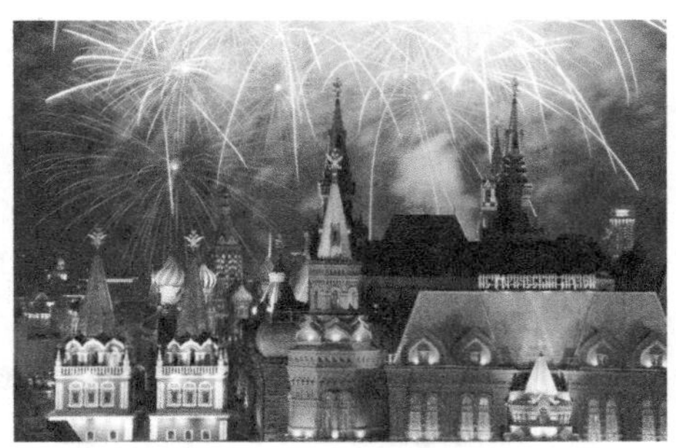

Fireworks over Kremlin, Russia

Historically, this piece was written to commemorate the 70th anniversary of the Russian victory over the French and Napoleon in Moscow. This piece is unique as it contains canons firing, fireworks, and church bells ringing. Tchaikovsky wrote specific parts in the music for these strange musical items. In reality, the Russian Army was severely outnumbered and short on equipment and supplies. There is no doubt that prayer, courage, and perseverance helped the Russians to victory. Musically, this piece contains the "Czar's Hymn" and "La Marseillaise" the French National Anthem.

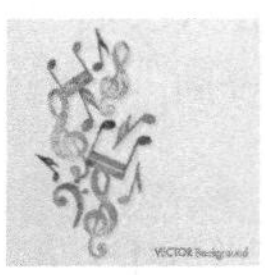

Listening Box 46

Type in 1812 and under Track results choose 1812 Overture Op. 49-Finale. Selection is on disc 2, Track 25.

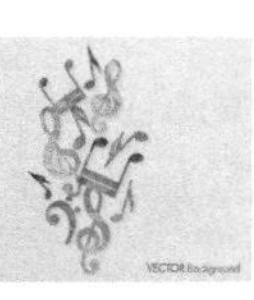

Listening Box 47

Type in Trepak and select top box Trepak, London Symphony Orchestra. Select Track 8. This selection is from The Nutcracker.

Summary of Unit 3, Chapter 6 Terms and Study Sheet

Terms

Capriccio: Music that is very lively and generally free form. The term can apply to instrumental, vocal or keyboard music.

Concert Overture: An individual instrumental concert piece that stands alone and does not come before an opera or show.

Nationalism: Nationalism in music is when composers choose to incorporate elements of their country into their musical works. In essence, they showcase and promote their country.

Tone Poem: Basically a one movement orchestral work. Sometimes referred to as a symphonic poem or one movement symphony.

Note: It is important to note that in this period of music history there were many countries that were creating nationalism in music. Some of them are Italy, Czech Republic, Scandinavia, Hungary, Spain, England, and the United States.

Composers: As previously stated, for this style period I am focusing on "The Five." They are Mily Balakirev, Alexander Borodin, Cesar Cui, Modest Mussorgsky, and Nikolai Rimsky-Korsakov.

Summary of Listeners Toolbox

Nationalism in music brings us in sound a composer's strong feelings for his country. Often times we analyze music for its own sake and rarely do we discuss the feelings of the composer. Nationalism is a good time to break from that mentality and concern ourselves with the composer's feelings. This time period gives us many sound points of view, larger orchestras, and program music in various categories.

Questions

How do you feel about nationalistic music in our country? Do we have too much, too little, or are we unaware of the music that exists?

To The Student: The instructor may add or delete study items at his or her discretion.

Unit 3, Chapter 6 Listening Box Playlist

LB42: Type in Alexander Borodin and select top box Alexander Borodin. Go to Track 4, Polovtsian Dance No. 17 (Stranger in Paradise). For the second listening go to Track 12, Borodin: Polovtsain Dance. If you are a Sarah Brightman fan, type in Stranger in Paradise and under Track Results select Sarah Brightman, then select Track 12. She has a wonderful arrangement of this song.

LB43: Type in Festival at Baghdad and select the top box, Festival at Baghdad—The Sea. Select Track 4. This movement contains the Scheherezade theme, shipwreck music, musical statements from other movements and has a very tranquil ending.

LB44: Type in Flight of the Bumblebee and under Track Results, The London Symphony Orchestra select Track 11. This piece is from Korsakov's opera, the Tale of Tsar Sultan.

LB45: Type in Fandango asturiano and under Track Results select New York Philharmonic. Choose Track 9.

LB46: Type in 1812 and under Track Results choose 1812 Overture Op. 49—Finale. Selection is on disc 2, Track 25.

LB47: Type in Trepak and select top box Trepak, London Symphony Orchestra. Select Track 8.

CHAPTER 7 OPERA

What Do We Find in This Period?

Music: The concept of opera started in Florence, Italy, around 1573, by an elitist group called the Camerata. Their purpose was to start a new type of vocal music. Their research took them to ancient Greek dramas, but they found no music. They collectively decided to take some of these stories and write original music for them. Because of this, the first categorical name for opera was musical drama. The first opera composer in music history was Jacopo Peri and he was a member of the Camerata. His first opera Dafne, 1597, met with a terrible fate as the music was lost. On the brighter side, the 455 page libretto still survives intact. Peri's second opera, Euridice, was written in 1600, and became the first opera for which we have music. Euridice was performed at the wedding of Marie de Medici and Henry IV, in 1600.

Additional opera points: Claudio Monteverdi invented the overture which is instrumental music that comes before the opera begins. It was designed to set a mood and give the listener songs he/she will hear later in full production.

Venice, Italy, becomes the city with the most opera houses and the first was Teatro San Cassiano, which opened in 1637.

Texture: Homophonic.

Forms: Opera, which includes recitative and aria.

Composers: Gioacchino Rossini, Gaetano Donizetti, Vincenzo Bellini, Giuseppe Verdi, Giacomo Puccini, George Bizet, and Richard Wagner. Needless to say, we have many more opera composers, but in the interest of brevity, I will cite just a few listed.

Travel to: Italy, France, and Germany.

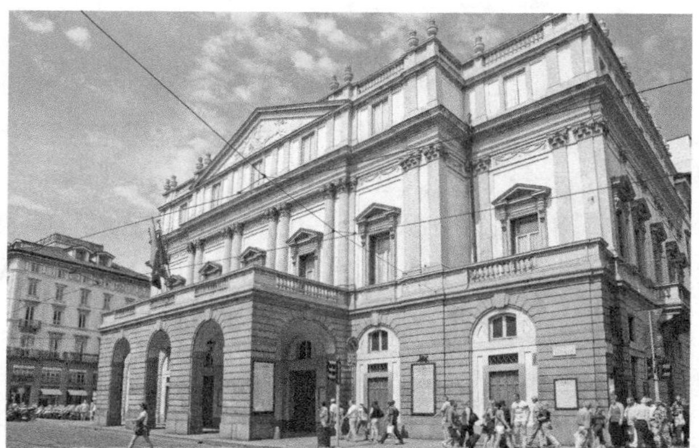

La Scala, Milan, Italy

Giuseppe Verdi (1813–1901)

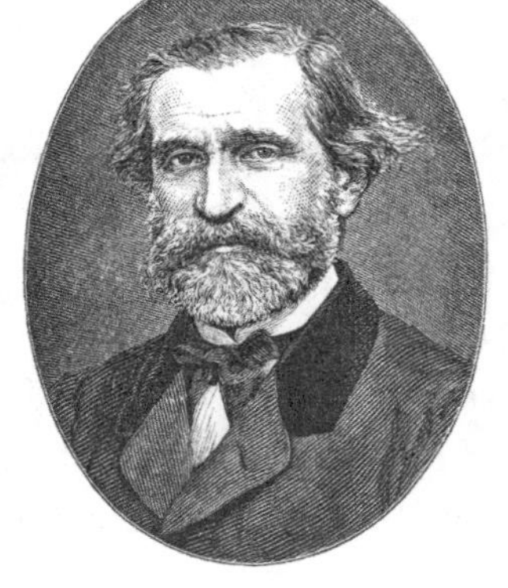
©Stocksnapper/Shutterstock.com

1. Born in Le Roncole, Italy.
2. Verdi showed early interest and talent in music and at the age of 8 became the church organist, which was a paid job.
3. By his own admission, he wrote many different pieces which added to his knowledge of composition.
4. Verdi always had his sights set on Milan, but when he applied to attend the Conservatory, he was turned down because his piano skills were substandard. At this point, he realized he needed to make influential contacts to become successful and he took private lessons from noted teachers.
5. In 1836, he married Margherita Barezzi, a former student and they had two children, Virginia (1837) and Icilio (1838). Unfortunately, both children died young, Virginia in 1838 and Icilio in 1839. More tragedy struck as his wife passed at the age of 26, in 1840, from encephalitis.
6. After Margherita passed, Verdi had a long relationship with Giuseppina Strepponi, a vocalist, whose voice quality eventually declined. This relationship was not looked upon favorably as the couple were not married, but living together. This all changes in 1859, when Verdi married Strepponi.
7. Verdi was very political and he made several nationalistic references in his operas. He was influential in the Risorgimento (unification) of Italy. For all his political discourse, he was ultimately appointed to the Parliament and Senate.
8. In his last years he showed his philanthropic side as he established Casa di Riposo per Musicisti (a rest home for retired musicians) and the building of a hospital at Villanova sull' Arda.
9. He passed in January, 1901, from a stroke.
10. Some of his most important compositions are:

    Operas: Nabucco (1842), Ernani (1844), Attila (1847), Macbeth (1847), Rigoletto (1851), Il trovatore (1853), La traviata (1853), Un ballo in maschera (1859), La forza del destino (1862), Don Carlos (1867), Aida (1871), Otello (1887), and Falstaff (1893)

    Sacred Music: Requiem (1874), Quattro pezzi sacri (Four Sacred Pieces 1889–1897).

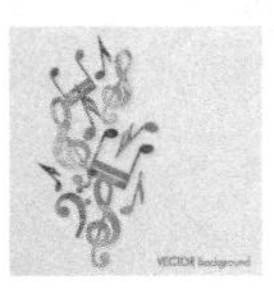

Listening Box 48

Type in Triumphal March and select top box, Verdi: Triumphal March. Selection is on disc 2, Track 19.

Note: This selection is from Verdi's opera Aida, where in the second act Radames leads the Egyptian Army on its return following their victory over the Ethiopians.

Giacomo Puccini (1858–1924)

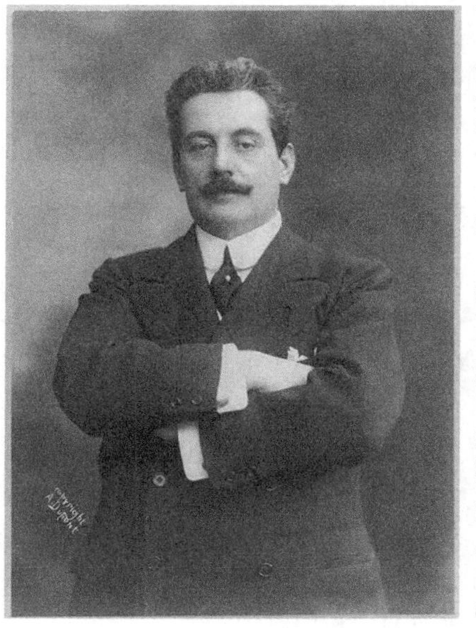
Giacomo Puccini. c1908. Library of Congress Prints and Photographs Division. Retrieved from http://www.loc.gov/pictures/item/2005685154/.

1. Born in Lucca, Italy.
2. Orphaned at the age of 5, Puccini studied music with some of his father's former pupils.
3. In 1880, he entered the Milan Conservatory and received his diploma in 1883. His music was influenced by Verdi, Wagner, Debussy, and Stravinsky.
4. The noted publisher, Giulio Ricordi, loved Puccini's early music and became a lifelong friend and patron.
5. In his personal life, Giacomo had trouble as after his mother's death he fled Lucca with Elvira Gemignani, a married women, and her daughter, Fosca. From this relationship a son Antonio was born in 1886 and the couple finally married in 1904, after the death of Elvira's husband.
6. The Puccini's had a somewhat tumultuous relationship as Elvira was very jealous and Giacomo traveled extensively.
7. Throughout his lifetime he composed many popular operas that are frequently performed in today's opera houses.
8. His final opera, Turandot, was incomplete as Puccini wound up with throat cancer and was sent to Brussels for surgery. He passed a few days later.
9. Some of his most important compositions are:

   Operas: Le Villi (1884), Edgar (1889), Manon Lescout (1893), La bohème (1896), Tosca (1900), Madama Butterfly (1904), La fanciulla del West (1910), Il tabarro (the clock, 1916), La Rondine (1917), Il trittico, which is a collection of three one act operas (Il tabarro, Suor Angelica and Gianni Schicchi, 1918), and Turandot (1926). He also wrote songs for piano and voice.

Note: The story of Puccini's opera La bohème, 1896, became the story line for the Broadway musical Rent, by Jonathan Larson in 1996. Larson changes some facts from the original opera in which Mimi is dying from aids and not tuberculosis and Roger is a drug addict who is HIV-positive.

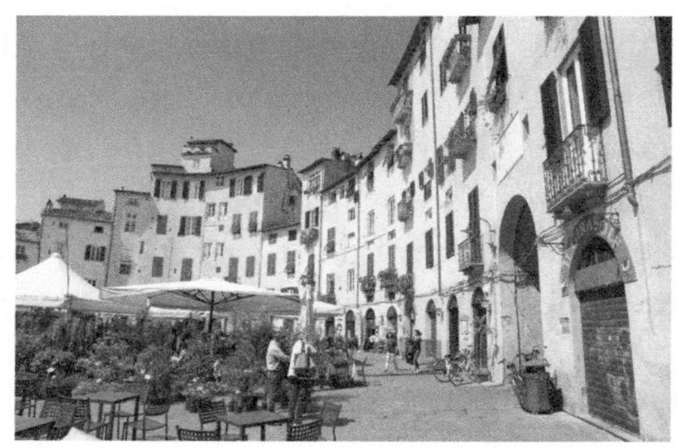

Piazza Santa Maria, Lucca, Italy

Turandot, Giacomo Puccini (1924)

Story Synopsis

As a youth, Princess Turandot witnessed the beating and murder of a female relative. She vowed as she got older to avenge the death of her relative and she invents a brutal scheme to accomplish this. In order to win the favors of the Princess, a man must first strike a gong to signal he is ready. He then has to be of noble birth and solve three riddles. Turandot's three ministers, Ping, Pang, and Pong, have seen much bloodshed as many men were not able to solve the riddles. On one occasion, Prince Calaf strikes the gong which signals he is ready. Turandot's three assistants, plus her father, try to convince Calaf to change his mind. He tells them no and is asked the following riddles: "What is born each night and dies at dawn?" Calaf answers, "Hope" which was correct. Next, "What flickers red and warm like a flame, yet is not fire?" Calaf answers "Blood" which was correct. Last, "What is like ice yet burns?" Calaf answers "Turandot" which was correct. Now, the Princess starts to panic and asks her father if there is any way she can get out of this situation. Her father states that she has made a deal and must stick to her end of the bargain.

In order to appease Turandot, Calaf gives her an option to get out of the deal, which is she now has to marry him. He says that if she answers his question correctly, he is prepared to die. If she does not, she will have to marry him. Calaf asks her, "What is my name?" The Princess has until dawn to answer correctly. There is a decree that no one shall sleep until Turandot knows his name. The penalty if she does not learn his name is that everyone in the city will be killed. At this point, chaos ensues and Ping, Pang, and Pong try to convince Calaf to withdraw from his staunch position. In addition, the crowd threatens Calaf with daggers, but Calaf turns down the ministers and the crowd. He tells all, only he knows his name. In the end, only Turandot and Calaf remain as he calls her the Princess of Death and kisses her. Turandot is stunned and begins to cry as this is the first time she had been kissed. Calaf tells her his real name. As Calaf sits on the throne, Turandot turns to the crowd and tells them the stranger's name is "Love."

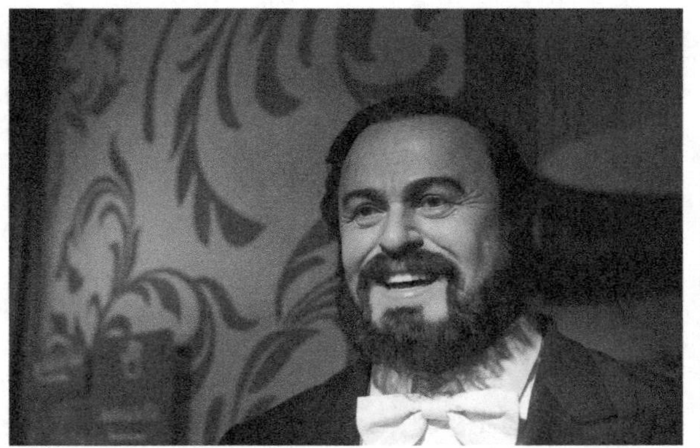

A Waxwork of Pavarotti, Bangkok, Thailand

Listening Box 49

Type in Nessun Dorma and under Track results select Nessun Dorma, Luciano Pavarotti. Selection is Track 1.

Nessun Dorma: This is one of opera's most famous tenor arias, so I wanted to provide you with a text translation.

Nessun dorma! Nessun dorma!
Tu pure, o Principessa,
Nella tua fredda stanza,
guardi le stelle
che tremano d'amore, e di speranza
Ma il mio mistero è chiuso in me;
Il nome mio nessun saprà!
No, No! Sulla tua bocca
Lo diro quando la luce splenderà!
Ed il mio bacio scioglierà
il silenzio che ti fa mia!

None shall sleep! None shall sleep!
Even you, O Princess,
in your cold bedroom,
watch the stars
that tremble with love and with hope
But my secret is hidden within me;
None will know my name!
No, No! On your mouth
I will say it when the light shines!
And my kiss will dissolve
the silence that makes you mine!

A chorus of women sing:

Il nome suo nessun saprà,
E noi dovrem, ahimè, morir, morir!

no one will know his name,
and we will have to, alas, die, die!

Calaf is now certain of victory and he sings:

Dilegua, o notte!
Tramontate, stelle!
Tramontate, stelle!
All'alba vincerò!
Vincerò! Vincerò!

Vanish, o night!
Fade, you stars!
Fade, you stars!
At dawn, I will win!
I will win! I will win!

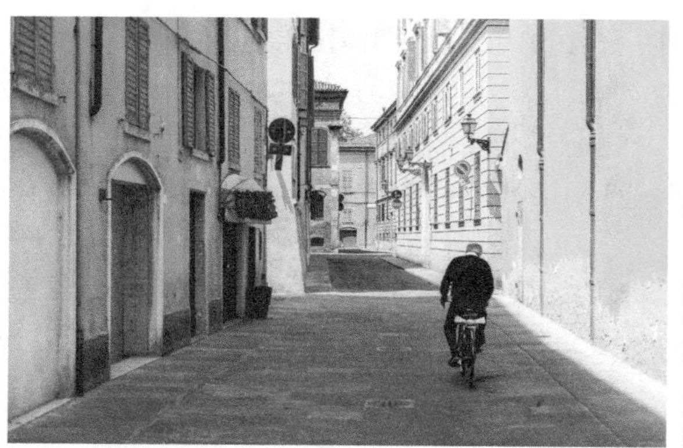

Modena, Italy, birthplace of Luciano Pavarotti

Georges Bizet (1838–1875)

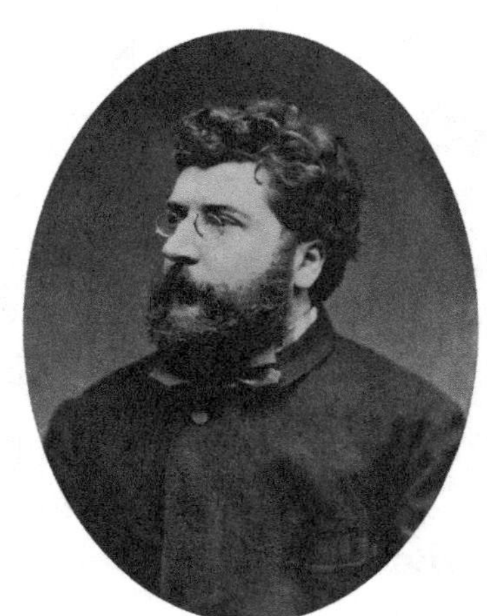
©Everett Historical/Shutterstock.com

1. Born in Paris, France.
2. Georges came from a musical background as his mother was a pianist and his father was a composer and a vocal teacher.
3. Bizet showed early signs of musical talent and his parents enrolled him at the Paris Conservatory. At the age of 14, he won first prize in piano.
4. In 1857, he won the Offenbach Prize and the Prestigious Prix de Rome, but did not concertize frequently even though he was a skilled pianist.
5. Bizet realized he could not make a living writing music, so in the lean years, he took students in piano and composition. Although he was an educated and skilled performer, his music was not very popular and mostly neglected.
6. In 1869, he married Geneviève Halèvy, despite objections from her mother and other family members. This marriage produced one son.
7. In 1870, Bizet joined the National Guard as part of the national fervor with Napoleon declaring war in July, 1870. After a while, Bizet became critical of poor equipment and enthusiasm waned as France lost several battles.
8. Throughout his life, Bizet was afflicted with a chronic throat problem. He was a heavy smoker.
9. Due to a lack of professional success and illness, he suffered severe depression. He eventually passed in 1875 from heart failure.
10. Some of his most important compositions are:

    Operas: Le Docteur miracle (1857), Les pècheurs de perles (1863), La jolie fille de Perth (1867), Djamileh (1872), and Carmen (1875)

    Cantatas: David (1856), Clovis et Clothilde (1857), and Te Deum (1858)
    Orchestral: Symphony No. 1 (1855), Vasco da Gama (1859), Souvenirs de Rome (1869), and L' Arlèsienne Suites 1 and 2 (1872)

    Piano Music: More than 150 pieces which included Jeux d' enfants (1872).

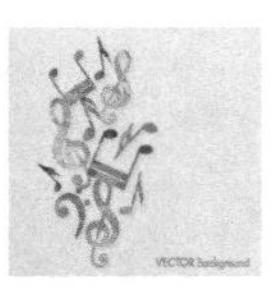

Listening Box 50

Type in Toreador Song and select top box, Bizet: Toreador Song. Select disc 1, Track 9. For the second listening select disc 2, Track 8, Habanera.

Note: Bizet really captures Spanish flavors in these listenings. I am sure you have heard these melodies, but are unaware they actually come from an opera.

Richard Wagner (1813–1883)

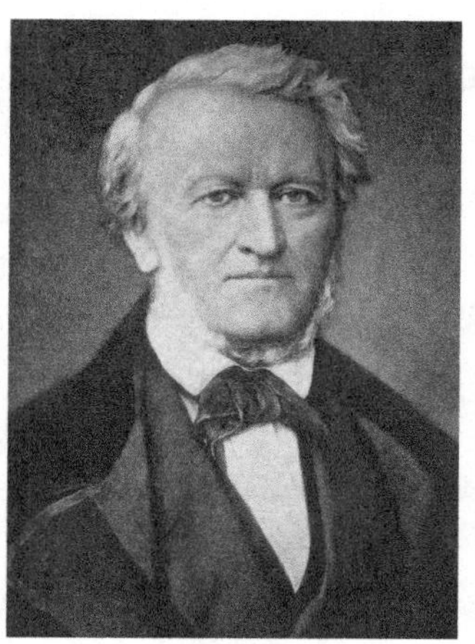
©Everett Historical/Shutterstock.com

1. Born in Leipzig, Germany.
2. Wagner's father passed away six months after Richard was born. His mother eventually went to live with a family friend, Ludwig Geyer, who was an actor and playwright.
3. Wagner showed early interest in literature and attended several boarding schools. He wanted to become a playwright himself.
4. Between 1828 and 1831, he studied harmony, but it was a performance by soprano Wilhelmine Schroder-Devrient that changed his thinking and his life.
5. In 1831, Wagner attended Leipzig University where he studied composition among other things. At this point, he was firmly convinced of setting drama to music. In fact, he wrote the stories (libretti) as well as the music for his operas. One of his compositional innovations was called the leitmotif. Leitmotifs are short musical melodies associated with characters, places, forces of nature that are used for identification.
6. In 1833, he secured a position as a rehearsal director for a small church in Leipzig. He wound up meeting and had an affair with Minna, one of the sopranos. Eventually, the couple married, but in truth, the marriage was plagued with infidelities on both sides.
7. In his lifetime, Wagner was known as a political activist, often calling for revolution. Because of his political positions, he was forced to leave Germany and he went to Switzerland, where he remained in exile for 12 years. This separation took its toll on his marriage, which finally ended. He continued having affairs with various women, some of which were his friend's wives.
8. One of the first things "Mad King Ludwig" did after he was crowned was to bring Wagner to Munich to produce operas. It was here that Wagner met Cosima Liszt, Franz Liszt's daughter, they started a relationship, and eventually married. A son Helferich Siegfried was born to the couple in 1869, before they married.
9. Wagner's opera productions were excessive and he constantly needed additional financing. Cosima was a good business woman and was able to convince the King he should subsidize and support Wagner's work.
10. In 1871, Wagner and the family moved to Bayreuth as he wanted to build an opera house for just his productions. Land was donated, but financial contributions were slow in coming. In time, the King gave in and provided additional subsidy for Festspielhaus which was completed in 1875. Festspielhaus finally opened in August, 1876.

11. In late 1882, after a Bayreuth Festival, exhausted and not feeling well, Wagner and the family went to Venice, Italy, for the winter. He suffered from several angina attacks and finally passed in February, 1883. His body was taken down the Grand Canal and transported to Germany where he was buried in a garden at Villa Wahnfried in Bayreuth.

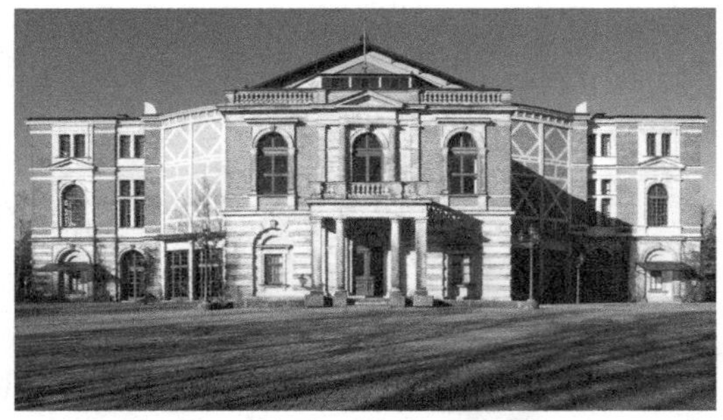

Festspielhaus, Bayreuth, Germany

12. Some of his most important compositions are:

Operas: Rienzi (1842), The Flying Dutchman (1843), Tannhäuser (1845), Lohengrin (1850), Tristan und Isolde (1865), The Meistersingers of Nuremberg (1868), The Ring of the Nebelung, a collection of four operas combined. They are: The Rhine Gold (1869), The Valkyrie (1870), Siegfried (1876), Twilight of the Gods (Götterdämmerung) (1876), and Parsifal (1882)

Orchestral: Symphony No. 1 in C major (1832), Symphony in E major (incomplete) (1834), Siegfried Idyll (1870), Grand Festival March (to celebrate the signing of the Declaration of Independence) (1876), and various overtures and concert overtures. In addition, he wrote piano music, chamber music, and songs.

Note: One of the compositional devices Wagner used frequently was the chromatic scale. The scale is made up of all half-steps. The following diagram explains this perfectly. Start on your left and as you ascend, the notes are C-C♯-D-D♯-E-F-F♯-G-G♯-A-A♯-B-C. As you descend, the notes are C-B-Bb-A-Ab-G-Gb-F-E-Eb-D-Db-C. What is meant by all half-steps is that you do not skip any notes as you ascend or descend.

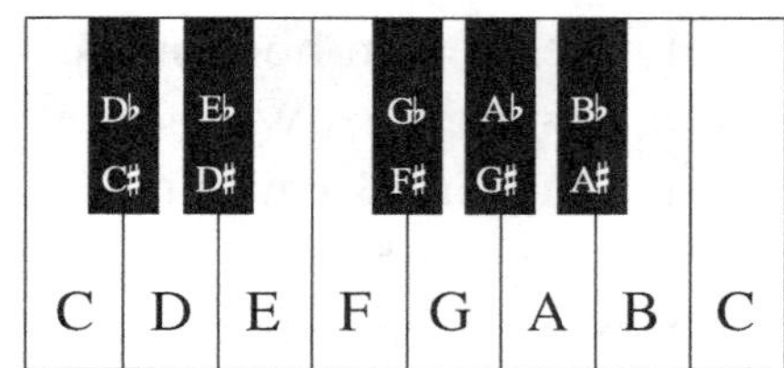

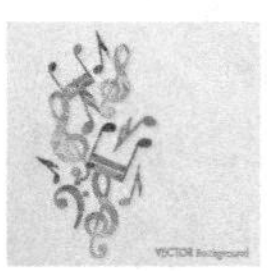

Listening Box 51

Type in Flying Dutchman Overture and under Track Results choose third selection, Flying Dutchman Overture, from Lo . . . Selection is on disc 2, No. 1.

Note: This is a good arrangement, heavy brass with good woodwind, string and percussion writing. One of your main listening objectives is to see if you can hear the extensive use of the chromatic scale.

There are several vocal groups that have become very popular singing opera songs as well as new songs in an operatic style. Probably, the first group to gain recognition is the Three Tenors. The members are Plácido Domingo, José Carreras, and Luciano Pavarotti. Sadly, Pavarotti passed in 2007. Their first concert as a group was in Rome, Italy, on the night before the Italia 90 World Cup. The album recorded this evening became the largest selling album of classical music. The conductor is Zubin Mehta. **Pictured from left to right are Domingo, Carreras, Pavarotti, and Mehta**

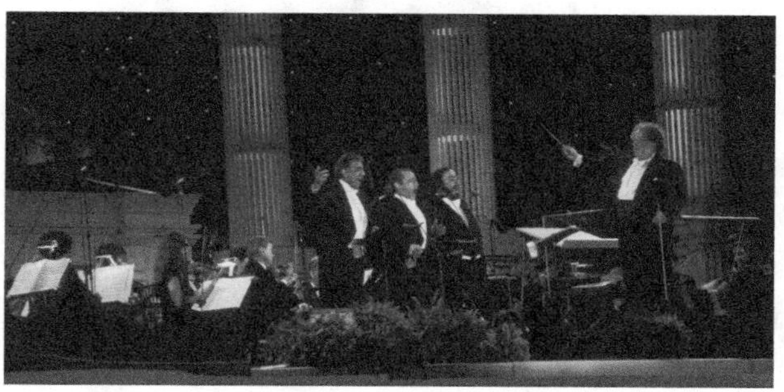

©Ron Galella/WireImage/Getty Images

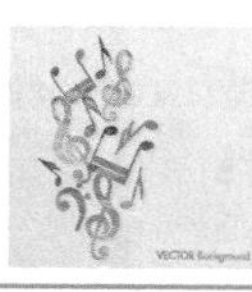

Listening Box 52

Type in Three Tenors and under Albums choose The Three Tenors in Concert, 1994. Select Track 7, My Way and Track 14, America.

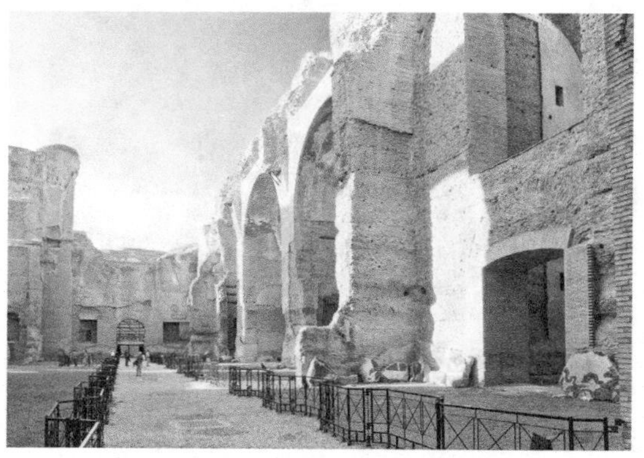

©Viacheslav Lopatin/Shutterstock.com

Baths of Caracalla, Rome, Italy. One of many places the Three Tenor's performed

IL Divo is another exceptional vocal group that has won many awards. It was started in the United Kingdom in 2003. In Italian, IL Divo means divine performer. The group members are Urs Bühler (Swiss), Carlos Marín (Spanish), Sébastien Izambard (French), and David Miller (American).

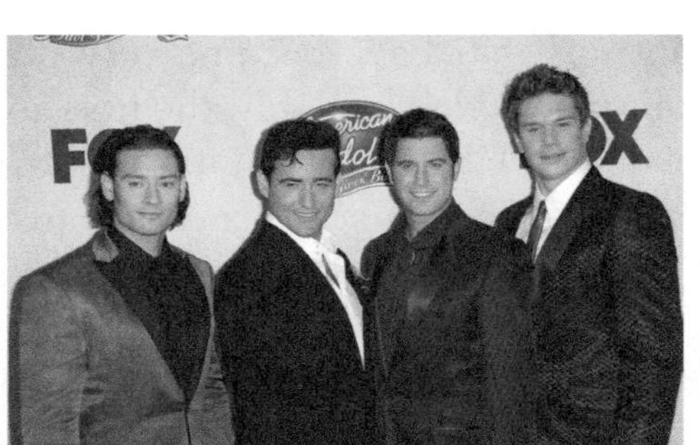

IL Divo; Pictured from left are: Bühler, Marín, Izambard, and Miller

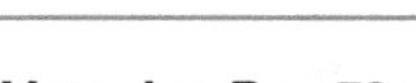

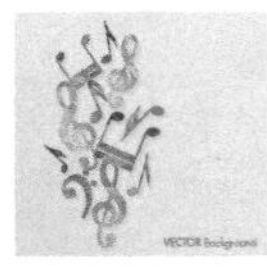

Listening Box 53

Type in Il Divo and underArtists choose Il Divo-Crossover Classical. Select Track 2, Amazing Grace and Track 7, A Whole New World.

IL Volo got started quite by accident. Each member was a vocal contestant on Italian television. The director, Robert Ceni, realized their talent and decided to put them together as kind of a young Three Tenors, in 2010. The rest is history! The members are Piero Barone, Ignazio Boschetto, and Gianluca Ginoble.

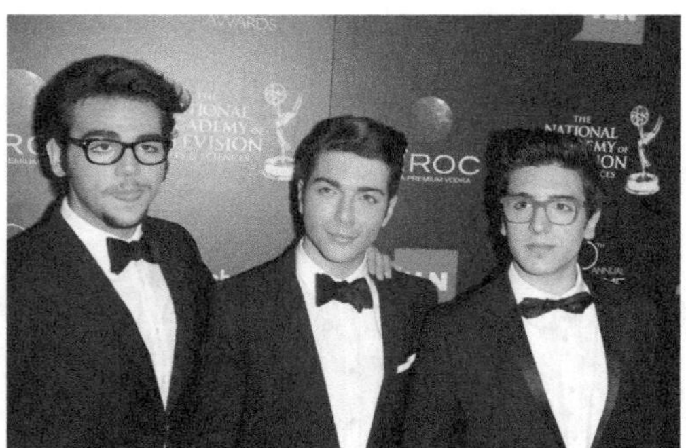

IL Volo (means "the flight") Pictured from left are Boschetto, Ginoble, and Barone

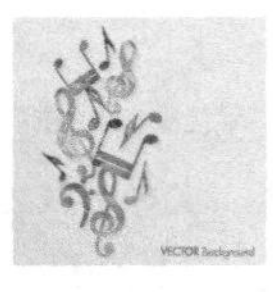

Listening Box 54

Type in Il Volo and under Top Result choose 'O Solo Mio.' Select Track 6, Smile.

Summary of Unit 3, Chapter 7 Terms and Study Sheet

Terms

The following opera terms have been previously discussed, but will be restated here.

Aria: A vocal solo.

Recitative: A speech-like style of singing.

Libretto: The book or story of an opera or oratorio.

Castrato: A surgically altered male that sang high parts in operas.

Music drama: The first categorical name for opera.

Leitmotif: Short musical melodies associated with characters, places, forces of nature, which are used for identification purposes.

Composers: The composers highlighted in this chapter are *Giuseppe Verdi, Giacomo Puccini, Georges Bizet, and Richard Wagner.*

Featured Artists: The Three Tenors, IL Divo, and IL Volo

Summary of Listeners Toolbox

Opera can take you in many directions, so you have to be flexible as a listener. For example, when listening to Bizet's, Carmen, you get many Spanish flavors. When listening to Wagner, you often get heavy orchestration along with chromaticism and leitmotifs. Italian opera composers are known for writing beautiful melodies. My overall suggestions are to take opera in small doses and learn the story first. I would start with groups like IL Divo and IL Volo.

Questions

Besides being in a foreign language, what do you think contributes to many young people not liking this music? What do you think opera administrators and performers can do to make opera more enjoyable for young listeners?

To The Student: The instructor may add or delete study items at his or her discretion.

Unit 3, Chapter 7 Listening Box Playlist

LB48: Type in Triumphal March and select top box, Verdi: Triumphal March. Selection is on disc 2, Track 19.

LB49: Type in Nessun Dorma and under Track Results select Nessun Dorma, Luciano Pavarotti. Selection is Track 1.

LB50: Type in Toreador Song and select top box, Bizet: Toreador Song. Select disc 1, Track 9. Also, for the second listening select disc 2, Track 8, Habanera.

LB51: Type in Flying Dutchman Overture and under Track Results choose third selection, Flying Dutchman Overture from Lo . . . . Selection is on disc 2, No. 1.

LB52: Type in Three Tenors and under Albums choose The Three Tenors in Concert, 1994. Select Track 7, My Way and Track 14, America.

LB53: Type in Il Divo and under Artists choose Il Divo-Crossover Classical. Select Track 2, Amazing Grace and Track 7, A Whole New World.

LB54: Type in IL Volo and under Top Result choose 'O solo mio.' Select Track 6, Smile.

CHAPTER 8 IMPRESSIONISM (1880–1920)

Music: Impressionism started in Paris, France, as an artistic idea. The original concept was to get away from Germanic influences and not sound like the old composers. Impressionistic music is music that appeals to the senses. The original founder of Impressionism was Claude Debussy, who was friendly with some impressionistic painters. He decided that it was possible to take the artistic concepts and apply them to his art form. There is no doubt he changed the direction of music.

Characteristics of this music as defined by Debussy: avoid hard outlines, deemphasize the rhythm section, use unconventional scales such as chromatic, pentatonic, and whole tone. Instrumentally, Debussy preferred strings, woodwinds, the harp, and the French horn. He used brass and percussion sparingly.

Texture: Homophonic

Forms: Prelude, Nocturne, Gigue, Ballade, Tone Poem

Composers: Claude Debussy and Maurice Ravel

Travel To: Paris and France

Note: Claude Monet started the concept of Impressionism in art with his ground breaking work, Impression, soliel levant (Impression, Sunrise) in 1872. This work was a depiction of the port of Le Havre. Often, impressionistic painters came under criticism for works that appeared unfinished or lacking in descriptive detail. Apparently, the critics did not understand that impressionism was more concerned with one's "impression" of an artistic work rather than accurate detail.

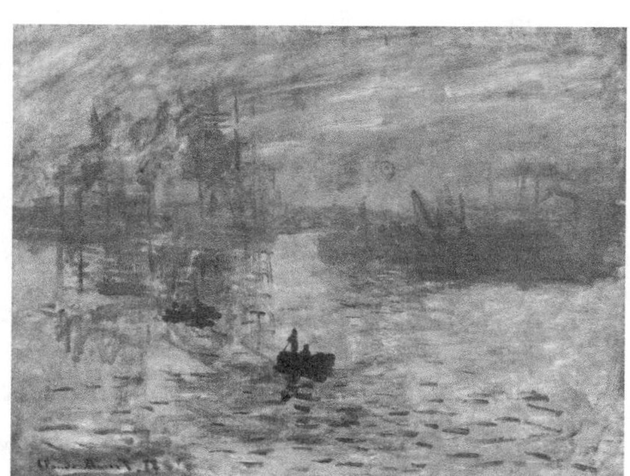

Impression, soliel levant, Claude Monet

Claude Debussy (de-byoo-see) (1862–1918)

1. Born in Saint-Germain-en-Laye, France.
2. One of the five children, he started taking piano lessons at the age of 7.

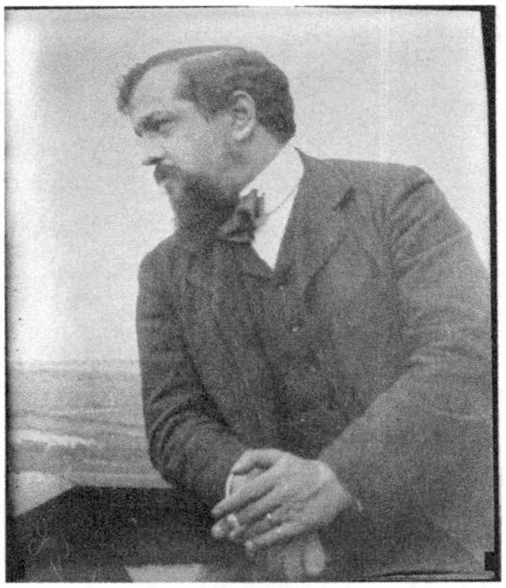

3. At the age of 10, Claude entered the Paris Conservatoire where he spent the next eleven years studying piano, harmony and theory, music history, and composition.
4. He had difficulty with some instructors as his compositions did not reflect the old style and were quite dissonant in some parts.
5. In 1884, he won the Prix de Rome and won a scholarship to Académie des Beaux-Arts. At the Académie, he once again was criticized for being unconventional.
6. After many tempestuous affairs, Debussy finally married Rosalie Texier, in 1899. Rosalie could not bear children and Claude wound up having a secret relationship with Emma Bardac, a married woman. Eventually, Debussy wrote to Rosalie from Dieppe, a coastal community in northern France, explaining their marriage was over, but never mentioned he was with Bardac. Upon hearing the news, Texier attempted suicide by shooting herself. She did survive, but the bullet remained in her for life.

Library of Congress, Prints & Photographs Division, photograph by Harris & Ewing, LC-DIG-hec-23688

7. In time, both Debussy and Bardac got divorced and in 1905, Emma was pregnant and gave birth to their only child, a daughter, Claud-Emma. The couple finally married in 1908.
8. Tragedy struck the Debussy household in 1909, as Claude was diagnosed with cancer. For the next nine years he had many treatments and operations. He finally passed in 1918. Not even a year later, his daughter passed from diphtheria, in 1919.
9. Some of his most important compositions are:

   Orchestral: Trois Scènes au crepuscule (1892–1893), Prelude to the Afternoon of a faun (1894), Nocturnes: Nuages (Clouds), Fêtes (Festivals), Siren (Sirens) (1897–1899), Le roi Lear (1904), La Mer (1903–1905), Images; Gigues (1902–1905), Ibéria (1905–1908), Ronde de Printemps (1905–1909)

   Ballet: Khamma (1911–1912), Jeux (1912–1913)

   Opera: Pelléas et Mélisande (1893–1902)

   Chamber Music: Piano trio in G Major (1879), String Quartet in G minor (1893), Syrinx (a nymph) for Flute (1913), Sonata for cello (1915), Sonata for Flute, Viola and Harp (1915), Sonata for Violin and Piano (1916–1917)

   Piano Music: Reverie (1890), Clair de Lune (1905), Estampes (1903), Children's corner (1906–1908), Préludes, Book 1 (1909–1910), Préludes, Book 2 (1912–1913), Études (1915)

   Choral Music: La Demoiselle élue (The Chosen Maid, 1888). Also, many songs for voice and piano.

As previously mentioned, Debussy preferred to use unconventional scales. I will explain the three scales he frequently used and show how they are constructed.

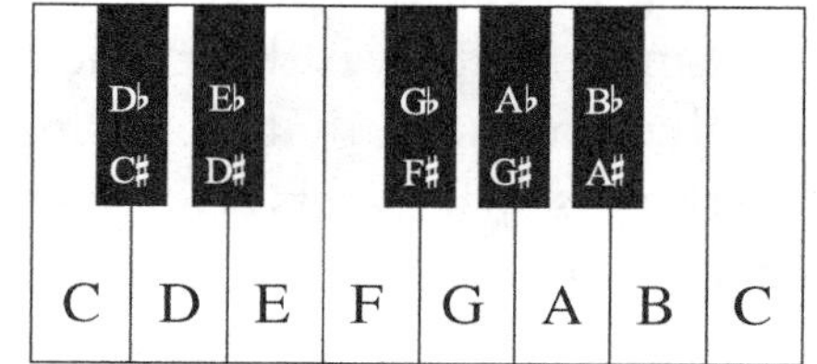

Chromatic Scale: The chromatic scale is made up of all half-steps. This basically means you do not skip over any notes. Remember ascending, C-C♯-D-D♯-E-F-F♯-G-G♯-A-A♯-B-C. Remember descending, C-B-Bb-A-Ab-G-Gb-F-E-Eb-D-Db-C.

Pentatonic Scale: The pentatonic scale has five different notes. The whole step pattern is, one whole, one whole, one whole plus a half, one whole. So reading from left to right the notes are C, D, E, G, A, and octave C.

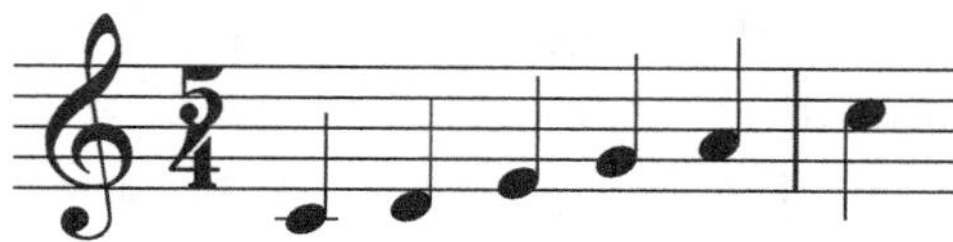

Whole Tone Scale: This scale is also unique as it is made up of all whole steps. Reading from left to right the notes are C-D-E-F♯-G♯-A♯-C.

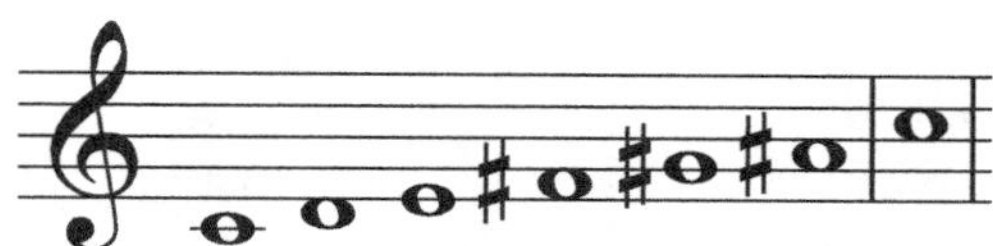

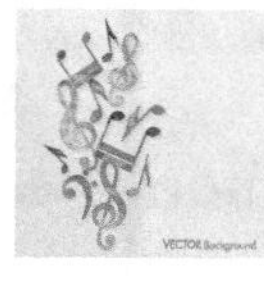

Listening Box 55

Type in Debussy Piano Music and under Album Results choose Clair de Lune, Reverie—Debussy: Select Track 1, Clair de Lune. Then select Track 2, Reverie. These are both good examples of impressionistic piano music.

Next Listening: Type in Prelude to the Afternoon of a Faun. Choose top box with the same name. Select Track 1.

Synopsis of Prelude to the Afternoon of a Faun

Debussy was inspired by a poem written by Stéphan Mallarmé in 1876. The poem is about a mythical half-man, half-animal forest creature. The creature awakens from a dream of lovely nymphs and seems to be confused and disoriented. He is feeling the warmth of the afternoon and he decides to go back to sleep. Musically, Debussy opens and closes the piece with a flute playing a chromatic melody. Throughout the piece there are sprays of orchestral color. Notice the lack of a solid steady rhythm which gives the music a floating feeling. I am firmly convinced that this constant lack of a steady rhythm is what sets Debussy's music apart from other composers.

Debussy house in Saint Germain en Laye

Maurice Ravel (1875–1937)

1. Born in Ciboure, France.
2. Ravel's interest in music was cultivated by his father who was an engineer and not a musician.
3. Maurice began piano lessons at the age of 7 and started studying composition, harmony, and counterpoint at the age of 12.
4. In 1889, while not considered to be a great pianist, he started giving public concerts. In the same year, he entered the Paris Conservatoire and two years later, won the school's piano competition.
5. At the Conservatoire, Ravel was considered a musical outcast and was expelled, in 1895. He was readmitted in 1897 and studied composition with Gabriel Fauré, only to be expelled again in 1900.
6. During the early 1900s, Ravel became friendly with Claude Debussy and Igor Stravinsky. Over the years, his relationship with Debussy dissolved as there were factions on both sides trying to claim which composer was better.
7. Maurice's personal life is covered in secret. He never married and it was said that he frequented brothels, as he never felt comfortable with women. Because of these feelings toward women, some thought he might be homosexual.
8. In 1915, Ravel joins the French Army as an ambulance driver, at the age of 40. He was eventually offered the Legion of Honor award in 1920, but declined the offer.
9. In 1917, with the passing of his mother and the extreme suffering of the French people during the war, Ravel suffered deep depression, which drastically slowed down his composition production.
10. In the 1920s, he toured many countries and his fee was a minimum $10,000 and a good supply of his favorite cigarettes.
11. In 1932, he received a head injury from a car accident and by 1937 he was still suffering from that injury.

12. In 1937, Ravel underwent neurosurgery and showed some improvement, but this was short-lived. He eventually passed in December, 1937, and was buried next to his parents.
13. Some of his most important compositions are:

    Orchestral: Alborada del gracioso (1905), Rhapsodie espagnole(1908), La Valse (1920), Bolero (1928), Piano Concerto in D Major for left hand (1930), Piano Concert in G Major (1931)

    Operas: The Child and the Spells (1925), L' Heure espagnole (1909)

    Songs: Shéhérazade with Orch (1903), Histoires Naturelles (1906), Chants Populaires (1910)

    Ballet: Mother Goose (1912), Daphnis et Chloé (1912)

    Chamber Music: String Quartet (1903), Trio for Violin, Cello and Piano (1914)

    Piano Music: Pavane for a Dead Princess (1899), Jeux d'eau (1901), Sonatine (1905), Miroirs (1905), Valses nobles et sentimentales (1911), Le tombeau de Couperin (1917).

Le Belvèdère in Montfort—l' Amaury, Ravel's last residence

Boléro (1928)

Bolero was commissioned by Russian actress and dancer, Ida Rubinstein. Ravel's concept was to constantly repeat the melody without developing it. He combines this idea with gradually increasing the volume of the orchestra. The blueprint of this piece is as follows: (1) There are two main melodies A&B. (2) The piece is written in triple meter, ¾. (3) The composer starts with individual instruments over rhythm, then goes to full sections over rhythm. (4) The piece in sound is one big crescendo. (5) At the end of the piece, the composer changes scale from C to E, which gives the piece a lift.

Note: This piece is not really an Impressionistic piece, but I selected it as it is Ravel's most famous work.

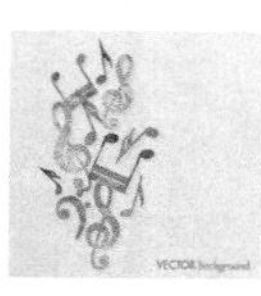

Listening Box 56

Type in Bolero Ravel and under Track Results choose Bolero, Hamburg Symphony Orchestra. Select Track 1.

Summary of Unit 3, Chapter 8 Terms and Study Sheet

Terms

Prelude: A prelude is a short instrumental piece that is often used as an introduction to a larger work. It can also be a piece that stands on its own.

Gigue: A gigue is a Baroque dance, usually in a fast tempo.

Ballade: Previously explained in Chapter 5.

Nocturne: Previously explained in Chapter 5.

Tone Poem: Previously explained in Chapter 7.

Composers: Claude Debussy and Maurice Ravel.

Summary of Listeners Toolbox

Impressionism in music is quite different than many other types of music. It is designed to appeal to your senses and conjure up your imagination. This music allows for the listener to put themselves and their ideas into a musical piece. In most cases, the very essence of a lack of solid symmetrical rhythms causes some confusion and unrest while listening. You may be right or wrong, but the main idea is to jump in and get your feet wet.

Questions

Have you heard Impressionistic types of music before in a modern setting? Where do you think would be the most likely settings for Impressionism in today's world? Do you think young people are culturally literate enough to deal with Impressionism? Since Impressionism started out as an artistic idea, do you think the composers did just as good a job as the painters?

To The Student: The instructor may add or delete study items at his or her discretion.

Unit 3, Chapter 8 Listening Box Playlist

LB55: Type in Debussy Piano Music and under Album Results, choose Clair de Lune, Reverie—Debussy: select Track 1, Clair de Lune. Then select Track 2, Reverie. These are both good examples of Impressionistic piano music.

Next listening: Type in Prelude to the Afternoon of a Faun. Choose top box with the same name. Select Track 1.

LB56: Type in Bolero Ravel and under Track Results choose Bolero, Hamburg Symphony Orchestra. Select Track 1.

CHAPTER 9 TWENTIETH CENTURY—IGOR STRAVINSKY (1882—1971)

For information on music of the twentieth century, I have chosen a different format and just one composer, Igor Stravinsky. It is his style of composition and his use of various compositional techniques that makes him the foremost composer of this period and a trendsetter.

Compositional Techniques Used by Stravinsky and Their Meanings

Polytonality: Polytonality occurs when you have two scales or keys sounding at the same time.

Polyrhythms: Polyrhythms occur when you have two different rhythms sounding at the same time. This is a technique Stravinsky learned from the early African tribal rhythms.

Polychords: Polychords occur when you have two different chords sounding at the same time. For example, an F sharp chord against a C chord.

Polymeters: Polymeters occur when you have two different meters sounding together. For example, triple meter against quadruple meter.

Ostinato: Ostinati (plural) are recurring melodic and rhythmic ideas.

Note: One of Stravinsky's most notable compositional innovations is his use of unpredictable rhythmic patterns and accents. These techniques create a drive and excitement to his music and caused him great consternation as they were not always graciously accepted by musicians and the general public.

Stravinsky Conducting, 1965

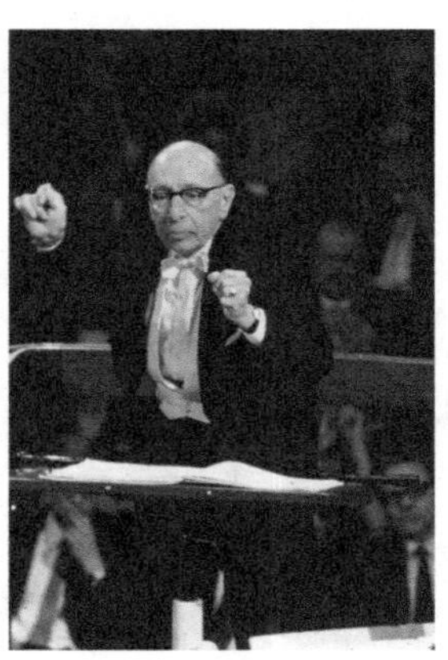

1. Born in Oranienbaum, Russia, but was brought up in St. Petersburg.
2. In his early years he studied piano and music theory, but his parents wanted him to study law.
3. In 1901, he enters the University of St. Petersburg to study law, but attended very few classes.
4. In 1902, Stravinsky goes to stay with Rimsky-Korsakov, the noted Russian composer, and Korsakov convinced

Igor to study composition privately rather than at the Conservatoire. He studied composition with Korsakov until Korsakov's death in 1908.

5. In 1906, he married Yekaterina Nosenko (Katya), a childhood sweetheart and second cousin. Their first two children were Fyodor (1907), a son, and Ludmila (1908), a daughter.
6. In 1908, at the first performance of his composition, The Firebird, was a distant cousin Sergei Diaghilev. Diaghilev, an opera and ballet impresario was himself planning to present Russian opera and ballet in Paris, at the Ballets Russes. He commissioned Stravinsky to write a full length ballet of The Firebird.
7. In 1910, The Firebird premiered with great success and this launched Stravinsky's career. In 1911, he wrote Petrushka and in 1913, he wrote Le Sacre du printemps (The Rite of Spring), also ballets.
8. With the breakout of World War I, Stravinsky moved to Switzerland. Here, a second son Sviatoslav was born. In 1914, a second daughter, Maria Milena was born in Lausanne.
9. The years between 1915 and 1920 were very lean for Stravinsky due to the war and the Russian Revolution. Igor turned to Swiss philanthropist Werner Reinhart for financial help. The two men established a very close relationship as Werner loved Stravinsky's music and he continued to subsidize the composer on several projects.
10. In 1921, Paris, Igor met Vera de Bosset and they started an affair even though both were married. Stravinsky led a double life until his wife died in 1939.
11. The years 1938 and 1939 were hard for Stravinsky as his wife, eldest daughter, and mother all passed.
12. World War II broke out in 1939 and Stravinsky came to the US alone to fulfill a commitment with Harvard University. Vera eventually joined him and they married in 1940.
13. Stravinsky settled in California, made many artistic friends, and became a US citizen in 1945.
14. In 1959, he received Denmark's highest musical honor, The Sonning Award. In 1969, he moved to the Essex House, in New York City, his final residence. He passed in 1971, at the age of 88 of heart failure.
15. Some of his most important compositions are:

    Ballets: Firebird (1910), Petrushka (1911), The Rite of Spring (1913), Pulcinella (1920), The Wedding (1923), Appolo Musagetes (1928), The Fairy's Kiss (1928), The Card Party (1937), Orpheus (1947), Agon (1957)

    Musical-theater: The Soldier's Tale (1918)

    Operas: Oedipus Rex (1927), The Rake's Progress (1951)

    Orchestral: Symphonies of Wind Instruments (1920), Violin Concerto (1931), Dumbarton Oaks Concerto (1938), Symphony in C (1940), Symphony in Three Movements (1945), Ebony Concerto for Clarinet (1945), Concerto for Strings (1946)

Choral Music: Symphony of Psalms (1930), Mass (1948), Cantata (1952), Threni (1958), A Sermon, a Narrative, and a Prayer (1961), Requiem Canticles (1966)

Piano Music: Sonata (1924), Concerto (1925), Sonata for 2 Pianos (1944)

Vocal Music: Pribaoutki (1914), Abraham and Isaac (1963).

History of the Rite of Spring

The Rite of Spring is a ballet written by Igor Stravinsky in 1913. It was written in two sections, The Adoration of the Earth and The Sacrifice. At its premiere in Paris, the audience was totally shocked by the music and choreography and they started a riot. People were screaming to stop the performance, some people who were protesting got slapped on the face and some others tore out the theater seats. Eventually, the riot spilled onto the Paris streets and about forty people were arrested. Stravinsky was in the audience and was so angry that he got up from his seat and left the building. As he was leaving, he turned to the audience and told them to "go to hell."

The Rite of Spring, Igor Stravinsky, "Sacrificial Dance" From Part II: The Sacrifice

Synopsis of the Sacrifice

A Sage and young women are standing around a fire near the sacred mound. One girl will be chosen and sacrificed to ensure the earth's fertility. As the girls dance in circles, one is left standing. At this point, she realizes she is the "chosen one." Honoring the chosen one, all dance vigorously into a frenzied climax. Finally, the chosen one dances feverishly until she collapses and dies. The men carry her body to the sacred mound as an offering to the gods of fertility.

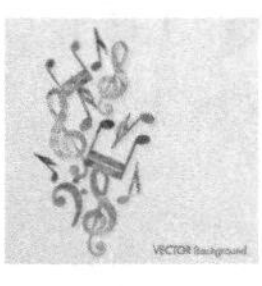

Listening Box 57

Type in Sacrificial Dance and choose top box, Sacrificial Dance (Chosen One). Selection is Track 29.

Note to Listeners: This piece is highly rhythmic and contains a great amount of ostinati. It is probably going to sound very modern to you as Stravinsky seems to use the entire orchestra as one percussion instrument. There is no doubt you have heard this style of music in the movies.

Summary of Unit 3, Chapter 9 Terms and Study Sheet

Terms

All of the following terms were explained at the beginning of the chapter.

Polytonality

Polyrhythms

Polychords

Polymeters

Ostinato

Composer: Igor Stravinsky

Summary of Listeners Toolbox

As previously stated, Stravinsky's music is highly rhythmic with unpredictable accents. Often it seems that he uses the orchestra as one big percussion instrument. The tricks to listening to his music are to hear these rhythms and accents plus all of the "poly" terms I have listed earlier. Better understanding will come with listening to his music multiple times.

Questions

After listening to the Sacrificial Dance, do you think the audience was justified in protesting? Do you think modern composers have copied Stravinsky's style, especially in movies? As the general public thought his music was dissonant and unacceptable, do you feel modern day audiences would find his music less offensive?

To The Student: The instructor may add or delete study items at his or her discretion.

Unit 3, Chapter 9 Listening Box Playlist

LB57: Type in Sacrificial Dance and choose top box, Sacrificial Dance (Chosen One). Selection is Track 29.

UNIT 4

Jazz

Unit Purpose

Understanding Jazz from the late 1600s to the present.

CHAPTER 1 JAZZ ORIGINS AND NEW ORLEANS

What Do We Find in This Period?

Music: Jazz was created in America by the descendants of the slaves who were brought here from West Africa in the 1600s and 1700s. Traders realized that music could help ease the trip of the captives and demanded their agents select some musicians from the tribes that were raided. As time passed in America, music became a mainstay in the lives of the slaves and many of the elements they used were passed down through generations. These elements become very important in the overall development of mainstream American music. It is amazing, but understandable, that these slaves were unaware that their culture and music traditions would help create the one truly American art form, Jazz.

Texture: Texture includes such elements as polyrhythms, call and response, syncopation, improvisation and riff, among other things.

Forms: Early forms included, but were not limited to, ragtime, the cakewalk, Dixieland and the blues. Later forms included, but were not limited to, swing, be-bop, fusion and free style.

Composers: There are too many composers and artists to list here and I will highlight a few as we go along.

Travel to: West Africa and the United States.

Call and Response: African vocal music employed a great deal of call and response. The process used in call and response is when the leader sings a phrase and the group answers immediately. This type of vocal response permeates several types of music such as gospel, rock 'n' roll, and rhythm and blues.

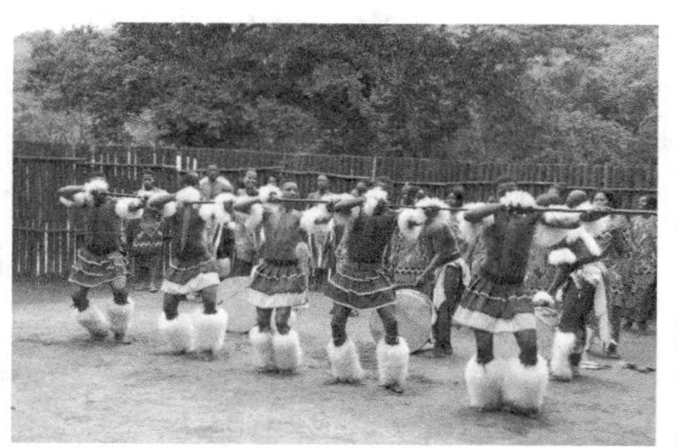

Swazi Tribal Dancers

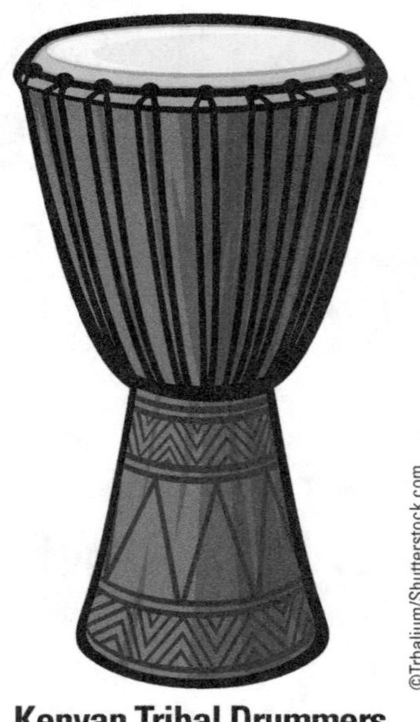

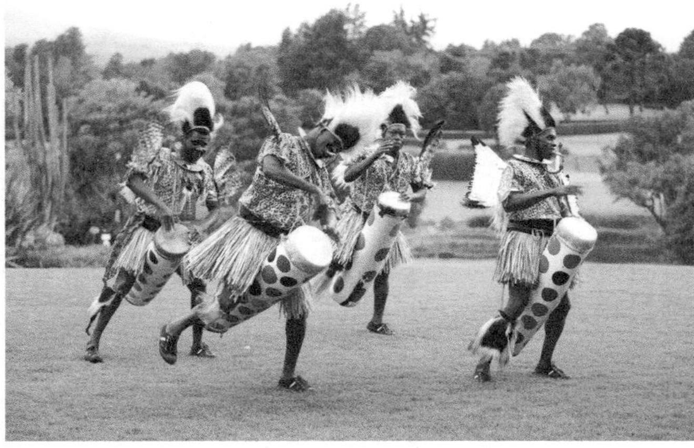

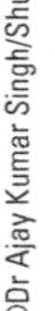

Kenyan Tribal Drummers

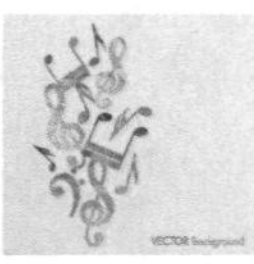

Listening Box 1

Type in Tribal Music and under Track results, choose the first selection, Tribal Music-Africa (African Drums Music). Select Track 4, Ghana-African Drums Conga Drums and Bongos. Also, select Track 9, Tribal Music-Africa. In both these selections, you will hear much repetition and several different rhythms going on at the same time.

Characteristics of Early Jazz: New Orleans

1. African drum music (previously mentioned)
2. Rhythmic work songs (plantation songs)
3. Negro spirituals (church)
4. Early Blues: probably started out as an unaccompanied moan, closely related to the work song
5. Early Ragtime: The first written pre-jazz form. This form spread throughout the country by means of piano player rolls.

Popular instruments of this period: Banjo, Trumpet, Piano, Trombone, Drums, Clarinet, Saxophone, Tuba, and Bass. **Note**: All instruments were acoustical, there were no electric instruments.

Early Jazz Pioneers: Scott Joplin (piano), Louis Armstrong (trumpet), Buddy Bolden (trumpet), Joe Oliver (trumpet). In early Jazz, the lead trumpet player in the band was given the complimentary name "King."

Early Brass Bands: The Eureka Brass Band, the Imperial Marching Band.

Early Regular Bands: Original Superior Orchestra, Original Creole Orchestra, Original Dixieland Jazz Band.

Performance Note: During the day, musicians played on riverboats. At night, they worked in café's playing Jazz. Also, since Jazz was played in bars into the early morning hours, it was considered the "Devil's" music. Besides nightclub bands there were funeral and marching bands.

Scott Joplin (1867/1868–1917)

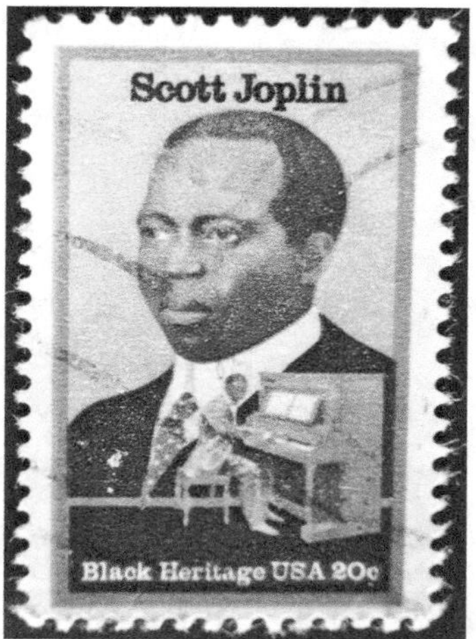

©neftali/Shutterstock.com

1. Born in Texarkana, Texas.
2. Because of his many ragtime compositions, he was known as the "King of Ragtime."
3. He was the second of six children and his parents were musical people in that his father played violin and his mother sang and played banjo. Neither parent was a professional musician.
4. Joplin played piano, guitar, violin, mandolin, banjo, cornet, and he also sang. He received most of his piano training from a private teacher who knew he was poor and did not charge him for the lessons.
5. Scott worked as a laborer with the railroad, but eventually gave that up to become a full time musician.
6. In 1893, he goes to the Chicago World's Fair and he performs with his own band.
7. In 1894, he moves to Sedalia, Missouri, and earns a living as a teacher of piano and composition.
8. By 1897, his style of music, ragtime, had become very popular with the general public.
9. His personal life was not great as he was married several times. His daughter from the first marriage only lived a few months. In 1904, his second wife dies ten months after the wedding. In 1909, he marries for the third time in New York City.
10. Joplin had moved to New York as he thought this would be the best city to get his opera Treemonisha, published. He could find no financial backers for this work and decided to put his own money into the project. He put on a small production of the opera and invited potential backers. The work was not favorably met and these potential backers walked out of the performance. This reaction caused great depression and he eventually had a breakdown.
11. Somewhere along the line he gets the disease syphilis which causes dementia and insanity. In 1917, he is put into the Manhattan State Hospital. He dies there at age 49 and is buried in a pauper's grave without a marker. It is not until 1974, that

his grave is properly marked at his burial site at Saint Michael's Cemetery in East Elmhurst, Queens, New York.

12. Some of his most important compositions are: Maple Leaf Rag (1899), The Entertainer (1902), The Strenuous Life (1902), Gladiolus Rag (1907), Sugarcane Rag (1908, Wall Street Rag (1909). **Opera:** Treemonisha.

Ragtime Note: Ragtime is syncopated music written mostly for piano. It's most important characteristic is its "ragged" rhythm.

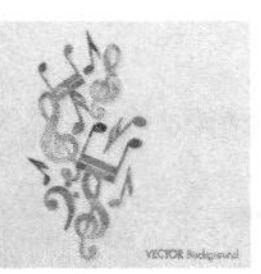

Listening Box 2

Type in Scott Joplin and under Album Results choose Scott Joplin Ragtime Piano (Amy Isla). Select Track 1, The Entertainer (used in the movie, "The Sting," in 1973). Also, Track 4, Maple Leaf Rag. These listening are great examples of stride piano.

Social Functions: The Cakewalk

At social functions slave couples often did a dance called the cakewalk. This dance goes back to the late 1800s and was primarily danced to on plantations in Southern states. One of the interesting innovations used by the couples was a high-kicking movement which was supposed to reflect the pomposity of the plantation owner. To add difficulty and interest to the high step, the couples would put buckets of water on their heads. The couple who spilled the least amount of water would win the prize which was a cake. As the dance became more popular, it was performed in Minstrel shows exclusively by men. Eventually, women were added to the shows and that made many step innovations possible. In time, the cakewalk became very popular throughout the country.

Gospel Music

A Christian music praising God and Jesus. Other topics are mostly life issues.

Outline

1. African American roots with Christian lyrics.
2. This genre of music can be traced back to the seventeenth century.
3. The original songs were hymns using call and response and much repetition. In performance, heavy vocals and harmony were used as well as hand clapping and foot stomping for rhythm.
4. Originally, Gospel was sung a cappella as choruses were added much later.
5. Music recording increased Gospel's audiences and by the mid-to-late 1940s, Gospel was going mainstream with public concerts.

6. Some categories of Gospel are: Southern Gospel, Gospel Blues, Progressive Southern Gospel (newer) and Christian Country Music.

Note 1: It is important to note that as Gospel progresses, more jazz elements were added to the music. This is interesting in that as previously stated, jazz was considered the "devils" music.

Note 2: In order to give you a more up to date sound, I have chosen Kirk Franklin for the listening examples.

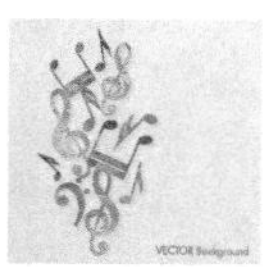

Listening Box 3

Type in Kirk Franklin and under Artist Results choose Kirk Franklin Christian R&B. Select Track 13, Brighter Day. Also, select Track 27, Before I Die.

The Blues

A style of music that is based on a certain scale, a certain chord progression and improvisation.

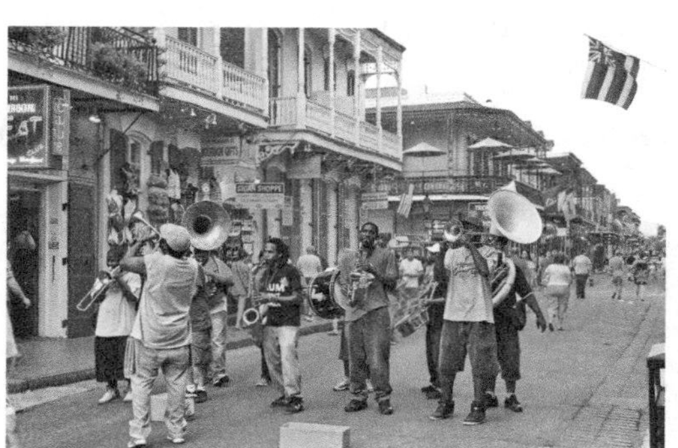

New Orleans

Outline

1. Blues can be traced back to the late nineteenth century and its first appearance was probably after the emancipation of slavery.
2. Musical elements that contributed to the blues genre were Negro Spirituals, Work Songs, Plantation Songs, and European Folk Music.
3. Blues music represents a down trodden way of life with seemingly little hope for recovery. When someone is not feeling well, you might have heard them say they are feeling "blue." or I'm feeling "blue" today.
4. Musical structure revolves around a scale (the blues scale) which has a lowered third note, lowered fifth note, and a lowered seventh note. Also included is a twelve-bar (measures) blues chord progression.
5. Improvisation is a key element of performance. The performer creates something new based on the melody, the scale, and the chordal harmony.

Example of a Major Scale: C-D-E-F-G-A-B-C

Example of a Blues Scale: C-D-Eb-F-Gb-A-Bb-C. Notice that in the blues scale the third note E is lowered to Eb, the fifth note G is lowered to Gb, and the seventh note B is lowered to Bb as compared to the major scale.

Example of Blues Harmony: Chords take the number of the scale note. For example, in the aforementioned major scale, C is the first note so the chord above this note is called a one chord. The note F is the fourth note of the scale and the chord above this note is called a four chord. Reading from left to right, a typical twelve-bar blues progression would look like this: I – I – I – I7 – IV7 – IV7 – I – I – V7 – V7 – I – I

Some Famous Blues Musicians

W.C. Handy (1873–1958): Known as the "Father of the Blues." Some of his famous compositions are: Memphis Blues (1912), St. Louis Blues (1914), and Beale Street Blues (1913).

Ma Rainey (1886–1939): (Real name Gertrude Pridgett), had a very strong voice and was known as "The Mother of the Blues." Some of her most popular recordings are: Bo-weevil Blues and Moonshine Blues (1923), See… See Rider Blues (1924), Black Bottom (1927) and Soon This Morning (1927).

Bessie Smith (1894–1937): Known as, "The Empress of the Blues," some of her famous recordings are: Gulf Coast Blues and Downhearted Blues (1923) and After You've Gone (1927).

Louis Armstrong (1901–1971): Known for his trumpet playing and being a pioneer of scat singing.

B.B. King (1925–2015): Known for being one of the greatest blues guitar players in music history. It is unbelievable, but he did not read music.

Louis "Satchmo" Armstrong (1901–1971) and "B.B." King (1925–2015)

I wanted to present Louis Armstrong and "B.B." King in a different way. Rather than give an outline of each musician's life, I am choosing to list several musical examples which I feel represent some of their work. It is my hope, these examples will stimulate class discussion and further research into the lives of these two incredible musicians.

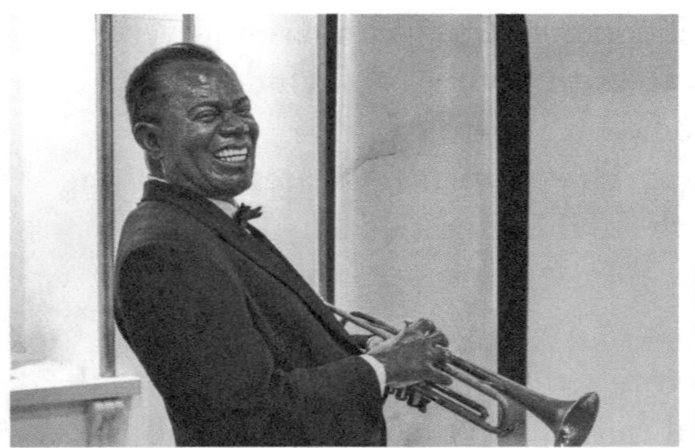

Wax Portrait of Louis Armstrong

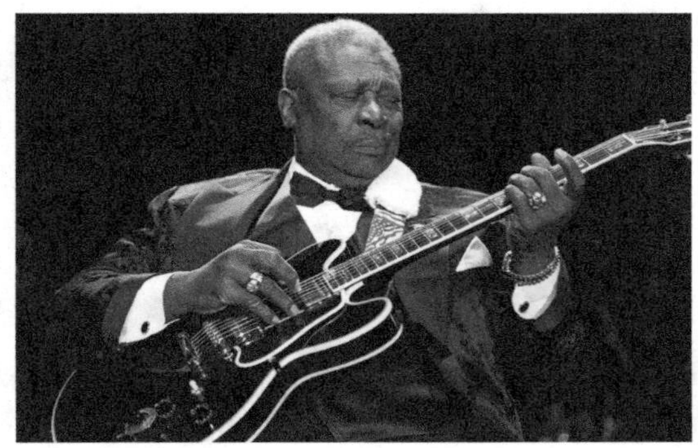

Riley "B.B." King

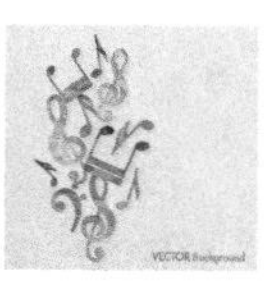

Listening Box 4

Type in St. Louis Blues and under Track Results choose St. Louis Blues, Louis Armstrong. Select Track 1, St. Louis Blues.

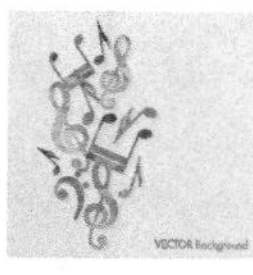

Listening Box 5

Type in B.B. King and under Album Results choose B.B. King Greatest Hits. Select Track 2, Every Day I Have the Blues. Select Track 8, Why I Sing the Blues. Select Track 19, B.B. Boogie.

Summary of Unit 4, Chapter 1 Terms and Study Sheet

Terms

Blues: A style of music, which has a specific scale and chord pattern and often uses improvisation in performance. Song subjects usually speak about a hard life.

Cakewalk: A high-kicking dance done by slave couples at social functions.

Call and Response: Is when a leader at a musical or religious function makes a vocal statement and the group immediately responds.

Gospel: Vocal music which has a positive message or effect.

Improvisation: The art of musically creating something extemporaneously without previous preparation.

Riff: A riff is a jazz ostinato which employs a recurring melodic and rhythmic pattern.

Ragtime: Is syncopated music written mostly for piano. Its most important characteristic is the "ragged" rhythm.

Composers and Musicians: Scott Joplin, W.C. Handy, Louis Armstrong, B.B. King. Ma Rainey and Bessie Smith.

Summary of Listeners Toolbox

Listening to Ragtime, Gospel, and Blues presents the listener with many challenges. Some key aspects of listening to these styles are the melody, the rhythm, the harmony and improvisation. As you listen, you may need to ask the instructor to clarify some issues.

To The Student: The instructor may add or delete study items at his or her discretion.

Unit 4, Chapter 1 Listening Box Playlist

LB1: Type in Tribal Music and under Track Results choose first selection, Tribal Music-Africa (African Drum Music). Select Track 4, Ghana-African Drums Conga Drums and Bongos. Also, select Track 9, Tribal Music-Africa.

LB2: Type in Scott Joplin and under Album Results choose Scott Joplin Ragtime Piano (Amy Isla). Select Track 1, the Entertainer (used in the movie "The Sting," in 1973). Also, Track 4, Maple Leaf Rag.

LB3: Type in Kirk Franklin and under Artist Results choose Kirk Franklin Christian R&B. Select Track 13, Brighter Day and Track 27, Before I Die.

LB4: Type in St. Louis Blues and under Track Results choose St. Louis Blues, Louis Armstrong. Select Track 6, St Louis Blues. 2

LB5: Type B.B. King and under Album Results choose B.B. King Greatest Hits. Select Track 2, Every Day I Have The Blues, Track 8, Why I Sing The Blues and Track 19 B.B. King Boogie.

CHAPTER 2 CHICAGO, THE GOLDEN AGE OF JAZZ, 1920s

What Do We Find in This Period?

Music: Chicago was the capitol city of Jazz during the period that followed World War I. This period is often referred to as, "The Jazz Age." As Jazz grew in the United States, it basically formed the letter T as it went from New Orleans, to Chicago, to Los Angeles, and to New York. There were two major changes in Jazz as it reached Chicago: (1) Marching bands were virtually eliminated as Chicago was a big and busy city. (2) Show business enters the Jazz world as it is now being played in theatrical settings such as on stage, ballrooms and amusement parks. Another big boost for Jazz is the beginning of the recording industry.

Texture: Improvisation

Forms: Stride piano, blues, and ragtime (discussed in Chapter 1)

Composers and Musicians: Jelly Roll Morton (piano), Johnny Dodds (clarinet), Earl Hines (piano), Ma Rainey (singer), Bessie Smith (singer), W.C. Handy (piano and blues composer), Blind Lemon Jefferson (guitar and blues singer), Bix Beiderbecke (trumpet), Thomas "Fats" Waller (piano), and Art Tatum (piano).

Travel to: Chicago, USA

The Recording Industry

A big advancement in music was the emergence of the recording industry in the 1920s. Some of the early labels were: Paramount, Perfect, Vocalion, Brunswick, Columbia, and Victor (British).

Notes on the Recording Process

1. Early recordings were made haphazardly by small companies.
2. Beginning recordings were made in warehouses.

3. In a recording studio of the 1920s, the acoustical horn was put in the center of the room and served as a giant ear into which musical sounds were directed. The players lined up at the most suitable angle and hoped for the best.
4. By the late 1920s, the improved electrical process came into full use.

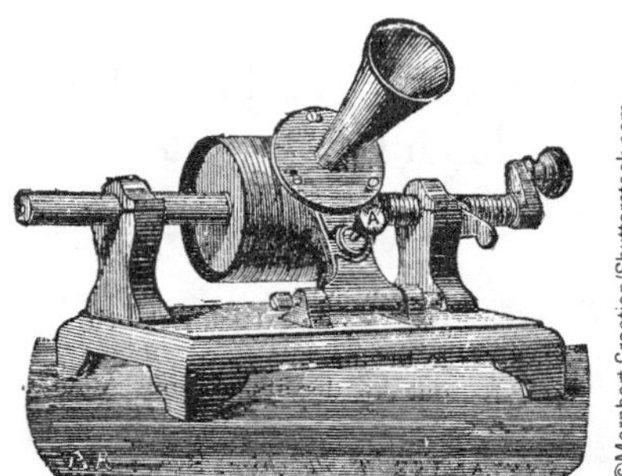

©Morphart Creation/Shutterstock.com

Edison's Original Phonograph

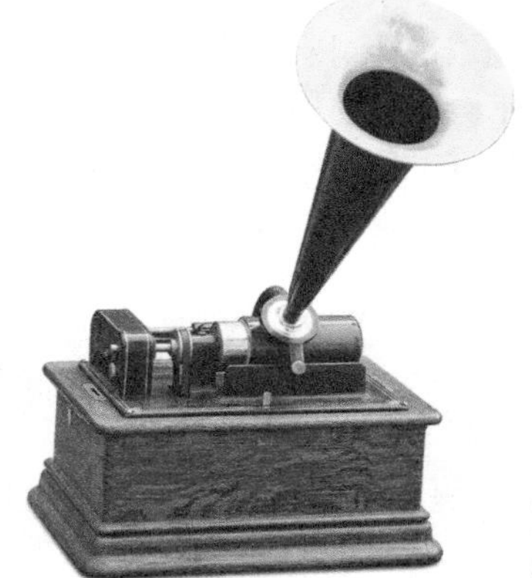

©Dja65/Shutterstock.com

Edison's more advanced machine

The Jukebox

As recordings improved, there was a need for getting music out to the general public on a larger scale. Enter the jukebox, in the 1930s, where people could put in a coin or two and hear their favorite song or artist. The Wurlitzer Company was a groundbreaker in supplying the jukebox.

Note: These machines are getting to be extinct as individuals now get their music on iPods, cell phones, and other devices.

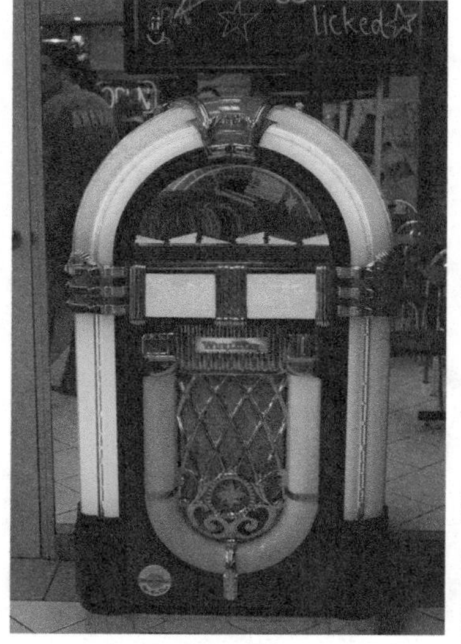

©Joe Kucharski/Shutterstock.com

The Wurlitzer Jukebox

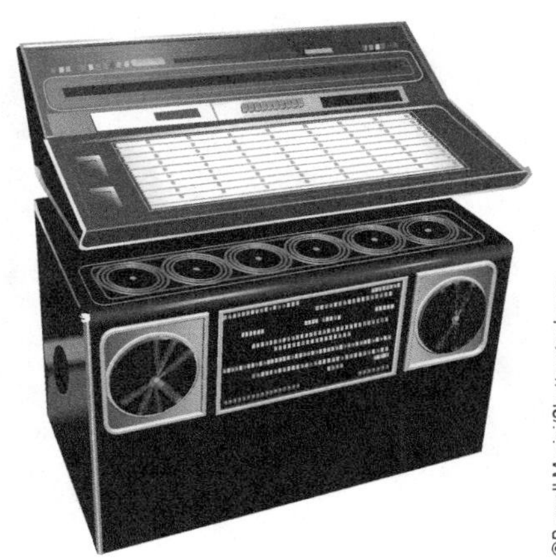

©Russell Marini/Shutterstock.com

A more modern version

Stride Piano

The term stride piano describes a certain technique used when playing the instrument. Originally called Harlem Stride Piano, it pretty much developed in larger cities during the 1920s and 1930s. The characteristic feature of playing this style is to get the left hand moving. The player generally plays a single note or an octave on the first beat and a chord on the second beat. This process is repeated on the third and fourth beats. Layered over the rhythm are the melody and improvisations. This music is generally busy sounding with a bright feel.

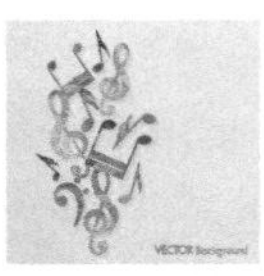

Listening Box 6

Type in stride piano and under Album Results select Stride Piano ... & More, Jon Brosseau. Select Track 1, Darktown Strutter's Ball. Also, select Track 2, Muskrat Ramble.

Note: Anyone of these tracks are good examples of stride piano playing.

Summary of Unit 4, Chapter 2 Terms and Study Sheet

Terms

Stride Piano: Stride piano is essentially a style and technique of piano playing.

Edison Phonographs

Wurlitzer Juke Boxes

Composers and Musicians: Listed on the first page of this chapter.

Summary of Listeners Toolbox

The main essence of this chapter is stride piano playing. As previously stated, special attention should be paid to the movement of the left hand.

Questions

What is your opinion of stride piano playing? Does the style sound very old to you? Do you like it enough to listen further?

To The Student: The instructor may add or delete study items at his or her discretion.

Unit 4, Chapter 2 Listening Box Playlist

LB6: Type in Stride Piano and under Album Results choose Stride Piano .... & More, Jon Brosseau. Select Track 1, Darktown Strutters Ball and Track 2, Muskrat Ramble.

CHAPTER 3 THE YEARS WHEN SWING WAS KING (THE BIG BAND)

What Do We Find in This Period?

Music: The 1930s was a very exciting time for Jazz as we have the emergence of the big band. The time period was actually called, "The Swing Era." What actually caused the big band development was a need to fill the larger dance halls. Since one trumpet, saxophone, or trombone were not enough to get a big sound, we get the beginning of sections. There were two very important developments in this era that got Jazz music to the general public. They were the advancement of the recording industry and the growth of network broadcasting (radio).

Texture: Homophonic

Forms: Big Band Jazz

Composers and Musicians

For this category, I will supply a list of the most famous band leaders of the 1930s and 1940s.

1. Duke Ellington
2. Benny Goodman
3. Fletcher Henderson
4. Tommy Dorsey
5. Glenn Miller
6. Artie Shaw
7. Lionel Hampton
8. Gene Krupa
9. Harry James
10. Count Basie
11. Woody Herman
12. Chick Webb
13. John 'Dizzy' Gillespie
14. Cab Calloway

Note: I would also like to cite two very important female vocalists, Billie Holiday and Ella Fitzgerald.

Travel to: Several states within the United States

Important General Information for This Era

1. In this era, black and white musicians began to integrate. The Jimmy Lunceford Band was the first integrated Jazz band.
2. New York City had many Jazz clubs and became very important to Jazz musicians as they tried to advance their careers.
3. 52nd Street in New York City became known as, "Swing Street."
4. Harlem, became the main focal point of New York Jazz. The famous Apollo Theater is in Harlem.
5. The electric guitar started to become popular in Jazz. Some early electric guitar players were: Charlie Christian, George Barnes, Eldon Shamblin, and Leonard Ware. Although Charlie Christian was not the first electric guitar player, he is given credit for paving the way for the electric guitar sound.

The Four Sections of a Big Band

1. Saxophones (5)
2. Trumpets (4)
3. Trombones (4)
4. Rhythm Section: Piano, Bass, Drums, and Guitar

It is interesting to note that in early Jazz bands there was no bass or guitar. Those parts were played by the tuba, which was replaced by the bass and the banjo, which was replaced by the guitar.

Glen Miller (1904–1944)

I have chosen Glen Miller and his music to represent the entire Swing Era of big band music. Needless to say, this is not done with disrespect to the other band leaders, but more of a representative sound of the times. Also, Miller was the best-selling recording artist from 1939 to 1943.

1. He was born in Clarinda, Iowa.
2. As a child he played mandolin, but switched to horn.
3. In 1923, he resigned from the Boyd Senter Orchestra and entered college. He dropped out of the University of Colorado after one year to pursue a career in music.
4. His overall skill set was in several categories. He was a trombonist, an arranger and composer and eventually a bandleader.

5. In 1939, he scored big with his performances at the Glen Island Casino in New York. The shows were broadcast over the radio which gave the band greater exposure and a larger listening audience.
6. In the early 1940s, Miller made several movies, but in 1942, he put all that aside and joined the Army. He was too old for combat and was transferred to the Army Air Force where he becomes leader of that band.
7. Tragedy strikes in 1944. He was stationed in England and got word the band was to do concerts in Paris, France. On December 15, 1944, he boards a transport plane headed for France to make arrangements for the band. Unfortunately, the plane gets lost over the English Channel and was never found. Miller left behind a wife and two children.
8. In 1954, a movie of his life was made and starred, Jimmy Stewart.
9. Some of his greatest hits are: In The Mood, Moonlight Serenade, A String of Pearls, American Patrol, Little Brown Jug, Sunrise Serenade, Stardust, Tuxedo Junction, Pennsylvania 6-5000, and many more.

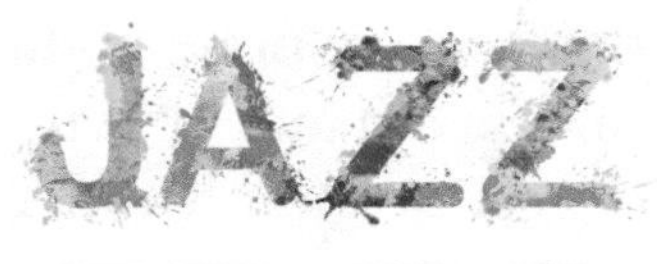

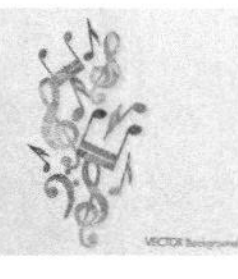

Listening Box 7

Type in Glen Miller and under Album Results choose Original Hits: Glen Miller. Select Disc 1, Track 20, American Patrol. Also, Disc 2, Track 13, In The Mood.

Ella Fitzgerald (1917–1996)

A wax figure of Ella

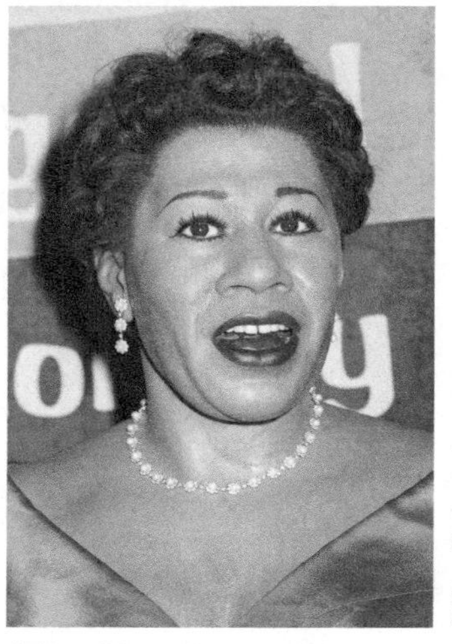

"The First Lady of Song"

1. Born in Newport News, Virginia.
2. Her parents split after she was born and her early life was a struggle.
3. She loved baseball and played in some local games. This caused her to think of herself as a tomboy. She also enjoyed singing and dancing.
4. In 1932, Ella's mother dies and she is forced to go live with her aunt. She is not happy here and is frequently absent from school. Eventually, she gets in trouble with the police and is sent to reform school.
5. In 1934, she enters an amateur night contest at the Apollo Theater in New York City and was very successful. This launches her career as she receives many offers.

6. What skyrocketed her career was a 1938 recording of a nursery rhyme, "A-Tisket, A-Tasket."
7. Her first marriage was to a dockworker, but when Ella finds out that the guy had a criminal past, she has the marriage annulled.
8. In the late 1940s, while on tour with Dizzy Gillespie, she falls in love with the bass player, Ray Brown. They marry and adopt a son, Ray Jr. In time, busy work schedules take their toll on the marriage and she divorces Brown in 1952.
9. As a person and musician, Ella was well loved and respected. In her career, which spanned six decades, she recorded over 200 albums and 2,000 songs. Internationally, she sold forty million records.
10. As her career advances, the awards start rolling in. She wins first place in the Downbeat Critic's Poll for eighteen consecutive years; she wins first place in the Playboy poll for thirteen consecutive years; the US National Medal in 1987; the Commander of Arts and Letters from France; Honorary Doctorate degrees from Dartmouth and Yale as well as other universities. If this is not enough, she also wins thirteen Grammy awards. Her final award was the Ford Freedom Award which is given to an African American whose contributions result in lasting change. This was awarded posthumously.
11. The last ten years of her life were not good health wise. In 1986, she undergoes quintuple by-pass surgery and was diagnosed with diabetes. As time passed, she suffered severe circulatory problems and ultimately, both her legs were amputated below the knees. For her last years, she spends most of the time sitting in the backyard with her son and granddaughter. She passes on June 15, 1996.
12. Some of her greatest hits are: As there are so many, I will list a few. Misty, A-Tisket, A-Tasket, Summertime, Manhattan and Someone to Watch Over Me.

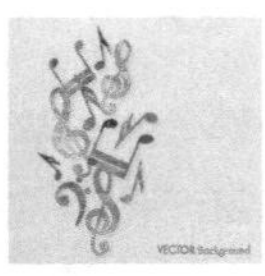

Listening Box 8

Type in Ella Fitzgerald and choose top box Artist, Ella Fitzgerald, Vocal Jazz. Select Track 12, Blue Skies.

Summary of Unit 4, Chapter 3 Terms and Study Sheet

Terms

Scat singing: An improvisational jazz vocal style of singing that uses syllables, not words.

The four sections of a big band: Saxophones, Trumpets, Trombones, and Rhythm (piano, bass, guitar, and drums).

Swing Era: In the 1930s, we have the emergence of the big band. This was called the Swing Era.

Composers and Musicians: Glen Miller and Ella Fitzgerald.

Questions

Is it possible to hear early jazz components in the Swing Era? What is your impression of scat singing? Do you enjoy hearing a big band sound?

Summary of Listeners Toolbox

The Swing Era in music presented a very lively big band style. Many people were attracted to this sound as it was also very danceable music. As you listen, see if you can relate to music that your parents and grandparents probably enjoyed.

To The Student: The instructor may add or delete study terms at his or her discretion.

Unit 4, Chapter 3 Listening Box Playlist

LB7: Type in Glen Miller and under Album Results choose Original Hits: Glen Miller. Select disc 1 Track 20, American Patrol and disc 2 Track 13, In The Mood.

LB8: Type in Ella Fitzgerald and choose top box Artist, Ella Fitzgerald, Vocal Jazz. Select Track 12, Blue Skies.

CHAPTER 4 DIFFERENT STYLES OF JAZZ AFTER WORLD WAR II

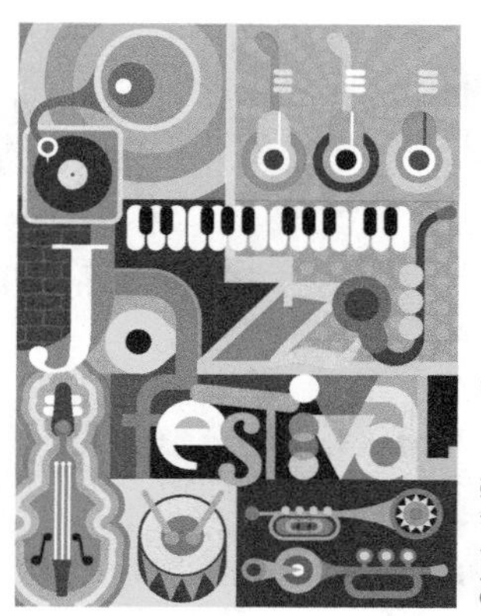

©danjazzia/Shutterstock.com

What Do We Find in This Period?

Music: From the late 1940s to the present, Jazz has undergone many changes. As referenced earlier, we have the emergence of different styles. I will give a short description of each and include listening examples.

Texture: Mainly homophonic as it exists in big band and small group arrangements.

Forms: Standard Jazz forms as well as free forms.

Composers and Musicians

I will list the important people in each category. The musicians cited will not represent a comprehensive list, but will be exemplary of the style.

Travel to: The United States

Bebop and Modern Jazz

Bebop of the 1940s and 1950s got its name from several factors. Instrumentally, it was used to describe the sound of large leaps "Be" (high) and "Bop" (low pitch). Vocally, it is related to nonsense syllables in scat singing. The term Bebop was used to describe Jazz music after World War II. As this style moved into the 1960s, it became known as Modern Jazz.

Some Popular Artists of This Style

Dizzy Gillespie (trumpet), Charlie Parker (saxophone), Stan Getz (saxophone), and Thelonious Monk (piano).

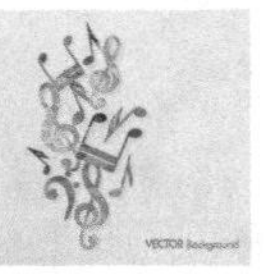

Listening Box 9

Type in Dizzy and under Artist Results choose Dizzy Gillespie, Bop. Select Track 4 Manteca; Track 8 Mas Que Nada; Track 13 Caravan and Track 24, 52nd Street Theme.

Note 1: Dizzy Gillespie was born in Cheraw, South Carolina, in 1917 and died in New Jersey, in 1993.

Note 2: 52nd Street in New York City was known as, "Swing Street."

West Coast Jazz

West Coast Jazz was also known as, "Cool Jazz" It was an alternative to the frenetic sound of Bebop. Musicians in Los Angeles created a more laid back airy sound which gave rise to its categorical name.

Some Popular Artists of This Style

Miles Davis (trumpet), Quincy Jones (trumpet), Gerry Mulligan (baritone sax), Dave Brubeck (piano), and Chet Baker (trumpet).

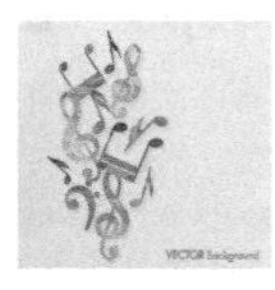

Listening Box 10

Type in Gerry Mulligan and under Artist Results choose Gerry Mulligan, Cool/West Coast Jazz. Select Track1, Walkin' Shoes and Track 8, Ornithology.

"Avant Garde" or Free Style Jazz

I call this experimental Jazz as the performers completely changed structural ground rules and tried to get away from the older sound. They employed more complex rhythms, they changed conventional scale and tonal structures by using atonal elements. They often used strange chords and many melodies had no tonal center. All these changes made it very difficult for the listener.

Some Popular Artists of This Era

John Coltrane (saxophone), Ornette Coleman (saxophone), Nat Adderly (trumpet), and "Cannonball' Adderly (saxophone).

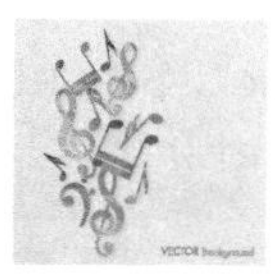

Listening Box 11

Type in Ornette Coleman and under Artist Results choose Ornette Coleman, Free Jazz. Select Track 1, Tears Inside and Track 3, Blues Connotation.

Hard Bop

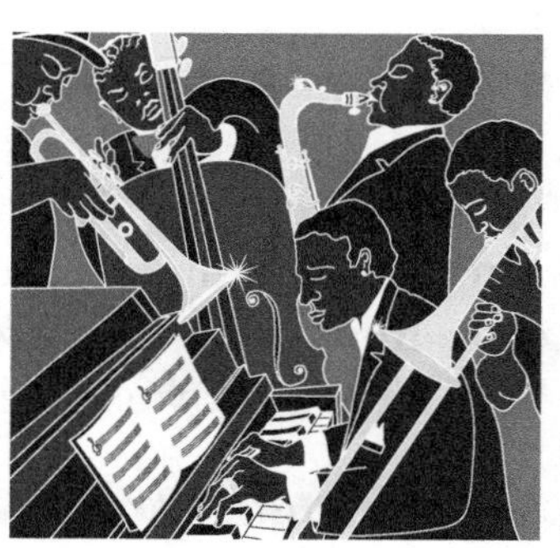

©isaxar/Shutterstock.com

Hard Bop basically returned to traditional Jazz, but added some different elements such as gospel and soul music.

Some Popular Artists of This Style

Horace Silver (piano), Oscar Peterson (piano), Ahmad Jamal (piano), and Charlie Mingus (bass).

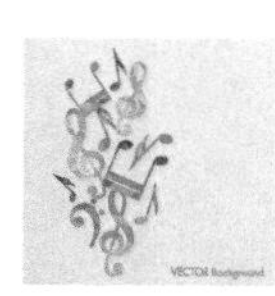

Listening Box 12

Type in Oscar Peterson and under Album Results choose Essential Oscar Peterson—The Swinger. Select Track 1, Something's Coming and Track 2, Blues for Big Scotia.

Jazz–Rock Fusion

This style blends Jazz and Rock elements. Jazz musicians had an increasingly difficult time getting work, so many decided to combine the popular elements of Rock 'n' Roll with Jazz. This resulted in a very unique sound which became popular with the general public.

Some Popular Artists of This Style

Chick Corea (piano), Jimi Hendricks (guitar), Chicago (band), and Blood Sweat and Tears (band).

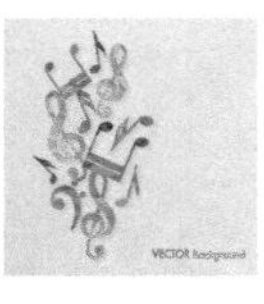

Listening Box 13

Type in Chicago and choose top box Artist, Chicago Lite Rock. Select Track 5, Saturday in the Park and Track 8, Hard Habit to Break.

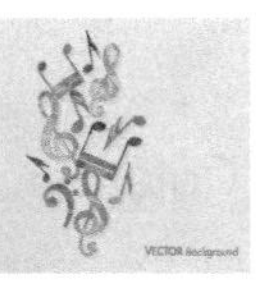

Listening Box 14

Type in Blood Sweat & Tears and under Artist Results choose Blood Sweat & Tears, Jazz Rock. Select Track 1, You Made Me So Very Happy and Track 2, Spinning Wheel.

Smooth Jazz

Smooth Jazz is closer to what the average listener would enjoy. The overall sound is less frantic, smoother, and more relaxing. The improvisations are more melodic and less dissonant. Sometimes smooth jazz is referred to as elevator or dentist music, but categorically, it is cooler than easy listening. This style was very popular in the 1960s and 1970s. In the 1980s, it was basically a commercial form of jazz fusion.

Some Popular Artists of This Style

Chuck Mangione (trumpet and flugelhorn), George Benson (guitar), Grover Washington (saxophone and vocals), and Wes Montgomery (guitar).

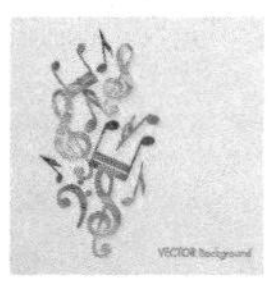

Listening Box 15

Type in Chuck Mangione and at top under Artist choose Chuck Mangione, Jazz Instrumental Pop. Select Track 1, Feels So Good; Track 3, Give It All You Got and Track 4, Land of Make Believe.

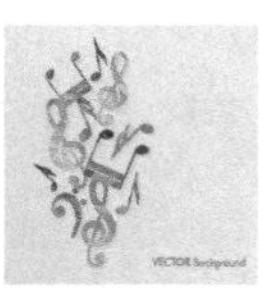

Listening Box 16

Type in George Benson and under Artist Resultschoose George Benson, Pop-Jazz. Select Track 2, Breezin' and Track 5, The Masquerade.

Jazz from the 1980s to Today

In this time frame, many musicians tried to restore the older sound and structure of Jazz as they felt it was being listened to by ever increasing diminishing audiences. Some different elements, such as synthesizers were used, but many musicians were criticized for limiting the growth of Jazz. People like Wynton Marsalis, Director of Jazz at Lincoln Center, helped turn things around as he reignited Jazz on the concert stage. At this time in Jazz history, there is no one style that dominates, but we do see electronic instruments in groups which give a modern feel and sound.

Some Popular Artists of This Style

Wynton Marsalis (trumpet), Harry Connick Jr. (piano and vocals), and Diana Krall (piano and vocals).

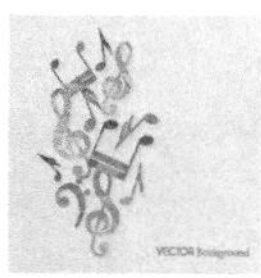

Listening Box 17

Type in Wynton Marsalis and choose top box Artist, Wynton Marsalis, Post Bop. Select Track 15, Caravan and Track 10, My Ideal.

Latin Jazz

Latin Jazz can easily be traced back to the early 1940s, but its greatest awareness and success came after World War II. It is basically a jazz style over Latin rhythms. Besides good rhythms, it includes improvisation, repetition, and syncopation. The two main categories are:

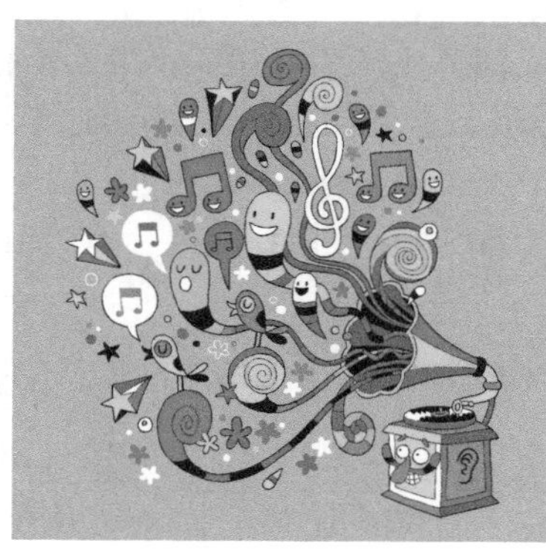

©Alias Ching/Shutterstock.com

1. **Afro-Brazilian Jazz**: This style features samba and bossa nova rhythms.
2. **Afro-Cuban Jazz**: This style includes popular Cuban dance rhythms.

Some Popular Artists of This Style

Antonio Carlos Jobim (Brazilian guitarist), Airto Moreira (Brazilian percussionist), and Tito Puente (drummer).

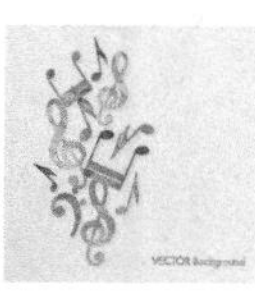

Listening Box 18

Type in Tito Puente and under Artist Results choose Tito Puente, Latin and World Jazz. Select Track 2, Ran KanKan and Track 3, Oye Como Va.

Summary of Unit 4, Chapter 4 Terms and Study Sheet

Terms

Bebop and Modern Jazz

West Coast Jazz

"Avant Garde" or Free Jazz

Hard Bop

Jazz–Rock Fusion

Smooth Jazz

Jazz from the 1980s to today

Latin Jazz

Note: All terms were previously discussed, please refer to those explanations.

Composers and Musicians

Dizzy Gillespie, Charlie Parker, Stan Getz, Thelonious Monk, Miles Davis, Quincy Jones, Gerry Mulligan, Dave Brubeck, Chet Baker, John Coltrane, Ornette Coleman, Nat Adderly, "Cannonball" Adderly, Chick Corea, Jimi Hendricks, Chicago (band), Blood sweat & Tears (band), Chuck Mangione, George Benson, Grover Washington, Wes Montgomery, Wynton Marsalis, Harry Connick Jr, Diana Krall, Antonio Carlos Jobim, Airto Moreira, and Tito Puente.

Summary of Listeners Toolbox

In Jazz music from the 1980s to today you are probably not going to hear many new styles. What has been added are electronic instruments such as the synthesizer. The best way to understand Jazz is to keep listening and don't be overwhelmed by improvisations.

Questions

As you listen to the different Jazz styles, have you decided which one is your favorite? As a category, did you find Jazz interesting?

To The Student: The instructor may add or delete study items at his or her discretion.

History Note: In 1987, the House and Senate passed a bill declaring Jazz a rare and valuable national American treasure.

Unit 4, Chapter 4 Listening Box Playlist

LB9: Type in Dizzy and under Artist Results choose Dizzy Gillespie, Bop. Select Track 4, Manteca; Track 8 Mas Que Nada; Track 13 Caravan and Track 24, 52nd St. Theme.

LB10: Type in Gerry Mulligan and under Artist Results choose Gerry Mulligan, Cool / West Coast Jazz. Select Track 1, Walkin' Shoes and Track 8, Ornithology.

LB11: Type in Ornette Coleman and under Album Results choose Ornette Coleman, Free Jazz. Select Track 1, Tears Inside and Track 3, Blues Connotation.

LB12: Type in Oscar Peterson and under Album Results choose Essential Oscar Peterson—The Swinger. Select Track 1, Something's Coming and Track 2, Blues for Big Scotia.

LB13: Type in Chicago and choose top box Artist, Chicago, Lite Rock. Select Track 5, Saturday in The Park and Track 8, Hard Habit To Break.

LB14: Type in Blood Sweat & Tears and under Artist Results choose Blood Sweat & Tears, Jazz Rock. Select Track 1, You Made Me So Very Happy and Track 2, Spinning Wheel.

LB15: Type in Chuck Mangione and at top under Artist choose Chuck Mangione, Jazz Instrumental Pop. Select Track 1, Feels So Good; Track 3, Give It All You Got and Track 4, Land of Make Believe.

LB16: Type in George Benson and under Artist Resultschoose George Benson, Pop-Jazz. Select Track 2, Breezin' and Track 5, The Masquerade.

LB17: Type in Wynton Marsalis and choose top box Artist, Wynton Marsalis, Post Bop. Select Track 15, Caravan and Track 10, My ideal.

LB18: Type in Tito Puente and under Artist Results choose Tito Puente, Latin and World Jazz. Select Track 2, Ran KanKan and Track 3, Oye Como Va.

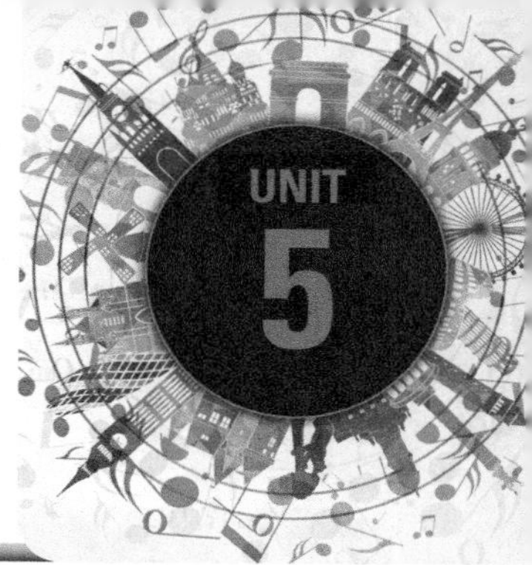

Americana

Unit Purpose

First, to clarify a constant mistake made in the singing of the Star Spangled Banner and second, to showcase four American composers.

CHAPTER 1 THE NATIONAL ANTHEM

What Do We Find in This Period?

Music: I wanted to explain and clarify a constant mistake in the singing of the Star Spangled Banner. Believe it or not, this mistake is made by many so called stars and musicians.

Also, we have studied the music of many European composers and I thought it would be a good idea to showcase a few of our own greats. All listenings will be orchestral, with the exception of the Star Spangled Banner.

Texture: Homophonic

Forms: Anthem, piano concerto, suite, overture

Composers: Ferde Grofé, George Gershwin, Aaron Copland, Leonard Bernstein

Travel to: New York City, Lawrence, Mass., Arizona, Lisbon

The Star Spangled Banner

1. The words come from a poem, "Defence of Fort M'Henry," by Francis Scott Key, 1814.
2. Francis Scott Key was a lawyer, author, and amateur poet.
3. The music comes from a British composer John Stafford Smith, who wrote the melody for a men's social club called the Anacreontic Society. The song was originally called, "The Anacreontic Song," or "To Anacreon in Heaven." This music was set to Key's poem and was later named, "The Star Spangled Banner."
4. It was made the official National Anthem in 1931, through a Congressional resolution signed by President Woodrow Wilson.

Lyrics for the first stanza:

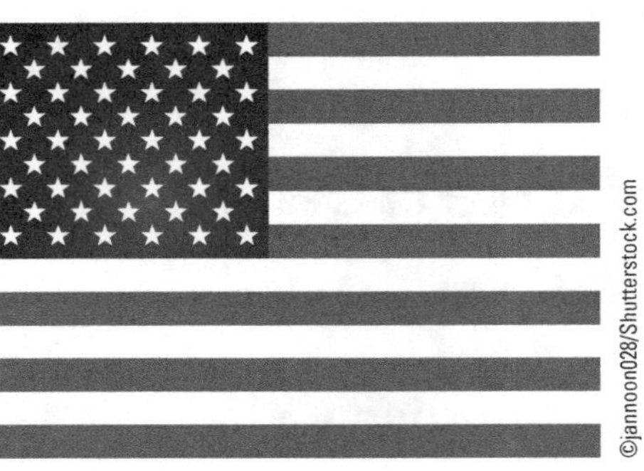
©jannoon028/Shutterstock.com

Oh, say can you see by the dawn's early light

What so proudly we hailed at the twilight's last gleaming?

Whose broad stripes and bright stars thru the perilous fight,

O'er the ramparts we watched were so gallantly streaming?

And the rocket's red glare, the bombs bursting in air,

Gave proof through the night that our flag was still there.

Oh, say does that star-spangled **Banner** yet wave

O'er the land of the free and the home of the brave?

Note: Notice I put the word Banner in bold with a capital B. I did this to highlight where the problem is. Most people add notes on the word banner that are not supposed to be there. In the listening example provided, notice that the second note on the word banner jumps from the first note. If you are having trouble hearing or understanding this, your instructor will explain.

Star Spangled Banner: The Correct Way

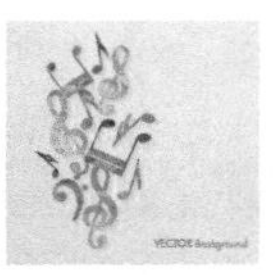

Listening Box 1

Type in Star Spangled Banner and under Artist Results, choose National Anthem-Star Spangle..., Christian/Gospel. Select the only choice. Also, under Track Results choose Star Spangled Banner, Lee Greenwood.

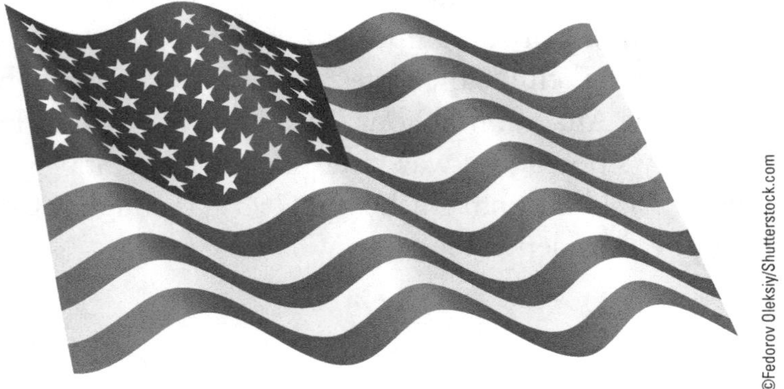
©Fedorov Oleksiy/Shutterstock.com

Star Spangled Banner: The Incorrect Way

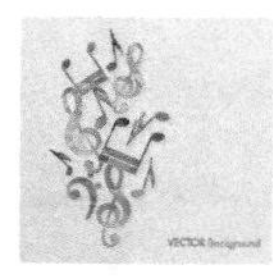

Listening Box 2

Type in Star Spangled Banner and under Track Results, choose the Star Spangled Banner, Whitney Houston.

Note: Whitney is singing with four beats in a measure and there are supposed to be only three.

CHAPTER 2 AMERICAN COMPOSERS

Ferde Grofé (1892–1972)

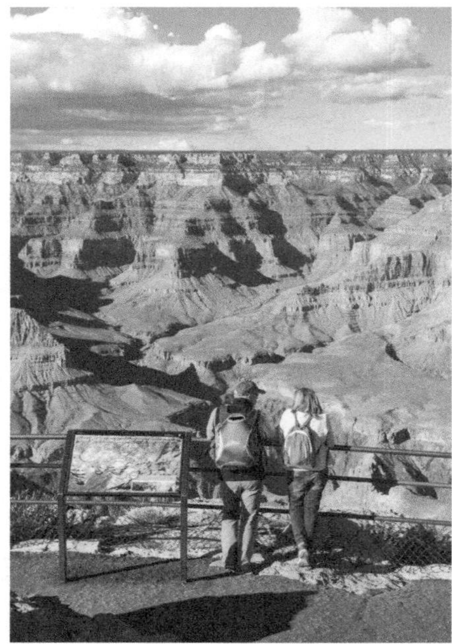
Grand Canyon

©Yongyut Kumsri/Shutterstock.com

1. Born in New York City.
2. Grofé came from a family of musicians and after his father died, his mother took him to Germany to study music. He played piano, several string instruments, and several brass instruments. In addition, he was a composer, arranger, and conductor.
3. He left home at age 14 and worked many different jobs. He enjoyed playing in night clubs and at age 15, he was playing in dance bands. He wrote his first commissioned work at age 17.
4. From the early 1920s to the 1930s, he played for Paul Whiteman and was his arranger.
5. Musically, there was not much Grofé did not do. He wrote music for films, worked on radio shows as a conductor, played classical and jazz piano, and eventually was employed at the Juilliard School of Music, where he taught composition.
6. His personal life was not always together as he was married three times and when he passed away in 1972, he left behind a wife and four children.
7. Some of his most important compositions are: **Suites**: The Mississippi (1925), The Grand Canyon (1931), Madison Square Garden (1930s), Death Valley (1949), Hudson River (1955), Niagara Falls (1960–1961), World's Fair (1964), and Hawiian (1965). **Ballets**: Tabloid Ballet (1930), Jungle Ballet (1937), and Hollywood Ballet (1938). **Movie Scores**: Early To Bed (1928; silent movie), The Jazz Singer (1928; the first talking movie), Redemption (1930), Diamond Jim (1935), Rocketship X-M (1950), The Return of Jesse James (1950), and A Christmas Story (1983; musical excerpts were taken from The Grand Canyon Suite). He also wrote works for concert band, chamber music, and music for solo instruments.

Suite: A suite is an orchestral composition with several sections that generally have the same theme or topic. For example, Grofé's Grand Canyon Suite is in five sections and they are: Sunrise, Painted Desert, On the Trail, Sunset, and Cloudburst. Obviously, Grofé is musically describing these phenomena at the canyon.

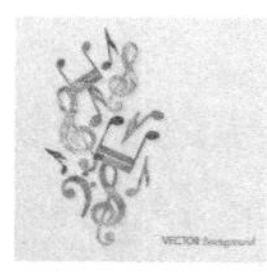

Listening Box 3

Type in Grand Canyon Suite and under Track Results, choose first Grand Canyon suite - Grand Canyo..., Leonard Bernstein. Select Track 3, On the Trail. When time permits, listen to the first five tracks which represent the entire suite.

George Gershwin (1898–1937)

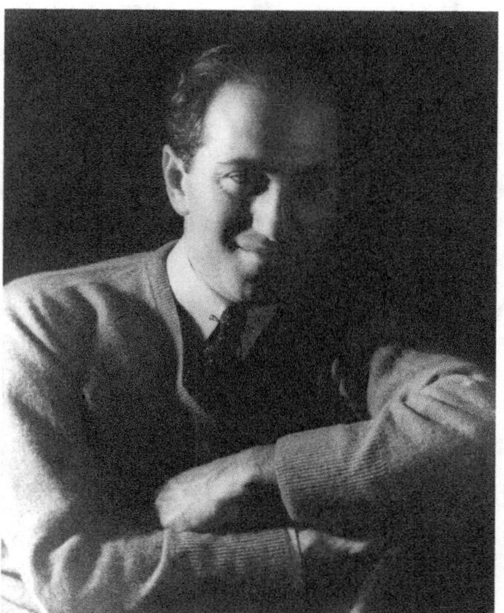

©Everett Historical/Shutterstock.com

1. Born in New York City.
2. He was born of Russian-Jewish parents who fled Russia because of Anti-Jewish sentiment.
3. George did not get interested in music till age 10 when he became fascinated with the piano that was bought for his older brother Ira. It seems Ira was not thrilled with piano lessons and became very happy when George took over.
4. In the early years, Gershwin had several piano teachers and eventually studied composition with Rubin Goldmark and Henry Cowell.
5. He had very little interest in school and left at age 15. At this young age he found his niche as a "song plugger," for J.H. Remick and Company and made $15 a week.
6. His first big national hit was "Swanee," in 1919, which was sung by Al Jolson. He also made a lot of money making piano player rolls.
7. He was a very prolific Broadway Show writer, which I will cite later.
8. George ventured to Paris in the mid-1920s to shore up his classical composition skills. He applied to be a student of both Nadia Boulanger and Maurice Ravel. He was turned down by both as they thought heavy classical training would ruin his jazz style.
9. In his career he did write a few operas and film scores, but he was mostly noted for Broadway Shows and individual hits.
10. One of his prized compositions was the opera "Porgy and Bess," composed in 1935. As this was the Depression Era, the work was not a commercial success and he decides to move to Hollywood to write movie scores.

11. George never married, but had a ten-year relationship with composer Kay Swift. She eventually divorced her husband in hopes of marrying George, but his mother Rose wasn't happy with Kay because she was not Jewish.
12. It is important to note Gershwin collaborated on many projects with his older brother Ira, who was a lyricist.
13. In his last years, he suffered from severe headaches and he passed away in 1937, from a brain tumor.
14. Some of his most important compositions are: **Orchestral**: Rhapsody in Blue (1924), Piano Concerto in F (1925), and an American in Paris (1928). **Solo Piano**: Three Preludes (1926) and George Gershwin Song Book (1932). **Operas**: Blue Monday (1932) and Porgy and Bess (1935). **Some Broadway Shows**: George White's Scandals (1920–24), Lady Be Good (1924), Oh-Kay! (1926), Strike Up the Band (1927), Girl Crazy (1930), Of Thee I Sing (1931), Pardon My English (1933), and Let 'Em Eat Cake (1933). **Films**: Delicious (1931), Shall We Dance (1937), A Damsel in Distress (1937), and The Goldwyn Follies (1938 and posthumously released).

Rhapsody in Blue (1924)—Gershwin

Rhapsody in Blue is an exceptional and trendsetting piece. Composed by Gershwin and arranged by Grofé in a five-week period of time, it is known as the first example of orchestral jazz. Apparently, Paul Whiteman, who was a popular band leader at the time, approached concert hall managers and board members about the idea of putting jazz on the concert stage. This idea was not favorably met as the piece was arranged for solo piano and jazz band. Eventually, theater administration was convinced and the piece premiered on February 12, 1924, at the Aeolian Hall in New York City, with Gershwin at the piano. At this first performance, Gershwin improvised some of the piano parts and a specific piano part was written later on. Grofé arranged this piece several times after the first performance. In 1926, he arranged it for show orchestra and in 1942, for full orchestra. This piece has gone down in music history as one of the most popular by any composer.

What to listen for: The opening clarinet solo, the great piano playing, the many syncopated rhythms, the great arrangement, and the few beautiful melodies.

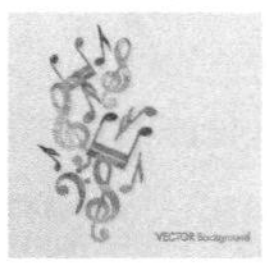

Listening Box 4

Type in Rhapsody in Blue and choose top box Track. Select Track 5, Rhapsody in Blue.

Porgy and Bess (1935)—Gershwin

Porgy and Bess was written in 1934 and first performed in 1935. Gershwin teamed up with Dubose Heyward and his sister Dorothy to write this opera. Gershwin wrote the music and the Heywards, the libretto. George's brother Ira also wrote lyrics to some songs. The Heywards were wealthy white people who were interested in African-American culture and lived in Charleston, South Carolina. In order to get the culture of the Gullah community correct, Gershwin and the Heywards spent time on Folly Beach. They spoke to people, went to religious services, and generally participated in different events.

After the amazing overture, the opera opens in a neighborhood town called Catfish Row with the song, "Summertime." The story is about Porgy, a crippled beggar and Bess, a street woman, whose lover Crown is very jealous and violent. Bess tries to break away from Crown as she learns he is wanted for murder. Porgy is willing to overlook Bess's past and offers her shelter. Their relationship is threatened for the following reasons: the disapproval of town's people, the constant presence of Sportin' Life, Bess being a drug dealer, and the return of Crown.

As the story moves forward in Act 3, Crown and Porgy have a confrontation and Porgy kills Crown. Porgy is eventually put in jail for refusing to identify Crown's body. Sportin' Life tells Bess that Porgy is going to be in jail for a long time, and he tries to convince Bess to go to New York with him. Bess is reluctant, but goes. After a week, Porgy is released from jail and finds out that Bess has gone to New York with Sportin' Life. Porgy prays to God and heads for New York.

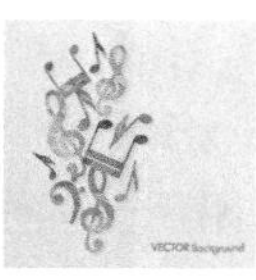

Listening Box 5

Type in Oscar Peterson and under Artist Results, choose Oscar Peterson, Jazz Piano. Select Track 2, Summertime. Also, Track 14, It Ain't Necessarily So.

Aaron Copland (1900–1990)

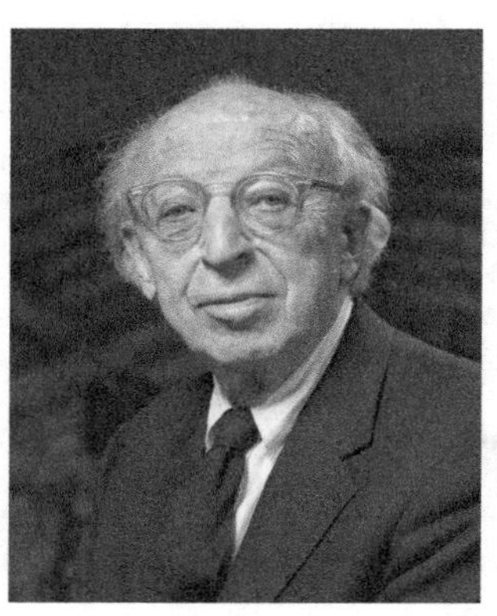

©Mikey Adair/Hulton Archive/Getty Images

1. Born in New York City.
2. Copland's skill set is viewed in many areas. He was a composer, writer, conductor, and teacher. One of his most famous pupils was Leonard Bernstein.
3. Aaron's musical talent was recognized at an early age and he was given piano lessons by his sister, Laurine. By age 15, he was studying composition, harmony, and theory with Rubin Goldmark.

4. His father was not interested in music and wanted him to go to college. His mother sang, played piano, and made sure he took music lessons.
5. His friend Aaron Schaffer convinced him to study in Paris. He eventually studied with the famed Nadia Boulanger for three years.
6. In the mid-1920s, Copland returned home and decided to be a full-time composer. He did not make much money, but he was persistent.
7. After meeting Alfred Stieglitz and his colleagues, Copland was convinced his music should reflect the ideas of American Democracy. Later in life, he was known as the "Dean of American Composers," as much of his music reflects American Nationalism.
8. His overall compositional techniques included jazz, twelve tone row, as well as conventional forms.
9. While never joining any political party, he did support the Communist Party USA and thought American policies were stifling to artists. This affiliation caused him great consternation and he was constantly investigated by the FBI. Copland was put on a list of 151 artists that the FBI thought had Communist associations. The investigations stopped in 1955 and were totally closed twenty years later.
10. Copland's personal life reveals some interesting facts. He was an agnostic and a homosexual. He had relationships with many men, but was very secretive about this lifestyle.
11. Two of the most important career highlights occurred when he received commissions to write ballet music for Agnes de Mille (Rodeo) and Martha Graham (Appalachian Spring).
12. In his later life, he gave up composing and conducted mostly his music.
13. Some of his most important compositions are: **Ballets**: Billy the Kid (1938), Rodeo (1942), Appalachian Spring (1944). **Film Music**: Of Mice and Men (1939), Our Town (1940), Red Pony (1948), The Heiress (1949). **Opera**: The Tender Land (1955). **Songs**: Twelve Poems of Emily Dickenson (1950), Old American songs. **Orchestral Music**: Music for Theater (1925), Piano Concerto (1926), Symphonies: No. 1 (1928), No. 2 (1933), and No. 3 (1946), El Salón Mexico (1936), An Outdoor Overture (1938), Quiet City (1940), Lincoln Portrait (1942), Fanfare for the Common Man (1942), Clarinet Concerto (1948), Orchestral Variations (1957), Music for a Great City (1964), Inscape (1967), Three Latin American sketches (1972). He also wrote chamber and piano music.

Fanfare for the Common Man (1942)—Copland

Fanfare: A fanfare is usually a short composition scored for brass and percussion. It is designed to be an attention getter. Most often it is associated with a certain theme or event such as the Olympics. Fanfare for the Common Man was commissioned by Eugene Goosens, conductor of the Cincinnati Symphony Orchestra, in 1942. It was written out of respect for and recognition of the US entry into World War II.

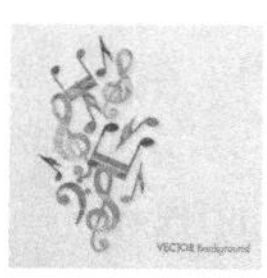

Listening Box 6

Type in Fanfare for the Common Man and under Album Results, choose Copland Conducts Copland – Expan...Various Artists. Select Track 1, Fanfare for the Common Man.

Rodeo—Ballet (1942)—Copland

Hoe-Down: The last section of the ballet is the Hoe-Down scene. This part is about a cowgirl who is interested in the head championship roper. At first, she tries to get his attention by showing her skills as a rider. Unfortunately, he does not pay attention. At the end of the ballet, she shows up in a beautiful dress in the Hoe-Down scene and basically has to fight off the competing cowboys. At last, she catches the eye of the head wrangler and he asks her to dance. The remaining dancers join the couple in a real upbeat and wild Hoe-Down.

Listening Note: In this section, Copland tries to capture the sound, spirit, and thinking of the country fiddlers. He does this with syncopation and exciting dance rhythms. This music has been used in many ways, including modern-day product commercials. I'm sure you will recognize it.

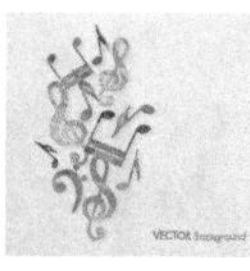

Listening Box 7

Type in Hoe-Down and choose top box Track, Hoe-Down, Aaron Copland. Select track 5, Hoe-Down.

Leonard Bernstein (1918–1990)

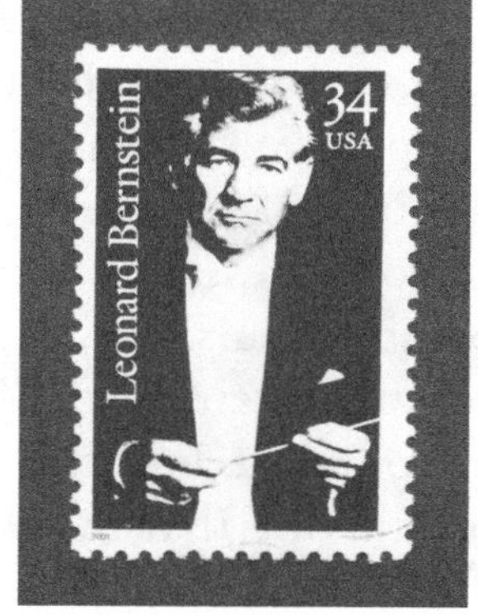

©catwalker/Shutterstock.com

1. Born in Lawrence, Massachusetts.
2. A super talented musician who was a conductor, composer, author, lecturer, and pianist.
3. Bernstein studied piano in his early years and after high school graduation in 1935, he entered Harvard University as a music major.
4. In 1939, after graduating Harvard, he entered the Curtis Institute of Music, Philadelphia. At Curtis, he studied conducting, orchestration, piano, counterpoint, and score reading.
5. After leaving Curtis, he moves to New York taking on different jobs such as arranging and music transcription.
6. In 1943, he was appointed assistant conductor of the New York Philharmonic. As luck would have it, guest conductor Bruno Walter became ill and Bernstein got his first big break conducting.

7. From the 1940s to the end of his life, Lenny conducted all over the world. Some of his favorite countries were Israel, Czech Republic, Austria, France, England and the US, to name a few.
8. In 1951, he married Felicia Cohn Montealegre and they eventually had three children, Jamie, Alexander, and Nina. Bernstein was also homosexual and apparently his wife knew of this lifestyle.
9. He was appointed permanent conductor of the New York Philharmonic in 1958 and held that position until 1968.
10. Some of his affluent and influential friends were Adolph Green, Betty Comden, Judy Holiday, Aaron Copland, Dimitri Mitropoulos, Nadia Boulanger, Serge Koussevitzky, and Jerome Robbins, again, to name a few.
11. Bernstein was a heavy smoker and in his later years developed cancer. He passed away in 1990, and a huge funeral procession brought him to his final resting place in Brooklyn, New York.
12. Some of his most important compositions are: **Musicals**: On the Town (1944),Wonderful Town (1953),West Side Story (1957), 1600 Pennsylvania Avenue (1976). **Ballet**: Fancy Free (1944), Facsimile (1946), Dybbuk (1974). **Opera**: Trouble in Tahiti (1952), Candide (1956), A Quiet Place (1983). **Films**: On the Town (1949), On the Waterfront (1954), West Side Story (1961). **Incidental and Theater**: Peter Pan (1950), The Lark (1955), The Firstborn (1958), Mass (1971), "Side by Side by Sondheim" (1976). **Orchestral**: Symphony No. 1 (1942), Symphony No. 2 (1949), Symphony No. 3 (1963), Songfest (1977), Slaval (1977), Halil (1981). **Chamber Music**: Piano Trio (1937), Sonata for Clarinet and Piano (1942), Brass Music (1959), Dance Suite (1988). He also wrote vocal and piano music.

Candide (1956)—Bernstein

Candide was written by Voltaire and published in 1759. The overall theme of the story is mindless optimism. Candide, illegitimate son of the Baron's sister, travels from Westphalia, Germany, with Cunégonde, the Baron's daughter, and Professor Pangloss, in search of "the best of all possible worlds." As they travel to places like Lisbon, Paris, Buenos Aires, and Venice, they endure much hardship. They are confronted with the Spanish Inquisition, the rape of Cunégonde, the plague, an earthquake, and slavery. They eventually return to Westphalia and realize perfection can never be attained. A person has to do the best they can and hope everything works out. Voltaire himself challenged the thinking that these horrific events could happen "in the best of all possible worlds." After encountering so many misfortunes, Candide, Cunégonde, and Professor Pangloss are not the same naïve people they were before they left Westphalia. More tragedy strikes as Cunégonde becomes a slave and turns very ugly. Candide is in pursuit to find her and when he does, he vows to marry her regardless of what she looks like. Candide concludes that hard work is the only way of making life bearable.

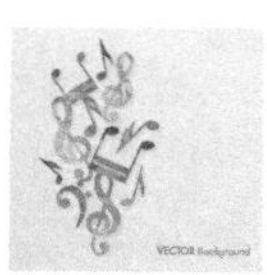

Listening Box 8

Type in Overture to Candide and choose top box Track, Leonard Bernstein (bonus track). Select Track 1, Overture.

Listening Note: As you know, the overture is the musical material that comes before the curtain opens and the story begins. Listen to the big orchestral sound and syncopations Bernstein uses to set the mood.

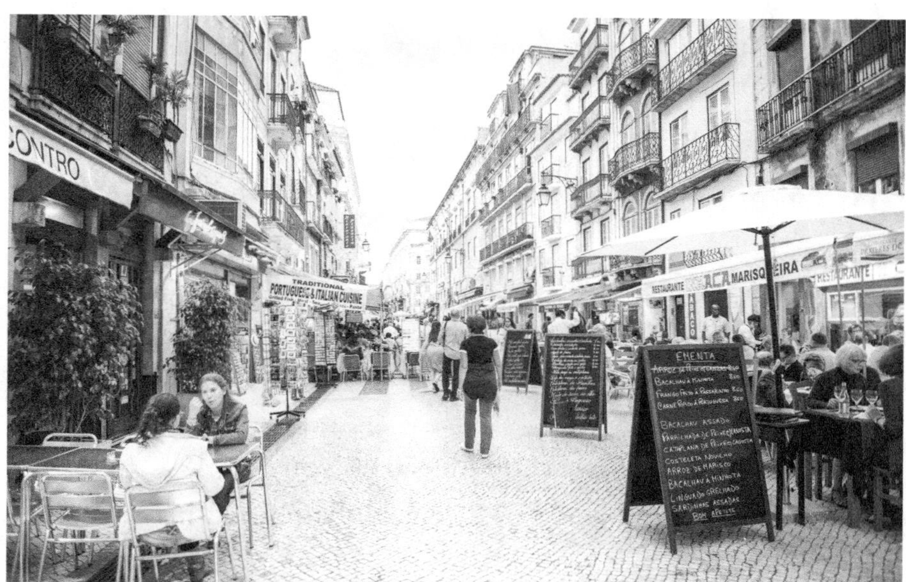

Lisbon, Portugal

Summary of Unit 5, Chapters 1 and 2 Terms and Study Sheet

Terms

Anthem: An anthem is usually a vocal composition with a religious or political lyric.

National Anthem: A National Anthem is the official song of a nation or country.

Suite: A suite is an orchestral composition with several sections that generally have the same theme or topic.

Rhapsody: A rhapsody is an orchestral composition with irregular form that often incorporates improvisation.

Fanfare: A fanfare is usually a short composition scored for brass and percussion. It is designed to be an attention getter.

Composers: Ferde Grofé, George Gershwin, Aaron Copland, and Leonard Bernstein.

Summary of Listeners Toolbox

The listenings in these two chapters are orchestral and have many different flavors. A personal assignment for you is to see if you can pick out in sound as many different instruments as possible.

Question

Of the four composers listed above, whose music do you prefer?

To The Student: The instructor may add or delete study items at his or her discretion.

Unit 5, Chapters 1 and 2 Listening Box Playlist

LB1: Type in Star Spangled Banner and under Artist Results, choose National Anthem – Star Spangle... Christian/Gospel. Select the only choice. Also, under Track Results, choose Star Spangled Banner, Lee Greenwood.

LB2: Type in Star Spangled Banner and under Track Results, choose The Star Spangled Banner, Whitney Houston.

LB3: Type in Grand Canyon Suite and under Track Results, choose first Grand Canyon Suite-Grand Canyon..., Leonard Bernstein. Select Track 3, On the Trail. I suggest you listen to the first five tracks as they represent the entire suite.

LB4: Type in Rhapsody in Blue and choose top box Track. Select Track 5, Rhapsody in Blue.

LB5: Type in Oscar Peterson and under Artist Results, choose Oscar Peterson, Jazz Piano. Select Track 2, Summertime. Also, Track 14, It Ain't Necessarily So.

LB6: Type in Fanfare for the Common Man and under Album Results, choose Copland conducts Copland - Expan...Various Artists. Select Track1, Fanfare for the Common Man.

LB7: Type in Hoe-Down and choose top box Track, Hoe-Down, Aaron Copland. Select Track 5, Hoe-Down.

LB8: Type in Overture to Candide and choose top box Track 1, Leonard Bernstein (Bonus Track). Select Track 1, Overture.

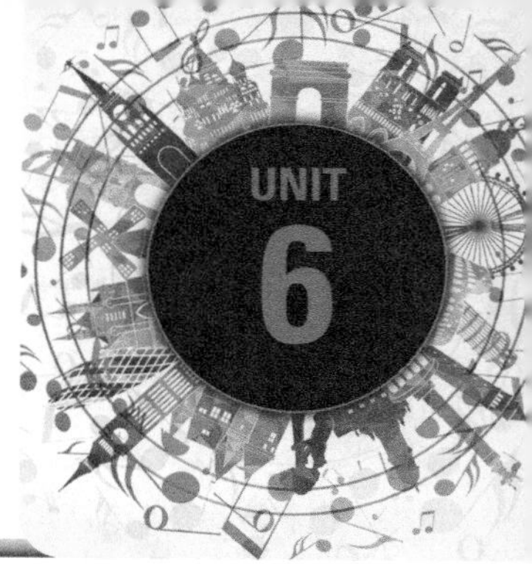

Broadway Shows

Unit Purpose

To present and explain the development of Broadway Shows.

CHAPTER 1 EARLY BEGINNINGS

What Do We Find in This Period?

Music: Broadway Show music is very diverse and enhances a multitude of subjects. It has grown and changed as society progresses and newer shows have added things like synthesizers to be up to date.

Texture: Homophonic

Forms: Comic opera, ballad opera, operetta, minstrelsy, vaudeville, burlesque, extravaganzas and spectacles, revue

Composers: There are too many to list here and I will cite some as we go along.

Travel to: New York City, Kentucky, Mississippi, Venice, Austria, France and London.

Broadway Shows have been around a long time and I am still amazed at how many people have not seen a live performance. There are many early elements that contributed to the development of the modern Broadway Show. They are comic opera, ballad opera, operetta, minstrelsy, vaudeville, burlesque, extravaganzas and spectacles, and the revue.

1. **Comic Opera:** In comic opera, comedy was emphasized over romance.
2. **Ballad Opera:** In ballad opera, popular songs of the day were featured. The style was very popular with the general public.
3. **Operetta:** The operetta included spoken dialogue and subjects like love and adventure. The overall presentation was lighthearted and fanciful.
4. **Minstrelsy:** Minstrels go back to tenth-century France. Back then, minstrels were poets, musicians, storytellers, and jugglers. They performed anywhere they could and strangely, society treated them as outcasts.
5. **Minstrels in America:** In the 1800s, slaves put on shows for entertainment. These shows were also used as a means of preserving their culture. The shows included

such things as solo songs, comedy, dancing, juggling, magic, and acting out of the story line.

6. **Vaudeville:** Vaudeville was a variety show which featured novelty acts plus song and dance. As this style evolved, African-Americans participated, but the shows were segregated.
7. **Vaudeville Roots:** Vaudeville roots go back to fifteenth-century France. Villagers entertained themselves and individual performers and sketches were added later. In America, 1865, Tony Pastor opened a variety theater in New Jersey. He featured all clean entertainment and smoking was not allowed.
8. **Burlesque:** In the mid to late 1800s, burlesque started as naughty entertainment for men. This was a raunchy style show which included comedy and sexual connotations. After World War I, comedy was replaced with vulgar sexuality. Because of this, burlesque never recovered.
9. **Extravaganzas and Spectacles:** These were huge variety shows with large casts. The Hippodrome Theater (1905–1935), took up an entire block on 6th avenue between 43rd and 44th streets in New York City. Thousands of people could enjoy shows in this theater which included water ballets, cavalry fights, floods, fires, and mock wars. Unfortunately, The Great Depression affected economics and paying customers decreased.

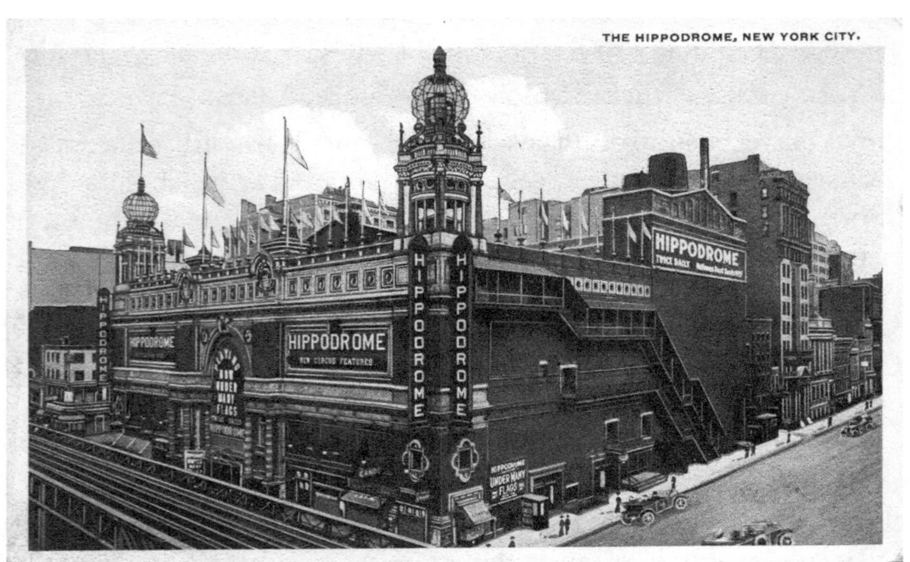

10. **The Revue:** The Revue is another type of spectacular show which featured star performers, dramatic sketches, and comedy routines. Revues debuted in 1894, with "The Passion Show." On Broadway, the longest running revue was Ziegfield Follies (1907–1931).

Florenz Ziegfield (1867–1932)

Ziegfield was a trendsetter with great ideas and insight for spectacular shows. His shows were dedicated to the glorification of women. He was basically a star maker and launched such entertainers as Fanny Brice, Barbara Stanwyck, Ed Wynn, Eddie Cantor, and Will Rogers.

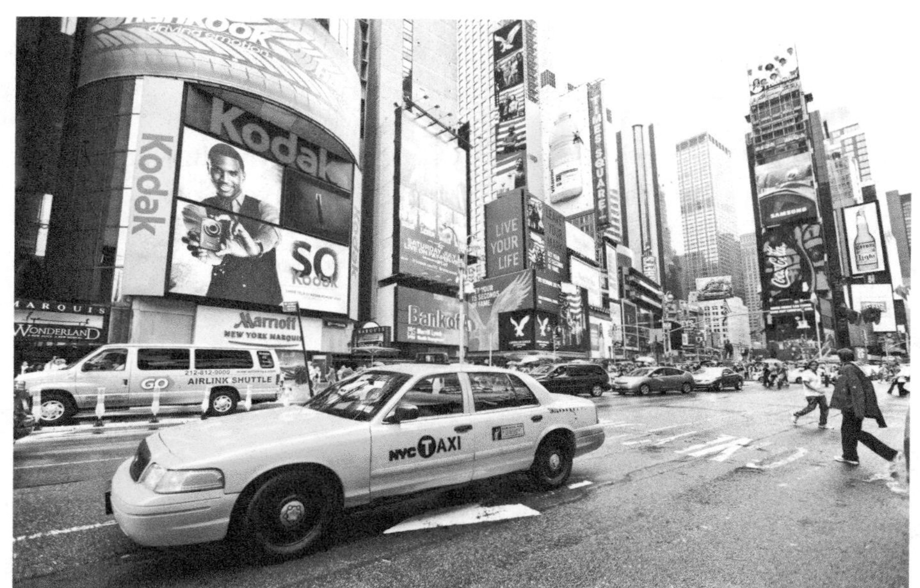

©Andrey Bayda/Shutterstock.com

Times Square—Theater District—New York

Note: There is no doubt that minstrel shows of the 1800s were the first musical theater in America. These shows were made popular by African Americans and white people eventually followed the format and formed their own touring companies. It is important to cite a few American composers who wrote songs for minstrel shows. As time passed, many of these songs became individual hits.

1. Dan Emmett (1815–1904)
2. Stephen Foster (1826–1864)
3. James A. Bland (1854–1911)

Of the three composers mentioned, I will highlight the songs of Stephen Foster (1826–1864).

Foster wrote Oh! Susanna (1848), Camptown Races (1850), Old Folks at Home (1851), Old Black Joe (1853), My Old Kentucky Home (1853), Jeanie with the Light Brown Hair (1854), and Beautiful Dreamer (1864). These aforementioned songs are but a few of many and Foster was North America's most successful songwriter. He passed at the young age of 38, in a charity ward in New York.

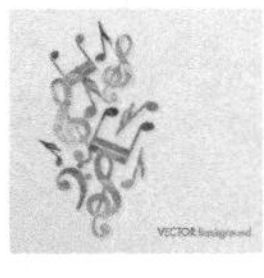

Listening Box 1

Type in Traditional Songs of Stephen Foster and under Album Results, choose Traditional Songs of Stephen Foster, Various Artists. Select Track 1, Oh! Susanna; Track 2, My Old Kentucky Home; Track 5, Ring Ring de Banjo; and Track 8, Camptown Races.

Note: As the Kentucky Derby takes place at Churchill Downs, in Kentucky, it is customary and appropriate that My Old Kentucky Home is always played.

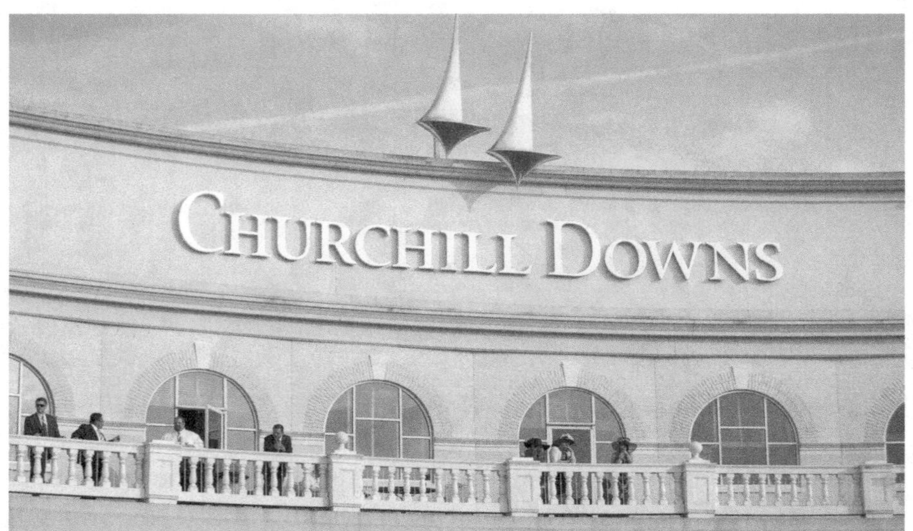

Churchill Downs, Louisville, Kentucky

Unit 6, Chapter 1 Listening Box Playlist

LB1: Type in Traditional Songs of Stephen Foster and under Album Results, choose Traditional Songs of Stephen Foster, Various Artists. Select Track 1, Oh! Susanna; Track 2, My Old Kentucky Home; Track 5, Ring Ring de Banjo; and Track 8, Camptown Races.

CHAPTER 2 MODERN BROADWAY SHOWS (MUSICALS FROM THE EARLY 1900s)

The term Broadway represents the Theater District in New York City. New York was and still is a trendsetting city when it comes to producing shows. The show tradition of the city can be traced back to the mid and late 1700s. Many early shows were Shakespearian plays and ballad operas. Along with Lincoln Center and Radio City Music Hall, the Theater District represents the best place to see musicals.

Note: I will separate the Modern Broadway Show into two categories, early and more current.

Early Broadway From the 1900s

As previously stated, The Great Depression wreaked havoc on Broadway, but as we get into the 1940s, things start looking brighter. Probably the one show that put Broadway back on the map was Oklahoma!, first performed in March, 1943, and written by Richard Rodgers and Oscar Hammerstein. This show lasted for 2,212 performances and represents the first collaboration for these two men.

Overall, there were many composers and lyricists that contributed to the growth of Broadway. Some of them are George M. Cohan (1878–1942), Jerome Kern (1885–1945), Irving Berlin (1888–1989), Cole Porter (1891–1964), George Gershwin (1898–1937), Richard Rodgers (1902–1979), Ira Gershwin (1896–1983, lyricist), and Oscar Hammerstein (1895–1960, lyricist).

In presenting some of these great musicians, I am going to use a different format. As I would like to use as many songs as time and space permit, I will shorten the biographical notes.

George M. Cohan (1878–1942)

Cohan performed in vaudeville as a child with his parents and sister. The show family was known as "The Four Cohans." George was very talented and in his lifetime wrote over 300 songs. In the music industry he was also known as a singer, producer, actor, dancer, and playwright. I would like to feature two of his songs, "Give My Regards to Broadway" and "Yankee Doodle Dandy." These songs are from the show George M1, a story about his life.

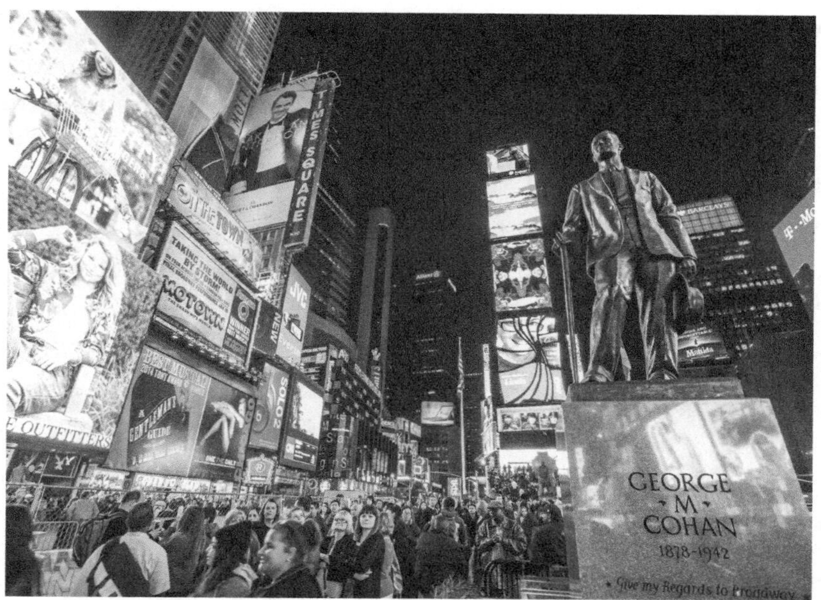

George M. Cohan Statue, Broadway, New York

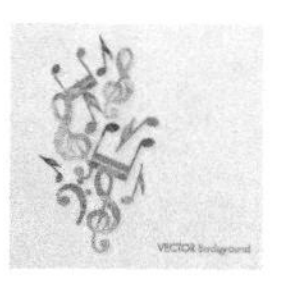

Listening Box 2

Type in George M. Cohan and choose top box George M! Various Artists. Select Track 7, Give My Regards to Broadway and Track 12, Finale: Yankee Doodle Dandy.

Note: As the show George M! is the story of his life and music, all selections represent his artistry.

Some of his most famous shows are The Governor's Son (1901), Little Johnny Jones (1904), Seven Keys to Baldpate (1913), Going Up (1917), The Royal Vagabond (1919), Madeline and the Movies (1922), The Merry Malones (1927), and The Return of the Vagabond (1940). Admittedly, this is a very short list of the shows Cohan either wrote, starred in, produced, composed music for, or directed.

Jerome Kern (1885–1945)

Kern learned piano and organ from his mother who was an accomplished musician. His father wanted him to go into the family business, but Jerome was not interested. 1902 was his senior year in high school and he decided to leave before graduation. He eventually continued his education at the New York College of Music, where he studied piano, theory and composition. In his lifetime he wrote music for film, shows, and over 700 songs.

Of all his shows I will list, probably the most popular one is Show Boat. The show is in two acts and is about the lives of the people working on the Cotton Blossom, a Mississippi River show boat. The main themes of the show include racial prejudice and lasting love.

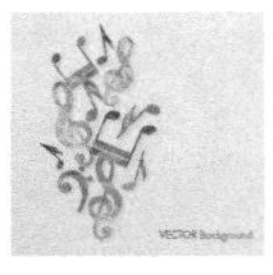

Listening Box 3

Type in Show Boat and under Album Results, choose Show Boat, Jerome Kern. Select Track 3, Ol' Man River and Track 4, Can't Help Lovin' Dat Man.

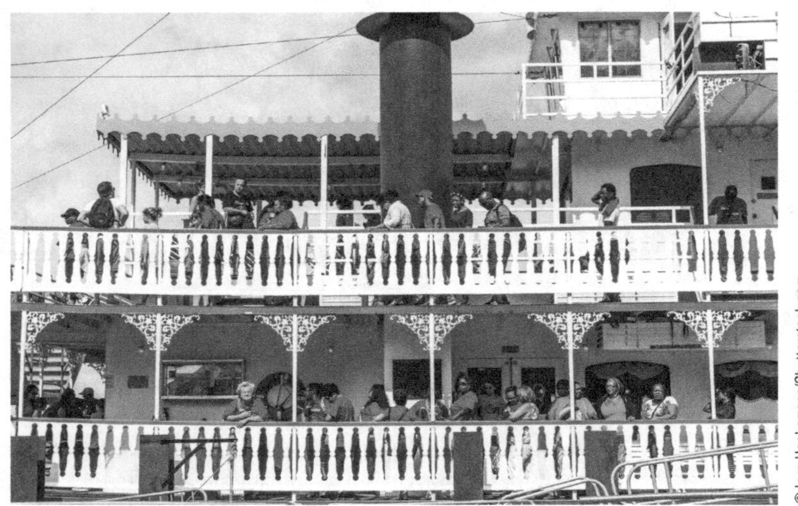

Mississippi River Boat

Some of his most famous shows are Nobody Home (1915), Very Good Eddie (1915), Have a Heart (1916), Oh, Boy! (1917), Oh, Lady, Lady (1918), The Night Boat (1920), Sally (1920), Good Morning Dearie (1921), The Cabaret Girl (1922), the Beauty Prize (1923), Sunny (1925), Show Boat (1927), The Cat and the Fiddle (1931), Music in the Air (1932), Roberta (1933), and Very Warm for May (1939).

Cole Porter (1891–1964)

Porter grew up in a wealthy family in Peru, Indiana. He started playing violin at six and piano at eight. His grandfather was very wealthy and subsidized his education at the Worcester Academy in Massachusetts, Yale, and Harvard. Cole was supposed to study law and his grandfather was never told he changed his major to music. At Yale, he wrote two football fighting songs, "Bulldog" and "Bingo Eli Yale." While in Paris he studied at ScholaCantorum to increase his knowledge of composition. In Paris, he met a wealthy American, Linda Lee Thomas, a divorcee. They eventually married in 1919. She was aware of his homosexuality, but accepted this lifestyle. Together, Cole and Linda loved the lavish lifestyle and rented in Paris and Venice. In 1937, he had a tragic horseback-riding accident in New York. He had many operations and eventually lost his right leg. Needless to say, this changed his whole life, which for the most part was lived at a very high social level. Musically, he wrote for films and many shows, but he is most noted for the individual songs that came out of these shows. He was very witty and clever and wrote the words to his songs. His songs dealt mainly with love, relationships, wealth, and lavish spending.

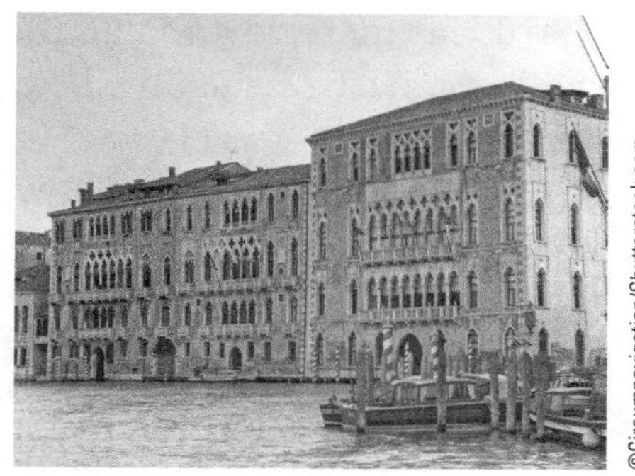

Ca' Rezzonico, Venice (on the Right)

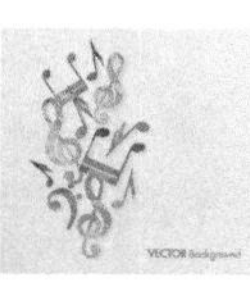

Listening Box 4

Type in Cole Porter and choose top box Anything Goes, Cole Porter. Select Track1, Prelude (From "Anything Goes") and Track 10, It's Delovely (From "Red, Hot and Blue").

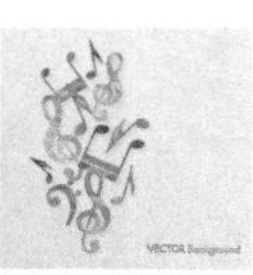

Listening Box 5

Type in Cole Porter and under Playlist Results, choose Frank Sinatra Sings Cole Porter. Select Track 1, I've Got You Under My Skin and Track 3, Night and Day.

Some of his most famous shows are See America First (1916), Greenwich Village Follies (1924), Paris (1928), Fifty Million Frenchmen (1929), The New Yorkers (1930), Gay Divorce (1932), Anything Goes (1934), Jubilee (1935), Leave It to Me (1938), Du Barry Was a Lady (1939), Panama Hattie (1940), Kiss Me Kate (1948), Can-Can (1953), Silk Stockings (1955).

Richard Rodgers (1902–1979)

Rodgers was born in New York City. He started playing piano at age six and after high school attended Columbia University. He moved on from Columbia and attended the Institute of Musical Art (now Juilliard). In his lifetime he composed music for movies, television, and 43 shows, which produced over 900 songs. His first two lyricist partners were Lorenz Hart and Oscar Hammerstein. He met Hart in 1919 and their first show, "The Garrick Gaieties," was a hit and produced the song "Manhattan," which launched both their careers. As time passed, Hart began to experience health and reliability problems, so in 1943, Rodgers collaborated with Oscar Hammerstein on Oklahoma! This show was a monster hit and probably launched the best composer-lyricist team in Broadway history. Hammerstein passed away in 1960, and Rodgers collaborated with Stephen Sondheim on the show, "Do I Hear a Waltz." He later collaborated with Martin Charnin and Sheldon Harnick.

Richard was married and had three daughters; only two survived, Mary and Linda. After surviving cancer of the jaw, he passed away in 1979 from a heart attack, and his ashes were scattered at sea. He was one of two people who won an EGOT, which stands for Emmy, Grammy, Oscar, and Tony awards. He also won two Pulitzer Prizes, one in 1944, for Oklahoma! and one in 1950, for South Pacific.

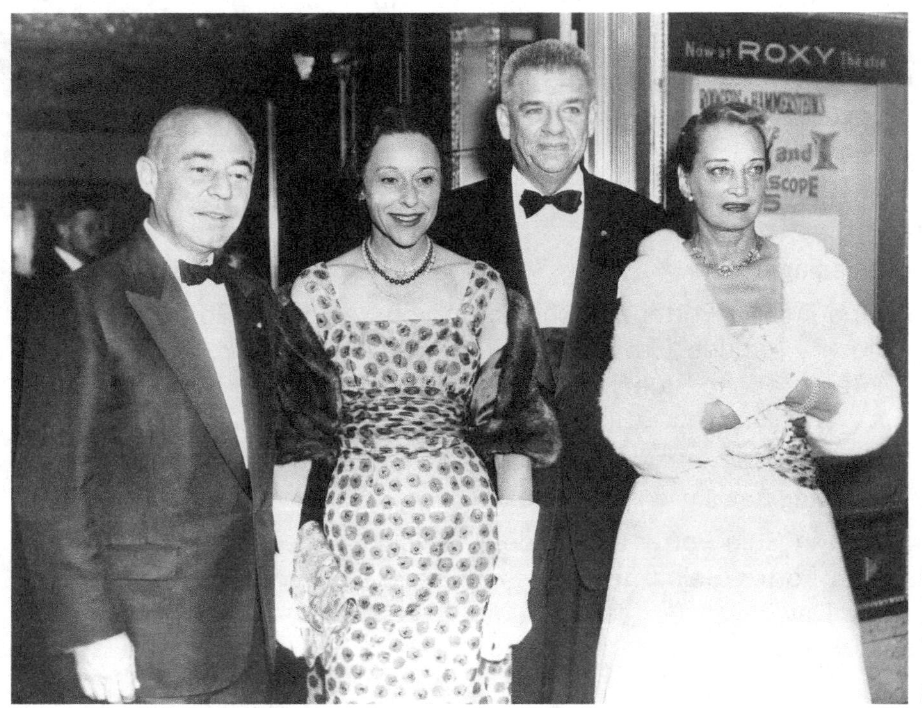

Richard and Dorothy Rodgers, Oscar and Dorothy Hammerstein (1956)

Show collaborations with Lorenz Hart: The Garrick Gaieties (1925–1926),A Connecticut Yankee (1927), Jumbo (1935), On Your Toes (1936), Babes in Arms (1937), I Married an Angel (1938), The Boys from Syracuse (1938), Pal Joey (1940-41), By Jupiter (1942).

Show collaborations with Oscar Hammerstein: Oklahoma! (1943), Carousel (1945), South Pacific (1949), The King and I (1951), Cinderella (1957), Flower Drum Song (1958), The Sound of Music (1959).

The Sound of Music by Richard Rodgers and Oscar Hammerstein (1959)

The Cast

1. Maria Rainer—a postulant at Nonnberg Abbey
2. Captain Georg von Trapp—father of seven children and a military person
3. Max Detweiler—von Trapp's friend, music agent, and producer

4. **Mother Abbess**—head of Nonnberg Abbey
5. **Baroness Elsa Schraeder**—Captain von Trapp's would be fiancée
6. **Rolf Gruber**—17-year-old Nazi delivery boy in love with Liesl
7. **Sister Bertha**—mistress of novices
8. **Sister Margareta**—mistress of postulants
9. **Sister Sophia**—sister at Abbey
10. **Herr Zeller**—the Gauleiter (an unpleasant person in charge of a district in Nazi Germany)
11. **Franz**—Captain von Trapp's butler
12. **Frau Schmidt**—Captain von Trapp's housekeeper

The Children

1. **Leisl von Trapp, 16**
2. **Freidrich von Trapp, 14**
3. **Louisa von Trapp, 13**
4. **Kurt von Trapp, 11**
5. **Brigitta von Trapp, 10**
6. **Marta von Trapp, 7**
7. **Gretl von Trapp, 5**

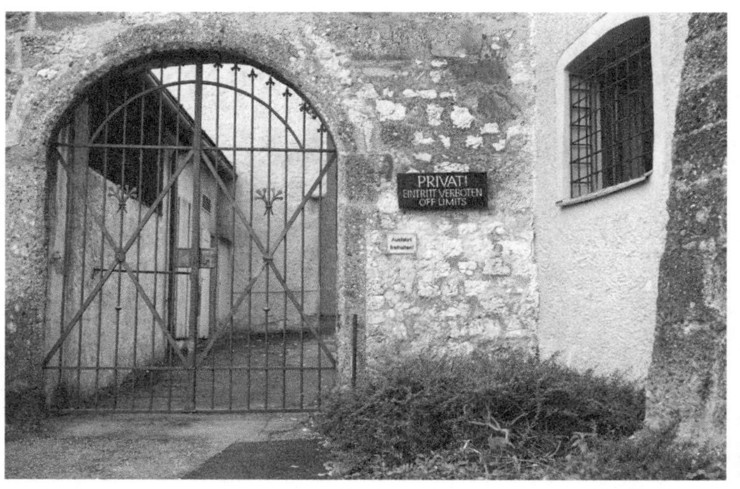

©EQRoy/Shutterstock.com

Nonnberg Abbey, Salzburg, Austria

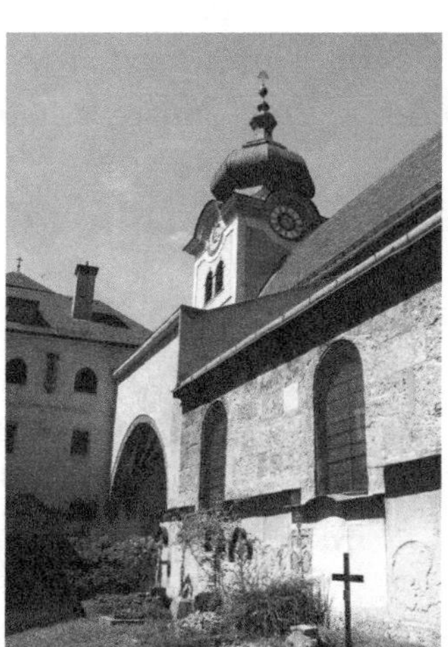

©Tupungato/Shutterstock.com

The Abbey and Cemetery

Synopsis of the Sound of Music

The story is about Maria who is trying to decide whether she wants to become a nun and her eventual association with the von Trapp family. As she is not doing well at the Abbey, she grudgingly accepts a job as governess for the von Trapp family. Captain von Trapp is a single parent with seven children. He is very strict and has many rules. At first, the children treat Maria poorly, but she continually shows her love and care for them. Maria is more lenient with the rules, which upsets the Captain. As time passes, Maria falls in love with the Captain and this causes a stir with von Trapp's supposed fiancée, Baroness Schraeder. The Captain and Maria eventually get married at the delight of the children and the dismay of the Baroness.

The Captain is ordered to take a commission in the German Navy, but he is not in agreement with the Nazis. Ultimately, he and Maria plan to escape Austria with the children. At the end of the show, a talent contest is planned and the singing von Trapps participate. With the help of Max Detweiler, the family friend and master of ceremonies, the von Trapps plan their escape from the show. Max does his best to stall the announcement of the contest winners, which gives the family time to escape. Finally, Max announces that the von Trapp family has won first prize. The family does not appear on stage to accept the prize and the Nazis become very suspicious. Frantically, they start their search and wind up at the Abbey where the von Trapps are hiding. In the end, the family safely leaves Austria and goes to Switzerland. They eventually come to America.

In Real Life

1. The family went to Italy, London, and then came to the United States.
2. Maria and the Captain married in 1927. His first wife died in 1922. He was 25 years older than Maria.
3. Maria and the Captain spent time in Austria before escaping.
4. The von Trapps left Austria in 1938 and settled in Stowe, Vermont. Maria and the Captain had three children, Rosemarie, Eleonore, and Johannes.
5. The Captain died in 1947, and their home was turned into a twenty-seven-room ski lodge.
6. In 1980, the lodge was destroyed by fire and was re-built in 1983, with 93 rooms.
7. Maria von Trapp died in 1987 and thirty-two family members shared in ownership. In 1994, Johannes von Trapp wanted to buy out all the owners which caused disagreement and legal proceedings. The case was eventually decided by the Supreme Court of Vermont.

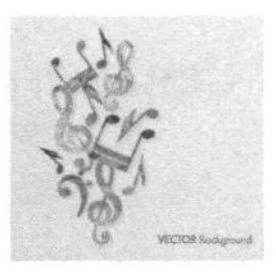

Listening Box 6

Type in The Sound of Music and under Album Results, choose The Sound of Music (Music from the...), Various Artists. Select Track 2, The Sound of Music; Track 4, My Favorite Things; Track 5, Do-Re-Mi; Track 13, Climb Every Mountain; Track 19, Edelweiss.

Unit 6, Chapter 2 Listening Box Playlist

LB2: Type in George M. Cohan and choose top box George M! Various Artists. Select Track 7, Give My Regards to Broadway and Track 12, Finale: Yankee Doodle Dandy.

LB3: Type in Show Boat and under Album Results, choose Show Boat, Jerome Kern. Select Track 3, Ol' Man River and Track 4, Can't Help Lovin' Dat Man.

LB4: Type in Cole Porter and choose top box Anything Goes, Cole Porter. Select Track 1, Prelude (From "Anything Goes") and Track 10, It's Delovely (From "Red, Hot and Blue").

LB5: Type in Cole Porter and under Playlist Results, choose Frank Sinatra Sings Cole Porter. Select Track 1, I've Got You Under My Skin and Track 3, Night and Day.

LB 6: Type in The Sound of Music and under Album Results, choose The Sound of Music (music from the...), Various Artists. Select Track 2, The Sound of music; Track4, My Favorite things; Track 5, Do-Re-Me; Track 13 Climb Every Mountain; Track 19, Edelweiss.

CHAPTER 3 MODERN BROADWAY SHOWS (MUSICALS FROM THE 1980s)

As Broadway Shows advanced in time, creative subjects are drawn from many areas. For example, comic strips, historical themes, animals, Hollywood, pop music, dance, opera, and revivals. In conjunction with new themes, synthesizers and special effects machines added new musical dimension and visual experiences.

Cats by Andrew Lloyd Webber and Lyrics by T.S. Eliot, Trevor Nunn, and Richard Stilgoe (1982, Broadway)

This is an extraordinary show about cats that is based on the 1939 book by T.S. Eliot, *Old Possum's Book of Practical Cats*. The show includes almost forty different cats, an unbelievable score by Lloyd Webber, and probably the most incredible make-up of any show. It is hard to imagine, but each cat has a different look.

Some of the Important Cats

1. **Old Dueteronomy:** the oldest cat and he gets to choose which cat goes on to a new life at the Jellicle Ball
2. **Grizabella:** the glamour cat
3. **Rum Tum Tugger:** a flashy tom cat
4. **Victoria:** a pure white cat that dances very well
5. **Asparagus/Gus:** the old theater cat
6. **Macavity:** the troublemaker cat
7. **Mistoffelees:** the magic cat
8. **Munkustrap:** a tom cat and the show's narrator
9. **Skimbleshanks:** the railway cat who basically lives on trains and has become the mascot of the train station
10. **Bustopher Jones:** the twenty-five-pound education cat

Synopsis of Cats

The story revolves around a bunch of cats who belong to a group called Jellicle. Once a year, at the Jellicle Ball, Old Deuteronomy selects a cat who is spared and goes on to a new life. In this show, he selects Grizabella, the glamour cat who is now old and who has been mistreated by all the cats. Perhaps her mistreatment is justified because she wasn't very pleasant in her younger days to her fellow peers. Nevertheless, Old Dueteronomy selects her and the rest of the cats join in her send-off to a new life. Also interesting is how each of the cats is presented to the audience, displaying their different characteristics as they speak of the lives they have led. This show has great music and plenty of dancing and should be on your list of must see.

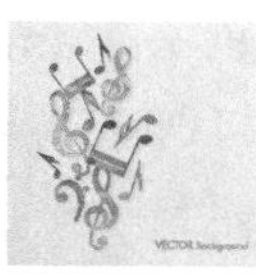

Listening Box 7

Type in Cats the Musical and choose the top box Memory, Cats the Musical. Select Track 3, The Rum Tum Tugger; Track 5, Old Deuteronomy; Track 10, Mr. Mistoffelees; Track 11, Memory.

Les Misérables by Claude-Michel Schönberg, Alain Boublil, and Jean-Marc Natel (1987)

Les Misérables is based on the novel of the same name by Victor Hugo. The book was published in 1862 and the story was first presented in film in 1935. It initially appeared on Broadway in 1987. Since then, it is still shown around the world. The latest film version was in 2012 and starred Hugh Jackman, Russel Crowe, Anne Hathaway, and Amanda Seyfried, to name a few.

The Cast

1. **Jean Valjean/Monsieur Madeleine:** put in prison for stealing bread to feed his sister's family, he eventually turns his life around and becomes a factory owner and Mayor of the town
2. **Inspector Javert:** the police
3. **Bishop of Digne:** the clergy
4. **Gavroche:** factory foreman, urchin; dies on barricade
5. **Fantine:** factory worker, single mom to Cosette; dies early in show
6. **Cosette:** Fantine's daughter
7. **The Thénardiers:** innkeepers
8. **Eponine:** daughter of the Thénardiers
9. **Marius:** student revolutionary
10. **Enjolras:** student revolutionary

Synopsis of Les Misérables

This is a story about Jean Valjean, a peasant who served 19 years in prison for stealing bread to feed his sister's family. He received a five-year sentence, but he kept breaking his parole orders and consequently fourteen years were added to his sentence.

After being released from prison by Javert, Valjean has difficulty finding work. He eventually meets the Bishop of Digne who invites him in for food and a night's sleep. Valjean repays the Bishop by stealing his silver and flees the Bishop's residence during the night. Valjean is caught by the police and is returned to face the Bishop. In an incredible show of mercy, the Bishop tells the police that Valjean did not steal the silver and as a matter of fact left so quickly, he forgot two candlesticks. At this point, the police reluctantly leave and the Bishop makes Valjean promise he will sell the silver and turn his life around.

Valjean, who was prisoner 24601, sells the silver, opens a factory, and changes his name to Monsieur Madeleine. He is very successful and eventually becomes the mayor of the town.

One of the workers in the factory is a woman by the name of Fantine who is a single mother to Cosette. Life is a struggle for Fantine, and she has to let Cosette live with the Thénardiers who are innkeepers. At work, Fantine has to constantly reject the advances of the foreman Gavroche. Eventually, she gets into an altercation with him and she loses her job. Now destitute for money, she sells her hair and locket and turns to prostitution. She becomes very ill and Valjean realizing he did nothing to help her, promises that he will take care of Cosette. Fantine passes away and Valjean buys Cosette from the Thénardiers.

Valjean is constantly being chased by Javert and at one point they meet, but Valjean escapes. As many people are in poverty and suffering, Valjean helps the student revolutionaries prepare for their fight against the government and the army.

Cosette is now a grown lady and is in love with Marius, one of the student revolutionaries. It is also revealed that Eponine, daughter of the Thénardiers, is also in love with Marius. Collectively, the students and townspeople build a huge barricade in anticipation of a big fight against the army. Javert claims to be a rebel, but is actually spying on the rebels for the government. This activity is exposed and the rebels hold him captive where he meets Valjean again. Valjean is ordered to dispose of Javert, but lets him go.

As the fight breaks out at the barricade, the rebels are grossly outnumbered and several people get killed. Among them is Eponine, which totally destroys Marius as she is his good friend. During the battle, Marius is severely wounded and is saved by Valjean as both men try to escape through the sewer system. They finally make it to the exit only to be greeted by Javert. Valjean convinces Javert to let him take Marius to the hospital and promises to return to have a final face to face.

Javert, who has spent so many years hunting for Valjean, cannot live with himself for letting him go. He commits suicide by jumping into the river.

Marius survives his wounds and is reunited with Cosette. Valjean is fearful that Cosette will find out about his past and leaves without saying anything to her. Cosette is completely distraught but is comforted by Marius who explains it is all for the best. On a happier note, Cosette and Marius get married and Valjean does not attend as he is very ill and hiding out at the convent. At the wedding reception, Marius gets Mr. Thénardier to tell him where Valjean is and both Marius and Cosette leave for the convent. When they find Valjean, he does not have much time to live. Valjean finally passes and both Cosette and Marius are heartbroken. Marius realizes that it is just he and Cosette that are left and they must start a new life.

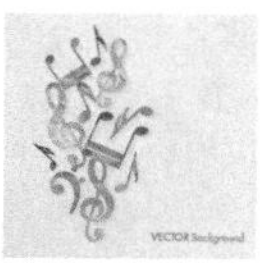

Listening Box 8

Type in Les Misérables and choose top box Les Misérables, Alain Boublil. Select Track 1, Overture/Work Song; Track 15, Red and Black; Track 16, Do You Hear The People Sing?

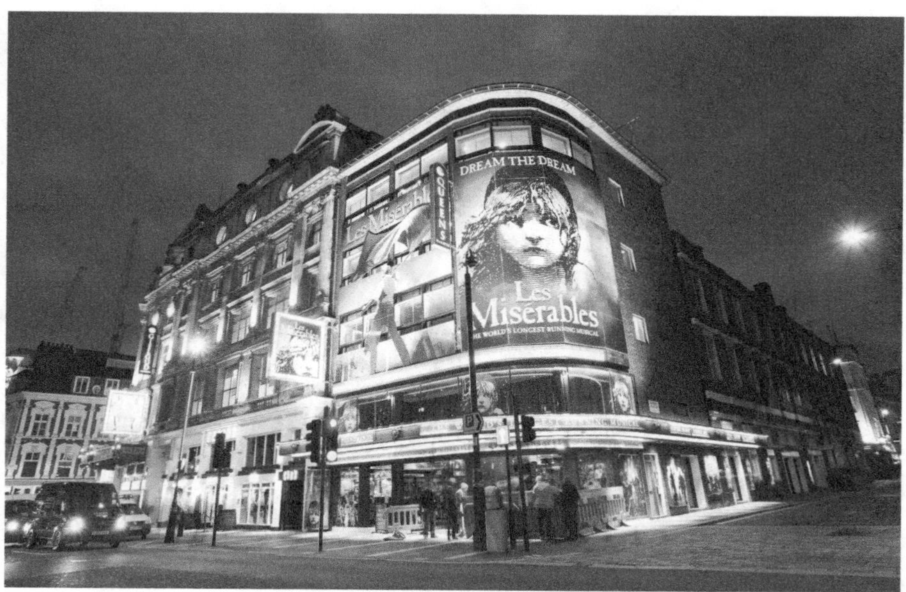

Queen's Theater, London

Bring in 'da Noise, Bring in 'da Funk (1995 Off Broadway–1996 Broadway)

Music by: Daryl Waters, Zane Mark, Ann Duquesnay

Lyrics by: Reg E. Gaines, George C. Wolf, Ann Duquesnay

Choreography: Savion Glover

This is a very unique and different Broadway Show. It traces the history of African-Americans through tap dancing and covers the time period from slavery to today. The show includes such elements as hip-hop, funk, soul, and gospel. Musically, the audience is treated to great rhythmic and dancing displays. For a more up-to-date sound, synthesizers are used. The show opened off-Broadway in November, 1995, and closed in January, 1996. It re-opened in April, 1996, on Broadway and closed January, 1999, after 1135 performances.

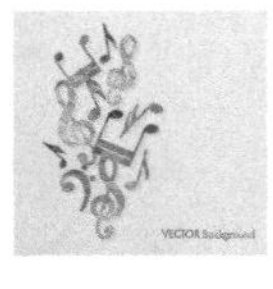

Listening Box 9

Type in Bring in 'da Noise and choose top box Bring in 'da Noise, Bring in 'da Funk. Select Track 25, Bring in 'da Noise, Bring in 'da Funk; Track 5, Pan Handlers; Track 9, Industrialization; Track 13, Now that's Tap; and Track 24, Hittin'.

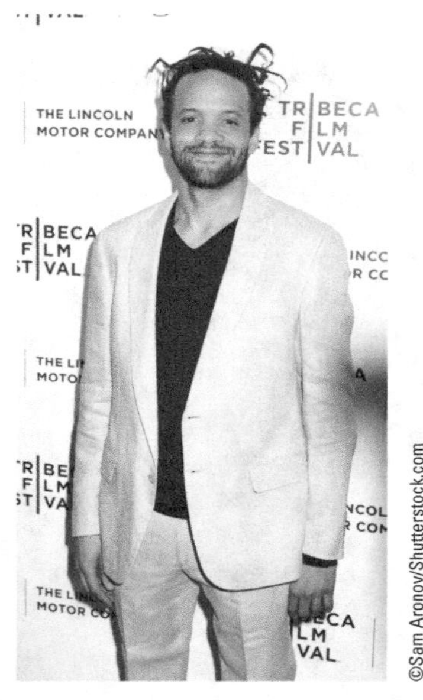

©Sam Aronov/Shutterstock.com

Savion Glover

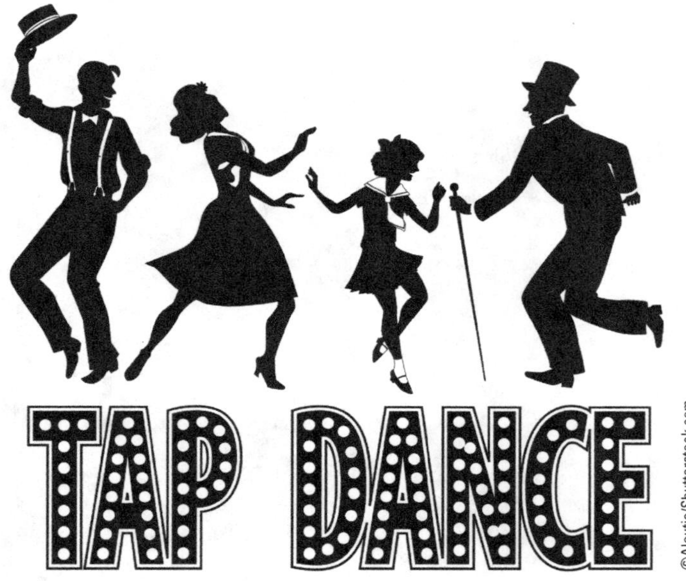

©Aleutie/Shutterstock.com

Prominent Composers and Lyricists and Some of Their More Popular Shows

Richard Adler and Jerry Ross: Pajama Game (1954), Damn Yankees (1955)

Leonard Bernstein: On the Town (1944), Wonderful Town (1953), West Side Story (1957)

Alain Boublil and Claude-Michel Schönberg: Les Misérables (1987), Miss Saigon (1990)

Jerry Bock and Sheldon Harnick: Fiorello! (1959), Tenderloin (1960), She Loves Me (1963), Fiddler on the Roof (1964)

Marvin Hamlisch and Edward Kleban: A Chorus Line (1975)

Jerry Herman: Milk and Honey (1961), Hello Dolly! (1964), Mame (1966), Mack & Mabel (1974), La Cage aux Folles (1983)

Tom Jones and Harvey Schmidt: The Fantasticks (1960), 110 in the Shade (1963), I Do! I Do! (1966)

John Kander and Fred Ebb: Cabaret (1966), Zorba (1968), Chicago (1975), Woman of the Year (1981), Kiss of the Spider Woman (1993), Curtains (2006)

Burton Lane and E.Y. Harburg: Finnian's Rainbow (1947), On a Clear Day You Can See Forever (1965, with **Alan Jay Lerner**)

Frank Loesser: Where's Charley (1948), Guys and Dolls (1950), Most Happy Fella (1956), How to Succeed in Business Without Really Trying (1961)

Alan Menken and Howard Ashman: Beauty and the Beast (1994)

Julie Styne collaborated with Betty Comden, Adolph Green, and others: Peter Pan (1954), Bells Are Ringing (1958), Do Re Mi (1960), Subways Are for Sleeping (1961), Gentlemen Prefer Blondes (1949, with Leo Robin), Funny Girl (1961, with Bob Merrill), Gypsy (1958, with Stephen Sondheim)

Andrew Lloyd Weber and Tim Rice: Joseph and the Amazing Technicolor Dreamcoat (1968), Jesus Christ Superstar (1971), Evita (1976), Cats (1981), Starlight Express (1984), Phantom of the Opera (1986, with **Charles Hart** and **Richard Stilgoe**), Sunset Boulevard (1993, with **Don Black**), Bombay Dreams (2004, with **Don Black**), The Woman in White (2005, with **David Zippel**)

Meredith Wilson: The Music Man (1957), The Unsinkable Molly Brown (1960), Here's Love (1963)

Unit 6, Chapter 3 Listening Box Playlist

LB7: Type in Cats the Musical and choose the top box Memory, Cats the Musical. Select Track 3, Rum Tum Tugger; Track 5, Old Deuteronomy; Track 10, Mr. Mistoffelees; Track 11, Memory.

LB8: Type in Les Misérables and choose Les Misérables, Alain Boublil. Select Overture/ Work Song; Track 15, Red and Black; Track 16, Do You Hear The People Sing?

LB9: Type in Bring in 'da Noise and choose top box Bring in 'da Noise Bring in 'da Funk. Select Track 25, Bring in 'da Noise Bring in 'da Funk; Track 5, Pan Handlers; Track 9, Industrialization; Track 13, Now That's Tap; and Track 24, Hittin'.

Summary of Unit 6, Chapters 1–3 Terms and Study Sheet

Terms: (All these terms have been previously explained)

Comic Opera	Vaudeville
Ballad Opera	Vaudeville roots
Operetta	Burlesque
Minstrelsy	Extravaganzas and Spectacles
Minstrels in America	The Revue

Composers and Lyricists

Dan Emmett, Stephen Foster, James A Bland, George M. Cohan, Jerome Kern, Cole Porter, Richard Rodgers, Oscar Hammerstein, Andrew Lloyd Webber, Trevor Nunn, Richard Stilgoe, Claude-Michel Schönberg, Alain Boublil, Marc Natel, Daryl Waters, Zane Mark, Ann Duquesnay, Reg E. Gaines, George C. Wolf, and Savion Glover (Choreography).

Summary of Listeners Toolbox

Broadway shows cover so many different styles, so the listener has to be prepared for anything. The best thing to do is go to as many shows as possible and absorb all the flavors.

Question

Of the Broadway Shows presented in these chapters, which one do you like best? Consider story and music.

To The Student: The instructor may add or delete study items at his or her discretion.

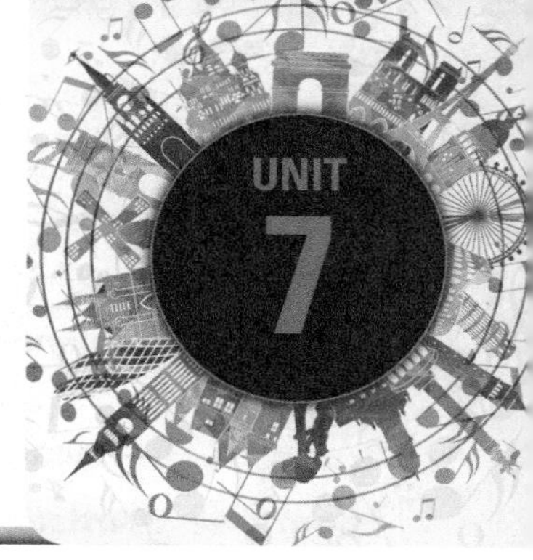

Rock 'n' Roll—Top 40—Country—Gospel

Unit Purpose

To present Rock 'n' Roll, Top 40, Country, and Gospel Music.

CHAPTER 1 EARLY HISTORY AND THE 1950s AND 1960s

What Do We Find in This Period?

Music: It is claimed by many that the musical concept of Rock 'n' Roll started in the late 1940s and early 1950s. It was the coming together of many elements that created this new style. The categorical term Rock 'n' Roll is attributed to Alan Freed, a Cleveland, Ohio, disc jockey. An early television personality was Dick Clark, who hosted the very popular American Bandstand. The general public loved this new genre of music because you could listen to, sing, or dance to the music. As Rock 'n' Roll moved from the 1950s to the 1960s, we experienced a new phenomenon: the British Invasion with such groups as the Beatles. Overall, there were many cultural things that contributed to the direction of this music. Teenagers and race played big parts in influencing song subjects. The early dance craze was the "sock-hop," which began as a dance held in the school gymnasium. Young dancers had to take off their shoes so as not to scuff up the gym floor. For some reason, most of the dancers wore heavy white sox. As time passed, the newer dances were the twist, funk, disco, house, techno, and hip-hop. Of course, our present popular category is Rap, which is often described as music of the street, or "the hood."

The instrumentation of early Rock 'n' Roll bands was fashioned after the rhythm section of the jazz band which included piano, bass, guitar, and drums. Often times a tenor saxophone was added and it was used as a melodic lead or solo instrument. As time progressed, the guitar was featured more and some groups like the Beatles initially did not use keyboard at all.

Texture: Homophonic

Forms and influences: Rhythm and blues, blues, soul, gospel, jazz, boogie-woogie, country and folk, heavy metal, soft rock, rap and hip-hop, grunge, alternative, and pop punk. African-American and big band influences contributed greatly.

Composers/Artists: Since there are so many, I will cite some of the main contributors in each decade.

Travel to: Many US cities and England

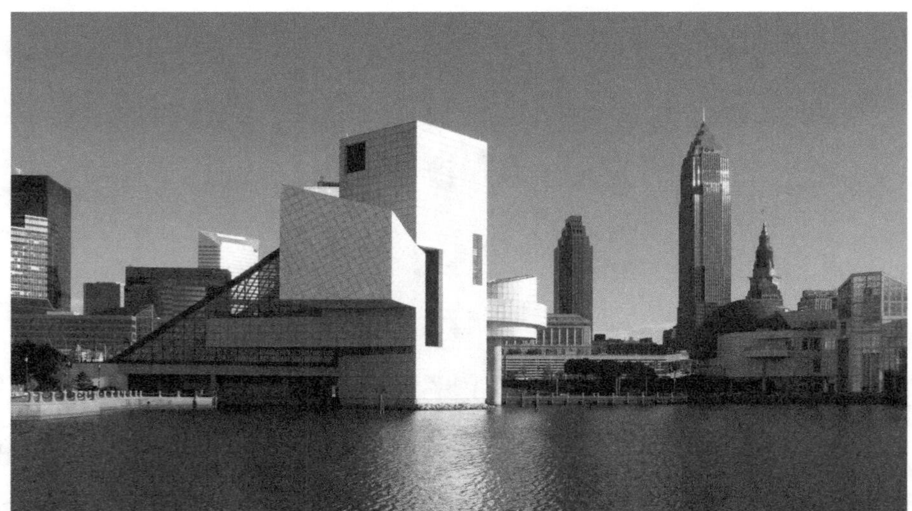

©Amy Nichole Harris/Shutterstock.com

Rock 'n' Roll Hall of Fame, Cleveland, Ohio

The 1950s

Some highlights of music in the 1950s:

1. Alan Freed, a disc jockey from Cleveland, began to play rhythm and blues records on his radio show. He eventually called the show, "The Moondog House," and he was known as, "The King of the Moondoggers." Freed recognized early on that teenagers were a vast and receptive audience. Most of his music selections and radio programs catered to teenagers. He was also very clever in introducing black music to white audiences and vice versa. He was a constant advocate for young causes and was loved by many.
2. In the 1950s, the electric guitar became commercially available and this development had a great impact on musical sound.
3. The 78 RPM record was replaced by the LP. LP stands for long play and was a great advancement in recording. The 78 record had only one song per side. The LP was an invention by a scientist at Columbia University, New York. The new

process was called microgrooves and enabled production people to put five songs on each side of the vinyl.

4. Another important individual who was very influential in promoting Rock 'n' Roll was Dick Clark. He was affiliated with the show American Bandstand from 1956 to 1989. The show was broadcast from a studio which held about 200 teenagers who were on five days a week dancing to the current hits.
5. There are three main categories in 1950s Rock 'n' Roll. They are Rhythm and blues, Rockabilly, and Doo-Wop.
6. Some of the most famous Rhythm and Blues artists and groups are Bill Haley and the Comets, The Drifters, the Dominos, The Platters, B. B. King, Chuck Berry, Little Richard, Fats Domino, and Lloyd Price.
7. Some of the most famous Rockabilly artists are Elvis Presley, Jerry Lee Lewis, Carl Perkins, Johnny Cash, and Buddy Holly.
8. Some of the most famous Doo-Wop groups are The Orioles, The Penguins, The Five Satins, The Moonglows, The Del-Vikings, The Diamonds, Frankie Lymon and the Teenagers, Johnny Maestro and the Brooklyn Bridge, The Cadillacs.

The Rhythm and Blues Category

In the R and B category there is no question that one group put Rock 'n' Roll on the map. That group is Bill Haley and the Comets. Their first big hit was "Crazy Man Crazy," in 1953, but the tune that launched the musical genre was "Rock Around the Clock," in 1955.

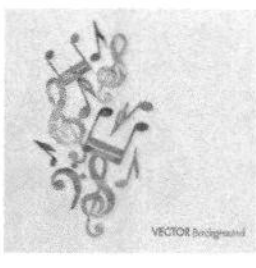

Listening Box 1

Type in Bill Haley and under Album Results, choose the Platinum Collection, Bill Haley and the Comets. Select Track 1, Rock Around the Clock and Track 2, Shake, Rattle & Roll.

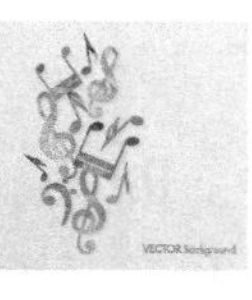

Listening Box 2

Type in Little Richard and under Album Results, choose the essential Little Richard, Little Richard. Select Track 1, Tutti Frutti; Track 2, Long Tall Sally, and Track 5, Good Golly Miss Molly.

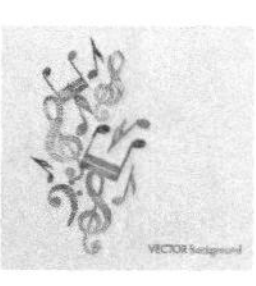

Listening Box 3

Type in Chuck Berry and under Album results, choose The Great Twenty-Eight, Chuck Berry. Select Track 1, Maybellene; Track 6, Roll Over Beethoven; Track 13, Johnny B. Goode.

The Rockabilly Category

Rockabilly music combines country roots with rhythm and blues. It was a style predominantly sung by white singers, but not exclusively. Probably the single most successful individual in all of the 1950s music industry was Elvis Presley. He captivated female audiences all over the world with looks, music, and body movements. There is no question that he sold more music and was the highest earner of all musicians of the day.

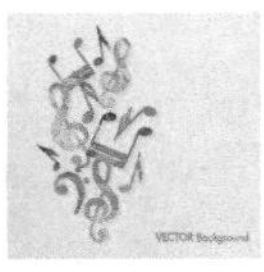

Listening Box 4

Type in Elvis Presley and under Album Results, choose The Essential Elvis Presley, Various Artists. Select Disc 1, Track 6, Blue Suede Shoes; Track 7, Hound Dog; Track 12, Jailhouse Rock.

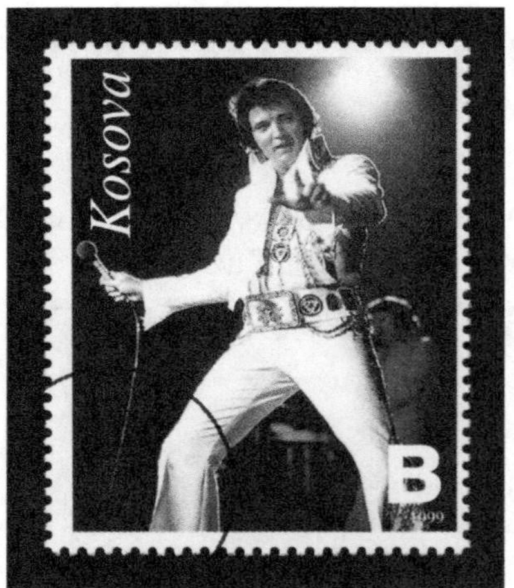

©BekehStock/Shutterstock.com

Elvis Presley

©Malgorzata Litkowska/Shutterstock.com

Graceland, Memphis, Tennessee

The Doo-Wop Category

The Doo-Wop sound of Rock 'n' Roll featured group harmony and nonsense syllables. It was a style that caused a lot of young teenage guys to try by the corner candy store. Believe it or not, some of these local groups became famous.

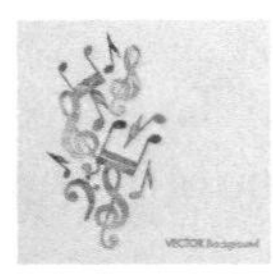

Listening Box 5

Type in The Del-Vikings and choose the top box Whispering Bells, The Del-Vikings. Select Track 1, Come Go With Me and Track 3, Whispering Bells.

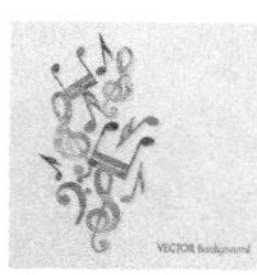

Listening Box 6

Type in The Penguins and choose top box The Penguins, Doo-Wop. Select Track 1, Earth Angel (Will You Be Mine Version 1).

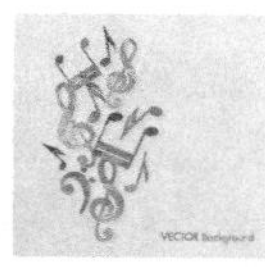

Listening Box 7

Type in The Cadillacs and under Album Results, choose The Cadillacs Meet The Orioles, Various Artists. Select Track 1, Speedo; Track 3, Zoom.

The 1960s

Some highlights of music in the 1960s:

1. There was a new movement in music called the British Invasion. Early groups such as The Beatles and Rolling Stones made their way to America and became instant sensations as they performed for massive audiences.
2. The themes for early Rock songs were often about love and relationships. In the 1960s, social commentary and politics entered the picture.
3. The Beatles did not use a keyboard in much of their early music and this created a more metallic sound which eventually led to Heavy Metal.
4. Television became a big factor in promoting music and two of the main shows were American Bandstand and The Ed Sullivan Show.
5. In 1967, outdoor festivals began with the Monterey Pop Festival. Over 50,000 people attended each day for three days.
6. In 1969, the Woodstock Music and Art Fair took place in Bethel, New York. This festival drew over 500,000 people.
7. The top money earners of the decade were The Beatles and Elvis Presley.
8. Some of the most famous British Invasion bands are The Beatles, The Rolling Stones, The Doors, The Who, The Animals, The Yardbirds, and Herman's Hermits.
9. Some of the most famous girl groups are The Shirelles, The Supremes, The Dixie Cups, The Chiffons, The Ronettes, and The Shangri-Las.
10. Some of the most famous Motown artists and groups are Stevie Wonder, Smokey Robinson, Marvin Gaye, The Jackson Five, The Temptations, The Marvelettes, and Gladys Knight and The Pips.
11. Some of the most famous Psychedelic Rock groups are The Grateful Dead, Pink Floyd, and Jefferson Airplane.
12. Some of the most famous Hard Rock bands are Cream, Led Zeppelin, Deep Purple, and Vanilla Fudge. Also, Jimi Hendrix fits into this category.
13. One of the most famous Bubble Gum rock bands is The Monkees.

The British Invasion—The Beatles

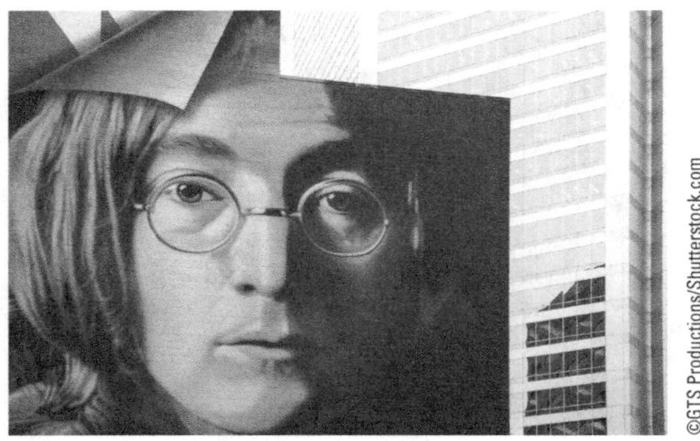

©GTS Productions/Shutterstock.com

Poster of John Lennon

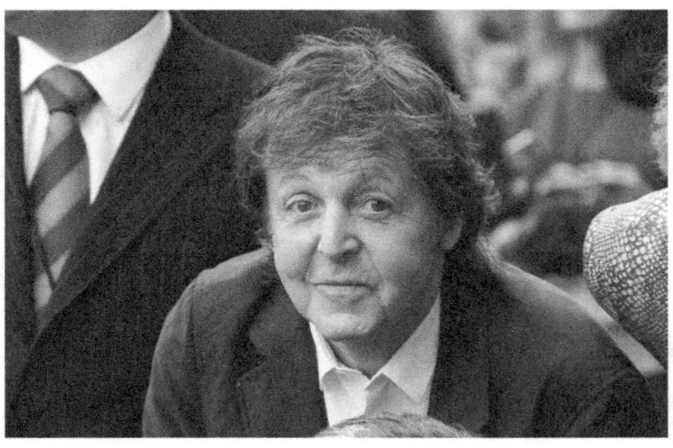

©s_bukley/Shutterstock.com

Paul McCartney

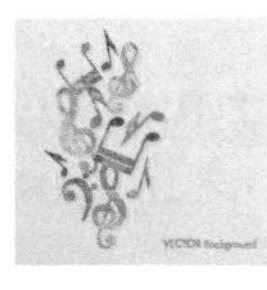

Listening Box 8

Type in The Beatles and under Album Results, choose the red album with the yellow number 1. Select Track 3, She Loves You; Track 4, I Want To Hold Your Hand; Track 6, A Hard Day's Night; and Track 27, The Long and Winding Road.

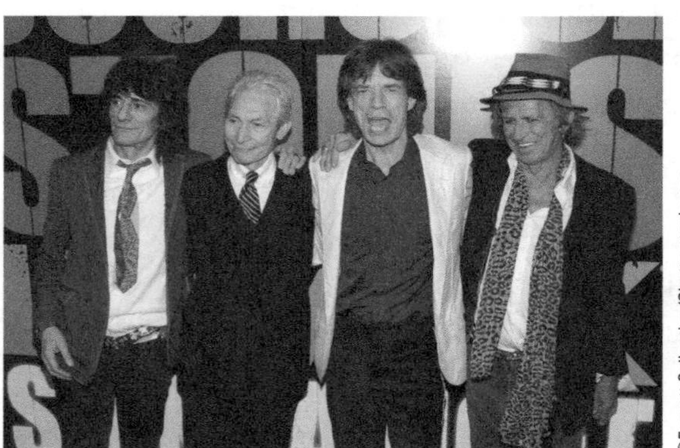

©Everett Collection/Shutterstock.com

The Rolling Stones

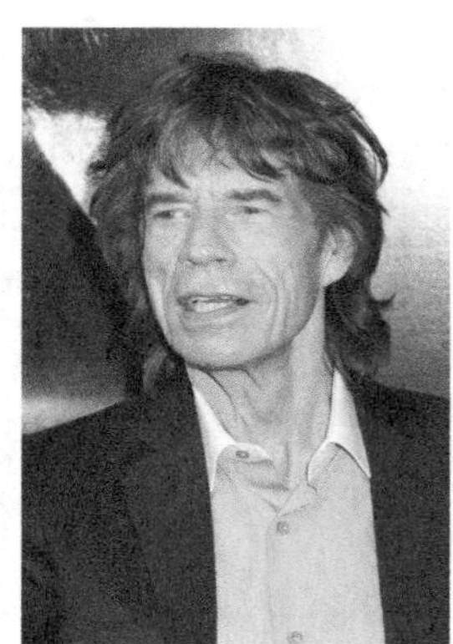

©JStone/Shutterstock.com

Mick Jagger

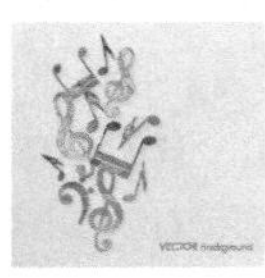

Listening Box 9

Type in The Rolling Stones and under Track Results, choose Beast of Burden, The Rolling Stones. Select Track 4, It's Only Rock 'n' Roll.

Girl Groups—The Supremes (Featuring Diana Ross)

The Supremes started out as a four-member group in the late 1950s. They recorded for the Motown Company. By 1962, they were down to three members and remained that way until 1970, when Diana Ross left for a solo career and was replaced.

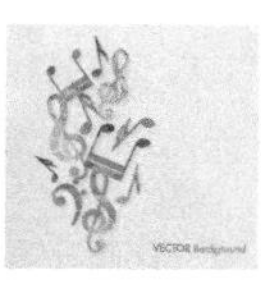

Listening Box 10

Type in The Supremes and under Track Results, choose I Hear a Symphony, The Supremes. Select disc 1, Track 12, Stop! In The Name of Love; Track 17, I Hear a Symphony; and Track 20, You Can't Hurry Love.

Motown

Motown is short for "Motor Town," which referred to the car industry in Detroit, Michigan. Motown was started in 1959 by Berry Gordy, and the company was called Tamla Records. In 1960, the name was changed to Motown Record Corporation. The main concern of the company was to produce and promote African American talent. I will cite a few of the greats who recorded for this company and some of their hits.

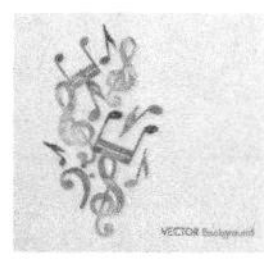

Listening Box 11

Type in The Definitive Collection and under Album Results, choose The Definitive Collection, Stevie Wonder. Select Track 5, For Once in My Life; Track 8, You Are The Sunshine of My Life; Track 19, I Just Called to Say I Love You.

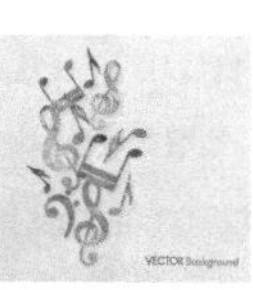

Listening Box 12

Type in Gladys Knight and choose top box Midnight Train to Georgia, Gladys Knight. Select Track 7, Midnight Train to Georgia; Track 9, Best Thing That Ever Happened to Me; Track 15, The Way We Were/Try to Remember.

Psychedelic Rock

Psychedelic Rock is music that was inspired by mind-altering drugs, namely LSD which stands for lysergic acid diethylamide also known as acid, a mind altering drug, that was

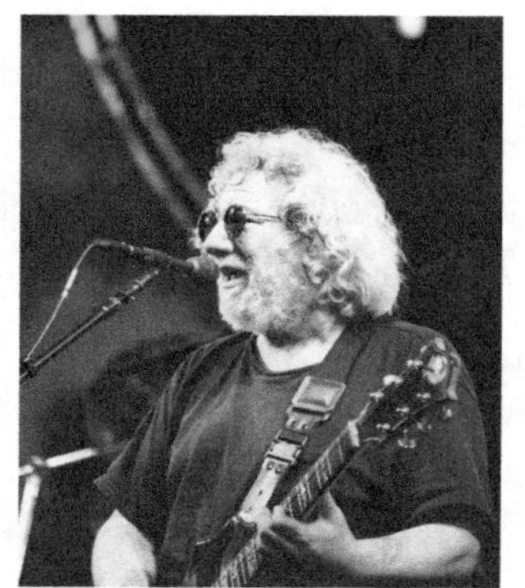

The Grateful Dead (Jerry Garcia)

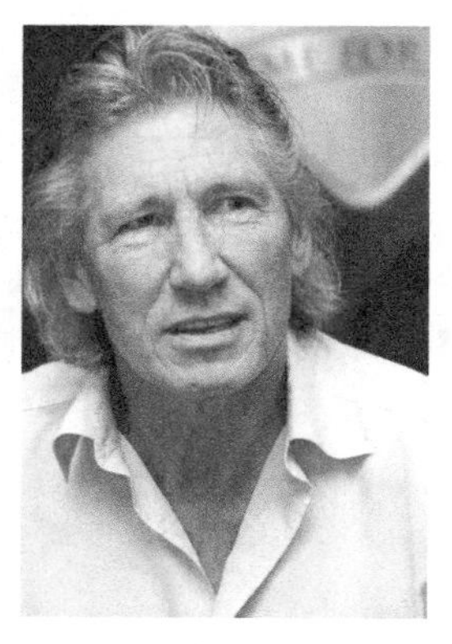

Pink Floyd (Roger Waters)

popular in this era. The music tried to alter the mind as did the drugs. This style of music was definitely influenced by the concepts of Eastern mysticism and incorporated things such as Eastern scales (ragas).

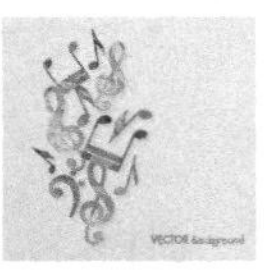

Listening Box 13

Type in The Grateful Dead and under Album Results, choose The Best of The Grateful Dead. Select Track 4, Dark Star; Track 7, Uncle John's Band; Track 10, Truckin'.

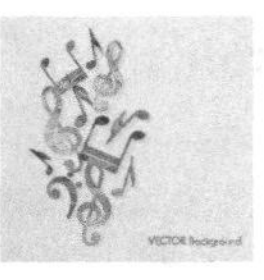

Listening Box 14

Type in Pink Floyd and under Artist Results, choose Pink Floyd, Art & Progressive Rock. Select Track 3, Another Brick in the Wall; Track 5, Time; Track 6, Money.

Hard Rock—Heavy Metal

The concept of Heavy Metal started in the late 1960s, predominantly in Britain. Some of the elements that are included in this genre are blues, psychedelic rock, heavy guitar playing, very loud sound, and a harmonic device called power chords. The performance style is definitely designed to project strong and macho. Heavy Metal music is often used to psyche up sports teams before they go out and do battle.

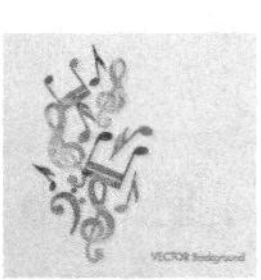

Listening Box 15

Type in Led Zeppelin and choose top box Black Dog, Led Zeppelin. Select Disc 1, Track 4, Stairway to Heaven; Track 8, When the Levee Breaks.

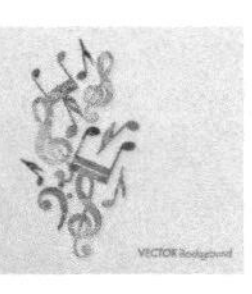

Listening Box 16

Type in Black Sabbath and under Artist Results, choose Black Sabbath, Metal. Select Track 1, Iron Man; Track 2, Paranoid; Track 6, Heaven and Hell.

Unit 7, Chapter 1 Listening Box Playlist

LB1: Type in Bill Haley and under Album Results, choose The Platinum Collection, Bill Haley & The Comets. Select Track 1, Rock Around the Clock; Track 2, Shake, Rattle and Roll.

LB2: Type in Little Richard and under Album Results, choose The Essential Little Richard, Little Richard. Select Track 1, Tutti Frutti; Track 2, Long Tall Sally; Track 5, Good Golly Miss Molly.

LB3: Type in Chuck Berry and under Album Results, choose The Great Twenty—Eight, Chuck Berry. Select Track 1, Maybellene; Track 6, Roll Over Beethoven; Track 13, Johnny B. Goode.

LB4: Type in Elvis Presley and under Album Results, choose The Essential Elvis Pressley, Various Artists. Select disc 1, Track 6, Blue Suede Shoes; Track 7, Hound Dog; Track 12, Jailhouse Rock.

LB5: Type in the Del-Vikings and choose top box Whispering Bells, The Del-Vikings. Select Track 1, Come Go With Me; Track 3, Whispering Bells.

LB6: Type in The Penguins and choose top box The Penguins, Doo-Wop. Select Track 1, Earth Angel (Will You Be Mine) (Version 1).

LB7: Type in The Cadillacs and under Album Results, choose The Cadillacs Meet the Orioles, Various Artists. Select Track 1, Speedo; Track 3, Zoom.

LB8: Type in The Beatles and under Album Results, choose the Red Album with the yellow number 1. Select Track 3, She Loves You; Track 4, I Want To Hold Your Hand; Track 6, A Hard Day's Night; Track 27, The Long and Winding Road.

LB9: Type in The Rolling Stones and under Track Results, choose Beast of Burden, The Rolling Stones. Select Track 4, It's Only Rock 'n' Roll.

LB10: Type in The Supremes and under Track Results, choose I Hear a Symphony, The Supremes. Select disc 1, Track 12, Stop! In The Name of Love; Track 17, I Hear a Symphony; Track 20, You Can't Hurry Love.

LB11: Type in The Definitive Collection and under Album Results, choose The Definitive Collection, Stevie Wonder. Select Track 5, For Once in My Life; Track 8, You Are The Sunshine of My Life; Track 19, I Just Called to Say I Love You.

LB12: Type in Gladys Knight and choose top box Midnight Train to Georgia, Gladys Knight. Select Track 7, Midnight Train to Georgia; Track 9, Best Thing That Ever Happened to Me; Track 15, The Way We Were / Try To Remember.

LB13: Type in The Grateful Dead and under Album Results, choose the Best of The Grateful Dead. Select Track 4, Dark Star; Track 7, Uncle John's Band; Track 10, Truckin'.

LB14: Type in Pink Floyd and under Artist Results, choose Pink Floyd, Art and Progressive Rock. Select Track 3, Another Brick in The Wall; Track 5, Time; Track 6, Money.

LB15: Type in Led Zeppelin and choose top box Black Dog, Led Zeppelin. Select disc 1, Track 4, Stairway to Heaven; Track 8, When The Levee Breaks.

LB16: Type in Black Sabbath and under Artist Results, choose Black Sabbath, Metal. Select Track 1, Iron Man; Track 2, Paranoid; Track 6, Heaven and Hell.

CHAPTER 2 THE 1970s AND 1980s

Some highlights of music in the 1970s:

1. Psychedelic Rock declined and was transformed into Progressive Rock. There was also a move to emphasize Heavy Metal.
2. Sports arenas became new venues for touring bands.
3. There was a clear distinction between Top 40 and Rock 'n' Roll.
4. Live performance albums became very popular with the general public.
5. The 1970s brought us more singer/songwriters.
6. In the late 1970s we get the emergence of New Wave, which added synthesizers to the mix.
7. With all the new transformations in Rock of the 1970s, there is no question Disco dominated.

Some of the popular styles in the 1970s and some of their artists:

Soft Rock: Billy Joel, Elton John, Fleetwood Mac

Arena Rock/Heavy Metal: Deep Purple, Queen, Van Halen

Heartland Rock: Credence Clearwater Revival, Bruce Springsteen

Progressive Rock: Genesis, Emerson, Lake & Palmer

Southern Rock: The Allman Brothers, Charlie Daniels, Lynyrd Skynyrd

Country Rock: The Eagles, Crosby, Stills and Nash

Punk Rock: The Ramones, The Damned

New Wave: Blondie, Elvis Costello, Talking Heads

Note: This is by no means a complete list, but should give you a good idea of categories and artists in the 1970s. Also, you will find the appropriate music categories for the listening boxes listed earlier.

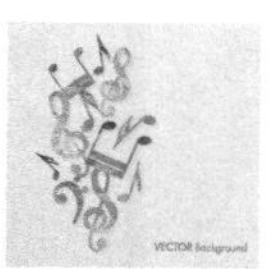

Listening Box 17

Type in The Very Best of Fleetwood Mac and choose the top box with the same name. Select disc 1, Track 1, Monday Morning and disc 2, Track 2, Don't Stop.

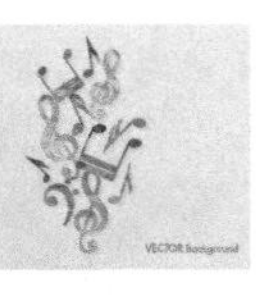

Listening Box 18

Type in Bayou Country and choose top box Proud Mary, Credence Clearwater Revival. Select Track 1, Born on the Bayou; Track 6, Proud Mary.

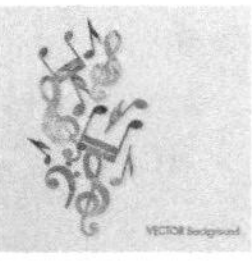

Listening Box 19

Type in Emerson, Lake & Palmer and under Album Results, choose Works, Vol. 1, Emerson, Lake & Palmer. Select Track 5, Nobody Loves You Like I Do; Track 13, Fanfare for the Common Man.

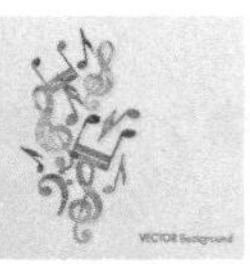

Listening Box 20

Type in Billy Joel and choose top box Honesty, Billy Joel. Select Track 1, Piano Man; Track 9, Movin' Out (Anthony's Song); Track 11, Just The Way You Are; Track 12, Honesty.

Some highlights of music in the 1980s

1. In 1981, MTV was born.
2. In 1984, VH1 was born.
3. Music videos started to flood the market and brought a new music presence to the general public.
4. More success for female artists was achieved.
5. Many more concerts and other projects were done for charity.
6. A definite awareness of a new style of music called Rap.
7. House and Techno music began in the 1980s and are essentially electronic dance music.

Some of the popular styles in the 1980s and some of their artists:

Rap/Hip-Hop: LL Cool J, Ice T, Beastie Boys

R&B/Blues: Michael Jackson, Prince, Whitney Houston, Lionel Richie

Pop: Madonna, Kenny Rogers, Phil Collins

New Wave: Talking Heads, The Police, Depeche Mode

Heavy Metal: Iron Maiden, Judas Priest, Ozzy Osbourne, Def Leppard

Note: Once again, this is by no means a complete list, but should give you a good idea of categories and artists of the 1980s. Also, you will find the appropriate music categories for the listening boxes listed earlier.

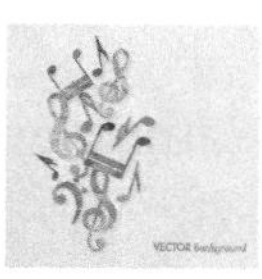

Listening Box 21

Type in Michael Jackson and under Album Results, choose Thriller, Michael Jackson. Select Track 1, Wanna be Startin' Somethin'; Track 4, Thriller; Track 6, Billy Jean.

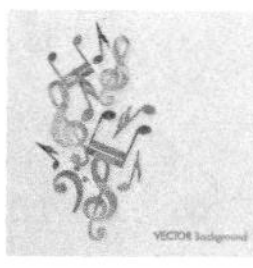

Listening Box 22

Type in LL Cool J and under Playlist Results, choose LL Cool J's Blueprint. Select Track 2, I Need a Beat; Track 3, I Can't Live Without My Radio.

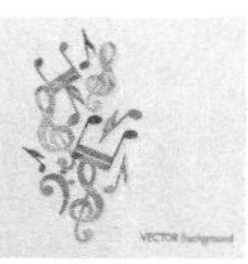

Listening Box 23

Type in Judas Priest and choose top box Painkiller, Judas Priest. Select Track 1, Painkiller; Track 2, Hell Patrol; Track 5, Metal Melt Down.

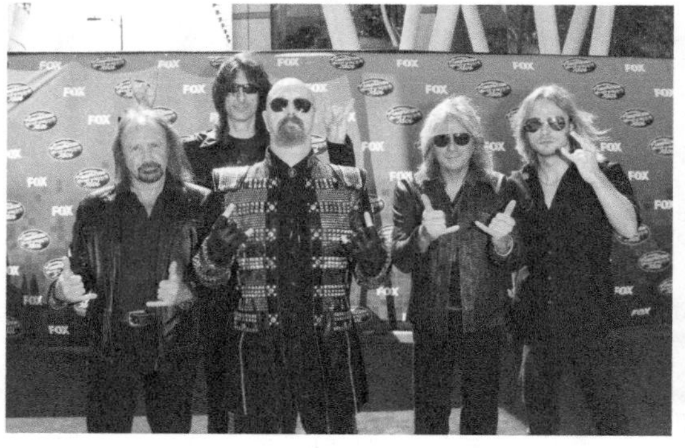

©s_bukley/Shutterstock.com

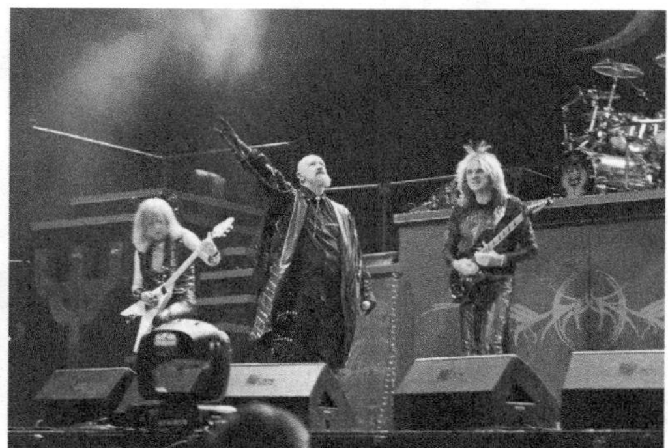

©Narcis Parfenti/Shutterstock.com

Judas Priest

Unit 7, Chapter 2 Listening Box Playlist

LB17: Type in The Very Best of Fleetwood Mac and choose top box with the same name. Select disc 1, Track 1, Monday Morning; disc 2, Track 2, Don't Stop.

LB18: Type in Bayou Country and choose top box Proud Mary, Credence Clearwater Revival. Select Track 1, Born on the Bayou; Track 6, Proud Mary.

LB19: Type in Emerson, Lake & Palmer and under Album Results, choose Works, Vol. 1, Emerson, Lake & Palmer. Select Track 5, Nobody Loves You Like I do; Track 13, Fanfare for The Common Man.

LB20: Type in Billy Joel and choose top box Honesty, Billy Joel. Select Track 1, Piano Man; Track 9, Movin' Out; Track 11, Just The Way You Are; Track 12, Honesty.

LB21: Type in Michael Jackson and under Album Results, choose Thriller, Michael Jackson. Select Track 1, Wanna Be Startin' Somethin', Track 4, Thriller; Track 6, Billy Jean.

LB22: Type in LL Cool J and under Playlist Results, choose LL Cool J's Blueprint. Select Track 2, I Need a Beat; Track 3, I Can't Live Without My Radio.

LB23: Type in Judas Priest and choose top box Painkiller. Select Track 1, Painkiller; Track 2, Hell Patrol; Track 5, Metal Melt Down.

CHAPTER 3 THE 1990s AND 2000s

Some highlights of music in the 1990s:

1. Alternative subgenres like Grunge and Pop Punk were extremely popular in this decade.
2. Many artists were resistant to the demands of the big companies and decided to go in different directions.
3. Hip-Hop continued to expand.
4. Fusion genres expanded. For example, Jazz/Rock and Hip-Hop/Soul emerged.
5. Heavy Metal turned into Rap Metal or Rapcore.

Some of the popular styles in the 1990s and their artists:

Alternative: R.E.M., Smashing Pumpkins, Red Hot Chilli Peppers, Pearl Jam, Radiohead

Grunge: Nirvana, Alice in Chains, Stone Temple Pilots

Pop: Shania Twain, Whitney Houston, Britney Spears, Backstreet Boys, Destiny's Child, The Spice Girls, Celine Dion, Sting, Michael Bolton

Metal: Korn, Limp Bizkit, Nine Inch Nails, Metallica

Hip-Hop: Public Enemy, Tupac Shakur, Jay-Z, Coolio

Hard Rock: Guns 'n' Roses, Van Halen, Aerosmith, AC/DC, Creed, U2

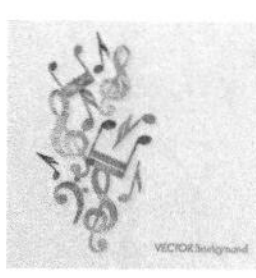

Listening Box 24

Type in Red Hot Chilli Peppers and under Track Results, choose Under The Bridge—Red Hot Chilli P ..., Primary Artist. Select Track 10, Under The Bridge.

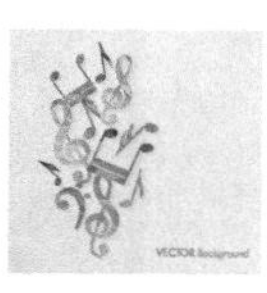

Listening Box 25

Type in Nirvana and choose top box Nirvana, Grunge. Select Track 15, All Apologies (Unplugged in New York).

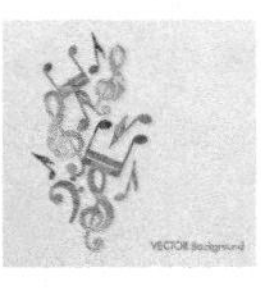

Listening Box 26

Type in Backstreet Boys and under Artist Results, choose Backstreet Boys, Pop. Select Track 5, Quit Playing Games (With My Heart); Track 12, We've Got it Goin' On.

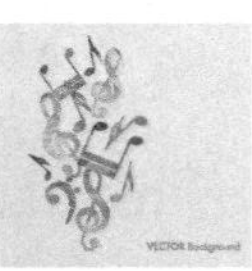

Listening Box 27

Type in Van Halen and choose top box Runnin' With The Devil, Van Halen. Select Track 1, Runnin' With The Devil; Track 7, Atomic Punk.

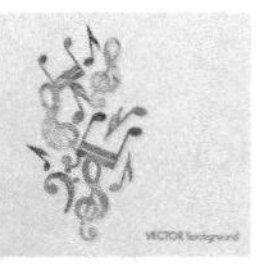

Listening Box 28

Type in Destiny's Child and under Artist Results, choose Destiny's Child, Contemporary R&B. Select Track 2, Survivor.

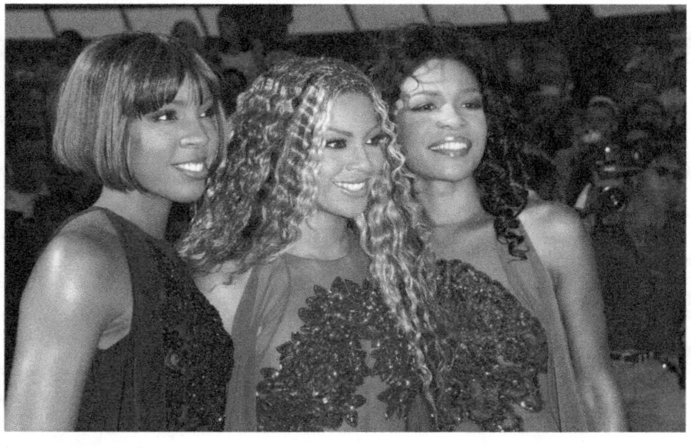

Destiny's Child

Some highlights of music in the 2000s:

1. There weren't many new styles in this period, but rather a convergence of older styles.
2. Rock declined as it gave way to Hip-Hop and Rap.
3. What really broke out in the 2000s are advances in new devices and their programs such as iTunes.
4. The internet played a major role in the globalization and distribution of music. YouTube became a major player in bringing music videos to the general public.
5. World situations such as the War on Terror and 911 greatly affected the economy which caused a downturn in music sales.

6. Musically, the Bass instrument was featured less and this gave a greater presence to the Drums. This created overall, a very loud sound.
7. The genres of Adult Contemporary and Country found great success in the 2000s.

Some popular artists of the decade:

Hip-Hop: Eminem, Kanye West, 50 Cent, Ludacris, Nas, T.I, Lil Wayne, Nelly, Drake, Outkast, Pitbull, FloRida, Usher, DMX, Rakim, Dr. Dre

Pop Female: Taylor Swift, Rihanna, Adele, Pink, Christina Aguilera, Lady Gaga, Beyoncé

Alternative Rock: Cold Play

Metal: Linkin Park, Tool

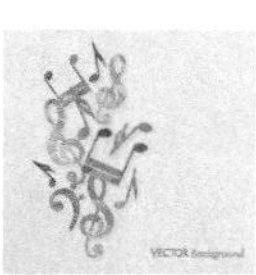

Listening Box 29

Type in Kanye West and choose top box Stronger, Kanye West. Select Track 3, Stronger.

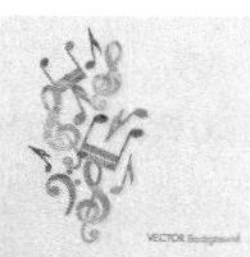

Listening Box 30

Type in Adele and choose top box Adele, Pop. Select Track 1, Hello; Track 2, When We Were Young.

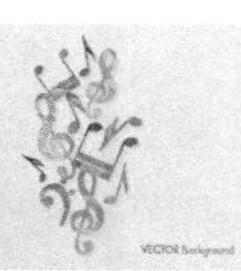

Listening Box 31

Type in Linkin Park and under Artist Results, choose Linkin Park, Alt Metal. Select Track 1, Numb; Track 2, In The End; Track 5, Somewhere I Belong.

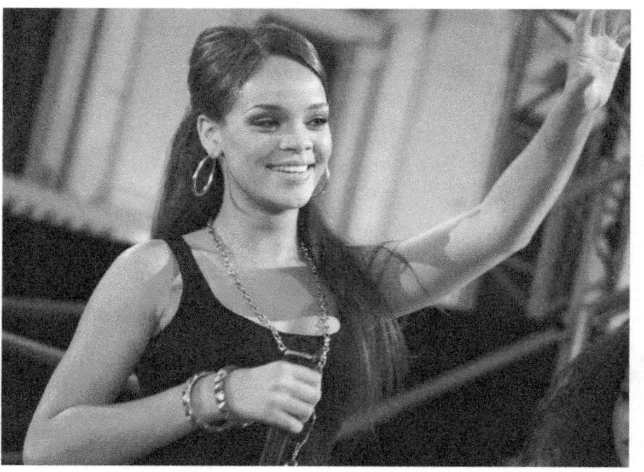

©Dino Geromella/Shutterstock.com

Rihanna

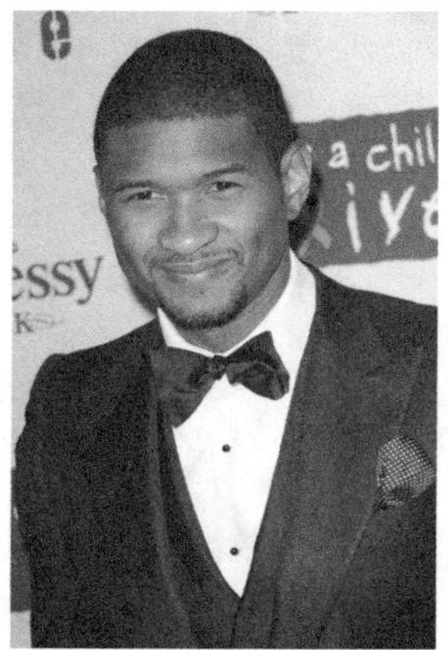

©Everett Collection/Shutterstock.com

Usher

Unit 7, Chapter 3 Listening Box Playlist

LB24: Type in Red Hot Chilli Peppers and under Track Results, choose Under the Bridge—Red Hot Chilli P . . ., Primary Artist. Select Track 10, Under the Bridge.

LB25: Type in Nirvana and choose top box Nirvana, Grunge. Select Track 15, All Apologies (Unplugged in New York).

LB26: Type in Backstreet Boys and under Artist Results, choose Backstreet Boys, Pop. Select Track 5, Quit Playing Games (With My Heart); Track 12, We've Got it Goin' On.

LB27: Type in Van Halen and under Artist Results, choose Van Halen, Hard Rock. Select Track 1, Jump; Track 4, Runnin' With The Devil; Track 46, Atomic Punk. (This selection is five from the bottom of the list.)

LB28: Type in Destiny's Child and under Artist Results, choose Destiny's Child, Contemporary R&B. Select Track 2, Survivor.

LB29: Type in Kanye West and choose top box Stronger, Kanye West. Select Track 3, Stronger.

LB30: Type in Adele and choose top box Adele, Pop. Select Track 1, Hello; Track 2, When We Were Young.

LB31: Type in Linkin Park and under Artist Results, choose Linkin Park, Alt Metal. Select Track 1, Numb; Track 2, In The End; Track 5, Somewhere I Belong.

CHAPTER 4 COUNTRY MUSIC

Some highlights of Country Music:

1. Country Music started in the 1920s and was originally called Hillbilly Music.
2. Pretty much starting in the South by European immigrants, this genre has Irish and Celtic roots.
3. Early instruments used were fiddles, banjos, electric, and acoustic guitars.
4. Bluegrass and Honky Tonk were two important styles developed in the 1950s and 1960s.
5. The Nashville Sound really helped popularize Country with the general public.
6. The British Invasion of the 1960s caused the fusion between Country and Rock.
7. In the 1970s and 1980s, Country fused with Folk music by artists like John Denver.
8. In the 1990s, artists such as Garth Brooks and others were well received which further helped the popularity of the music.
9. In the 2000s, Country fused with Punk and Hip-Hop.

Note: I will list artists in old and new categories.

Older Artists: Waylon Jennings, Hank Williams, Buck Owens, Eddie Arnold, Johnny Cash, Dolly Parton, Willie Nelson

Newer Artists: Shania Twain, Carrie Underwood, Martina McBride, Tim McGraw, Faith Hill, Toby Keith, Alan Jackson, Garth Brooks, Kenny Rogers, Reba McEntire, Kenny Chesney, Blake Shelton, Randy Travis

Older Recordings

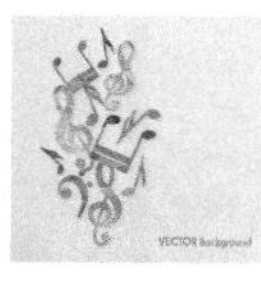

Listening Box 32

Type in Hank Williams and under Album Results, choose Hank Williams Greatest Collection, Hank Williams. Select Track 1, Your Cheatin' Heart; Track 4, Hey Good Lookin'.

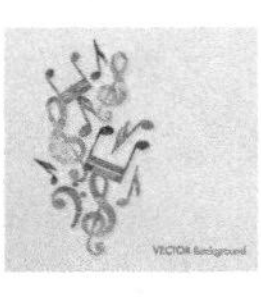

Listening Box 33

Type in Waylon Jennings and choose top box Waylon Jennings, Outlaw Country. Select Track 4, Theme from the Dukes of Hazzard (Good Ol' Boys); Track 5, Good Hearted Woman.

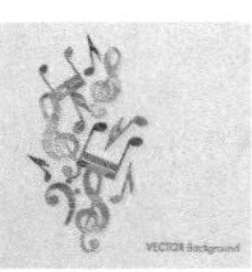

Listening Box 34

Type in Johnny Cash and choose top box Johnny Cash, Outlaw Country. Select Track 2, I Walk The Line; Track 3, Folsom Prison Blues (Live).

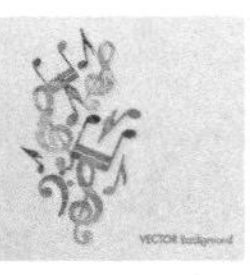

Listening Box 35

Type in Willie Nelson and under Artist Results, choose Willie Nelson, Outlaw Country. Select Track 1, Always on My Mind; Track 2, On The Road Again; Track 6, Georgia On My Mind; Track 7, City of New Orleans.

Newer Recordings

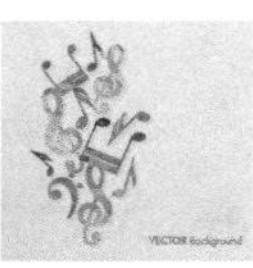

Listening Box 36

Type in Carrie Underwood and choose top box Heartbeat, Carrie Underwood. Select Track 1, Renegade Runaway; Track 3, Church Bells; Track 4, Heartbeat; Track 8, Chaser.

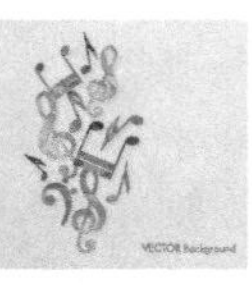

Listening Box 37

Type in Alan Jackson and under Album Results, choose 34 Number Ones, Alan Jackson. Select Track 24, Little Bitty; Track 33, It's Five O'Clock Somewhere (Alan Jackson and Jimmy Buffett).

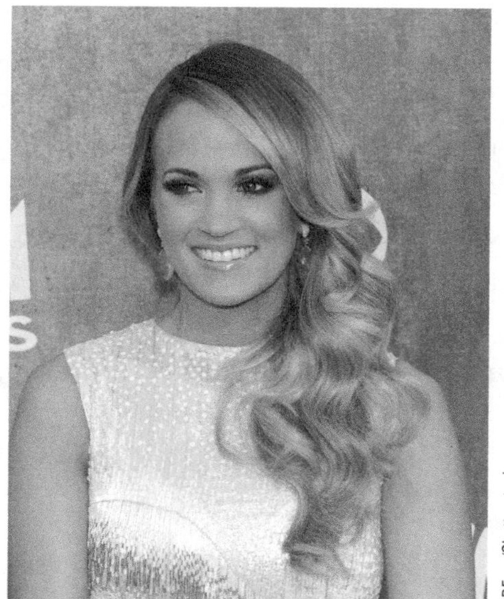
©DFree/Shutterstock.com

Carrie Underwood

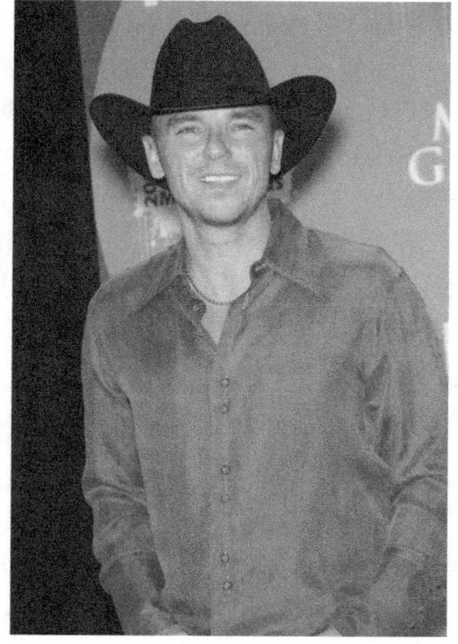
©Featureflash Photo Agency/Shutterstock.com

Kenny Chesney

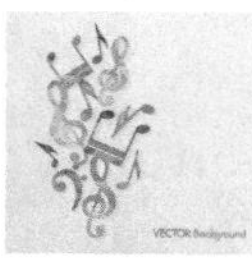

Listening Box 38

Type in Reba McEntire and choose top box Reba McEntire, Country Pop/ Cosmopolitan. Select Track 1, Fancy; Track 3, The Night The Lights Went Out in Georgia; Track 8, Is There Life Out There; Track 9, The Greatest Man I Never Knew.

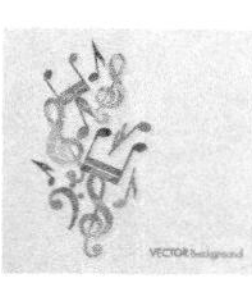

Listening Box 39

Type in Kenny Chesney and under Album Results, choose Greatest Hits, Kenny Chesney. Select Track 1, I Lost It; Track 2, Don't Happen Twice; Track 4, Fall in Love.

Unit 7, Chapter 4 Listening Box Playlist

LB32: Type in Hank Williams and under Album Results, choose Hank Williams Greatest Collection, Hank Williams. Select Track 1, Your Cheatin' Heart; Track 4, Hey, Good Lookin'.

LB33: Type in Waylon Jennings and choose top box Waylon Jennings, Outlaw Country. Select Track 4, Theme From The Dukes of Hazard (Good Ol' Boys); Track 5, Good Hearted Woman.

LB34: Type in Johnny Cash and choose top box Johnny Cash, Outlaw Country. Select Track 2, I Walk The Line; Track 3, Folsom Prison Blues (Live).

LB35: Type in Willie Nelson and under Artist Results, choose Willie Nelson, Outlaw Country. Select Track 1, Always On My Mind; Track 2, On The Road; Track 6, Georgia On My Mind; Track 7, City of New Orleans.

LB36: Type in Carrie Underwood and choose top box Heartbeat, Carrie Underwood. Select Track 1, Runaway Renegade; Track 3, Church Bells; Track 4, Heartbeat; Track 8, Chaser.

LB37: Type in Alan Jackson and under Album Results, choose 34 Number Ones, Alan Jackson. Select Track 24, Little Bitty; Track 33, It's Five O'Clock Somewhere (Alan Jackson and Jimmy Buffett).

LB38: Type in Reba McEntire and choose top box Reba McEntire, Country Pop/ Cosmopolitan. Select Track 1, Fancy; Track 3, The Night The Lights Went Out In Georgia; Track 8, Is There Life Out There; Track 9, The Greatest Man I Never Knew.

LB39: Type in Kenny Chesney and under Album Results, choose Greatest Hits, Kenny Chesney. Select Track 1, I Lost It; Track 2, Don't Happen Twice; Track 4, Fall In Love.

CHAPTER 5 GOSPEL MUSIC

Some highlights of Gospel Music:

1. While there is no specific date as to the beginning of Gospel Music, it is generally believed that it started in the 1800s.
2. The music has African American roots and early concepts were created by slaves.
3. Slaves were prohibited from playing or singing their traditional music by plantation owners. Also prohibited was the use of their traditional instruments. These restrictions caused a need to create a new music. Enter the Spiritual.
4. Spirituals are songs with Christian themes that stress worship, praise, atonement, salvation, hope, and thanks to God. It is in this context that the church becomes a sanctuary for slave expression. There is no question that Gospel is a descendant of the Spiritual and this music gives a Christian alternative to secular music.
5. Thomas Andrew Dorsey is known as the "Father of Gospel." He was a musician and composer and in his writings combined Christian elements with jazz and blues in the 1930s. Two of his most famous pieces are "Precious Lord" and "Peace in the Valley."
6. Performance of Gospel music in church was done by a cappella choirs. Their style was the old traditional call and response and rhythm was provided by hand clapping and foot stomping. Gospel music always contained harmony and strong vocals.
7. 1920s radio helped popularize Gospel and after World War II, we see an appearance of public Gospel concerts.

   A. Starting with the Spiritual, Gospel evolved through many styles. These styles are Traditional Gospel, Blues Gospel, Southern Gospel, Progressive Southern Gospel, Country Gospel, Contemporary Gospel, Bluegrass Gospel, Soul Gospel, Celtic Gospel, and Reggae Gospel.

   B. Some of the popular artists of Gospel are Thomas Andrew Dorsey, Mahalia Jackson, Albertina Walker, Aretha Franklin, Ray Charles, Little Richard, The Winans Family, Elvis Presley, Dolly Parton, Gladys Knight, Patti La Belle, Whitney Houston, Kirk Franklin, Annointed, Mary Mary, Tri-City Singers, Byron Cage, Shirley Caesar, Dorinda Clark-Cole, Rev. James Cleveland.

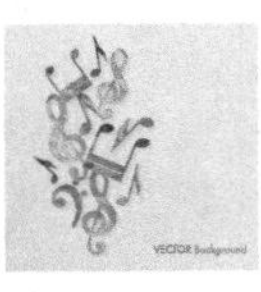

Listening Box 40

Type in Gospel Music and choose top box Gospel Music, Various Artists. Select Track 15, My God is Real, Mahalia Jackson.

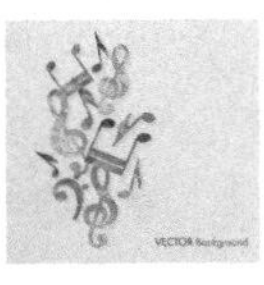

Listening Box 41

Type in Gospel Music and under Track Results, choose Amazing Grace, Black Gospel Music. Select Track 4, Amazing Grace.

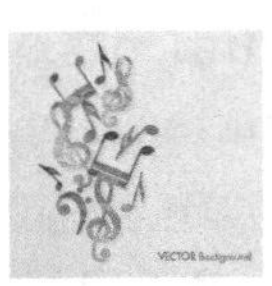

Listening Box 42

Type in Gospel Music and under Track Results choose Gospel Music, 116. Select Track 3, Gospel Music; Track 11, Stand Strong.

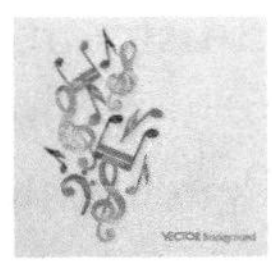

Listening Box 43

Type in Kirk Franklin and under Artist Results, choose Kirk Franklin, Christian R&B. Select Track1, I Smile; Track 11, Brighter Day.

Unit 7, Chapter 5 Listening Box Playlist

LB40: Type in Gospel Music and choose top box Gospel Music, Various Artists. Select Track 15, My God Is Real, Mahalia Jackson.

LB41: Type in Gospel Music and under Track Results, choose Amazing Grace, Black Gospel Music. Select Track 4, Amazing Grace.

LB42: Type in Gospel music and under Track Results, choose Gospel Music, 116. Select Track 3, Gospel Music; Track 11, Stand Strong.

LB43: Type in Kirk Franklin and under Artist Results, choose Kirk Franklin, Christian R&B. Select Track 1, I Smile; Track 11, Brighter Day.

Summary of Unit 7, Chapters 1–5 Terms and Study Sheet

Terms

Rhythm and Blues: Music with a heavy rhythm, blues scale, and blues chord progression.

Rockabilly: A blend of Country music and Rock 'n' Roll.

Doo-Wop: Music that featured group harmony and nonsense syllables.

British Invasion: A name given when British groups came to America and became popular (Beatles).

Motown: A company started by Berry Gordy to promote young African American talent.

Psychedelic Rock: Music inspired by psychedelic drugs and designed to alter the mind.

Hard Rock/Heavy Metal: Music that emphasizes loud amplification, distortion, and heavy drum beats. It is designed to exemplify macho.

Soft Rock: Music that put emphasis on melody, harmony, and a softer drum sound.

Heartland Rock: Music that has country elements, personal values, and Americana (Springsteen).

Progressive Rock: Started in England and used elements of Jazz and Classical music. It was designed to elevate the status and sophistication of Rock 'n' Roll.

Southern Rock: A style of music that was started in Southern states that combined elements of Country, Blues, and Rock 'n' Roll.

Country Rock: This music is a fusion of Country music and Rock 'n' Roll.

Punk: Music with a very hard sound that often had anti-political and anti-establishment lyrics.

New Wave: A derivative of Punk which uses heavy electrical elements and synthesizers.

Rap: Rap is a Hip-Hop style of music that uses a speech-like style of singing over rhythm. It is often called music of the "hood" or the "street."

Hip-Hop: A musical style created in the South Bronx, New York, this music contained elements of Rap, upbeat rhythms, and DJ sounds.

Alternative: This music provides an alternative to mainstream Rock 'n' Roll and includes more independent thinking and individuality to the music.

Grunge: Fuses Heavy Metal and Punk Rock (Nirvana and Stone Temple Pilots).

Country Music: Created in the South, it has elements of Folk and Blues music.

Gospel Music: Created in the South, it has African American roots and is a descendant of the Spiritual. This is a Christian style of music designed to be uplifting spiritually.

Artists

In this unit, artists have been presented in their representative categories. Please revisit the categories.

Summary of Listeners Toolbox

As you have seen and heard, many styles of popular music have been cited. Your job here is to understand the different elements of the various styles. This can be accomplished by continual listening.

Questions

After listening to the many styles, do you have a favorite? Which of the presented artists or groups represents your taste in music?

To The Student: The instructor may add or delete study items at his or her discretion.

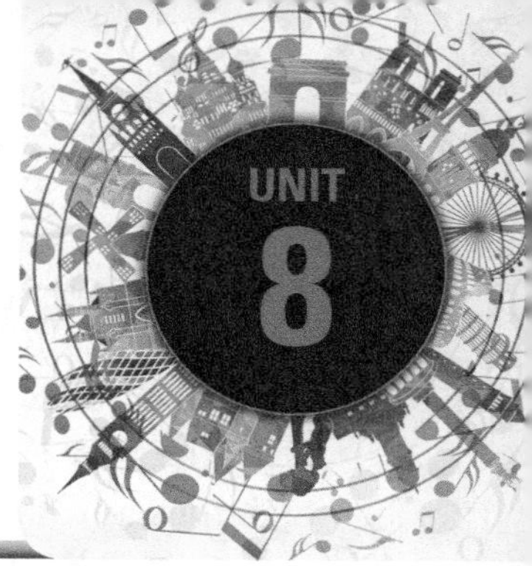

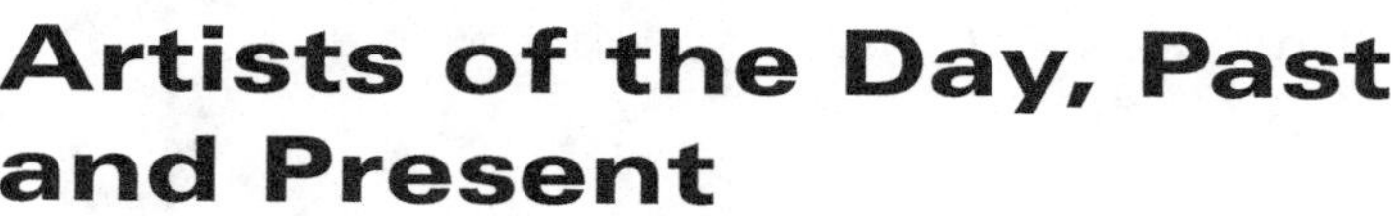

Artists of the Day, Past and Present

Unit Purpose

To present artists past and present who have made or are currently making enormous contributions to music.

CHAPTER 1 ARTISTS OF THE PAST

What Do We Find in This Period?

Music: With music from artists of the past, we find a great diversity in sound. There is a definite clarity of story line that is sometimes missing in the music of some of the present artists. There is less emphasis on the drummer and guitar player and more of an emphasis on feeling and various aspects of relationships. Also, we find evidence of silly songs as per Elvis Presley's "Houndog." Moreover, there was a great respect for the melody and the person singing it and there was almost never a time when the instruments overpowered the singer.

Texture: Homophonic

Forms and Styles: Most music was traditional A-B-A form and styles varied from Rhythm and Blues to Rock 'n' Roll. Jazz elements were also part of the mix.

Artists/Groups: Nat King Cole, Frank Sinatra, Tony Bennett, Ella Fitzgerald, Elvis Presley, The Beatles, Michael Jackson, Whitney Houston. I will cite five from this list.

Travel to: The United States and London

Frank Sinatra (1915–1998)

1. Born in Hoboken, New Jersey.
2. Although he never really learned how to read music, he was a master at translating the lyrics of his songs. He took elocution lessons from John Quinlan, a noted vocal coach.
3. He was a singer, producer, actor, and record company owner. His company was called Reprise Records, which he started in 1960.

4. At an early age, he was interested in the Big Band sound and basically his singing career started in bars and nightclubs which he often called "dives" or "joints."
5. In the late 1930s, he was the lead singer for Harry James and then switched to the Tommy Dorsey Band. In 1942, he left Dorsey to pursue a solo career.

6. From the years 1942–1945, his career really flourished and the phenomenon was called "Sinatramania."
7. In real life he had many nicknames, "Ol' Blue Eyes," "Bones," "Chairman of the Board," "Lady Macbeth." The Lady Macbeth name was given to him because of his obsession with cleanliness. It was said he changed clothes frequently and would take as many as twelve showers a day.
8. In 1946, he put out his first album called, "The Voice of Frank Sinatra," and in his career he sold over one hundred and fifty million records.
9. Paralleling his singing career was an acting career. His first movie was in 1941, "Las Vegas Nights." In 1953, he won an Oscar for his portrayal of Maggio in the film, "From Here to Eternity."
10. Sinatra's personal life is one that could fill a book without ever mentioning his music and acting careers. He was married four times and had three children with his first wife. He was accused, but never convicted, of having Mafia connections. He was a tough little guy who on occasion would get into fist fights, especially when he got drunk. Often he would battle with the press as he thought they were unfair to him about his personal life. Also, he would battle with photographers who constantly hounded him. He had a great love for his country and often spoke out for human rights. He was very vocal about racism against blacks and Italians.
11. On a more positive note, he was known throughout the world and was very generous with his money. He would often pay house and hospital bills for his friends who were having financial difficulty. He went to classical concerts when he could and often used this genre of music for relaxation.
12. Sinatra won many awards and was given several honorary doctorate degrees. One of the most prestigious awards was the Presidential Medal of Freedom given by President Ronald Reagan in 1983. His final touring concerts were in 1994, Japan. On his deathbed, his wife was encouraging him to fight and his last words were, "I'm losing."

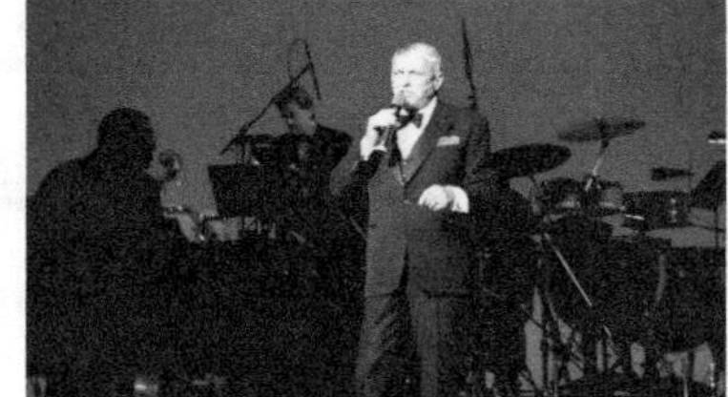

Sinatra Performing in Washington, DC, 1991

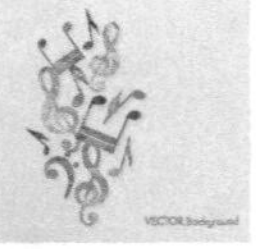

Listening Box 1

Type in Frank Sinatra and under Artist Results, choose Frank Sinatra, pop Standards. Select Track 3, Theme From New York, New York; Track 4, The Way You Look Tonight; Track 5, I've Got You Under My Skin; Track 6, My Way.

Nat King Cole (1919–1965)

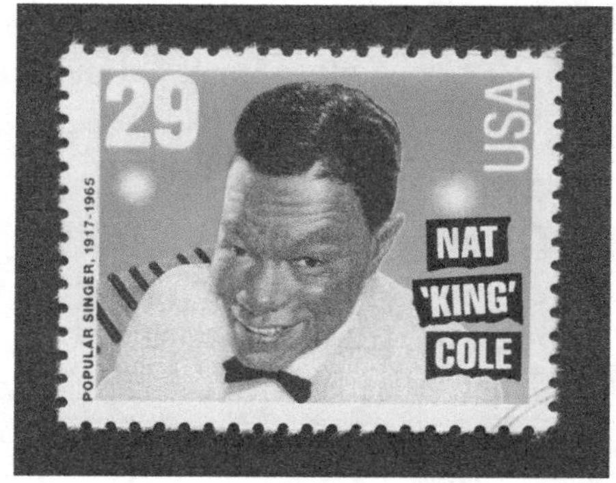

1. Born in Montgomery, Alabama.
2. His real last name was Coles, but his older brother Eddie, who was also a musician, decided to drop the s and Nat followed suit.
3. At age 4, he started to learn how to play organ and was given lessons by his mother who was church organist. At age 12, he began formal piano lessons. He studied classical music, but was mainly interested in Jazz.
4. In the early 1930s, he formed a trio which he called "King Cole Swingsters." This group played in many nightclubs and radio broadcasts.
5. "Jazz at the Philharmonic" is a series of Jazz concerts produced and promoted by the impresario Norman Granz. Nat Cole was one of the first musicians to play Jazz in a classical venue, Philharmonic Auditorium, Los Angeles, in 1944.
6. Nat was very shy about singing and felt awkward about what to do with his hands. No question, it was his deep baritone voice that made him a star.
7. Cole was the first African-American to host a television show on NBC, in 1956. It was called "The Nat King Cole Show." The show lasted two years, but was eventually dropped for lack of national sponsorship. Many big companies did not want to be associated with an African-American. Nat's historical line was "Madison Avenue is afraid of the dark."
8. Throughout his career he recorded many hits and sang at times in foreign languages such as Spanish and Portuguese. He never really understood the words, but sang them phonetically.
9. Nat made a few movies and tried Broadway, but his efforts were only minimally successful. By and large, he did recordings, concerts, and variety shows.
10. Cole's personal life had many ups and downs. He was married twice and had five children with the second wife, two of whom were adopted. He was a constant victim of racial prejudice, and members of the Ku Klux Klan put a burning cross on his front lawn and poisoned the dog. In 1956, he was attacked on stage in Birmingham, Alabama, by several white guys. He wasn't very vocal about the incident and was vilified by his own people and called an "uncle tom." He never went back to Alabama again.
11. In the end, after a remarkable career, Nat wound up with lung cancer and passed away in 1965.Two of his most famous recordings are Mona Lisa and The Christmas Song.

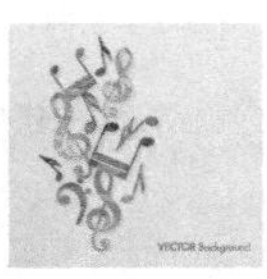

Listening Box 2

Type in Nat King Cole and under Artist Results, choose Nat King Cole, Jazz. Select Track 1, Love; Track 2, Unforgettable (with Natalie Cole); Track 3, Smile; Track 10, Mona Lisa.

Ray Charles (1930–2004)

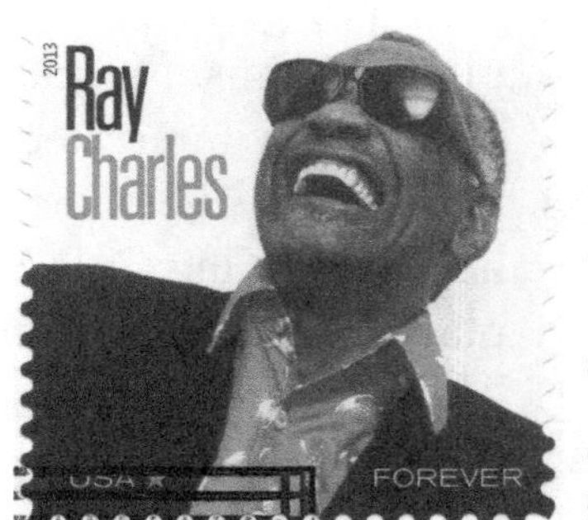

©Olga Popova/Shutterstock.com

1. Born in Albany, Georgia, but the family moved to Greenville, Florida, after he was born.
2. His real name was Raymond Charles Robinson. Robinson was dropped as there was a famous boxer of the day whose name was Sugar Ray Robinson. Obviously, this was done to avoid confusion.
3. Ray started to go blind by age 7 and he lived with his single mom and his brother George. Tragedy struck the family when at age 4 his brother drowned in a big laundry tub their mom used for washing clothes in order to earn money.
4. Ray's musical interest was influenced by Wylie Pitman, who owned the Red Wing Café. Pitman had a piano in the place and gave Ray his first lessons.
5. Being poor and uneducated, Ray's mom was constantly looking for a school that could address and accommodate Ray's blindness. She found the Florida School for the Deaf and Blind in St Augustine, Florida. Despite not being a happy camper at first, Ray attended from 1937 to 1945. At this school he learned to play different instruments as well as learning how to write music in Braille.
6. For much of the 1940s, Ray worked in many places and struggled to make a living. Around 1948, he moved to Seattle, Washington, with a friend and eventually met Quincy Jones, who at the time was fifteen years old.
7. The 1950s were very good to Ray after he signed with Atlantic Records. He contracted a female vocal group for backup vocals. They were called "The Cookies" and he renamed them "The Raelettes."
8. Although Ray is given credit for pioneering soul music in the 1950s, his music included Jazz, Gospel, Rock 'n' Roll, and R&B. As a matter of fact, Charles was vilified by his own people for combining Gospel with Jazz as Jazz was considered music of the devil.
9. From the late 1960s to the early 1980s, Ray's career was in decline. Many believe this decline was due to his addiction to heroin. He eventually went into rehab and was cured.
10. From the 1980s to the early 2000s, Ray was still a loved and respected musician. He actually had two nicknames, "The Genius" and "The High Priest of Soul."

11. Although difficult to separate the elements, Ray tried to keep his road life away from his home life. He was not good at doing this and was married twice and had twelve children with nine different women. While he was not around most of the time, it is said he was very generous and financially supported everyone.
12. As a victim of racism, Ray was active in civil rights. An incident in 1961, in Albany, Georgia, caused a stir. Ray was to do a concert at the Bell Auditorium. Apparently, the seating arrangements were not the same for blacks as for whites. In addition, only whites were allowed on the dance floor. Ray decided not to do the concert and was eventually sued by the promoter for breach of contract. In 1962, he was fined $757.00. In 1963, he returned to the desegregated Bell Auditorium with The Raelettes.

    As is portrayed in the movie Ray, he was never banned from playing music in Georgia. In fact, he was inducted into the State Music Hall of Fame in 1979, given a formal apology, and his version of "Georgia on My Mind" was made the state song.
13. In his lifetime, Ray won many awards. In 1986, he was inducted into the Rock 'n' Roll Hall of Fame and in the same year won Kennedy Center Honors. In 1991, he was given the Grammy Lifetime Achievement Award. The aforementioned awards are a few of many.
14. In 1986, Ray started a foundation for the hearing impaired. When asked why he chose hearing impaired over blindness, Ray stated that music had changed his life for the better and that he was grateful to be able to hear.
15. Ray passed away in 2004 and several albums were released after his death. They are Genius Loves Company (2004), Genius and Friends (2005), Ray Sings and Basie Swings (2006).

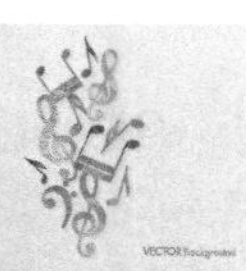

Listening Box 3

Type in Ray Charles and under Artist Results, choose Ray Charles, Rhythm & Blues. Select Track 1, Hit The Road Jack; Track 3, Georgia on My Mind; Track 7, America the Beautiful; Track 9, Unchain My Heart.

Note: The song "Georgia on My Mind" was written by Howard Hoagland "Hoagy" Carmichael (music) and Stuart Gorrell (words). It is often thought that Ray Charles wrote this song, but he did not.

Sammy Davis Jr. (1925–1990)

1. Born in Harlem, New York City.
2. His main talents were singing and dancing, but he was also noted for his comedy, drum playing, and impersonations. His nickname was "Mister Show Business."

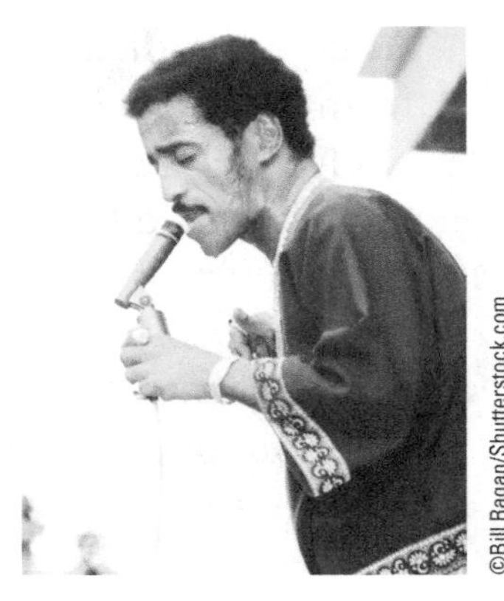
©Bill Ragan/Shutterstock.com

3. Sam's parents decided to split when he was 3. In order to not lose custody of his son, Sam's father took him on the road and the little guy performed with his father and uncle. The group was known as The Will Mastin Trio.
4. Like many black entertainers, Sammy was the victim of racial prejudice. This affected him greatly and he got involved in the Civil Rights Movement mentally, physically, and financially.
5. Sam served in the US Army during World War II in Special Services. After military service, he rejoined his father and uncle.
6. In the 1950s, Frank Sinatra formed a group of entertainers who performed together in places like Las Vegas. They included Sinatra, Dean Martin, Joey Bishop, and Peter Lawford. The group was originally called "The Clan," then "The Summit," but the press called them "The Rat Pack." Davis joined this group in 1959.
7. Besides a music career, Sam had an active movie career which started in 1933, when he was a child. His first big hit movie with The Rat Pack was "Ocean's 11" in 1960. The Pack made several other movies, "Sergeants 3" in 1962 and "Robin and the Seven Hoods" in 1964. He also won high praise for his role as Sportin' Life in "Porgy and Bess" in 1959.
8. In 1954, Sam was in a severe car accident and lost one eye. For many months, he wore an eye patch and eventually was fitted for a glass eye which he wore the rest of his life.
9. Sam was Christian by birth, but eventually converted to Judaism in 1961. In a comedic moment on the golf course, Sam was asked what his handicap was. He replied, and here I am paraphrasing, "I'm a black Jew with one eye, isn't that handicap enough?"
10. Politically, Sammy was a Democrat, but he caused a stir in 1972, when he openly supported Richard Nixon. Nixon loved Sam, especially for his stance on Civil Rights, and convinced him to do USO tours in South Vietnam for the troops. Davis and his wife were the first African-Americans to sleep at the White House at Nixon's request.
11. Davis's personal life and actions caused him trouble. In the late 1950s, he was having a relationship with Kim Novak, a white actress. He was advised to break the relationship, but did not. As a scare tactic, he was kidnapped and threatened about having his good eye knocked out. To show he was complying with this request, a hastily put together marriage was arranged to a black dancer which lasted only nine months. To make matters worse, Davis married May Britt, a white Swedish actress. Sammy's interracial marriages were in a way trendsetting as there were thirty-one states where they were forbidden. The Supreme Court eventually ruled these laws to be unconstitutional.

12. Sammy and May had three children, a daughter and two adopted sons. The marriage was not a great one and eventually, the couple divorced.
13. In 1970, Sam married for the last time to a dancer, Altovise Gore. They adopted a son, Manny.
14. In his lifetime, Sammy won many awards. Among them are a Tony Award for Best Actor in a musical, 1965; many Emmy Awards; many Grammy Awards; Civil Rights Awards and Kennedy Center Honors in 1987, to name a few.
15. Sam passed away in 1990 from throat cancer and besides leaving behind family, he left a musical legacy that not many can equal. As an entertainer he was always upbeat and yes he did like to drink and smoke. Nevertheless, he will always be remembered as "The Candy Man."

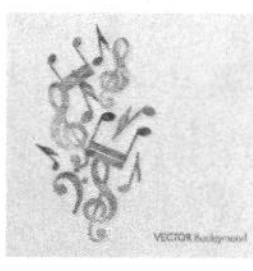

Listening Box 4

Type in Sammy Davis Jr. and under Album Results, choose Mr. Bojangles, Sammy Davis, Jr. Select Track 3, That's Entertainment; Track 4, The Birth of the Blues; Track 7, The Candy Man; Track 11, Mr. Bojangles.

Whitney Houston (1963–2012)

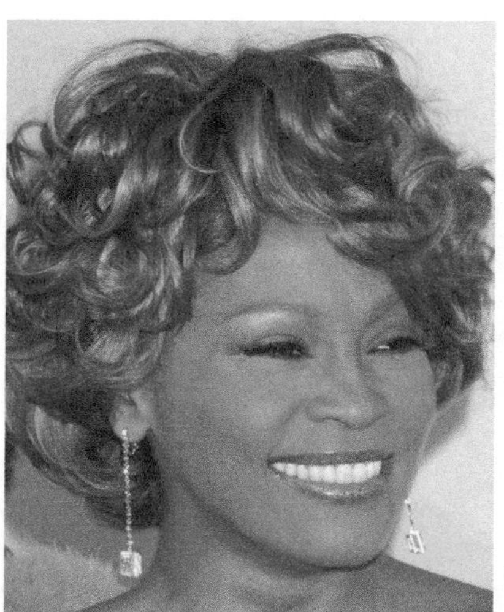

1. Born in Newark, New Jersey.
2. At an early age, Whitney was exposed to music by her mother Cissy, who was a professional singer.
3. At age 11, she was singing in the church choir and eventually started singing solo numbers. Her voice range was mezzo-soprano.
4. Whitney was very close to her mother and she often would accompany mom on her nightclub tours.
5. Starting at 15, Whitney sang backup vocals for Chaka Kahn, Jermaine Jackson, and Lou Rawls.
6. Most people know Whitney as a singer and actress, but she was also a model and record and film producer. She appeared in such magazines as Glamour, Seventeen, and Cosmopolitan.
7. Houston signed a record contract with Arista Records in 1983, but did not release her first album "Whitney Houston" until 1985. In 1986, this album topped the Billboard charts.
8. Her recording success was astronomical. She received awards for Best Female Act of All Time and numerous Billboard awards (thirty in total). She was one of music's top-selling performers and the only performer to have seven number one hits in Billboard's Top 100 Hits list. Some of her other awards include six

Grammys, two Emmys, and twenty-two American Music Awards. The general estimate for her career exceeds four hundred.

9. Some say Whitney's touring schedule was unequalled. She visited countries in Europe, the Middle East, and Asia. She also visited England and Russia besides all her tours in the United States.
10. As most people know, by the 1990s, Whitney turned to drugs. At this time, she became very unreliable and missed or was late for interviews and recording sessions. She also canceled many television appearances and her general attitude turned nasty. Some say this behavioral changed was induced by her then husband, Bobby Brown.
11. Whitney and Brown had a daughter, Bobbi Kristina. Eventually, they divorced in 2007, after much turmoil and controversy. Whitney does get custody of the child.
12. Of all her successes, probably the most significant was her starring role in the movie, "The Body Guard," with Kevin Costner. She was criticized for her acting, but the film was a huge box office success, grossing over four hundred million dollars worldwide. The most popular song to come out of the film is "I Will Always Love You," which was written and recorded by Dolly Parton in 1974.
13. Whitney Houston died on February 11, 2012, submerged in a hotel bathtub. The coroner's report stated she died from heart disease and cocaine use.

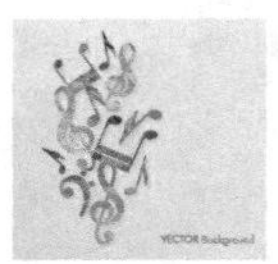

Listening Box 5

Type in Whitney Houston and under Album Results, choose The Greatest Hits, Whitney Houston. Select disc 1, Track 11, I Will Always Love You; disc 2, Track 7, Step By Step; Track 13, So Emotional; Track 15, How Will I Know.

Unit 8, Chapter 1 Listening Box Playlist

LB1: Type in Frank Sinatra and under Artist Results, choose Frank Sinatra, Pop Standards. Select Track 3, The Way You Look Tonight; Track 4, My Way; Track 5, I've Got You Under My Skin; Track 7, Theme from New York, New York.

LB2: Type in Nat King Cole and under Artist Results, choose Nat King Cole, Jazz. Select Track 1, Love; Track 2, Unforgettable (with Natalie Cole); Track 3, Smile; Track 13, Mona Lisa.

LB3: Type in Ray Charles and under Artist Results, choose Ray Charles, Rhythm & Blues. Select Track 1, Hit the Road Jack; Track 2, Georgia on My Mind; Track 6, America the Beautiful; Track 10, Unchain My Heart.

LB4: Type in Sammy Davis Jr. and under Album Results, choose Mr. Bojangles, Sammy Davis Jr. Select Track 3, That's Entertainment; Track 4, The Birth of the Blues; Track 7, The Candy Man; Track 11, Mr. Bojangles.

LB5: Type in Whitney Houston and under Album Results, choose The Greatest Hits, Whitney Houston. Select disc 1, Track 11, I Will Always Love You; disc 2, Track 7, Step by Step; Track 13, So Emotional; Track 15, How Will I Know.

CHAPTER 2 ARTISTS OF THE PRESENT

Note: I will cite five current artists from the following list: Beyoncé, Taylor Swift, Selena Gomez, Lady Gaga, Kendrik Lamar, Jay Z, Rihanna, Ariana Grande, Meghan Trainor, Justin Timberlake.

Beyoncé Knowles (1981–)

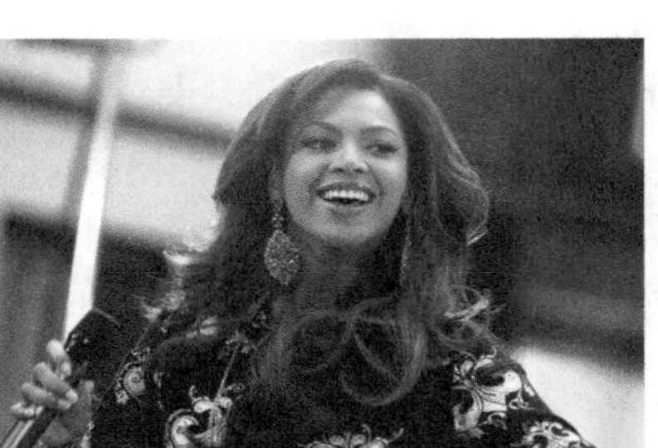

1. Born in Houston, Texas.
2. Most people know Beyoncé as a singer, but she is also an actress, songwriter, and record producer.
3. In elementary school, she was in dance classes and the dance teacher recognized she had a good singing voice and advised her to take singing lessons.
4. To further her singing studies, she enrolled in the high school for the performing and visual arts. At this time, she also sang in the church choir.
5. Her initial success came as a member of Destiny's Child, which was managed by her father Matthew. Some of the group's famous albums are Destiny's Child, Survivor, The Writing's on the Wall, and Destiny Fulfilled.
6. In 2003, she released her first solo album, Dangerously in Love, which earned her five Grammy Awards.
7. In 2008, she married Jay Z (Shawn Corey Carter) and their first child Blue Ivy, a girl, was born in 2012.
8. Beyoncé's list of accomplishments is staggering. Her awards include twenty Grammys, the Recording Industry of America Award, the Broadcast Film Critics Award, the World Music Award, the Billboard Millennium Award, Women of the Year, Top Female Vocalist. There is also a Beyoncé exhibit in the Rock 'n' Roll Hall of Fame. As the general public knows, she continues to tour, record, and add to her awards list.
9. Beyoncé's charity work must also be noted here. From 2005 and the founding of the Survivor Foundation, which provided housing for Hurricane Katrina victims, Beyoncé has been involved in many humanitarian causes. She has worked with the first lady on child obesity, with George Clooney for victims of the Haiti

earthquake, and in 2010, she and her mother opened a cosmetology center in Brooklyn, which provides a seven-month course in cosmetology for men and women. She has also spoken out about women empowerment and gun control.

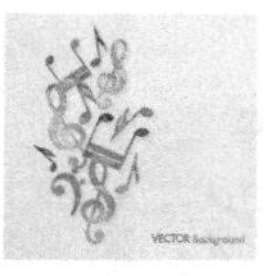

Listening Box 6

Type in Beyoncé and under Album Results, choose Beyoncé (Platinum Edition), Beyoncé. Select disc 1, Track 1, Pretty Hurts; Track 12, Superpower; Track 13, Heaven.

Taylor Swift (1989–)

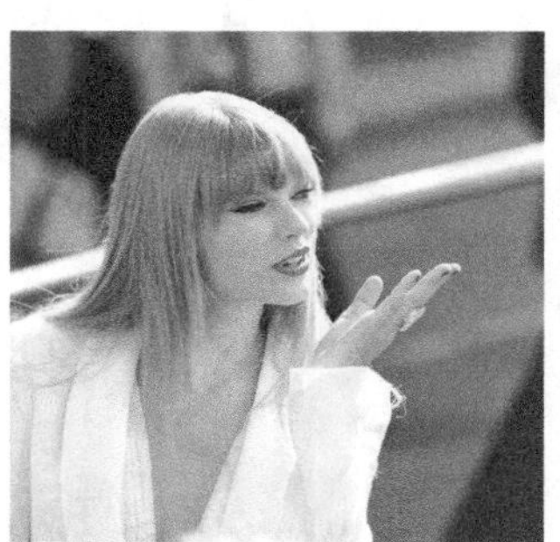

©Featureflash Photo Agency/Shutterstock.com

1. Born in Reading, Pennsylvania.
2. She is a singer, songwriter, and actress. She also owns her own management company.
3. Taylor knew at an early age she wanted to be a Country Music star. With total support from her family, Taylor, her brother Austin, and her parents moved to Hendersonville, Tennessee, when she was 14. Her touring schedule increased and she had to leave Hendersonville High to complete her last two years at The Aaron Academy, which offered home tutoring.
4. Rather than do other people's music, Taylor wanted to write her own and she collaborated with Liz Rose, who gave her writing lessons after school.
5. Taylor was very gifted at writing lyrics and she was good at writing "hooks," which are the catchy parts of the music that "hook" people into buying the song. Swift claimed that she was influenced by Shania Twain, Madonna, Stevie Nicks, and others.
6. Taylor moved to Nashville when she was 14, so she was in the heart of the Country Music capital.
7. In 2005, Swift was spotted in a Nashville café by an executive from Big Machine Records. She was one of the company's first signees. Her first album in 2006 was called Taylor Swift. She made many radio and television appearances to promote this album.
8. In 2008, Swift released her second album, Fearless, and now owns her own management company. She appears on several television shows and communicates with fans through social media to promote the album.
9. In 2010, she released her third album, Speak Now. This was a special project in that she wrote all fourteen songs. Again, she toured all over the world to promote the album.

10. In 2014, she released her fourth album, Red. For this album, she wrote more than half the songs. Musically, this album was thought by many to steer Taylor away from the Country sound and more toward the Pop sound.
11. Taylor's awards could probably fill a book as they categorically include nineteen American Music Awards, ten Grammys, eleven Country Music Association Awards, twenty-two Billboard Music Awards, to name a very few.
12. Swift is very generous with her money as she has given to arts in education, college music departments, the Nashville Symphony, the Seattle Symphony, and many schools that correct child illiteracy. She has also given to victims of weather disasters. Taylor is a generous and remarkable talent and as the saying goes, the beat goes on.

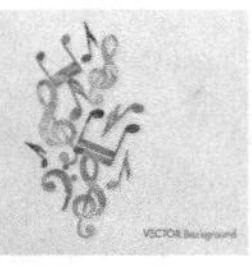

Listening Box 7

Type in Taylor Swift and under Playlist Results, choose Taylor Swift's Very Best. Select Track 1, Fifteen; Track 2, Tim McGraw; Track 3, Teardrops on My Guitar; Track 4, Fearless; Track 8, Our Song.

Selena Gomez (1992–)

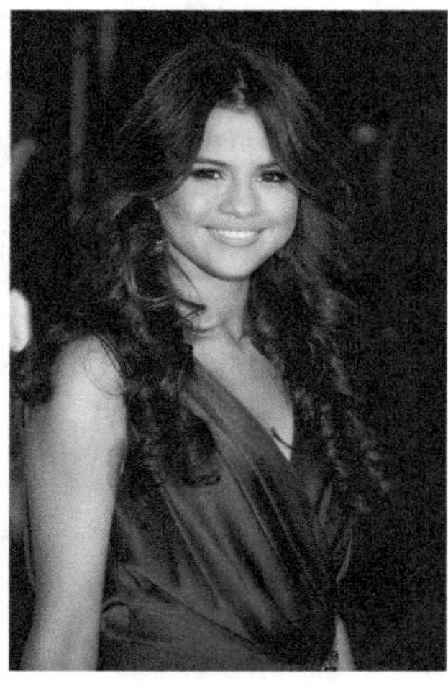

©Tinseltown/Shutterstock.com

1. Born in Prairie, Texas.
2. When Selena was born, her mother was just sixteen years old. Her parents divorced when she was 5 and life for her and her mother was a financial struggle.
3. In the early 2000s, she auditioned and became a cast member of Barney and Friends. In 2007, she became a Disney cast member in Wizards of Waverly Place.
4. Her singing career started in 2008, when she signed with Hollywood Records. At Hollywood, she worked with a band called The Scene and together they recorded several albums: Kiss & Tell (2009), A Year Without Rain (2010), When the Sun Goes Down (2011).
5. Selena also has a film acting career and she has appeared in Ramone and Beezus (2010), Monte Carlo (2011), Hotel Transylvania (2012), Spring Breakers (2013).
6. Her record company always had plans for her to go solo and her first solo album was called Stars Dance, in 2013. This album produced the hit "Come & Get It." Selena spent six years with Hollywood Records, and then in 2014, she signed with Interscope Records.
7. Selena's second solo album, Revival, in 2015, produced the hits "Good for You" and "Same Old Love."

8. In 2010, with her singing and acting careers flourishing, Selena decided to launch a fashion line of clothing. She called it "Dream Out Loud."
9. As is the case with many stars, Selena's philanthropic ventures are numerous. She has given to such organizations as UNICEF, St. Jude's Children's Hospital, Raise Hope for Congo, Island Dog, Disney's Friends for Change, and in 2012, she was named ambassador to the Ryan Seacrest Foundation.
10. Selena has always given credit to her strong mother and grandparents for love, support, and guidance. Unfortunately, in 2015, Selena was diagnosed with lupus and had to undergo chemotherapy treatments to cure the disease. As of this writing, she is still acting, singing, helping others, and getting on with life.

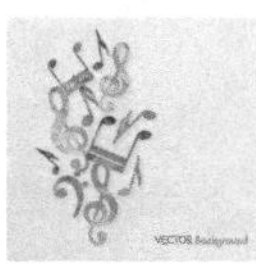

Listening Box 8

Type in Selena Gomez and under Album Results, choose For You, Selena Gomez. Select Track 1, The Heart Wants What It Wants; Track 2, Come and Get It; Track 3, Love You Like a Love Song; Track 5, Who Says.

Justin Timberlake (1981–)

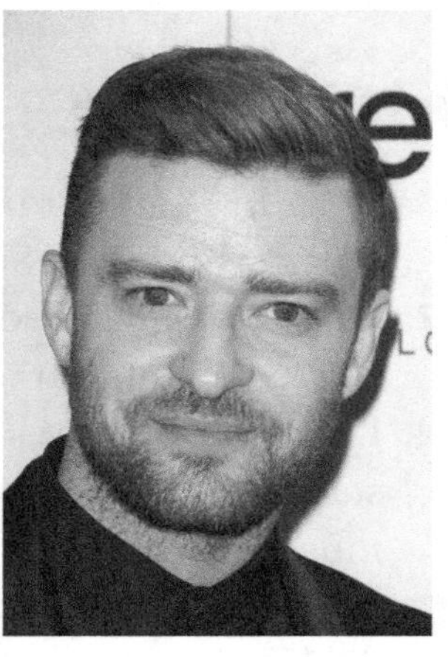

1. Born in Memphis, Tennessee.
2. Justin's music career gained momentum when he was a lead singer for NSYNC, which formed in 1995. The group's career began in Europe in 1996. It wasn't until 1998 that the group became famous in the United States.
3. Some of NSYNC's popular albums are NSYNC (1997), No Strings Attached (2000), Celebrity (2001). The Essential NSYNC was their third compilation album and released in 2014.
4. By the early 2000s, NSYNC's popularity declined and Timberlake decides to go solo. His first solo hit was "Like I Love You."
5. Justin's successful studio albums are Justified (2002), Future Sex/Love Sounds (2006), The 20/20 Experience (2013), The 20/20 Experience (2) (2013).
6. Timberlake also has an acting career. Some of the films he appeared in are Longshot (2000), Edison (2005), Alpha Dog (2006), Black Snake Moan (2007), Shrek the Third (2007), The Love Guru (2008), The Open Road (2009), Yogi Bear (2010), Bad Teacher (2011), Runner Runner (2013), Trolls (2016), to name a few.
7. As a businessman, he was involved in three restaurants, "Chi" in California and "Southern Hospitality" and "Destino" in New York. He also started a clothing line

with his friend Juan Ayala in 2005. He purchased, renovated, and eventually sold a golf course in Millington, Tennessee.

8. His personal awards are many and include four Emmys, three Brit Awards, nine Grammys, seven American Music Awards, ten Billboard Music Awards, and several MTV Video Awards.
9. Justin's philanthropic ventures are second to none. One of his first was NSYNC's "Challenge for the Children." The "Justin Timberlake Foundation" started out funding music in schools, but now has a broader scope. He has given money to Wildlife Warriors, The Memphis Rock 'n' Soul Museum, and the Memphis Music Foundation.
10. In his personal life, he had relationships with Cameron Diaz, Britney Spears, and others. He married Jessica Biel in 2012. They have a son Silas, born in 2015. Justin continues to sing, act and tour.

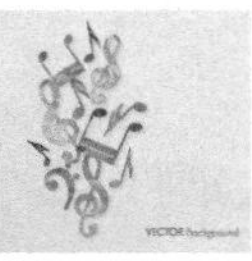

Listening Box 9

Type in Justin Timberlake and choose top box Justin Timberlake, Pop. Select Track 1, Mirrors; Track 6, What Goes Around . . . Comes Around; Track 8, Rock Your Baby; Track 9, My Love.

Lady Gaga (1986–)

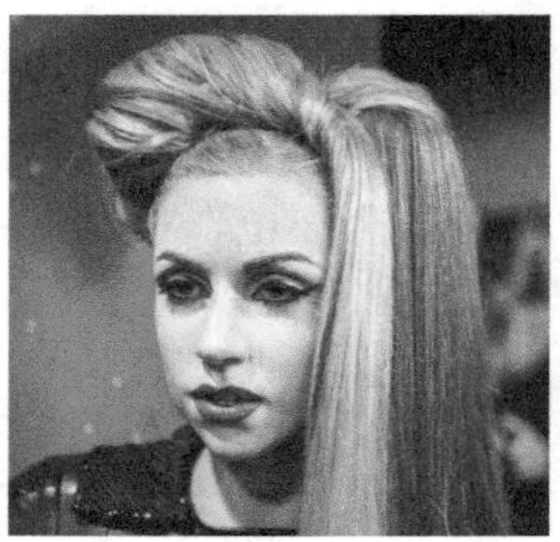

©Anton_Ivanov/Shutterstock.com

1. Born in Manhattan, New York City.
2. Her real name is Stefani Joanne Angelina Germanotta.
3. Gaga is a singer, songwriter, and actress who basically got started singing in nightclubs in New York.
4. Lady started playing piano at age 4 and in her early teens started to compose music. She participated in high school musical productions and auditioned for different shows, but was unsuccessful.
5. At 17, she enrolled in the CAP21 program at NYU, but only stayed for two years and left to concentrate on her music career.
6. In 2005, she formed her own band (SGBand) and a talent scout recommended her to music producer Rob Fusari. She eventually worked with a series of music people and record companies as a singer and songwriter.
7. In 2007, Fusari got his friend Vincent Herbert to sign Gaga to a contract for Streamline Records. At this time, Gaga continued to develop her style which is considered Glam Pop or Glam Rock.
8. In 2008, Lady moved to California and recorded her first album, The Fame, which produced several hit songs such as "Poker Face," "Just Dance," "Love Game,"

"Paparazzi," and "Eh, Eh (Nothing Else I Can Say)." This album sets her out on a world tour.

9. Some of Gaga's popular albums are Born This Way (2011), Artpop (2013), Cheek to Cheek (with Tony Bennett) (2014). She also made some compilation albums with Kon Live.
10. During the touring and making album years, Gaga found time to collaborate with such stars as Elton John and Tony Bennett.
11. Lady has made several television appearances on shows such as Saturday Night Live, The Sopranos, Boiling Points, Gossip Girls, American Idol, A Very Gaga Thanksgiving, and the Simpsons, to name a few.

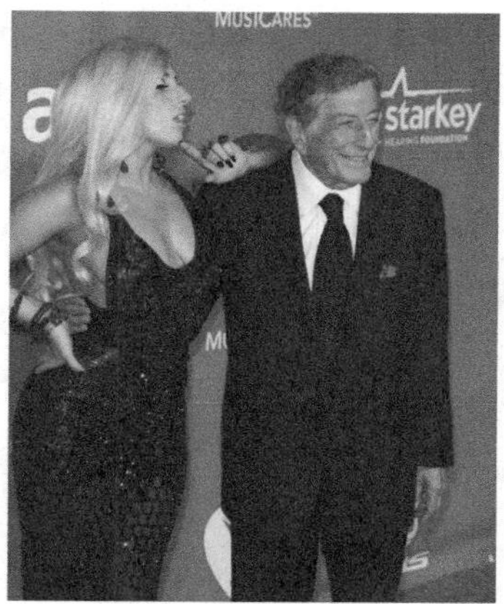

©Helga Esteb/Shutterstock.com

Lady Gaga and Tony Bennett

12. Her film credits include The Zen of Bennett, Katie Perry: Part of Me, Muppets Most Wanted, Sin City: A Dame to Kill For, and Jimmy Scott: The People's Designer.
13. Lady Gaga has contributed to many charitable organizations and causes. In 2012, she started The Born This Way Foundation, which is dedicated to helping young people overcome their academic, social, and personal feeling issues. She has given to the victims of the Haiti Earthquake, the victims of the Japanese Tsunami, the American Red Cross, and the fight against AIDS.
14. In her personal life, Gaga had several relationships, but got engaged to Taylor Kinney in 2015.
15. Her personal award achievements are Golden Globe Award, thirteen MTV Video Awards, six Grammy's, the Songwriters Hall of Fame Award, Council of Fashion Designers Award, Woman of the Year (2015), Billboard's Artist of the Year (2010), and Contemporary Icon Award (2015), to name a few.
16. At this time, Lady Gaga continues to write songs, perform, record, tour, and fill the world with good music.

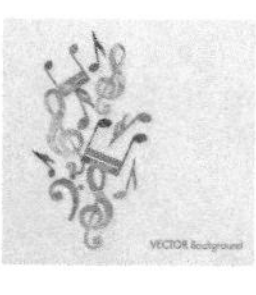

Listening Box 10

Type in Lady Gaga and under Artist results, choose Lady Gaga, Dance Pop. Select Track 3, Just Dance (Featuring Colby O'Donis); Track 5, Paparazzi; Track 7, Telephone (Featuring Beyoncé).

Note: I would be remiss if I did not take this opportunity to present the combining of the past and present. As many of you know, Lady Gaga and Tony Bennett combined talents making recordings and public appearances together. The public reaction was very positive and this merging put these two artists in a favorable new light. If for nothing else, it showed each artist is capable of going beyond who they are supposed to be, besides creating wonderful music. I am of the opinion that more of this should be done as it brings another dimension of music to the general public.

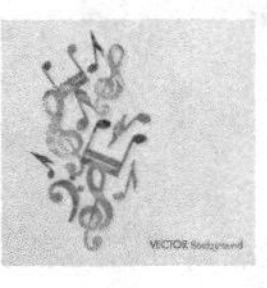

Listening Box 11

Type in Tony Bennett and Lady Gaga and choose top box Cheek to Cheek, Tony Bennett. Select Track 1, Anything Goes; Track 2, Cheek to Cheek; Track 9, I Won't Dance; Track 13, Let's Face the Music and Dance.

Unit 8, Chapter 2 Listening Box Playlist

LB6: Type in Beyoncé and under Album Results, choose Beyoncé (Platinum Edition), Beyoncé. Select disc 1, Track 1, Pretty Hurts; Track 12, Superpower; Track 13, Heaven.

LB7: Type in Taylor Swift and under Playlist Results, choose Taylor Swift's Very Best. Select Track 1, Fifteen; Track 2, Tim McGraw; Track 3, Teardrops on My Guitar; Track 4, Fearless; Track 8, Our Song.

LB8: Type in Selena Gomez and under Album Results, choose For You, Selena Gomez. Select Track 1, The Heart Wants What It Wants; Track 2, Come and Get It; Track 3, Love You Like A Love Song; Track 5, Who Says.

LB9: Type in Justin Timberlake and choose top box Justin Timberlake, Pop. Select Track 1, Mirrors, Track 5, What Goes Around . . . Comes Around; Track 8, Your Baby; Track 9, My Love.

LB10: Type in Lady Gaga and under Artist Results, choose Lady Gaga, Dance Pop. Select Track 3, Just Dance (Featuring Colby O'Donis); Track 5, Paparazzi; Track 7, Telephone (Featuring Beyoncé).

LB11: Type in Tony Bennett and Lady Gaga and choose top box Cheek to Cheek, Tony Bennett. Select Track 1, Anything Goes; Track 2, Cheek to Cheek; Track 9, I Won't Dance; Track 13, Let's Face the Music and Dance.

Summary of Unit 8, Chapters 1–2 Terms and Study Sheet

Terms: No new terms for this unit.

Artists: Frank Sinatra, Nat King Cole, Ray Charles, Sammy Davis Jr., Whitney Houston, Beyoncé, Taylor Swift, Selena Gomez, Justin Timberlake, Lady Gaga

Summary of Listeners Toolbox: Music of the past artists is different in many ways from the present artists. In particular, as you listen, see if you can pick out differences in instruments, overall volume of the music, and general style differences. This type of analysis should give you a clearer picture of what has come before as compared to what is now. Of course, if you have any questions, always consult with the instructor.

Questions: What is your general impression of the sound Lady Gaga and Tony Bennett get? Can you think of any other combinations of artists that could be as successful? Did listening to Bennett and Gaga change your mind about either artist?

To The Student: The instructor may add or delete study items at his or her discretion. As there are no new study terms, the instructor might add additional questions.

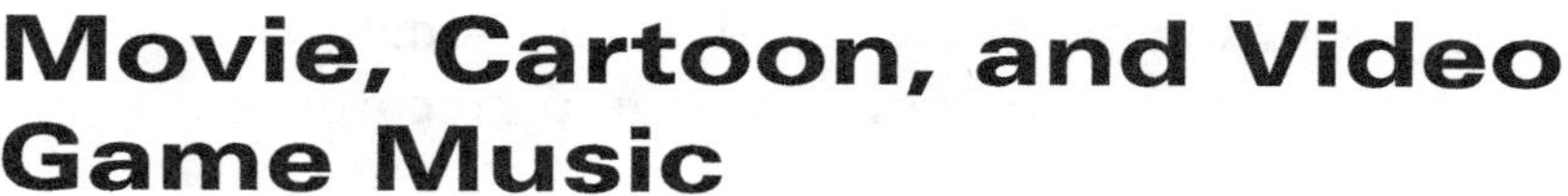

Movie, Cartoon, and Video Game Music

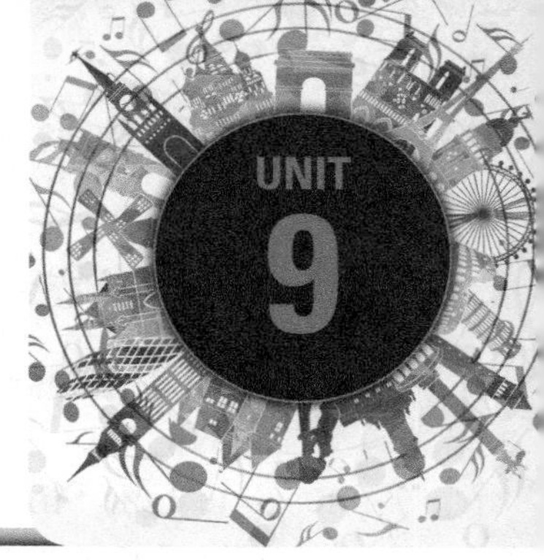

Unit Purpose

To present a brief history and sound examples of movie, cartoon, and video game music.

CHAPTER 1 THE MOVIES

There is no doubt that the progress of the movie industry depended on the advancement of the camera and film used in this device. Early technology in America probably dates back to 1888, with Thomas Edison. I will cite the early progress.

1. In 1888, Edison began designing machines capable of making and showing films.
2. In 1891, Edison along with his assistant, William Dickson, completed the design of the Kinetographic Camera and Kinetoscope. The Kinetoscope was a peephole video device that could be viewed by one person at a time.
3. In 1885, George Eastman and William Walker invent film rolls suitable for motion pictures.
4. In 1895, France, two brothers Auguste and Louis Lumière invented a camera, the Cinématographe, which enabled film to be viewed by many. The Lumières invented film perforation which was critical in advancing the film to the next images. They are also considered to be the first filmmakers in history.
5. In 1905, in Pittsburgh, Nickleodeon machines had the capability to show films. Nickle meaning 5 cents and "odeon," a Greek word meaning theater. These machines were put in storefronts, dance halls, and large venues. Viewer demand was so great that in 1907, movie theaters were built.
6. Believe it or not, movie making as we know it got started on the East Coast in New Jersey. In the early 1900s, Edison tried to monopolize the industry by putting a patent on everything, but was not successful.
7. From around 1908 to 1912, companies moved to the West Coast as they felt the East was getting too dangerous to make films. As time progressed in the West, several companies merged and Paramount, MGM, Fox, Universal, Warner Bros., and Goldwyn were left standing.

8. Through the World War I years, films had undergone many changes in lighting, subject matter, and time length. Viewing prices increased proportionately.
9. In 1914, Charles Russell used moving pictures with phonograph records in his movie The Photo-Drama of Creation.
10. The Jazz Singer (1927) is considered to be the first talking film. While mostly silent, it synchronized dialogue and singing. The first musically scored film was produced in France, in 1908. It was called, The Assassination of the Duke of Guise. By 1929, most all movies were "talkies."

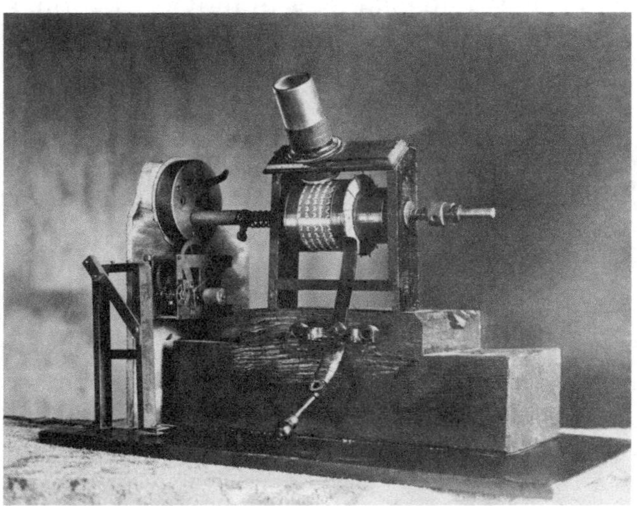

Edison's Kinetoscope

Hollywood's Golden Age (1930–1959)

The concept of Hollywood's Golden Age was based on the formation of motion picture studios and star making. Companies went to great lengths to sign good actors and actresses to long-term contracts in hopes of making them stars. Along with stars and in-house film making, companies made huge profits.

Some of the great male actors of the era are James Cagney, John Wayne, Humphrey Bogart, Clark Gable, Burt Lancaster, Kirk Douglas, Edward G. Robinson, James Stewart, Gregory Peck, Henry Fonda, Errol Flynn, Ernest Borgnine, and Marlon Brando. Needless to say, this is not a complete list.

Some of the great female actresses of the era are Lauren Bacall, Joan Crawford, Bette Davis, Doris Day, Ava Gardner, Katherine Hepburn, Elizabeth Taylor, Maureen O'Hara, Jane Russell, Barbara Stanwyck, Lucille Ball, and Rita Hayworth. Again, this is not a complete list.

Noted composers of film music in this era are Max Steiner (1888–1971), Alfred Newman (1900–1970), Franz Waxman (1906–1967), Dimitri Tiomkin (1894–1979).

Max Steiner (1888–1971)

1. Born in Austria.
2. Max studied at the Imperial Academy of Music.
3. His father was a theatrical impresario and got Max to conduct musical shows when he was 12 years old.
4. Steiner had gone to England to conduct shows and after staying for 8 years, he came to America in 1914, after World War I broke out.
5. Max spent many years in New York as a musical director, arranger, orchestrator, and conductor of Broadway Shows. He eventually moved to California to start writing music for movies.
6. His film-writing career started in the late 1920s. While not his first film credit, Steiner wrote his first original score for the movie Cimarron, in 1931. Max wrote over 300 film scores and was known as "the father of film music."

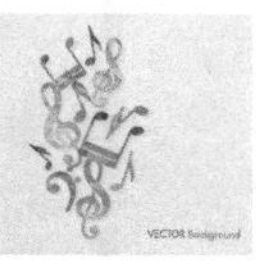

Listening Box 1

Type in Max Steiner and under Album Results, choose Gone with the Wind: Original Moti..., Max Steiner. Select Track 1, Main Title (This is from Gone with the Wind).

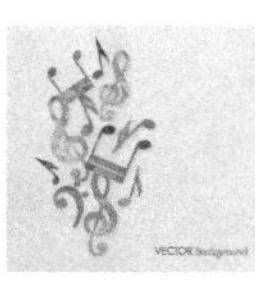

Listening Box 2

Type in Max Steiner and under Album Results, choose Silver Screen Magic, Max Steiner. Select Track 2, Death of a Scoundrel – Opening and Closing Themes; Track 7, Charge of the Light Brigade – Forward the Light Brigade.

Note: Any track on these albums represent good examples of early motion picture scores.

Dimitri Tiomkin (1894–1979)

1. Born in Kremenchuk, Poltava Governorate, Russian Empire (Now the Ukraine).
2. Dimitri started taking piano lessons from his mother at an early age.
3. As he got older, he studied music at the Saint Petersburg Conservatory. After his studies, he traveled to and worked in Berlin and Paris.
4. In the mid-1920s, Tiomkin moved to New York where he concertized in such places as Carnegie Hall.
5. In 1927, he married Albertina Rasch, an Austrian ballerina. The 1929 stock market crash took its toll on available work, which forced Tiomkin and his wife to move to California.

6. Dimitri's big break came from working with the famed director, Frank Capra, on the movie Lost Horizon in 1937. After this movie, Tiomkin became a very sought after composer.
7. Dimitri's scores were mostly written for Western movies as he always tried to capture the American frontier spirit.
8. In his lifetime, Tiomkin won several Oscars for best song and musical score. He also won many Golden Globe Awards.
9. After a long illustrious career, he eventually passed away in England, in 1979.

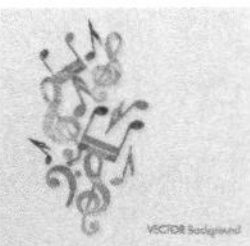

Listening Box 3

Type in Dimitri Tiomkin and under Album Results, choose The Alamo: The Essential Dimitri Ti...., Dimitri Tiomkin. Select disc 1, Track 1, Night Passage; Track 5, Wild Wild West – Main Theme; Track 9, Rawhide – Theme. Select disc 2, Track 1, Fall of the Roman Empire – Overture; Track 4, 55 Days at Peking – Overture; Track 12, High and Mighty – Main Theme.

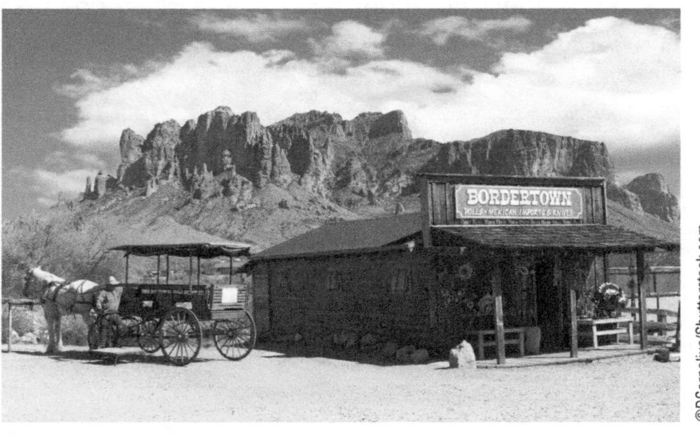

The Old Wild West

Film Animation and Music

1. The purpose of animation in film was to create movement with a succession of individual pictures, each slightly different.
2. An ancient form of animation goes back thousands of years as discovered artifacts showed different pictures of animals moving with different leg positions.
3. Modern day animation goes back to 1899, England, with a film called Matches. Believe it or not, the message of the film was about sending matches to the British troops who were fighting the Boer War in South Africa. The figures in the film were made out of matchsticks.

4. In 1900, the first animated film was Enchanted Drawing. In 1906, Humorous Phases of Funny Faces was the first totally animated film.
5. In 1932, The Academy of Motion Picture Arts and Sciences instituted the category of Animation Excellence. The first winner was Walt Disney, for Flowers and Trees.
6. As decades passed, computers revolutionized animation. Images could be made in 2D and 3D. Story lines were improved as professional screenwriters were hired. With James Cameron's film Avatar, 3D has gained new popularity.

Walt Disney (1901–1966)

1. Born in Chicago, Illinois.
2. Disney grew up on a farm and at an early age developed interest in drawing from a family friend.
3. Walt did not attend school until he was 8 years old and his family moved from Missouri to Kansas City where he was forced to repeat grades.
4. To earn money, Disney had his own paper route, which together with school, made him very tired. He would often sleep in class and frequently got low grades. He tried to further his drawing ambitions by attending the Kansas City Art Institute on Saturdays.
5. For business reasons, Walt's father moved the family to Chicago in 1917.
6. Walt's teenage years were really about him trying to find a direction. He attended high school and at night attended classes at the Chicago Academy of Fine Arts.
7. Disney decided to quit high school and join the Army. He was rejected because of his age. He and a friend decided to join the Red Cross. They wound up in France driving ambulances.
8. In 1920, he started his own Commercial Artists business with a friend. The concept of the business was to create cartoon characters based on fairy tales. These cartoons, called Laugh-O-Grams, became very popular and launched Disney into his own studio with the same name. As business grew, he hired several animators to help him complete the projects.
9. In 1923, Walt and his older brother Roy went to Hollywood and started their own cartoon studio. Some of their early successes were Alice Comedies, Oswald the Lucky Rabbit, and Mickey Mouse, whose original name was Mortimer. Besides Mickey, the Disney Company created such greats as Pluto, Goofy, and Donald Duck.
10. Walt's Snow White and the Seven Dwarfs took 3 years to make (1934–1937) and was the first animated film in Technicolor. Following successes were Bambi, Pinocchio, Fantasia (1940), Wind in the Willows, Peter Pan, Alice in Wonderland, Dumbo, Winnie the Pooh, Cinderella, Sleeping Beauty, Robin Hood, Roger Rabbit, The Little Mermaid, Beauty and the Beast, Aladdin, The Lion King, Pocahontas, and The Three Little Pigs.

11. As years passed, the Disney Company ventured out into new business areas such as theme parks, television (Mickey Mouse 1955), and, of course, currently, Disney Cruises. Disney theme parks have reached such places as Paris, Tokyo, Shanghai, and Hong Kong. In 1966, Walt Disney passed away from lung cancer, but in his lifetime won 22 Academy Awards and 7 Emmys.

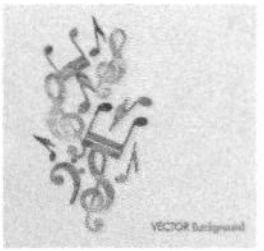

Listening Box 4

Type in Disney's and under Album Results, choose Disney's Greatest, Vol.1, Disney. Select Track 7, Circle of Life ("The Lion King" 1944); Track 8, Whole New World ("Aladdin" 1992); Track 9, Beauty and the Beast ("Beauty and the Beast" 1991); Track 12, Supercalifragilisticexpialidocious ("Mary Poppins" 1963); Track 16, You Can Fly! You Can Fly! ("Peter Pan" 1953); Track 17, Zip-A-Dee-Doo-Dah ("Song of the South" 1946); Track 18, Heigh-Ho ("Snow White" 1937); Track 20, When You Wish Upon a Star ("Pinocchio" 1940).

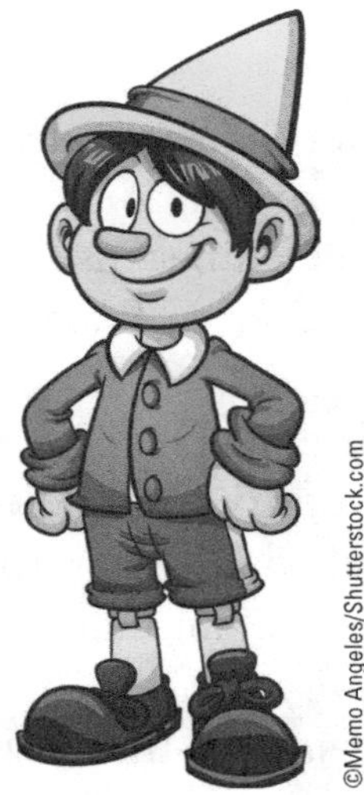

©Memo Angeles/Shutterstock.com

Pinocchio

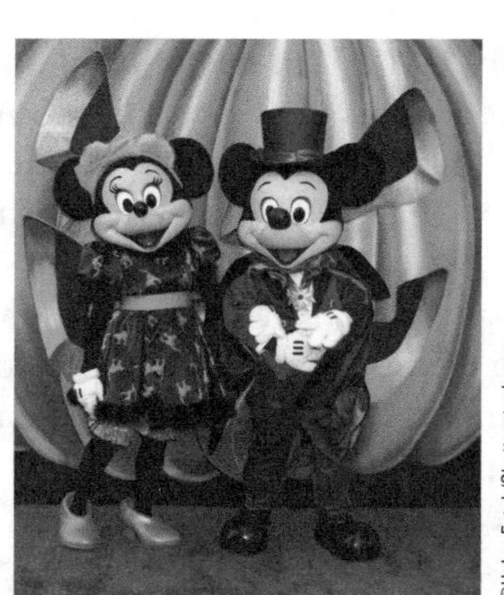

©Helga Esteb/Shutterstock.com

Mickey and Minnie

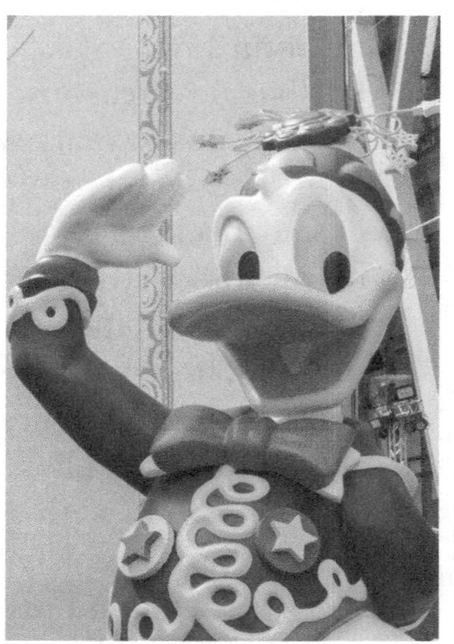

©jum ruji/Shutterstock.com

Donald Duck

Pixar

Pixar got its start in 1974, at NYIT (New York Institute of Technology). It remained as a computer graphics lab at NYIT from 1974 to 1979. It became part of Lucasfilm Computer Division from 1979 to 1986. It became its own corporation, Pixar, in 1986, under the leadership of Steve Jobs from Apple, Inc. In 2006, Pixar was purchased from Jobs by Disney for over 7 billion dollars. Some of the company's most famous film productions are Toy

Story (1995), A Bug's Life (1998), Finding Nemo (2003), Cars (2006), Ratatouille (2007), Monsters University (2013), Inside Out (2015), The Good Dinosaur (2015), to name a few.

Note: As is the case with all animated films, they have a musical score that highlights the action.

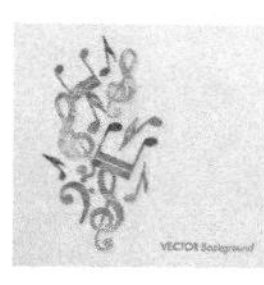

Listening Box 5

Type in Toy Story and choose top box, You've Got a Friend in Me, Randy Newman. Select Track 1, You've Got a friend in Me; Track 2, Strange Things; Track 3, I Will Go Sailing No More; Track 10, Mutants (True Instrumental).

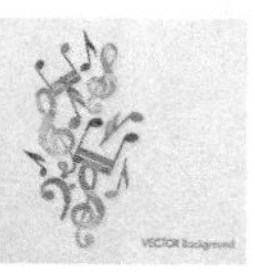

Listening Box 6

Type in Ratatouille and choose top box Ratatouille, Various Artists. Select Track 2, Welcome to Gusteau's (Score); Track 4, Granny Get Your Gun (Score); Track 5,100 Rat Dash (Score); Track 18, The Paper Chase; Track 24, Ratatouille Main Theme (Score).

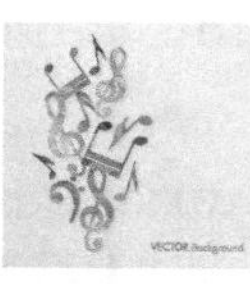

Listening Box 7

Type in Finding Nemo and choose top box Finding Nemo, Thomas Newman. Select Track 4, First Day; Track 7, The Divers; Track 9, Short-Term Dory; Track 11, Friends Not Food; Track 15, Foolproof.

DreamWorks and DreamWorks Animation

DreamWorks (SKG) was formed in 1994 by Steven Spielberg, Jeffrey Katzenberg, and David Geffen. The company began as a film production and film distribution enterprise. In 1995, DreamWorks bought shares in Pacific Data Images. In 2004, DreamWorks Animation became its own company and produced many high-earning animated films. Some of the most popular are: The Prince of Egypt (1998), Chicken Run (2000), Shrek (2001), Shrek 2 (2004), Shrek 3 (2007), Shrek Forever After (2010), Kung Fu Panda (2008), Kung Fu Panda 2 (2011), Kung Fu Panda 3 (2016), The Croods (2013), and Home (2015).

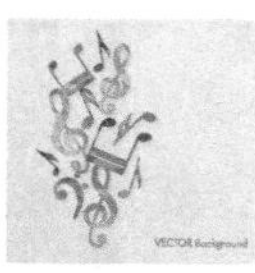

Listening Box 8

Type in Chicken Run and under Album Results choose Chicken Run, Harry Gregson – Williams (middle or second choice). Select Track 1, Opening Escape; Track 5, Chickens Are Not Organized; Track 7, Rocky and the Circus; Track 9, A Really Big Truck Arrives.

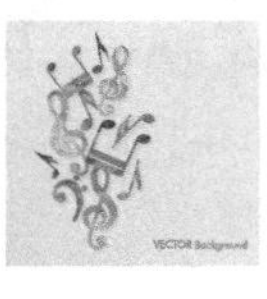

Listening Box 9

Type in Shrek and choose top box Shrek, Various Artists. Select Track 5, Funkytown; Track 6, I'm On My Way; Track 12, Fairy Godmother Song.

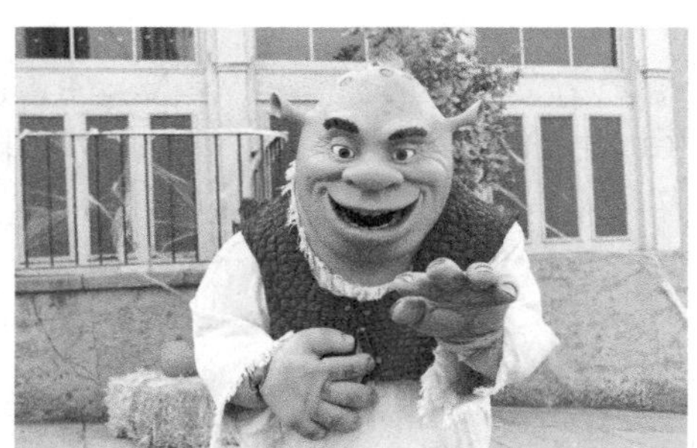

Shrek

Composers and Movie Scores After the Golden Age

For this section of the chapter, I will list famous composers and some of their popular film scores. I will not give biographical notes as I want to highlight the great music these people composed.

Composers: Elmer Bernstein (1922–2004), Henry Mancini (1924–1994), Maurice Jarré (1924–), Ennio Morricone (1928–), Jerry Goldsmith (1929–2004), Lalo Schifrin (1932–), John Williams (1932–), Quincy Jones (1933–), John Barry (1933–), Hans Zimmer (1957–).

Henry Mancini (1924–1994)

Some of Henry's most popular movie scores are: The Glen Miller Story (1953), Abbott and Costello Go to Mars (1953), Destry (1954), The Benny Goodman Story (1956), Breakfast at Tiffany's (1961), Days of Wine and Roses (1962), Hatari (1962), Two for the Road, (1967), Curse of the Pink Panther (1983), Son of the Pink Panther (1993).

Note: This is not a complete list. Also, this Listening Box contains some of Mancini's popular television themes.

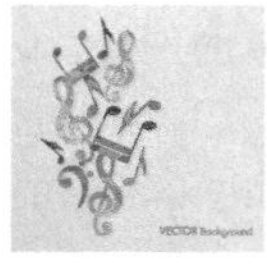

Listening Box 10

Type in Henry Mancini and under Album Results, choose Greatest Hits, Henry Mancini. Select Track 1, Peter Gunn; Track 4, Mr. Lucky; Track 6, Moon River; Track 7, Breakfast at Tiffany's; Track 10, Baby Elephant Walk.

Jerry Goldsmith (1929–2004)

Some of Jerry's most popular movie scores are: The Sand Pebbles (1966), Planet of the Apes (1968), Patton (1970), Logan's Run (1976), Alien (1979), Star Trek (The Moon Picture, 1979), Poltergeist (1982), First Blood (The first Rambo movie, 1982), Gremlins (1984), Air Force One (1997). For television, The Twilight Zone (1959).

Note: This is not a complete list.

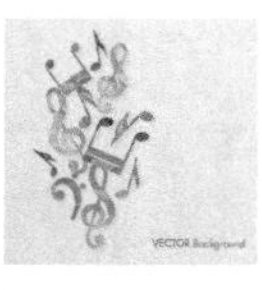

Listening Box 11

Type in Planet of the Apes and under Album Results, choose Planet of the Apes, Jerry Goldsmith, Select Track 3, Crash Landing; Track 6, the Clothes Snatchers; Track 7, The Hunt.

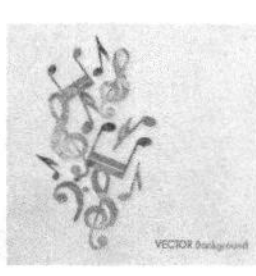

Listening Box 12

Type in Star Trek and under Album Results choose Star Trek: First Contact, Jerry Goldsmith. Select Track 1, Main Title/Locutus; Track 2, Red Alert; Track 11, End Credits.

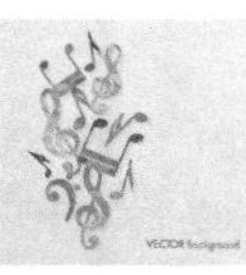

Listening Box 13

Type in First Blood and under Album Results, choose Rambo – First Blood II, Jerry Goldsmith. Select Track 1, Main Title; Track 3, Preparations; Track 4, The Jump; Track 13, Escape from Torture.

Quincy Jones (1933–)

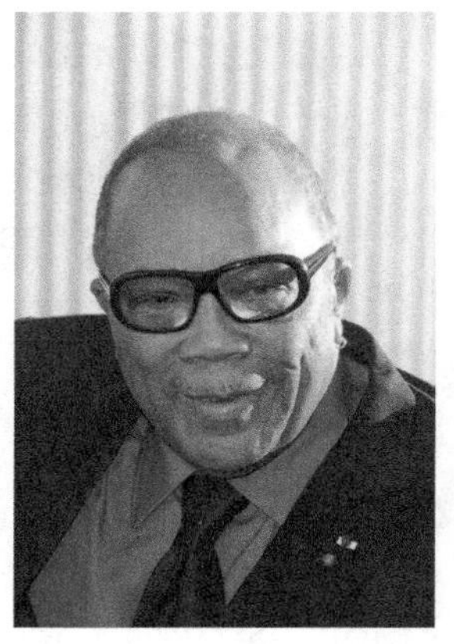

Some of Quincy's most popular movie scores are: The Pawnbroker (1964), In Cold Blood (1967), Enter Laughing (1967), In the Heat of the Night (1967), For Love of Ivy (1968), The Anderson Tapes, (1971), The Color Purple (1985), The Italian Job (2003). **Television:** Sanford and Son (1972–1977), Fresh Prince of Bel-Air (1990–1996).

Note: This is not a complete list.

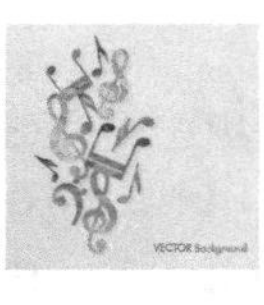

Listening Box 14

Type in The Pawnbroker and under Album Results, choose The Pawnbroker, Various Artists. Select Track 3, Harlem Drive; Track 8, Rack "Em Up; Track 9, Death Scene.

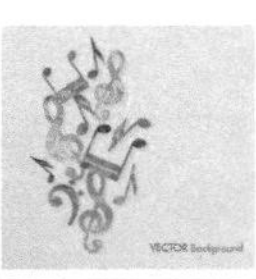

Listening Box 15

Type in Sanford and Son and under Track Results, choose Sanford and Son Theme, Quincy Jones. Select Track 8, Sanford and Son Theme.

Hans Zimmer (1957–)

Some of Hans's most popular movie scores are: Thelma and Louise (1991), The Lion King (1994), Gladiator (2000), Black Hawk Down (2001), Pearl Harbor (2001), The Last Samurai (2003), Pirates of the Caribbean (The Curse of the Black Pearl, 2003), The Da Vinci Code 92006), The Dark Knight (2008), Inception (2010).

Note: This is not a complete list.

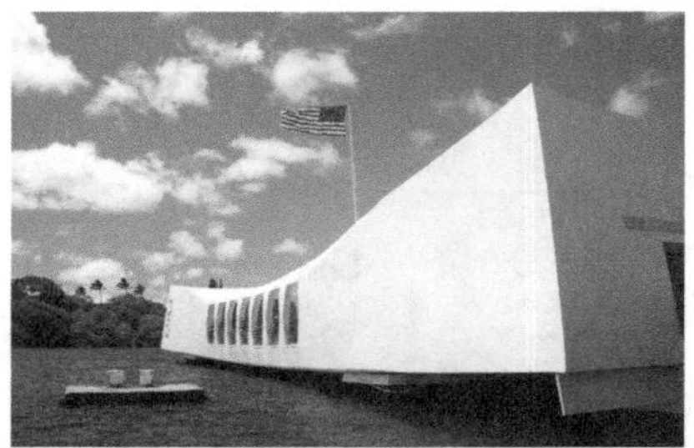

©Andre Nantel/Shutterstock.com

U.S.S. Arizona Memorial, Pearl Harbor, Hawaii

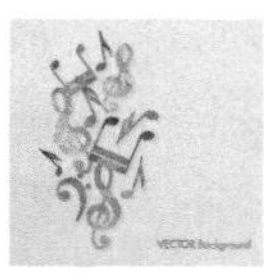

Listening Box 16

Type in Gladiator and choose top box Gladiator (2000), Hans Zimmer. Select Track 3, The Battle; Track 9, The Might of Rome; Track 12, Slaves to Rome; Track 13, Barbarian Horde.

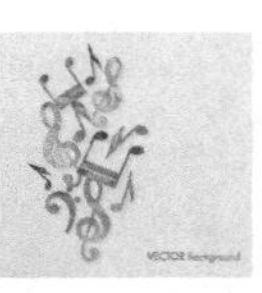

Listening Box 17

Type in Pearl Harbor and under Album Results choose Pearl Harbor – Original Motion Pictu… Various Artists. Select Track 1, There You'll Be (Faith Hill); Track 2, Tennessee; Track 7, December 7th; Track 8, War.

John Williams (1932–)

Some of John's most popular movie scores are: The Valley of the Dolls (1967), Fiddler on the Roof (1971), The Towering Inferno (1974), Jaws (1975), Superman (1978), The Empire Strikes Back (1980), Raiders of the Lost Ark (1981), E.T. the Extra-Terrestrial (1982), Return of the Jedi (1983), Indiana Jones and the Temple of Doom (1984), Home

Alone (1990), JFK (1991), Jurassic Park (1993), Schindler's List (1993), Saving Private Ryan (1998), Star Wars Episode 1: The Phantom Menace (1999), Harry Potter and the Sorcerer's Stone (2001), War of the Worlds (2005), Lincoln (2012), The BFG (2016).

Note: This is not a complete list.

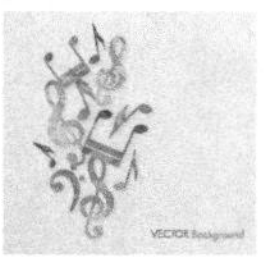

Listening Box 18

Type in Raiders of the Lost Ark and under Track results choose Raiders of the Lost Ark – Raiders of…, City of Prague Philharmonic. (**Note:** This will be your first choice and after you click on it, the picture will say, Film Music by John Williams). Select Track 1, Harry Potter and the Philosopher's Stone – Hedwig's Theme; Track 3, Star Wars: A New Hope; Track 5, Jaws; Track 7, E.T. The Extra-Terrestrial; Track 8, War of the Worlds – Suite; Track 10, Raiders of the Lost Ark; Track 12, Superman.

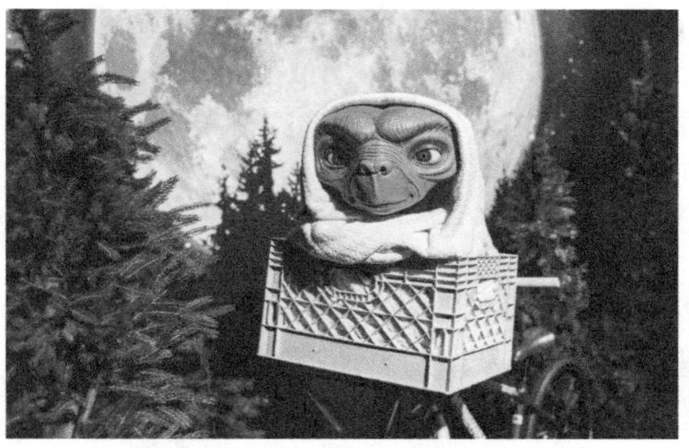

©Anton_Ivanov/Shutterstock.com

E.T. in Madame Tussauds Wax Museum, Times Square, New York

Star wars

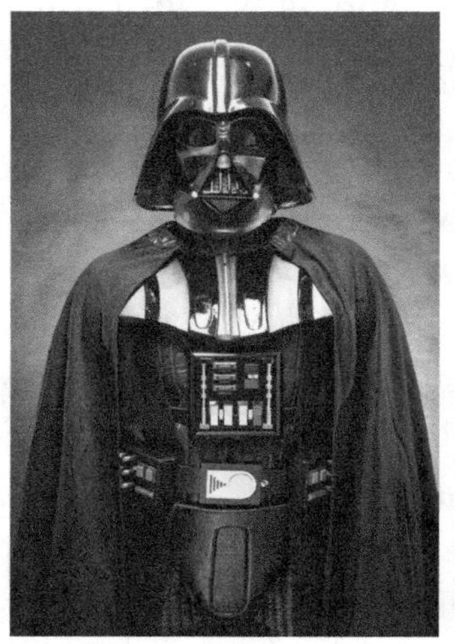

©Stefano Buttafoco/Shutterstock.com

Darth Vader

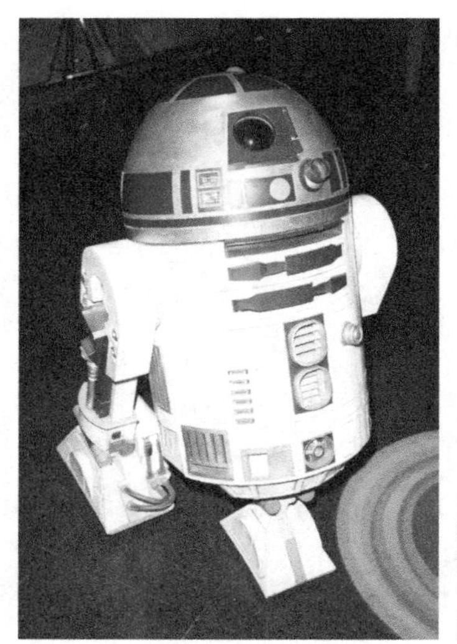

©Shelly Wall/Shutterstock.com

R2 – D2

Unit 9, Chapter 1 Listening Box Playlist

LB1: Type in Max Steiner and under Album Results, choose Gone with the Wind: Original Moti…, Max Steiner. Select Track 1, Main Title (This is from the movie Gone with the Wind).

LB2: Type in Max Steiner and under Album Results, choose Silver Screen Magic, Max Steiner. Select Track 2, Death of a Scoundrel – Opening and Closing Themes; Track 7, Charge of the Light Brigade – Forward The Light Brigade.

LB3: Type in Dimitri Tiomkin and under Album Results, choose The Alamo: The Essential Dimitri Ti…, Dimitri Tiomkin. Select disc 1, Track 1, Night Passage; Track 5, Wild Wild West – Main Theme; Track 9, Rawhide Theme. Select disc 2, Track 1, Fall of the Roman Empire – Overture; Track 4, 55 Days at Peking – Overture; Track 12, High and Mighty – Main Theme.

LB4: Type in Disney's and under Album Results, choose Disney's Greatest, Vol. 1, Disney. Select Track 7, Circle of Life ("The Lion King" 1994); Track 8, Whole New World ("Aladdin" 1992); Track 9, Beauty and the Beast ("Beauty and the Beast" 1991); Track 12, Supercalifragilisticexpialidocious ("Mary Poppins" 1963); Track 16, You Can Fly! You Can Fly! You Can Fly! ("Peter Pan" 1953); Track 17, Zip-A-Dee-Doo-Dah ("Song of the South" 1946); Track 18, Heigh-Ho ("Snow White" 1937); Track 20, When You Wish Upon a Star ("Pinocchio" 1940).

LB5: Type in Toy Story and choose top box, You've Got a Friend in Me, Randy Newman. Select Track 1, You've Got a Friend in Me; Track 2, Strange Things; Track 3, I Will Go Sailing No More; Track 10, Mutants (True Instrumental).

LB6: Type in Ratatouille and choose top box Ratatouille, Various Artists. Select Track 2, Welcome to Gusteau's (score); Track 4, Granny Get Your Gun (score); Track 5, 100 Rat Dash (score); Track 18, The Paper Chase; Track 24, Ratatouille Main Theme (score).

LB7: Type in Finding Nemo and choose top box Finding Nemo, Thomas Newman. Select Track 4, First Day; Track 7, The Divers; Track 9, Short-Term Dory; Track 11, Friends Not Food; Track 15, Foolproof.

LB8: Type in Chicken Run and under Album Results, choose Chicken Run, Harry Gregson-Williams (This will be your middle or second choice). Select Track 1, Opening Escape; Track 5, Chickens Are Not Organized; Track 7, Rocky and the Circus; Track 9, A Really Big Truck Arrives.

LB9: Type in Shrek and choose top box Shrek 2, Various Artists. Select Track 5, Funkytown; Track 6, I'm On My Way; Track 12, Fairy Godmother Song.

LB10: Type in Henry Mancini and under Album Results, choose Greatest Hits, Henry Mancini. Select Track 1, Peter Gunn; Track 4, Mr. Lucky; Track 6, Moon River; Track 7, Breakfast at Tiffany's; Track 10, Baby Elephant Walk.

LB11: Type in Planet of the Apes and under Album Results, choose Planet of the Apes, Jerry Goldsmith. Select Track 3, Crash Landing; Track 6, The Clothes Snatchers; Track 7, The Hunt.

LB12: Type in Star Trek and under Album Results, choose Star Trek: First Contact, Jerry Goldsmith. Select Track 1, Main Title/Locutus; Track 2, Red Alert; Track 11, End Credits.

LB13: Type in First Blood and under Album Results, choose Rambo – First Blood II, Jerry Goldsmith. Select Track 1, Main Title; Track 3, Preparations; Track 4, The Jump; Track 13, Escape from Torture.

LB14: Type in The Pawnbroker and under Album Results, choose The Pawnbroker, Various Artists. Select Track 3, Harlem Drive; Track 8, Rack 'Em Up; Track 9, Death Scene.

LB15: Type in Sanford and Son and under Track Results, choose Sanford and Son Theme, Quincy Jones. Select Track 8, Sanford and Son Theme.

LB16: Type in Gladiator and choose top box Gladiator (2000), Hans Zimmer. Select Track 3, The Battle; Track 9, The Might of Rome; Track 12, Slaves to Rome; Track 13, Barbarian Horde.

LB17: Type in Pearl Harbor and under Album Results choose Pearl Harbor – Original Motion Pictu…, Various Artists. Select Track 1, There You'll Be (Faith Hill); Track 2, Tennessee; Track 7, December 7th; Track 8, War.

LB18: Type in Raiders of the Lost Ark and under Track Results, choose Raiders of the Lost Ark – Raiders of…. City of Prague Philharmonic. (Note: This will be your first choice and after you click on it, the picture will say Film Music by John Williams). Select Track 1, Harry Potter and the Philosopher's Stone – Hedwig's Theme; Track 3, Star Wars: A New Hope; Track 5, Jaws; Track 7, E.T. The Extra-Terrestrial; Track 8, War of the Worlds – Suite; Track 10, Raiders of the Lost Ark; Track 12, Superman.

CHAPTER 2 CARTOONS: MORE FILM ANIMATION AND MUSIC

The origin of cartoons can be traced back to the Middle Ages. They were generally preparatory drawings done on very hard or sturdy paper. Their designs became finished products for larger works and things like stained glass. It wasn't until the nineteenth century that cartoons took on a humorous tone in newspapers and magazines. Great artists such as da Vinci and Raphael worked with cartoons. Subject matter for this medium often included comedy, politics, and science. In today's world, subjects like superheroes, animals, and space exploration have been added. Cartoons generally target younger audiences, but that being said, I believe they ignite the kid in all of us.

Note: All listening examples for this chapter will be taken from TV Theme Library – Hit Cartoon and Kid Show Themes.

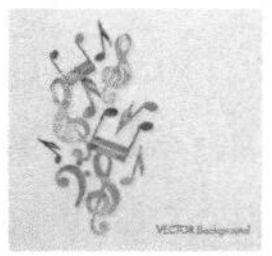

Listening Box 19

Type in TV Theme Library and under Album Results, choose TV Theme Library – Hit Cartoon and…, TV Theme Song Library (Your second choice). I will be using Tracks 1-2-6-7-8-9-10-12-13-14. It will not be necessary to sign into this site more than once. As a bit of a change to presentation, I will put the listening track number next to the picture name

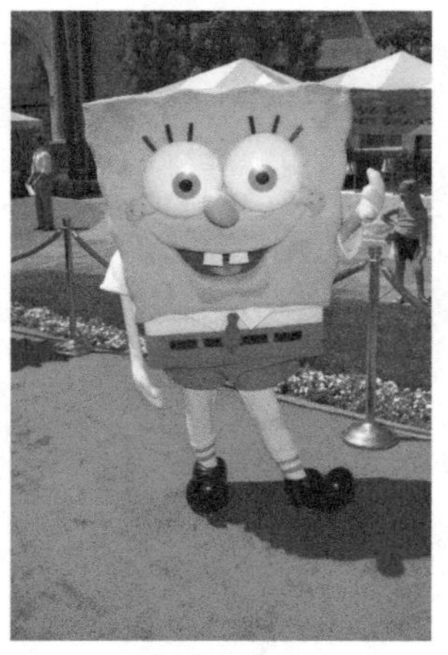

©Feature Flash Photo Agency/Shutterstock.com

Sponge Bob Square Pants – Track 1

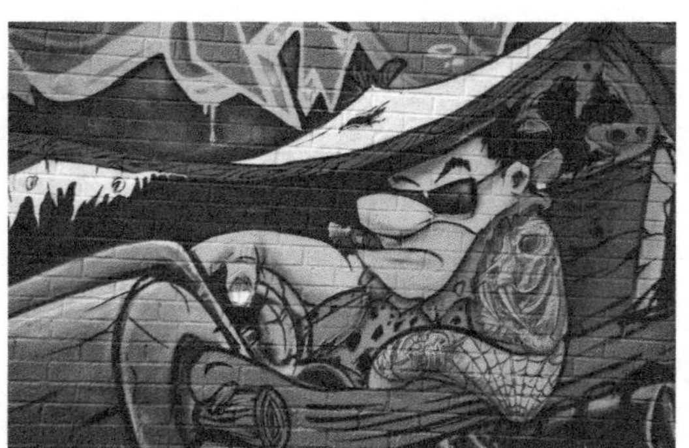

©meunierd/Shutterstock.com

Fred Flintstone – Track 2

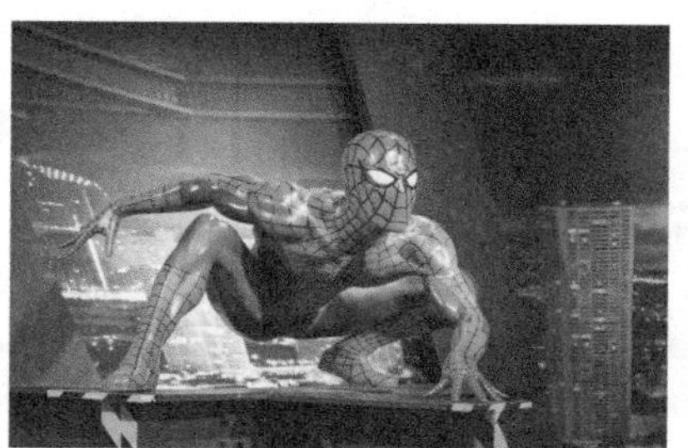

Spiderman – Track 7

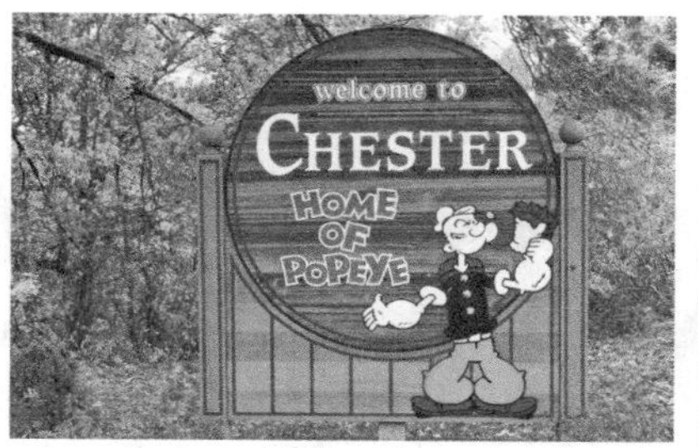

Popeye the Sailor Man – Track 10

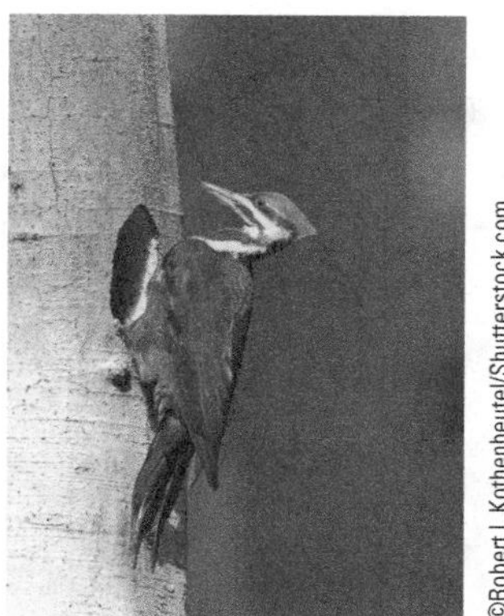

Woody Woodpecker – Track 12

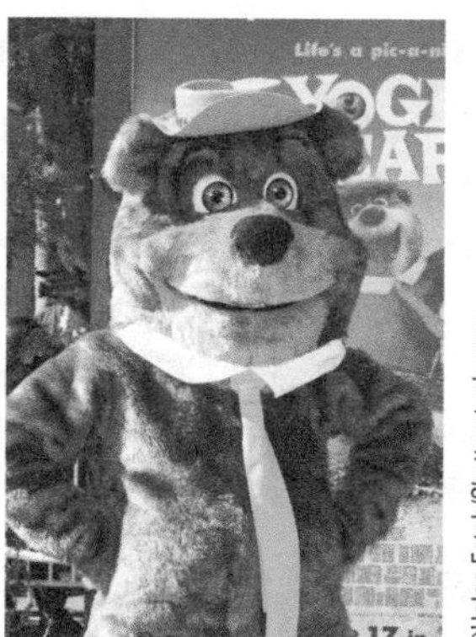

Yogi Bear – Track 13

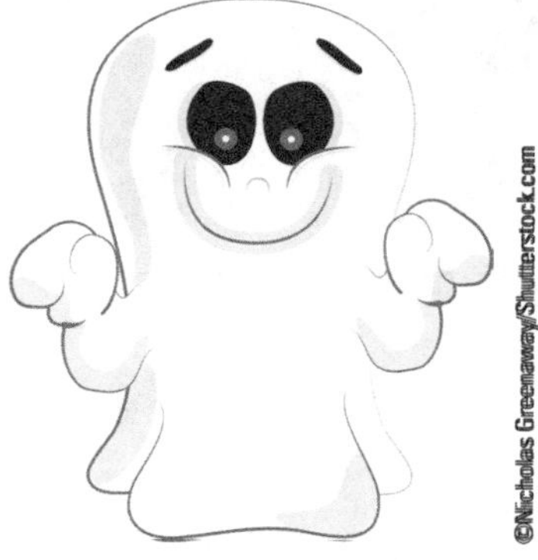

Casper the Friendly Ghost – Track 14

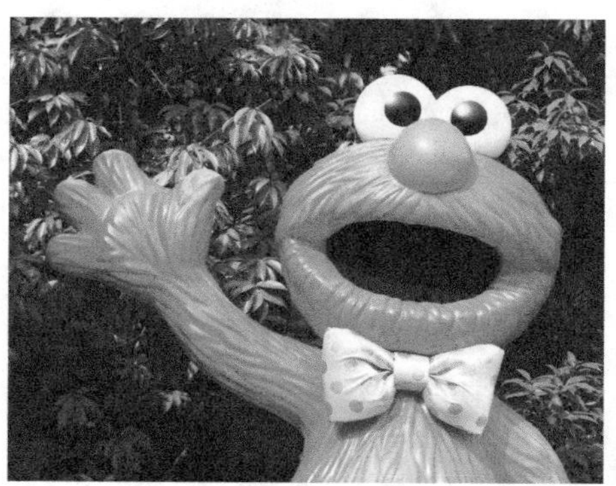

Elmo—Sesame Street – Track 6

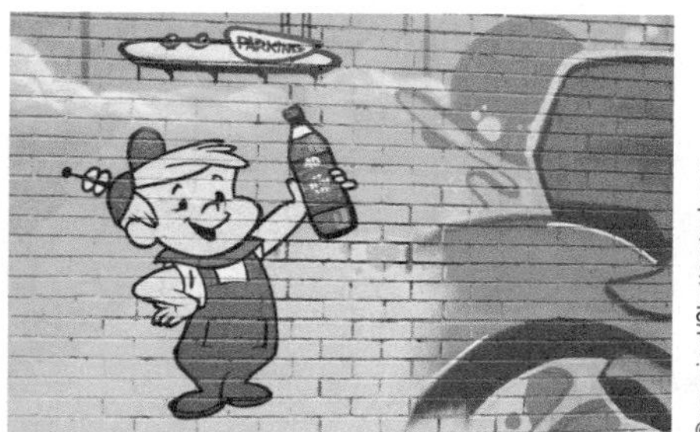

The Jetsons – Track 8

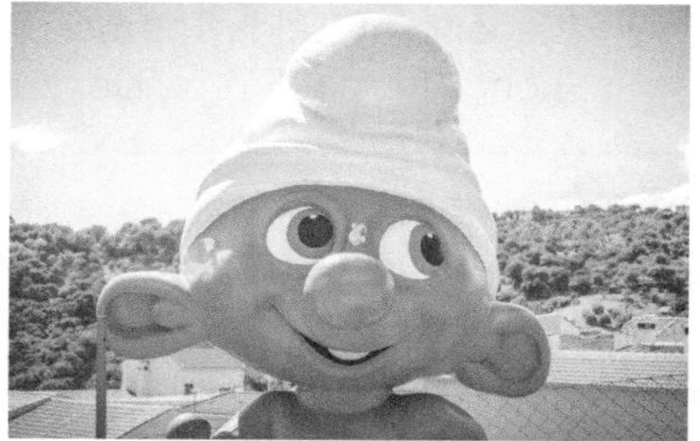

The Smurfs – Track 9

CHAPTER 3 VIDEO GAME MUSIC

Video games can be traced back to the 1950s, but they did not gain super popularity till the 1970s and 1980s. Video games are now at their highest level of use and popularity with inventions such as Xbox and mobile phones. Needless to say, computers have played a major role in the advancement of video games, and arcades were one of the first places the general public could play. Currently, Rap style is being used in the music to give an up-to-date sound. Companies like Microsoft, Sony, and Nintendo are major players in the video game industry.

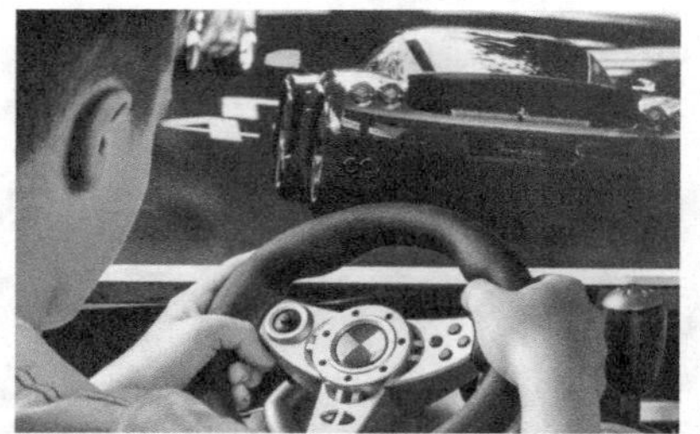

Teen Playing a Video Game

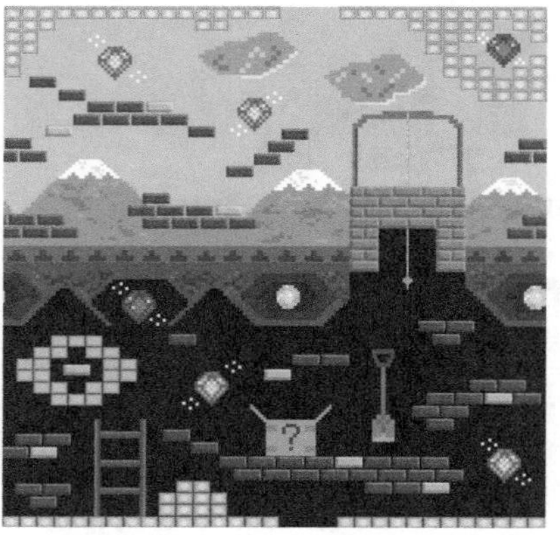

Seamless Pattern Video Gam

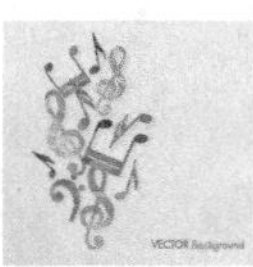

Listening Box 20

Type in Video Games and under Playlist Results, choose Nintendo Classics – Remixed. Select Track 1, Super Mario Bros. (Theme); Track 5, Metroid Theme (From "Metroid"); Track 6, The Legend of Zelda – Overworld; Track 7, #1 Legend of Zelda Theme Dubstep Remix (feat. Dubstep); Track 10, Donkey Kong Theme (From "Donkey Kong Country") (Cover).

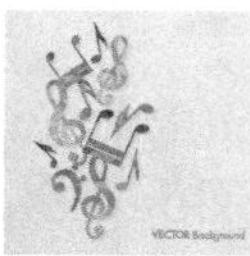

Listening Box 21

Type in The Greatest Video Game Music and choose the top box, The Greatest Video Game Music 2, Various Artists. Select Track 4, Final Fantasy Vii: One – Winged Angel; Track 8, Chrono Trigger: Main Theme; Track 13, Batman Arkham City: Main Theme.

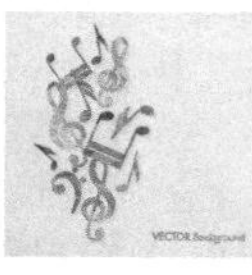

Listening Box 22

Type in The Greatest Video Game Music and under Album Results, choose The Greatest Video Game Music III…, M.O.D. Select Track 2, World of Warcraft – Invincible; Track 5, Dragon Age Inquisition – Main Theme. (These listenings are vocal editions.)

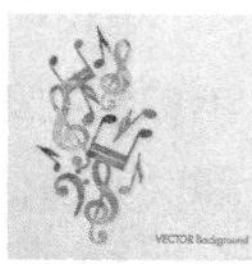

Listening Box 23

Type in The Greatest Video Game Music and under Album Results, choose Survival of the Fittest: The Greatest…Xsubn. Select Track 3, Digity Iglesia Technique; Track 6, Survival of the Fittest; Track 7, He's Gonna Bring the Party; Track 13, Spython (Retro). (This album contains great video game music that was never used.)

Unit 9, Chapters 2 and 3 Listening Box Playlist

LB19: Type in TV Theme Library and under Album Results, choose TV Theme Library – Hit Cartoon and...., TV Theme Song Library (Your second choice). I will be using Tracks 1-2-6-7-8-9-10-12-13-14. It will not be necessary to sign into this site more than once. As a bit of a change in presentation, I put the track number next to the picture name.

LB20: Type in Video Games and under Playlist Results choose Nintendo Classics-Remixed. Select Track1, Super Mario Bros. (Theme); Track 5, Metroid Theme (from"Metroid"); Track 6, The Legend of Zelda-Overworld; Track 7, #1 Legend of Zelda Theme Dubstep Remix (feat. Dubstep); Track 10, Donkey Kong Theme (from" Donkey Kong Country") (Cover).

LB21: Type in The Greatest Video Game Music and choose the top box, The Greatest Video Game Music 2, Various Artists. Select Track 4, Final Fantasy Vii: One-Winged Angel; Track 8, Chrono Trigger: Main Theme; Track 13, Batman Arkham City: Maim Theme.

LB22: Type in The Greatest Video Game Music and under Album Results choose The Greatest Video Game Music lll..., M.O.D. Select Track 2, World of Warcraft-Invincible; Track 5 Dragon Age Inquisition-Main Theme. (These listenings are vocal editions).

LB23: Type in The Greatest Video Game Music and under Album Results choose Survival of the Fittest: The Greatest....Xsubn. Select Track 3, Digity Iglesia Technique; Track 6, Survival of the Fittest; Track 7, He's Gonna Bring the Party; Track 13, Spython (Retro). This album contains great video game music that was never used.

Summary of Unit 9, Chapters 1-2-3 Terms and Study Sheet

Terms

Kinetoscope: An early peephole video device which could be viewed by one person at a time.

Kinetographic camera: An early movie camera.

Film animation: Creates movement in film with a succession of individual pictures, each slightly different.

Artists: Max Steiner, Dimitri Tiomkin, Walt Disney, Elmer Bernstein, Henry Mancini, Maurice Jarré, Ennio Morricone, Jerry Goldsmith, Lalo Schfrin, John Williams, Quincy Jones, John Barry, Hans Zimmer

Summary of Listeners Toolbox

Unit Nine is a very interesting unit in that I present some of the most up-to-date topics in music. The listener is obligated to think outside of the box in terms of different sounds. I'm firmly convinced that some of our most diverse music comes from the film industry. With the vast assortment of subjects to musically describe, the composers have an enormous task to do sound justice to the pictures. For the subjects contained in this unit, I suggest to the listener that you keep an open mind as you listen. Expand your horizons!

Questions: For Class Discussion

1. Do you think music helps or hinders a film?
2. Compare and contrast film music to cartoon music. Use provided sound examples to substantiate your answer.
3. In the categories of movie, cartoon, and video game music, which is your favorite and which is your least favorite?

To The Student: The instructor may add or delete study items at his or her discretion.

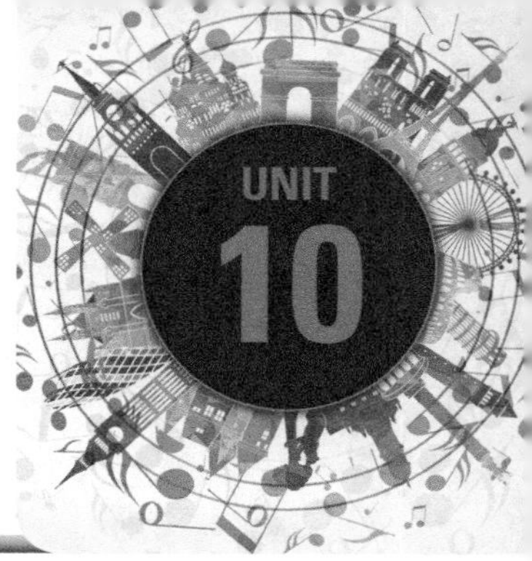

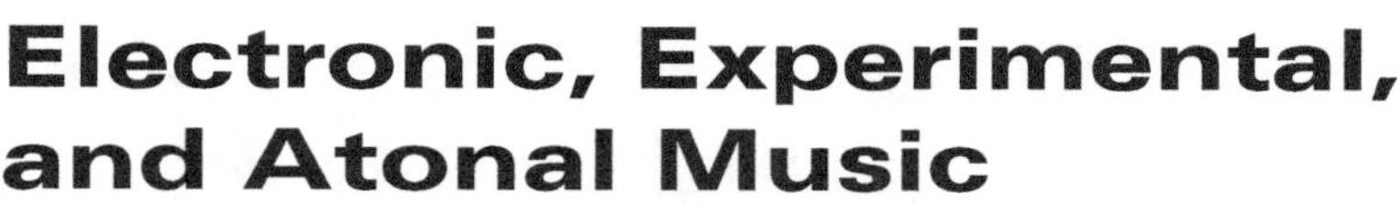

Electronic, Experimental, and Atonal Music

Unit Purpose

To present a brief history and sound examples of music that gives us a modern day sound.

CHAPTER 1 ELECTRONIC MUSIC

What Do We Find in This Period?

Music: With electronic, experimental, and atonal music, I am firmly convinced we have come full circle in the development of modern day music. I say this with the knowledge and respect I have for the unbelievable amount of possibilities computers and synthesizers can produce in sound. I think it is fair to say, sound combinations are limitless. Of course, we have to leave room for newer inventions which might make my previous statements obsolete.

Texture: Texture for electronic and experimental music is thought of differently than other types of music. For example, electronic music has no necessity for the ability to read music and generally depends on rhythm and a knowledge of the capabilities of the device being used. These electronic devices demand a different mentality when it comes to producing music.

Forms: As is the case with texture, forms in electronic, experimental, and atonal music are different from traditional music. Often times the development of a musical piece is based on electronic events rather than pure development of the melody. In the case of atonal music, often times different note systems are used and they are not thought of as scales.

Composers/Instrument Inventors: Thaddeus Cahill, Lee de Forest, Maurice Martenot, Léon Theremin, J.A. O'Neill, Laurens Hammond, John Cage, Vladimir Ussachevsky, Otto Luening, Milton Babbitt, Roger Sessions, Toru Takemitsu, Minao Shibata, Kuniharu Akiyama, Toshiro Mayuzumi, Pierre Boulez, and Edgard Varèse, to name a few.

Travel to: United States, France, Germany, Japan, Russia, Austria

A Modern Day Theremin

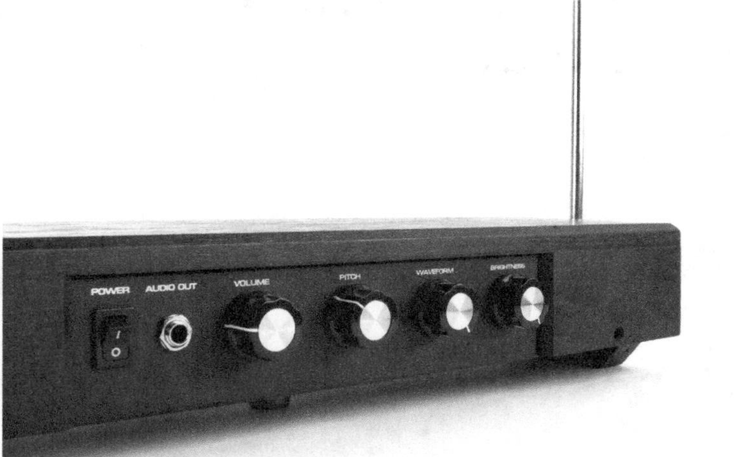

©Dmitry Nikolaev/Shutterstock.com

Electronic Music

1. Electronic music devices can be traced back to the late nineteenth century.
2. An original electronic music trendsetter was Léon Theremin with his invention of the Etherphone, which was later called the Theremin. This instrument, around 1920, was used for some of the earliest electronic compositions and was basically a sine-wave generator.
3. It was in the 1920s and 1930s that the first electronic compositions appeared.
4. In 1927, J.A. O'Neill invented a machine that used magnetic ribbon. This experiment was a commercial failure.
5. Around 1928, in Paris, France, Maurice Martenot invented the Ondes which was a Theremin-like instrument. This early device used the principles of varying oscillation frequency in vacuum tubes to produce sound.
6. In 1930, Laurens Hammond invented the Hammond Organ and this instrument was patented in 1934.
7. In 1942, the magnetic tape recorder and computer were invented. These devices opened doors to a wide range of new sounds.
8. One of the early concepts of electronic music was called Music Concrete, which started in France. Musicians took the tape recorder outside and recorded the sounds of the real or concrete world.
9. In the early 1950s, a major electronic music studio was built in Cologne. It was frequently used by early electronic music pioneers, Karlheinz Stockhausen and Gottfried Michael Koenig.

10. In 1946, the Sony Electronics Music Company was founded and this gave way to Japanese influence in electronic music. Toshiro Mayazumi introduced Music Concrete to Japan and some of his contemporaries were Toru Takemitsu, Joji Yuasa, Mineo Shibata, and Shiro Fukai.
11. In America, the concept of electronic music can be traced back to Thaddeus Cahill who invented the Telharmonium in 1895. This was an electromechanical instrument that Cahill worked on improving until 1912.
12. In the late 1930s, John Cage wrote five compositions under the title Imaginary Landscape. Probably his most famous was No. 4 for 12 radios.
13. In the 1950s, two universities combined talents to create electronic music. At Columbia University, Vladimir Ussachevsky and Otto Luening joined forces with Princeton University's Milton Babbitt and Roger Sessions. These four composers formed what was to become known as the Columbia–Princeton Electronic Music Center.
14. In 1958, the first synthesizer was made at Columbia–Princeton. A major contributor to the technology was Robert Moog who worked with voltage-controlled oscillators. Moog eventually went on to create his own company, Moog Music.
15. As time passed, research and development from several companies created some awesome synthesizers. For example, the Minimoog in the 1970s and 1980s, Yamaha GX-1, Prophet-5, and Yamaha's DX7, the first FM digital synthesizer. The first digital synthesizer was the Fairlight CMI in 1979. FM stands for frequency modulation.
16. A great addition and invention for electronic music is MIDI, which was born in 1980 and finalized in 1983. MIDI is an acronym which stands for Musical Instrument Digital Interface. It is a universal chord connection which enables devices to talk to each other when connected.
17. In the 2000s, computer technology put electronic music over the top and in many ways has surpassed synthesizer capabilities. Advances in the development of microprocessors and software have given such small devices as laptops, iPods, and iPads the ability to create great sound.

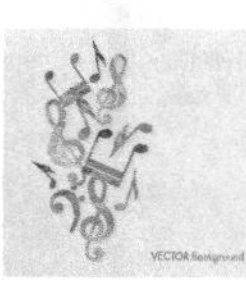

Listening Box 1

Type in Electronic Music and choose top box Electrospective: Electronic Music Since 1958, Various Artists. Select Track 2, Here Comes The Warm Jets; Track 3, The Things That Dream Are Made Of; Track 4, Planet Earth; Track 9, Kelley Watch The Stars; Track 15, One (Radio edit).

Note: The next Listening Box selections represent in sound electronic music that you might hear in a nightclub.

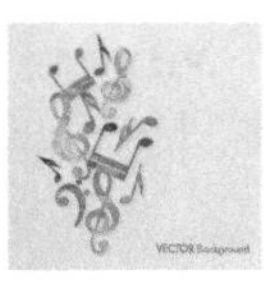

Listening Box 2

Type in Electronic Music and under Tracks, choose Hit Me, Club Bangers Academy. Select Track 1, The RezDeux; Track 2, Falling; Track 3, Glorious; Track 11, Rezerved.

Note: The next Listening Box selections represent in sound electronic music those you might hear in the movies.

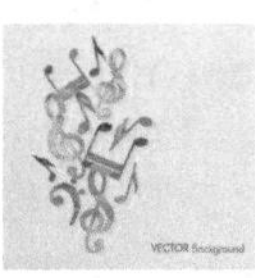

Listening Box 3

Type in Electronic Music and under Featured Playlists choose Electronic Music at the Movies (this will be your third choice). Select Track 3, Chase; Track 4, Main Theme; Track 10, Cellular Blur.

Note: If you are going to listen to all the selections at the same time, you only have to type in Electronic Music once, then follow the rest of the instructions.

DJ Mixer with Headphones Audio Equalizer

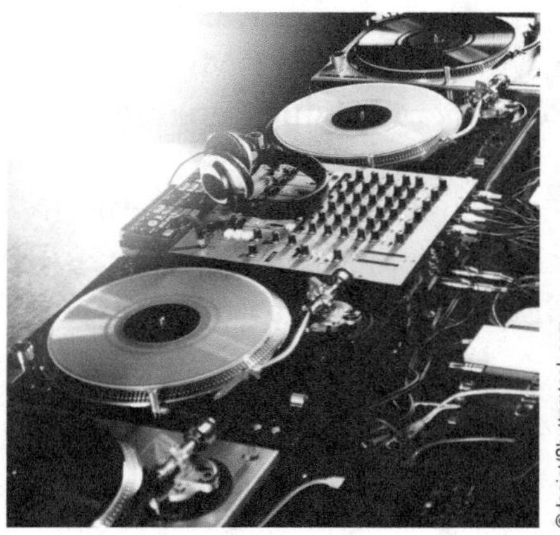

©dpaint/Shutterstock.com

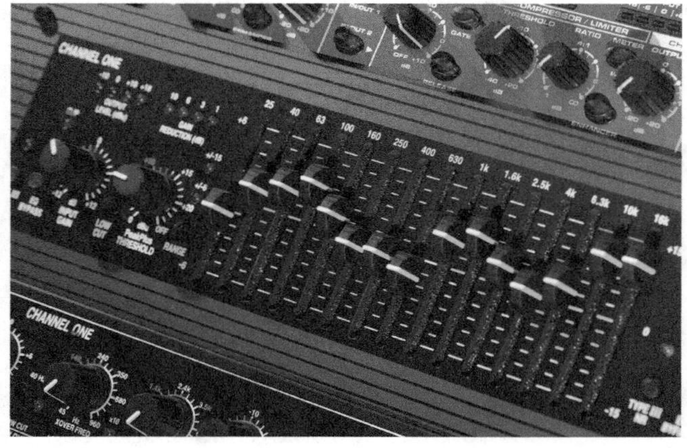

©Alexey Laputin/Shutterstock.com

Unit 10, Chapter 1 Listening Box Playlist

LB1: Type in Electronic Music and choose top box Electrospective: Electronic Music Since 1958, Various Artists. Select Track 2, Here Comes the Warm Jets; Track 3, The Things That Dreams Are Made Of; Track 4, Planet Earth; Track 9, Kelly Watch the Stars; Track 15, One (Radio Edit).

LB2: Type in Electronic Music and under Tracks, choose Hit Me, Club Bangers Academy. Select Track 1, The RezDeux; Track 2, Falling; Track3, Glorious; Track 11, Rezerved.

LB3: Type in Electronic Music and under Featured Playlists, choose Electronic Music at the Movies (This will be your third choice). Select Track 3, Chase; Track 4, Main Theme; Track 10, Cellular Blur.

CHAPTER 2 EXPERIMENTAL MUSIC

The basic concept of Experimental Music is to create pieces with unpredictable outcomes. This style can be traced back to the mid-twentieth century and involves many changes in music production, music notation, and music performance. There is no denying that although Electronic Music is a separate category, it certainly played a beginning role in the development of Experimental Music.

Unconventional Elements of Experimental Music

One of the most interesting elemental changes was how things were called. Terms like melody, harmony, and rhythm gave way to terms like musical events. Instruments and voices were sometimes called sound devices. Music Concrete, if you remember, was used to describe composers using a tape recorder to record the sounds of the outside world. Two very prominent terms in experimental music are chance and aleatoric.

Aleatoric Music is a performer-controlled music with precise notation. It is thought of as chance music in that the sound outcomes are unpredictable.

Chance Music is also performer-controlled music with less precise notation than Aleatoric Music. In this music, the performer has more of an ability to create and bring individuality to the piece. Like Aleatoric music, the sound outcomes are unpredictable.

More Unconventional Elements

1. Some music was written using diagrams rather than conventional notation.
2. Instruments and voices were used in unconventional ways.
3. Such devises as telephones, pots, and garbage pails were used as musical instruments.

Using the Piano and Stringed Instruments Unconventionally

Threnody to the Victims of Hiroshima [Krysztof Penderecki (Since 1933)]

This piece was written in 1960 and uses 52 stringed instruments in different ways. In this composition, Penderecki has players slapping the strings, playing on the tailpiece behind the bridge, and using all sorts of plucking and sliding motions. While this piece sounds extremely dissonant, its overall meaning is to convey the compassion Penderecki had for the Japanese people as they tried to survive the bombings of Hiroshima and Nagasaki in 1945. The word threnody means a song or a poem of lamentation.

Model of "Little Boy" the Atomic Bomb—The Explosion

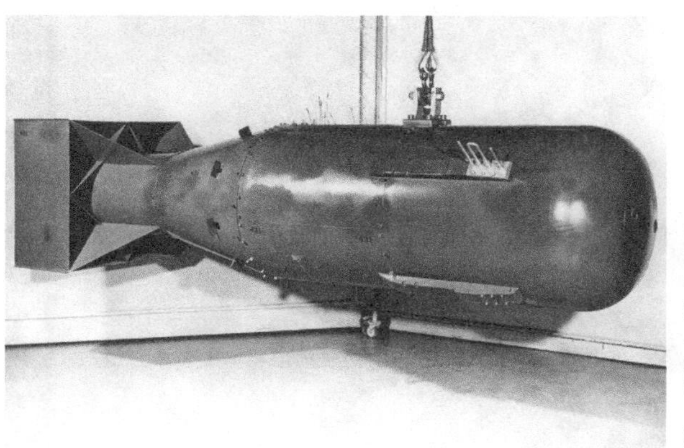

©Everett Historical/Shutterstock.com

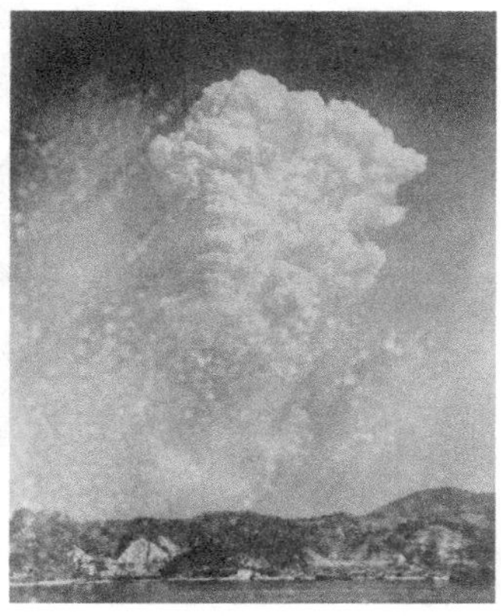

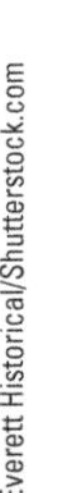

©Everett Historical/Shutterstock.com

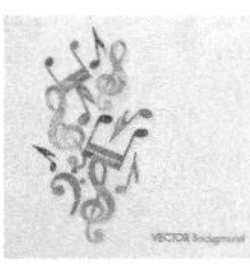

Listening Box 4

Type in Krzysztof Penderecki and choose top box Krzysztof Penderecki, 20th/21st Century. Select Track 1, Threnody To the Victims of Hiroshima.

The Banshee (Henry Cowell 1897–1965)

This piece was written in 1925 and the piano is used in a very different way. The first player sits at the piano, but does not play the keys, only uses the piano pedals. The second player uses sweeping motions on the strings to get specific sounds. This mode of playing the piano creates a very ethereal effect.

Note: In Irish folklore, the Banshee is a female spirit who is often seen as an ugly woman, but she can transform herself into a young and beautiful person if she chooses to do so. Her wailing is related to the death of a loved one. If the Banshee desires, she can appear before the death happens.

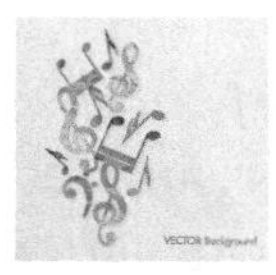

Listening Box 5

Type in Henry Cowell and under Tracks, choose The Banshee, Henry Cowell. Select Track 9, The Banshee.

A Howling Banshee

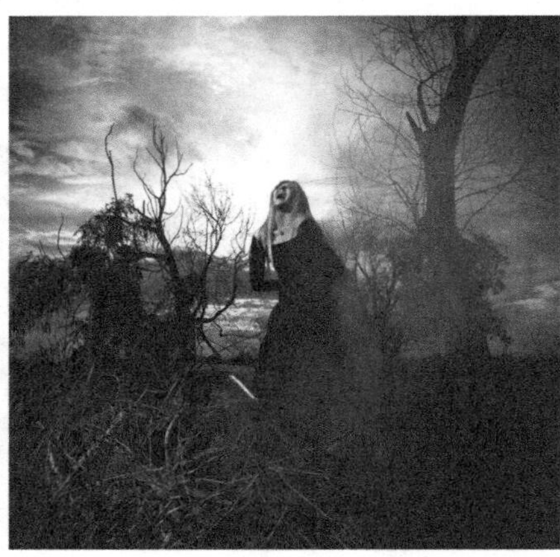

Eclat (Pierre Boulez 1925–2016)

Pierre Boulez was a French Experimentalist composer. Much of his music deals with the athematic style of composition. Athematic means a composition not based on melodies or themes. Eclat means Shine.

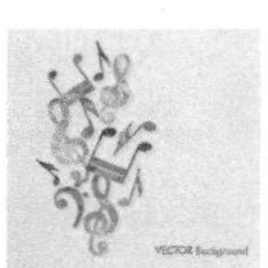

Listening Box 6

Type in Pierre Boulez and under Tracks, choose Eclat, Pierre Boulez. Select Track 1, Eclat; Track 3, Rituel (In Memory of Bruno Maderna).

Note: Admittedly, these are long listenings, but they are great examples of Experimental music. Also, Rituel means Ritual, and Bruno Maderna was an Italian conductor and composer.

Note: The Institute for Research and Coordination Acoustic Music was founded by Pierre Boulez and is in Paris, France. It is often referred to as IRCAM.

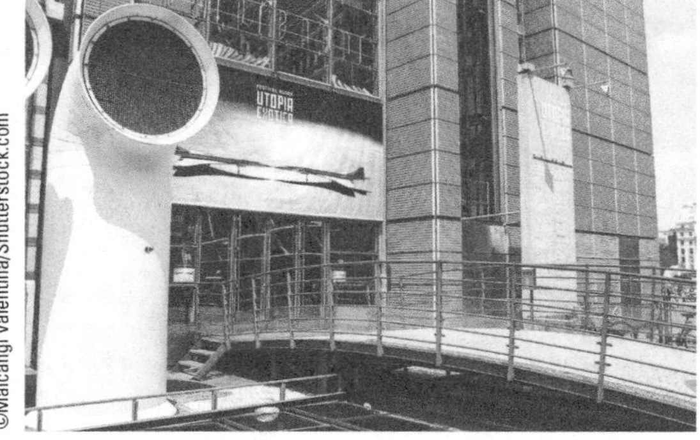

IRCAM

Zyklus (Karlheinz Stockhausen 1928–2007)

Karlheinz Stockhausen was a German composer who specialized in aleatoric, electronic, and serial music compositions. His piece Zyklus (1959) uses graphic notation and can start on any page. Also, it could be read upside down. These playing decisions are left up to the performer.

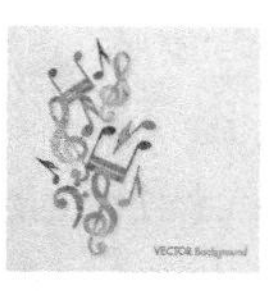

Listening Box 7

Type in Karlheinz Stockhausen and under Albums, choose Karlheinz Stockhausen: Spiral 1& Japan (this will be your second choice). Select disc 1, Track 1, Zyklus No. 9.

Gruppen (1955–1957), another Stockhausen piece, is interesting in that it was written for three orchestras that are placed in different locations of the concert hall.

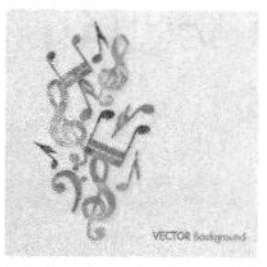

Listening Box 8

Type in Gruppen and choose top box GruppenfürdreiOrchester—WerkNr. 6. Select Track 2, GruppenfürdreiOrchester—WerkNr. 6.

Note: Zyklus means cycle and gruppen means groups in German.

It is often thought by many that Classical Music is always old and out of date sounding. This simply is not true and there is a category called Spooky Modern Classical. The sounds in this category provide the listener with a vast array of tonal permutations. There is no doubt the composers of this music were thinking outside the box. I will provide a few listening examples and I invite each one of you to be the judge.

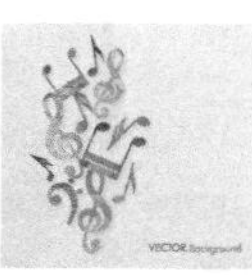

Listening Box 9

Type in Spooky Modern Classical and choose top box, Spooky Modern Classical. Select Track 2, 4. Rythmique; Track 17, Perpetual: Bad Idea.

Unit 10, Chapter 2 Listening Box Playlist

LB4: Type in Threnody to the Victims of Hiroshima and choose top box Threnody to the Victims of Hiroshima, Krakow Polish Radio Symphony Orchestra. Select Track 1, Threnody to the Victims of Hiroshima.

LB5: Type in Henry Cowell and under Tracks, choose The Banshee, Henry Cowell. Select Track 9, The Banshee.

LB6: Type in Pierre Boulez and under Tracks, choose Eclat, Pierre Boulez. Select Track 1, Eclat; Track 3, Rituel (In memory of Bruno Maderna).

LB7: Type in Karlheinz Stockhausen and under Albums, choose Karlheinz Stockhausen: Spiral 1+ Japan (This will be your second choice). Select Disc 1, Track 1, Zyklus No. 9.

LB8: Type in Gruppen and choose top box GruppenfürdreiOrchester – WerkNr. 6. Select Track 2, GruppenfürdreiOrchester – WerkNr. 6.

LB9: Type in Spooky Modern Classical and choose top box Spooky Modern Classical. Select Track 2, 4. Rhythmique; Track 17, Perpetual: Bad Idea.

CHAPTER 3 ATONALITY

Atonal Music is musical composition not based on a scale or key. One of the most outstanding composers in this category is Arnold Schoenberg. Atonality is one of the most distinct styles of the twentieth century.

Arnold Schoenberg (1874–1951)

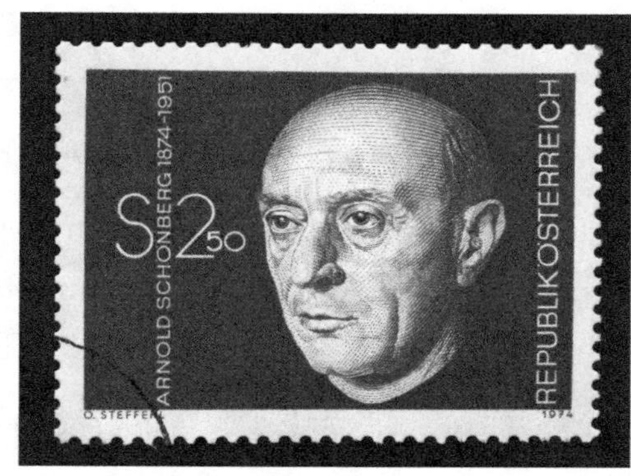

©Avonimir Atletic/Shutterstock.com

1. Born in Vienna, Austria.
2. Arnold was a composer and painter.
3. He was of the Jewish faith, but due to anti-Semitism, converted to Christianity in 1898. He eventually decided to stay true to his faith and returned to Judaism.
4. He was married in 1901 and fathered two children, Gertrud (1902–1947) and Georg (1906–1974). In 1908, his wife left him for several months and lived with a younger painter.
5. World War I brought crises to Schoenberg in that he was inducted into the Army at age 42. At this time, many of his compositions were not finished as much of his composing time was interrupted.
6. In 1923, his first wife died and in the same year he remarried.
7. Much of Arnold's music education came in the form of self-taught. In his early music writing years, his compositions were tonal in nature. He actually cemented in his concept of atonality in the Five Orchestral Pieces, Op.16, in 1909.
8. As previously stated, Schoenberg was a victim of anti-Semitism and he decided to come to America with his family in 1934.
9. His first teaching position was at the Malkin Conservatory in Boston. He eventually moved to California and secured teaching positions at the University of Southern California and the University of California.
10. Although Schoenberg influenced many young composers, his own music was not graciously accepted by the general public. He was also noted for being very

superstitious. Specifically, he was very fearful of the number 13. Ironically, he died on Friday, July 13, 1951, at age 76. Could it be that 76 (7 + 6) was his demise?

11. Some of his most important compositions are: **Orchestral:** Transfigured Night (1899), Pelleas und Melisande (1903), Five Orchestral Pieces, Op.16 (1909), Violin Concerto (1936), Piano Concerto (1942). **Piano:** Five Piano Pieces, Op. 23 (1920), Suite for Piano (1923). **Vocal:** Pierrot Lunaire, Op.21 (1912), Jacob's Ladder (unfinished oratorio, 1917), Expectation, Op. 17 (An opera, 1924).

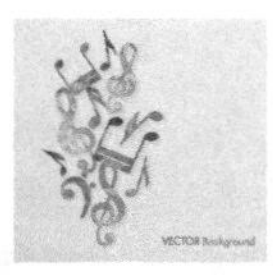

Listening Box 10

Type in Arnold Schoenberg and choose top box, Five Piano Pieces, Op.23 (Waltz). Select Track 14, Five Piano Pieces, Op. 23 (Sweepingly); Track 15, Five Piano Pieces, Op. 23 (Waltz).

Schoenberg and the Twelve-Tone Row

Schoenberg's contrivance of the Twelve-Tone Row is really another way of using the chromatic scale. Within the distance of an octave on the piano, there are 12 different notes, 7 white and 5 black. Schoenberg's formulated system for composing contends that no one note is more important than another, therefore all are equal. He also includes in his system the mandate of using all 12 notes, in any order, before repeating one. While this style of composition yields a more dissonant sound of music, when one analyzes the structure, it's clear that it is very organized.

In the first movement of Schoenberg's Suite for Piano, Op.25 (1923), the composer exposes the Twelve-Tone Row in the following order: E – F – G – Db – Gb – Eb – Ab – D – B – C – A – Bb. After the sound of the Bb we hear a repetition of the same note, but that is fine since all of the original 12 notes have been exposed. The following listening example will give you an accurate idea of how he puts this together.

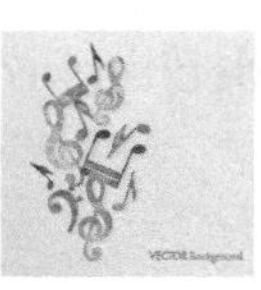

Listening Box 11

Type in Arnold Schoenberg and choose top box, Five Piano Pieces, Op.23 (Waltz). Select Track 16, Suite for Piano, Op. 25—Praleudium.

Note: If you are going to listen to Listening Box 1 and 2 at the same time, you only need to sign in once.

Anton Webern (1883–1945)

1. Born in Vienna, Austria.
2. Webern was a composer, conductor, and he played piano and cello.
3. He was a private pupil of Arnold Schoenberg.
4. His father was a mining engineer and his mother was an amateur pianist who gave him his first music lessons.
5. In the early 1900s, he entered the University of Vienna and eventually earned a PhD degree.
6. His early compositions were tonal, but he strayed away from this style in 1908–1909, with Stefan George songs.
7. In 1911, he married his first cousin and this did not have church approval. Anton and Wilhelmine had four children, three girls and one boy.
8. With the outbreak of World War I, Webern enlisted in the army, but was discharged after one year because of poor eyesight.
9. Webern was an excellent teacher, but never received any appointment at a university. He basically gave private lectures and lessons.
10. The Nazis labeled his music "degenerate art," and performances were banned.
11. In his early years, Webern was a Nazi sympathizer, but that changed with the outbreak of World War II.
12. In February, 1945, his only son Peter was killed by Nazi bombs while on a train.
13. After the death of his son, Webern left Vienna and moved to Mittersill, which is near Salzburg.
14. Unfortunately, in September, 1945, Webern was accidently shot in front of his house smoking a cigar, by an American soldier. The soldier that killed Webern was Pfc. Raymond Norwood Bell, a cook in the Army. Bell always felt guilty about this incident and died of alcoholism in 1955.

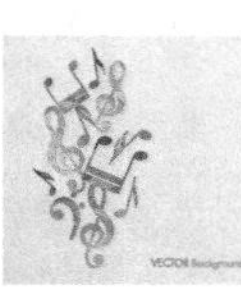

Listening Box 12

Type in Anton Webern and under Albums, choose Orchestral Music, Anton Webern. Select Track 1, Passacaglia, Op. 1; Track 8, Bewegt; Track 19, Variationen.

Passacaglia: The passacaglia is a dance form which can be traced back to seventeenth-century Spain. It was also popular in Italy and is usually written in ¾ time.

Bewegt: Means moves in German

Variationen: Variations

Steve Reich (1936–)

1. Born in New York City.
2. In his early years he studied piano and drums.
3. He eventually attended Cornell University and graduated in 1957.
4. After graduating Cornell, he studied composition with a private teacher and attended the Julliard School of Music. Later on, Reich moved to California where he earned a master's degree in composition from Mills College in Oakland.
5. His overall musical interest included 12-tone composition, minimalism, tape loops, and phasing.
6. Reich was interested in playing drums and in 1971, traveled to Ghana to study new techniques. On his return from Ghana, he wrote a 90-minute-long piece called "Drumming."
7. The 1980s reveal a more somber and dark style of Reich's compositions as he draws on his Judaic roots in the work "Tehillim," which means psalms in Hebrew.
8. The 1990s show several collaborations on opera with his wife Beryl, The Cave (1993), Three Tales (2002).
9. One of Reich's most famous and interesting pieces is WTC/911, which premiered in March 2011 at Duke University in North Carolina.
10. Some of his most important compositions are: It's Gonna Rain (1965), Come Out (1965), Pendulum Music (1968), Four Organs (1970), Clapping Music (1972), Different Trains (1988), WTC/911 (2011). **Opera**: The Cave (1993), Three Tales (2002).

Come Out—Steve Reich (1965)

Reich's piece Come Out is actually based on a crime which happened in Harlem, New York, in 1964. Six African-Americans were accused of murder, but only one was convicted. This group became known as the Harlem Six and one of its members, Daniel Hamm, punctured himself to highlight police brutality. He, Hamm, used the phrase, "I had to, like, open the bruise up, and let some of the bruise blood come out to show them." Reich took part of that phrase "come out to show them," and used such electronic composing techniques as tape looping and phasing to stress the meaning and importance of the words. As the phrase overlaps, it becomes blurry and unintelligible at the end.

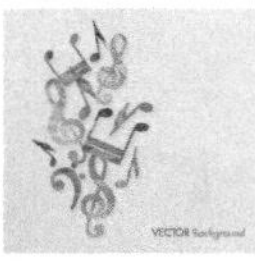

Listening Box 13

Type in Steve Reich and choose top box Clapping Music/1972, Steve Reich. Select Track 1, Come out/1996; Track 3, Clapping Music (1972). It's Gonna Rain Part 1 (1965).

Unit 10, Chapter 3 Listening Box Playlist

LB10: Type in Arnold Schoenberg and choose top box, Five Piano Pieces, Op. 23 (Waltz). Select Track 14, Five Piano Pieces, Op. 23 (Sweepingly); Track 15, Five Piano Pieces Op. 23 (Waltz).

LB11: Type in Arnold Schoenberg and choose top box, Five Piano Pieces, Op. 23 (Waltz). Select Track 16, Suite for Piano, Op. 25—Praleudium.

LB12: Type in Anton Webern and under Albums, choose Orchestral Music, Anton Webern. Select Track 1, Passacaglia, Op.1; Track 8, Bewegt; Track 19, Variationen.

LB13: Type in Steve Reich and choose top box Clapping Music/1972, Steve Reich. Select Track 1, Come Out/1996; Track 3, Clapping Music (1972), It's Gonna Rain Part 1 (1965).

Summary of Unit 10, Chapters 1–3 Terms and Study Sheet

Terms

Electronic Music
Theremin
Experimental Music
Atonality
Twelve-Tone Row
Passacaglia
Aleatoric Music
Chance Music
MIDI

Minimalism: The composer uses a small or limited amount of musical materials in a composition.

Note: All these terms have been previously explained with the exception of minimalism.

Composers: **From Chapter 2:** Krysztof Penderecki, Henry Cowell, Pierre Boulez, Karlheinz Stockhausen. **From Chapter 3:** Arnold Schoenberg, Anton Webern, Steve Reich.

Note: All composers from Chapter 1 have been previously listed.

Summary of Listeners Toolbox:

My number one suggestion when listening to the selections from these three chapters is to keep an open mind. I'm sure many of you will feel this music sounds strange. Consider the fact that all these composers are thinking outside the box of conventional sounding music. One of the things I try to do when listening to this type of music is to relate it to some of the movies I have seen. This approach provides for me a new meaning to the sound. I hope it does the same for you.

Questions: After listening, can you make any sense out of these diverse sounds? Would you say these composers have gone too far in trying to create new directions for music?

To The Student: The instructor may add or delete study items at his or her discretion.

Additional Paper Assignments

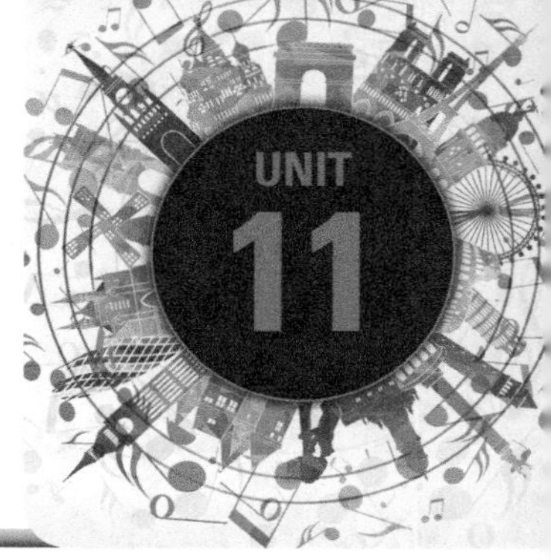

AMADEUS, IMMORTAL BELOVED REPORTS

A. **General Directions:**
Watch and review the movie "Amadeus" or "Immortal Beloved" and answer the five questions that are related to the movie.

B. **Include the following in your paper:** (Mozart—Amadeus)
  1. Characteristics and style(s) of the time period.
     What was going on?
     How did people dress?
  2. Give a general discussion of Mozart's adult life. **Be brief and concise!**
  3. Tell me about the relationship Mozart had with his wife and father.
  4. Give your overall impression of the movie as seen through Salieri's eyes. Include how Mozart's genius and musical expertise affected Salieri psychologically.
  5. Conclusion: Summarize the movie (How you view things).

C. **Include the following in your paper:** (Beethoven—Immortal Beloved)
  1. Characteristics and style(s) of the time period.
     What was going on?
     How did people dress?
  2. Give a general discussion of Beethoven's adult life. **Be brief and concise!**
  3. Tell me who you think Karl was.
  4. Tell me who the Immortal Beloved is. Since knowing who she is ties many loose ends together, tell me what some of the loose ends are.
  5. Conclusion: Summarize the movie (How you view things).

Directions: Papers must be typed (double space). Use Arial 11 or 12 font, one page maximum. Put your name along with the date at the top of the paper. Make sure the top margin is not too large. Do not rewrite the questions as this will cut down on the space you need for your answers.

Paper Due On:

DeLovely, Ray Reports

A. **General Directions:**
   Watch and review movie "DeLovely" or "Ray" and answer the five questions that are related to the movie.
B. **Include the following in your paper (Cole Porter—DeLovely)**
   1. Who was Cole Porter? What influences did he have on American popular music? (Example Broadway Shows).
   2. Cole Porter was a prolific songwriter. Tell me something about his songs. (Example, the inspiration for his songs).
   3. Although Cole Porter was married, he had numerous relationships with men. Tell me about his life with Linda, and how she handled the extramarital sexual exploitations.
   4. Tell me about Cole Porter's physical and emotional upheavals. For example: (a) separation from Linda; (b) the horse-riding accident; (c) the loss of his leg; (d) Linda's death; (e) the change of his religious views.
   5. Conclusion: Summarize the movie (How you view things).
C. **Include the following in your paper: (Ray—Ray Charles)**
   1. Who was Ray Charles? What influences did he have on American popular music?
   2. Tell me something about Ray as a father and husband. Did his extramarital relationships adversely affect his home life?
   3. Ray had some problem in the state of Georgia. Tell me about the problem, and eventually how this problem was reconciled.
   4. Everyone knows Ray Charles went blind as a young boy. Tell me what you think about how this malady affected his music, as well as his dependency on drugs.
   5. Conclusion: Summarize the movie (How you view things).

Directions: Papers must be typed and (double spaced). Use Arial 11 or 12 font, one page maximum. Put your name along with the date at the top of the paper. Make sure the top margin is not too large. Do not rewrite the questions as this will cut down on the space you need for your answers.

Paper Due On:

A Critique of Three Popular Songs

Directions:

1. Choose three popular songs. They may be from the same artist, or from two or three artists. You may use disc, video, or any other electronic device for information.
2. Write a two-paragraph description of each work using the following criteria:
   A. Title of song
   B. Artist/Artists
   C. Style
   D. Introduction
   E. Main Melody
   F. Rhythm
   G. Harmony
   H. Tone Color (Instr./Voices)
   I. Story Line, if a vocal
   J. Give your reason for choosing each song. Summarize.
3. You may choose to critique three classical pieces as another option. The same categories listed above apply here as well.

Note: All papers must be typed and stapled. Use Arial 11 or 12 font and the paper must be a maximum two pages.

Paper Due On:

Compare and Contrast—Berlioz and Stravinsky

Instructions: Listening

1. Listen to Berlioz's Symphonie Fantastique, movement five, "Dream of a Witche's Sabbath." As you listen, concentrate on the following: instruments, melody, tempo (speed), and the overall sound of the piece. As you listen, take notes.
2. Listen to Stravinsky's The Rite of Spring, "Sacrificial Dance." As you listen, concentrate on the following: instruments, melody, tempo (speed), and the overall sound of the piece. As you listen, take notes.

Writing: Paragraph 1

In paragraph 1, write down all the information you have about "Dream of a Witche's Sabbath."

Writing: Paragraph 2

In paragraph 2, write down all the information you have about "Sacrificial Dance."

Writing: Paragraph 3

In paragraph 3, compare and contrast both pieces and summarize as to which one you liked best.

Note: The paper should be typed using Arial 11 or 12 font. The paper should be a maximum one page.

Paper Due On:

Compare and Contrast—Mozart and Beethoven

Instructions: Listening

1. Listen to the first movement of Mozart's EineKleineNachtmusik (Allegro). As you listen, concentrate on the following: instruments, melody, tempo (speed), and the overall sound of the piece. As you listen, take notes.
2. Listen to the first movement of Beethoven's Fifth Symphony (Allegro con brio). As you listen, concentrate on the following: instruments, melody, tempo (speed), and the overall sound of the piece. As you listen, take notes.

Writing: Paragraph 1

In paragraph 1, write down all the information you have about the EineKleineNachtmusik (First Movement).

Writing: Paragraph 2

In paragraph 2, write down all the information you have about Beethoven's Fifth Symphony (First Movement).

Writing: Paragraph 3

In paragraph 3, compare and contrast both pieces and summarize as to which one you liked best.

Note: The paper should be typed using Arial 11 or 12 font. The paper should be a maximum one page.

Paper Due On:

An Additional Listening List

As most of our Classical Music concerts start from the Baroque Period, this list begins from the same point.

Baroque Music

Bach

St. Matthew Passion

Brandenburg Concertos (1–6)

Well-Tempered Clavier

Mass in B Minor

Little Fugue in G Minor

Toccata and Fugue in D Minor

Vivaldi

The Four Seasons

Handel

Water Music

Messiah

Music for Royal Fireworks

Giulio Cesare (opera)

Classical Music

Haydn

The Creation (oratorio)

The Seasons (oratorio)

Symphony No. 94 in G Major (Surprise)

Symphony No. 104 in D Major (London)

Mozart

Eine Kleine Nachtmusik (A Little Night Music)

Symphonies 39-40-41 (The Trilogy)

The Marriage of Figaro (overture)

Don Giovanni (opera), The Magic Flute (opera)

Requiem Mass (his last composition, which he never finished)

Beethoven

Symphonies 1-3-5-7-9
Sonata Pathétique Op.13, No. 8
Moonlight Sonata Op. 27, No. 14

Romantic Music

Berlioz

Symphonie Fantastique
Harold in Italy
Roman Carnival Overture

Liszt

Hungarian Rhapsodies
Symphonic Poems
Faust Symphony
Dante Symphony

Mendelssohn (Felix)

A Midsummer Night's Dream (overture)
Symphony No. 4, Italian

Schubert

"Ave Maria" (song)
Incidental Music to Rosamunde
Symphony No. 8 (unfinished)

Schumann

"Carnival" (piano)
"Papillons" (piano)
Symphony No.1 (Spring)

Chopin

Fantasie Impromptu (piano)
Piano Concertos No.1 and No. 2

Brahms

Academic Festival Overture
Piano Concerto No. 2 in B-flat Major
Violin Concerto
A German Requiem

Mahler

Symphonies 1-3-8

Strauss

Also Sprach Zarathustra
Till Eulenspiegel's Merry Pranks
Death and Transfiguration
Don Quixote
Don Juan

Russian Composers

Rimsky-Korsakov

Capriccio Espagnol
Scheherazade

Borodin

Prince Igor: "Polovtsian Dances"

Mussorgsky

Pictures at an Exhibition
A Night on Bald Mountain
Boris Godunov (opera)

Rachmaninov

Piano Concerto No. 1
Piano Concerto No. 2

Tchaikovsky

Sleeping Beauty (ballet music)
The Nutcracker (ballet music)
Swan Lake (ballet music)
1812 Overture
Romeo and Juliet
Capriccio Italien
Eugen Onegin (opera)
Piano Concerto No.1

Hungary

Bartok

Concerto for Orchestra
Music for Strings, Percussion, and Celeste
The Miraculous Mandarin (ballet)

Scandinavia

Sibelius

Finlandia

Italy

Respighi

Pines of Rome

Spain

Falla

The Three Cornered Hat

Opera—Italy

Donizetti

Linda di Chamonix

Rossini

William Tell
The Barber of Seville

Puccini

Turandot
Tosca
La bohème
Madama Butterfly

Verdi

Nabucco
Macbeth
IL Trovatore
La Traviata
Rigoletto
Don Carlos
Aida
Otello
Falstaff

France

Bizet

Carmen (opera)

Germany

Wagner

The Flying Dutchman (Overture)
The Ring of the Nibelung
Rienzi
Tannhäuser
Lohengrin
The Rhine Gold
Parsifal
The Valkyrie
Siegfried

Impressionism—France

Debussy

Prelude to the Afternoon of a Faun
La Mer
Images
Clair de lune (piano)

Ravel

Bolero
Scheherazade
Daphnis et Chloé
Suite No. 2

Atonal Music

Schoenberg

Suite for Piano

Berg

Wozzeck (opera)
Concerto for Violin and Orchestra

Stravinsky

The Firebird Suite
The Rite of Spring
Petrushka Suite
Pulcinella Suite
Ebony Concerto

Neoclassicism

Holst

The Planets
The Brook Green Suite
Moorside Suite

Four American Composers (Gershwin, Copland, Bernstein, Grofé)

Gershwin (George)

Rhapsody in Blue
An American in Paris
Porgy and Bess
Of Thee I Sing (musical)

Copland

Fanfare for the Common Man
Rodeo (ballet)
Lincoln Portrait (with narrator)
Billy the Kid (ballet)
Appalachian Spring (ballet)
El Salón México

Bernstein

West Side Story
Candide (overture)
Mass (theater piece)

Grofé

Grand Canyon Suite
Mississippi Suite
Madison Square Garden Suite
Kentucky Derby Suite
Yellowstone Suite
Hudson River Suite
Wheels for Orchestra (dedicated to the Ford dealers of America)
Lincoln's Gettysburg Address
March for Americans

A Random Selection of Composers and Their Interesting Compositions

Honegger

Pacific 231

Vaughan Williams

Fanatsia on "Greensleeves"

Britten

Young Person's Guide to the Orchestra (with narrator)

Prokofiev

Peter and the Wolf

Offenbach

Tales of Hoffman

Joplin

The Entertainer

Rodrigo

Concerto de Aranjuez

Broadway

Since there are so many wonderful shows and great composers, I will provide a "hand-picked" list that I honestly believe are trendsetters. Growing up in New York City gave me an opportunity to see most of these shows in person. I hope you enjoy my listening selections. To the artists and shows I omit, no disrespect is meant.

Leonard Bernstein—Stephen Sondheim

West Side Story (1957)

Jerry Bock—Sheldon Harnick

Fiddler on the Roof (1964)

Marvin Hamlisch—Edward Kleban

A Chorus Line (1975)

Jerry Herman

Hello! Dolly (1964)
Mame (1966)

Elton John—Tim Rice

Lion King (1997)
Aida (1999)

Tom Jones—Harvey Schmidt

The Fantasticks (1960)

John Kander—Fred Ebb

Zorba (1968)
Cabaret (1972)
Chicago (1975)

Burton Lane—Alan Jay Lerner

On a Clear Day You Can See Forever (1965)

Mitch Leigh

Man of La Mancha (1965)

Alan Jay Lerner—Frederick Loewe

My Fair Lady (1956)
Camelot (1960)

Frank Loesser

Guys and Dolls (1950)

Alan Menken

Beauty and the Beast (1994, video)

Cole Porter

Kiss Me Kate (1948)
Can Can (1953)

Richard Rodgers—Oscar Hammerstein

Oklahoma (1943)
Carousel (1945)
South Pacific (1949)
The King and I (1951)
The Sound of Music (1959)

Claude-Michel Schönberg, Alain Boublil, Jean-Marc Natel, Herbert Kretzmer

Les Miserables (1985)

Stephen Sondheim

A Little Night Music (1973)
Into the Woods (1988)

Charlie Strouse—Martin Charnin

Annie (1978)

Julie Styne—Betty Comden—Adolph Green

Peter Pan (1954)

Julie Styne—Stephen Sondheim

Gypsy (1959)

Julie Styne—Bob Merrill

Funny Girl (1964)

Andrew Lloyd Weber—Tim Rice

Jesus Christ Superstar (1971)
Evita (1979)
Cats (1981)
Phantom of the Opera (1988)

Meredith Wilson

The Music Man (1957)

Note: The following list of suggested groups and artists can be found on Napster. I will leave the individual song selections up to you.

Older Rock Groups

Bill Haley and The Comets
The Beatles
Credence Clearwater Revival
Van Halen
Pink Floyd
Kiss
AC/DC
Led Zeppelin
Red Hot Chilli Peppers
Matchbox Twenty
Nirvana
Rolling Stones
Grateful Dead
Journey

Jazz—Rock Fusion Groups

Chicago
Blood, Sweat, Tears
Earth, Wind, Fire

Older Male Vocalists

Frank Sinatra
Nat King Cole
Tony Bennett
Dean Martin
Sammy Davis Jr.

More Current

Andrea Bocelli
Michael Bublé
Harry Connick Jr.
Usher
Chris Brown

Older Female Vocalists

Ella Fitzgerald
Diana Ross
Whitney Houston
Madonna

More Current

Adele
Lady Gaga
Selena Gomez
Beyoncé

Glossary

A Cappella: Singing without instrumental accompaniment

Adagio: Slowly

Aleatoric: Performer controlled music with precise notation.

Allegro: Quickly, fast

Alternative: Provides an alternative to mainstream Rock 'n' Roll and includes more independent thinking and individuality to the music.

Alto: A voice range under soprano.

Antiphonal: Sound from different directions.

Aria: A vocal solo (male or female) usually found in an oratorio, cantata, or opera.

Arranger: An arranger is basically a composer who puts a new spin on the melody, harmony, and rhythm of a song.

Atonality: Music not based on a scale or key.

Avant Garde: French words that describe unconventional artists' and musicians' work.

Ballad Opera: A style of opera that introduced spoken dialogue between popular songs.

Ballade: Poetry put to music; also a piano composition in free-style.

Ballet: A story line set to dancing and music.

Baroque: A Portuguese word used to describe the historical time period from 1600 to 1750.

Bass Clef: A symbol that indicates mid to lower range notes.

Bass: A male voice range and the lowest in the chorus.

Beat: The rhythmic pulse.

Bebop: A Jazz style.

Blues: Vocal music started by African-Americans.

British Invasion: When rock and pop groups from England became popular in the United States (e.g., Beatles).

Cadence: A chord progression that comes after a musical section or phrase.

Cakewalk: A high kicking dance started on Southern plantations.

Call and Response: An African-American vocal style where the leader sings a phrase and the group responds.

Cantata: A vocal piece which can be sacred or secular with solo voices, instruments, and chorus.

Canzon: A song.

Capriccio: A free-form piece with an upbeat or lively feel.

Castrato: A surgically altered male who sang high parts in operas.

Chanson: A French song.

Chant: A single line of melody sung without instruments.

Chord: At least three notes sounding at the same time.

Chorus: A vocal group usually with four sections: Soprano, Alto, Tenor, Bass.

Chromatic Scale: A scale made up of half steps.

Classical Era: From 1750 to 1820.

Coda: A tag or tail song ending.

Comic Opera: A style of Italian opera popular in the eighteenth century.

Composer: A person who composes music, writes the actual notes.

Concerto Grosso: An instrumental piece in three sections for several solo instruments and orchestra.

Concerto: An instrumental piece in three sections for solo instrument and orchestra.

Concert Overture: An orchestral piece that stands alone and does not come before an opera.

Consonant: A pleasant sound without tension.

Counterpoint: Note against note.

Country Music: Created in the South, it has elements of Folk and Blues music.

Country Rock: A fusion of Country and Rock 'n' Roll.

Crescendo: To gradually get louder.

Decrescendo: To gradually get softer.

Development: A section in a piece where the main melody is changed with new material added.

Dissonant: A harsh sound with tension.

Doo-Wop: Vocal music with group harmony and nonsense syllables.

Duet: Two players

Electronic Music: Music produced from electronic instruments (e.g., synthesizers).

Enharmonic: Two notes that sound the same but are written differently.

Etude: A study piece, generally short.

Experimental Music: Music written in unconventional ways (unpredictable).

Exposition: Opening section of a fugue or sonata where the main melody is exposed.

Extravaganza: An elaborate and expensive show.

Fantasie: A piano piece that denotes whimsical or fantasy, usually short.

Film Animation: To create movement with a succession of pictures.

Flat: A music symbol that lowers a note one half step.

Forte: Means loud

Fugue: A composition which contains imitation, counterpoint, polyphonic texture.

Gospel: Christian Music created in the South.

Grunge: Fuses Heavy Metal and Punk Rock.

Hard Rock: Music that emphasizes loud amplification and distortion.

Harmony: A combination of notes that together create an agreeable sound.

Heartland Rock: Music with country values.

Hip-Hop: A style of music created in the Bronx, New York, with upbeat and DJ sounds.

Homophonic: A melody with harmonic accompaniment.

Idée fixe: A fixed idea in a piece, usually a melody.

Imitation: Repetition of musical elements in other parts.

Impromptu: A piano piece that sounds improvised but is written out.

Improvisation: Making music spontaneously without written notation.

Interval: The distance in pitch from one note to another.

Jazz Fusion: The blending of Jazz and Rock elements.

Key Signature: Tells the musician how many sharps or flats in a piece of music.

Kinetographic Camera: An early movie camera.

Kinetoscope: A peephole video device used to watch early movies.

Latin Jazz: Jazz with Latin rhythms and Latin instruments.

Ledger Lines: Shortened staff lines used to write notes above or below the staff.

Legato: Smooth and connected.

Libretto: The story of an opera.

Lied: The German term for Art Song.

Madrigal: Renaissance vocal music.

Maestoso: Majestic

Major: One of the basic scales used in Western Civilization music.

Mass: A religious celebration.

Mazurka: A Polish Dance in triple meter.

Meistersingers: German master singers of secular music, fourteenth, fifteenth, and sixteenth centuries.

Melisma: Singing several notes to one syllable.

Melody: An organized succession of tones that make sense when perceived as a group.

Meter: The organization of beats into groups.

Middle Ages: From 450 to 1450.

Minnesingers: Twelfth-century German singers of secular music.

Minor: One of the two basic scales used in Western Civilization music.

Minstrel: Tenth-century poets, story tellers, and musicians.

Minuet: A dance in ¾ time.

Monophonic: One single line of melody.

Motet: Sacred vocal music with polyphonic texture, thirteenth to seventeenth centuries.

Motive: The shortest kind of melody.

Motown: A music style and company created in the late 1950s to develop and promote African-American musicians.

Nationalism: Composers who displayed patriotism in their compositions.

Natural: A symbol that cancels out a sharp or flat.

New Wave: A derivative of Punk which uses heavy electrical elements and synthesizers.

Nocturne: A short piano piece inspired by association with nighttime.

Nonet: Nine player

Note: A symbol that indicates pitch and duration.

Octet: Eight players

Opera: Drama set to music with voices, orchestra, and sometimes dancing.

Operetta: Generally, a lighter opera with a spoken dialogue.

Oratorio: A vocal piece with a sacred subject, chorus, orchestra and vocal soloists. There is no special scenery, acting or costumes.

Organum: The beginning of harmony, polyphonic texture.

Ornamentation: Different ways a melody can be changed.

Ostinato: A recurring melodic and rhythmic pattern.

Overture: The musical material that comes before the show begins.

Phrase: Several melodic measures.

Piano: Means soft

Pizzicato: Plucking the strings

Polychords: Two different chords sounding at the same time.

Polymeters: Two different meters sounding at the same time.

Polyphonic: Two different independent melodies.

Polyrhythms: Two different rhythms sounding at the same time.

Polytonality: Two different scales or keys sounding at the same time.

Progressive Rock: Uses elements of Jazz and Classical music.

Psychedelic Rock: Music inspired by psychedelic drugs and designed to alter the mind.

Punk: Hard-sounding music with anti-political and anti-establishment lyrics.

Quartet: Four playerss

Quintet: Five players

Ragtime: Music with strong left-hand accompaniment and syncopation.

Rap: A speech-like style of singing over rhythm.

Recapitulation: A section in a piece of music where the main melody is restated.

Recitative: A speech-like style of singing found in operas and oratorios.

Renaissance: From 1450 to 1600.

Repetition: Refers to the repeating of a musical idea.

Requiem: A death Mass.

Rests: A symbol that indicates silence.

Revue: A large and costly variety show.

Rhythm: The pulse or beat of music.

Rhythm and Blues: A style of music which features rhythm and blues elements.

Rhythmic Ostinato: A constantly occurring rhythmic pattern.

Riff: Like ostinato, a recurring melodic and rhythmic pattern found in Jazz.

Rockabilly: A type of Rock 'n' Roll that has strong elements of country music.

Rondo: A return of the main theme.

Rubato: A deliberate unsteady tempo.

Sacred: Meaning religious.

Scale: A series of notes that ascend or descend depending on the specific pattern.

Scat Singing: A style of vocal singing that uses nonsense syllables.

Secular: Non-religious.

Septet: Seven players

Sequence: The same musical material repeated on different pitch levels.

Sextet: Six players

Sharp: A musical symbol that raises a note one half step.

Slur: A symbol indicating a group of notes be played smooth and together.

Soft Rock: A style of music that puts emphasis on melody and a softer sound.

Solo: Music featuring one performer.

Sonata Form: A section in Classical Music which has Exposition, Development, Recapitulation, and Coda.

Soprano: The highest vocal range.

Southern Rock: A style of Rock 'n' Roll that includes Country and Blues elements.

Spectacles: Probably the largest shows in terms of performers. Goes back to the early 1900s.

Staccato: Short and detached.

Staff: The five lines and four spaces that musical notes are put on.

Stretto: Close or tight entrances of the voice parts, usually found in a fugue.

Stride Piano: See Ragtime.

Swing Era: The big band era of the 1920s, 1930s, and 1940s.

Symphony: An orchestral work usually in four sections (movements).

Symphonic Poem: A one-movement symphony.

Syncopation: Accenting a normally weak beat.

Tempo: The speed of the music.

Tenor: A male voice range between alto and bass.

Texture: The blending of the musical elements.

Theme: Generally, a longer melody.

Theme and Variations: A melody and variety.

Tie: A symbol that connects two similar notes on the staff.

Time Signature: Two numbers on the staff that indicate how many beats in a measure and what kind of a note gets one beat.

Tone Poem: A one-movement symphony.

Tonic: The tonic is the first note of the scale that gives a feeling of home base

Treble Clef: A music symbol indicating a mid to high range.

Trill: A player or singer making two notes go back and forth in rapid succession.

Trio: Three players

Troubadours: Twelfth-century Knights in the courts of Southern France who sang secular music.

Trouvères: Twelfth-century Knights in the courts of Northern France who sang secular music.

Vaudeville: A variety show featuring several kinds of talent.

Vivace: Very lively, very fast.

Waltz: A dance in ¾ time.

Index

D

E

F

N

O

P

T

U

V

W

Y

Z